SPEAKING PICTURES

SPEAKING PICTURES

NEUROPSYCHOANALYSIS AND
AUTHORSHIP IN FILM AND LITERATURE

ALISTAIR FOX

INDIANA UNIVERSITY PRESS
Bloomington and Indianapolis

This book is a publication of

Indiana University Press
Office of Scholarly Publishing
Herman B Wells Library 350
1320 East 10th Street
Bloomington, Indiana 47405 USA

iupress.indiana.edu

© 2016 by Alistair Fox

All rights reserved

No part of this book may be reproduced or utilized in any form or by any means, electronic or mechanical, including photocopying and recording, or by any information storage and retrieval system, without permission in writing from the publisher. The Association of American University Presses' Resolution on Permissions constitutes the only exception to this prohibition.

The paper used in this publication meets the minimum requirements of the American National Standard for Information Sciences–Permanence of Paper for Printed Library Materials, ANSI Z39.48-1992.

Manufactured in the United States of America

Library of Congress Cataloging-in-Publication Data

Names: Fox, Alistair.
Title: Speaking pictures : neuropsychoanalysis and authorship in film and literature / Alistair Fox.
Description: Bloomington : Indiana University Press, 2016. | Includes bibliographical references and index.
Identifiers: LCCN 2015046899 | ISBN 9780253020871 (cl : alk. paper) | ISBN 9780253020918 (pb : alk. paper)
Subjects: LCSH: Fiction—Psychological aspects. | Authorship—Psychological aspects. | Psychology and literature. | Creation (Literary, artistic, etc.) | Motion pictures—Psychological aspects.
Classification: LCC PN3352.P7 F79 2016 | DDC 808.301/9—dc23 LC record available at http://lccn.loc.gov/2015046899

1 2 3 4 5 21 20 19 18 17 16

For my students

Poesy therefore is an art of imitation, for so Aristotle termeth it in his word *mimēsis*, that is to say, a representing, counterfeiting, or figuring forth—to speak metaphorically, a speaking picture—with this end, to teach and delight.

—Sir Philip Sidney, *An Apology for Poetry* (1581–1583)

When I think consciously I can think only one thought in any given moment. Yet an image ... simultaneously contains many thoughts. The image, worth a thousand words, is an unconscious organization.

—Christopher Bollas, *The Infinite Question* (2009)

CONTENTS

Acknowledgments   *xiii*

Introduction   1

1. Changing Configurations in Theories of Fictive
   Representation   9
   Embodied Fictions, or Fictions as Sign? Classical Perspectives   9
   The Effects of Christian Conversion: A Medieval Bifurcation   11
   The Renaissance Humanist Synthesis and Its Aftermath   12
   Neoclassicism versus Romanticism: A New Disjunction   15
   Displacing the Locations of Authority: Modernism and
       Postmodernism   17
   Renewed Allegoricizations: Psychoanalytic Theories of Interpretation   22
   Alternative Psychoanalytic Formulations: Object-Relations Theory   25
   Renewed Formalisms: Cognitive and Evolutionary Theories   27
   Neuropsychoanalysis and the Need for a New Synthesis   30

2. Why Does Fictive Representation Exist?   39
   Emotional Systems and the Human Brain   41
   Metaphorical Conceptualization   44
   Implicit and Explicit Memory   46
   Implications for Poststructuralist Critical Theory   48
   The Functions of Fictive Representation   49
   The Creation of Complex Models of Reality   50

3. The Wellsprings of Fictive Creativity   53
   Motivations Arising from the Basic Affects   53
   Psychological Motivations and Outcomes   55
   Emotional Perturbation as a Source of Creativity   59
   The Functions of Storytelling for the Collectivity   61
   The Preoccupations of Storytelling   62

4. The Materials of Fictive Invention   70
   The Building Blocks of Fictive Creativity   71
   The Montage Principle   72
   Visualization and Symbolization in the Encompassing of Complexity   74
   Discursive and Presentational Symbols in Shakespeare's *Romeo
       and Juliet*   76

	Visual and Verbal Interplay in Alexander Payne's "14ᵉ Arrondissement"	78
	Metaphor and Vitality Affects	81
	Vitality Affects in Cinematic Representations	85
	Evocative Objects, Networks of Association, and the Unconscious	89

5. **The Informing Role of Fantasy** — 95
   - The Nature of Fantasy — 95
   - The Mechanisms of Fantasy — 98
   - Fantasies and the Affective Systems — 99
   - The Functions of Fantasies — 101
   - Mechanisms of Displacement — 101
   - Fantasy and Visual Polysemia — 107

6. **The Shaping of Fictive Scenarios by the Author: Motivations, Strategies, and Outcomes** — 110
   - Determinants of Form — 112
   - Conversion of Metaphor into Plot: Preston's *Perfect Strangers*; Spenser's *Faerie Queene* — 113
   - Symbolic Mapping: The Films of Jane Campion — 118
   - Dichotomization: The Films of Bruno Dumont — 120
   - Symbolic Spatialization: Truffaut's *The Last Metro*; Panarello's *One Hundred Strokes* — 122

7. **The Exploitation of Generic Templates and Intertexts as Vehicles for Affect Regulation** — 128
   - The Nature and Function of Genres and Intertexts — 128
   - Triumph through Tragedy: John Milton's *Samson Agonistes* — 129
   - Containing Anxiety and Evacuating Fear: Contemporary American Blockbusters — 135
   - Enacting a Fantasy of Restitution: François Ozon's *The New Girlfriend* — 139
   - General Inferences — 142

8. **Theories of Reception in the Twentieth and Twenty-First Centuries** — 144
   - Reader-Response Theory versus the New Criticism — 145
   - Versions of Reader-Response Theory — 146
   - Psychoanalytic Accounts of Reception — 147
   - Cultural and Historical Materialist Perspectives — 148
   - Cognitivist Theories of Reception — 149
   - Embodied Simulation and the "Experiential Turn" — 151

CONTENTS　　xi

Hypnosis, Animality, and the "Body of Cinema" 153
Shortcomings in Contemporary Theories to Date 154

9. A Neuropsychoanalytic Theory of Reception 158
   The Nature of the Subject and Self-Formation 159
   Mirror Neurons 160
   Embodied Simulation, Agency, and Intentional Attunement 161
   The Intersubjective Transaction between the Author and
     Respondent 163
   The Role of "Interfantasy" 165
   The "Metabolizing" of Fictive Fantasies by the Respondent 166
   Motivations for the Respondent's Engagement with a Fictive
     Representation 168
   Evidence Derived from Self-Reports 170

10. Intersubjective Attunement, Filiation, and the Re-creative Process:
    Jules and Jim–from Henri-Pierre Roché to François Truffaut 174
    Unconscious Attraction and Networks of Filiation 175
    Truffaut's Encounter with Roché's Novel 180
    Clara Roché: A "Jocasta" Mother 182
    Janine Truffaut: The Queen of Indifference 184
    Multiple Identifications, Memories, and Emotions in Truffaut's *Jules
      and Jim* 187
    The Fantasmatic Scenario of Truffaut's *Jules and Jim* 191

11. The Conversion of Autobiographical Emotion into Symbolic
    Figuration: William Shakespeare's *Hamlet* 193
    The Vehicle for Fantasmatic Conversion: Belleforest's
      Account of Amleth 194
    Shakespeare's Alterations to the Source 197
    The Structural Shaping of the Representation 198
    Networks of Associative Metaphors 200
    Revelation of the Play's Affective Logic 202
    The Informing Fantasy 206
    The Link to Shakespeare's Biography 209
    The Centrality of *Hamlet* in Shakespeare's Personal Myth 211

12. Tracking a Personal Myth through an Oeuvre: The Films of
    François Ozon 215
    Charles Mauron and Psychocriticism: The Theory of Personal Myth 215
    A "Bulimic" Filmmaker: François Ozon 217

Recurring Images and Metaphors 218
Pairings and Doublings in Symbolic Configurations 224
"Cinegrams" and Repetitions in the Action 226
Fantasmatic Constructions 229
Strategies of Displacement 232
The Purposes of Ozon's Cinematic Fantasies 234

Conclusion 238

Notes 243
Select Bibliography 271
Filmography 281
Index 285

ACKNOWLEDGMENTS

I AM PARTICULARLY indebted to a number of people for the writing of this book. Chief among them is Raymond Bellour, whose work on the emotions and the effects of a cinematic representation on the spectator stimulated me to begin the line of enquiry that has eventuated in this study. My thanks go to him also for his hospitality and the many hours of conversation during which he freely imparted his insights. Equally important to my research has been the work of Anne Gillain, whose remarkable insights into the creative motivations and strategies of François Truffaut have been invaluable in helping me shape my own theory of authorship and of what takes place in the creative process. At one crucial point in this project, Norman Holland provided welcome support, and, like all scholars pursuing research on the psychological aspects of literature, I am indebted to his work on literature and the brain, and on reception.

At the University of Otago, several colleagues have acted as indispensable interlocutors: Dave Ciccoricco, whose expertise in cognitive literary studies meant that he was able to refer me to certain studies that have relevance to the topic, and Frédéric Dichtel, whose sharp interpretative insights allowed him to serve as a critical friend with respect to films we liked and my developing argument. I benefited, too, from the doctoral research of Sharon Matthews in her study of the plays of James K. Baxter, which, among other things, heightened my awareness of the continuing relevance of the psychocritical theory of Charles Mauron.

I would also like to thank Raina Polivka, my editor at Indiana University Press, whose input—in what is my third collaboration with her—ensured that this book will be a better one than it otherwise might have been.

Finally, my greatest debt, as always, is to my partner Hilary Radner for her encouragement and input into the evolution of my thinking. Not only does she possess an exceptional critical mind; her ability to see the potential implications of a line of thought is unrivaled. Without her, this book would never have been written.

SPEAKING PICTURES

Introduction

Throughout history, men and women have felt a need to represent their experience in images and to arrange those images in patterns that tell stories. Before the invention of writing, our ancestors transmitted stories orally from one generation to the next, and once people learned how to record words with written phonemic symbols, writing itself became a medium through which these stories could be conceived. Storytelling took a further leap forward with the invention of moving pictures, following the Lumière Brothers' public demonstration of their *cinématographe* in Paris in 1895, and it advanced still further with the introduction of "talkies." Today, using digital technology, people are consuming fiction to a greater extent than ever before: in the form of Hollywood special-effects blockbusters and genre films; in a plethora of television dramas and miniseries; in an unending stream of works of popular literature, ranging from chick lit through crime fiction to historical epics; in the films produced by a multitude of national cinemas; in videogames; and in cartoon strips and animated features.

The ubiquity of various forms of fictive representation and the universal appetite for them invites explanation. Why do authors feel a need to invent imaginative fictions? Why do we, as readers or spectators, find them so compelling and consume them so relentlessly? Classical writers believed that literature was pleasant and useful, Renaissance humanists thought its function was to teach and delight, while the mid-nineteenth-century poet Matthew Arnold, for whom the purpose of fiction was to "inspirit and rejoice," could predict that "more and more mankind will discover that we have to turn to poetry to interpret life for us, to console us, to sustain us."[1]

Since Arnold, however, academic studies of fictive representation, as a result of the popularity of various postmodernist theories, have lost any sense of these possible functions, even as more literary and cinematic works are being produced and consumed than at any other time in history. Starting in the late 1960s and for the next 30 years, postmodernism, animated by assumptions drawn from literary semiology, Lacanian psychoanalysis, and Althusserian Marxism, sought to dismantle the authority of "master narratives."[2] In literary and film theory, one consequence of this impulse has been a downgrading of the author, who is denied any status as an origin of, or delimiting constraint on, meaning in a text. Instead, poststructuralist approaches have privileged the reader/spectator, who is deemed to construct meaning as a result of the choices he or she makes in responding to the signifying indeterminacy of a text. Concurrently, cultural theory, believing that discourse writes the author and the reader, as well as the text and even the self (conceptualized as a "subject"), has diverted attention from the *content* of works of fiction toward their social and historical *contexts,* which are assumed to govern their production. In all cases, the effect has been a postmodernist tendency to dehumanize the study of cinema and literature. In addition, postmodern "deconstructors," to use a term employed by Christopher Butler, have become afraid to say what a text means because of an assumption that "the metaphorical characteristics of a language system will always ensure that it actually fails to command (or master) the subject matter which it purports to explain."[3]

Inevitably, a backlash began in the mid-1990s against postmodernist critical and cultural theory, promoted chiefly by cognitivist scholars who wanted literary and cinematic studies to become more empirically grounded, invoking scientific models derived from evolutionary biology, cognitive science, cognitive psychology, and computer science.[4] Whereas postmodernists privileged the reader and discursive contexts, "scientific" models privileged the text in terms of focusing on form and style. However antithetical they may seem, however, these counter-theory empirical approaches have proven no more capable of addressing the contribution of the original creator to a work of fiction than have the critical-cultural theories they oppose.

There is thus a pressing need for authorship—the dimension of fictive representation that has been missing from all theoretical accounts since the 1960s—to be addressed once more. The purpose of this book is to show how certain discoveries in affective neuroscience during the past two decades have made such an enterprise possible. I will consider examples drawn from cinema, literature, and theater, using the term "fictive representation" as a categorical designation to encompass them all, given that all three forms are manifestations of a larger phenomenon—namely, "storytelling" arising from imaginative invention and simulation—as against what the great Russian filmmaker and film theorist Sergei Eisenstein described as "an affidavit exposition" that works in accordance with "the informative logic of a plain statement recording events."[5]

There are good precedents for this. Two of the most important early film theorists, André Bazin and Eisenstein, recognized the intrinsic comparability of the psychological motivations, processes, and representational techniques in cinema, literature, and theater in key respects. Bazin, active during the 1940s and 1950s, went so far as to claim: "The truth is that the vast majority of images on the screen conform to the psychology of the theater or to the novel of classical analysis," owing to "a necessary and unambiguous causal relationship ... between feelings and their outward manifestations."[6] Similarly, Eisenstein regarded cinema as "the most modern form of an organic synthesis of art" in which "the method of art in general ... [becomes] analysable and graspable.... The method of cinema is like a magnifying glass, through which the method of each of them [the other arts] is visible, and the method of all of them taken together is the fundamental method of every art."[7] That method, for Eisenstein, involved "primal rhythmicality and the rhythmization indispensable in an affect," meaning that all forms of art mark "a reversion of our enlightened, modern intellect to the twilight stage of primitive thought," which "the *form* [my italics] in any given work at any given moment" allows us, in turn, to experience.[8] Regarding montage as at the heart of all forms of expressive art, Eisenstein concluded in 1939: "However diametrically opposite may be these spheres of art, eventually they are bound to become interrelated and unified by the method we now perceive."[9]

These insights have unfortunately been disparaged in the case of Bazin[10] and neglected in the case of Eisenstein.[11] Bazin's views became unfashionable for a time following the lurch of his colleagues toward Marxist materialism after the events in France of May 1968, whereas the essays in Eisenstein's *The Psychology of Composition*, written as part of a collaborative project with the neuropsychologist Alexander Luria,[12] were only compiled and translated after his death and finally published in 1987–by which time his extensive engagement with psychology and neuroscience had been largely overlooked. The findings of contemporary neuroscience since the mid-1990s, however, suggest that Bazin was right and that Eisenstein was well ahead of his time in positing a causative link between primitive affect and aesthetic form and in regarding this link as common to all of the arts.

Indeed, the recent discovery by contemporary neuroscientists of mirror neurons (discussed at length in chapter 9) lends support to the surmises of these earlier theorists by confirming that the psychological and somatic processes involved in the reception of cinema and literature–in terms of human brain behavior–are much the same irrespective of whether the representation is presented visually or verbally. There is, therefore, a great deal of sense in comparing the neuropsychological processes involved in fictive creativity across different forms of fictive representation, especially given that imaginative literary fiction invariably attempts to simulate a visual experience of the situations it evokes through verbal description, combined with the fact that the majority of people increasingly consume imaginative fictions via screens, whether in a cinema, on television, or on a computer.

Notwithstanding the new information about brain processes that neuroscience has been able to provide, the issues surrounding the author's creativity in fictive invention cannot be resolved with reference to neurobiology alone. Given the complexity introduced into human mental processes by the way memory works and the fact that the human brain has the ability to make "cinemalike editing choices," according to neuroscientist Antonio Damasio,[13] the processes involved in authorship can only be ascertained by marrying the findings of neuroscience with the insights of contemporary (post-Freudian) psychoanalysis. This is the approach I adopt in this book, responding to the call made by Eric Kandel, a distinguished Nobel Prize–winning neuroscientist, who in 1999 urged the marriage of psychoanalysis and neurobiology as a means of understanding the more complex operations of the human mind, which are far too complicated to be understood solely in terms of neuronal processes.[14] To develop this study, I draw on the work of other scholars who have begun to promote a synthesis of neuroscience and psychoanalysis in an emerging school of thought known as "neuropsychoanalysis."[15]

The need for a neuropsychoanalytic approach has been highlighted by the increasingly apparent shortcomings of cognitivist attempts to explain cinematic and literary representations. "Literary Darwinists," or "evolutionary critics," as they have become known, have proposed that fictive works are grounded in, and constrained by, biological and evolutionary conditions. This counters poststructuralist and cultural constructivist assumptions that meaning is subjectively and discursively produced.[16] The limitations of this approach, however, which treat the creation and reception of fiction as a wholly cognitive act, likening the human mind to a computer, are that they grossly underestimate the generative input of the emotions, assigning them instead a merely reactive, evaluative function. Although some cognitivists have since tried to rectify this excessive emphasis on cognition at the expense of emotion by accepting the "embodied nature of cognition generally,"[17] they still underestimate, and cannot account for, the unconscious processes that are equally apparent in the authoring of fiction. This is a major drawback of any account of fictive creation given that neuroscientists estimate that at least 90 percent of the operations of the mind are "largely nonconscious, internal, and unrevealed," becoming known only through "a narrow window of consciousness."[18] Consequently, cognitive approaches have been unable to provide a satisfactory explanation of the agentive input of the author, which remains a mystery and is largely ignored. As Isabel Jaén and Julien Jacques Simon, in their overview of the development of cognitive literary studies, acknowledge, some fundamental questions have been left unanswered: "How do we build a theory that integrates all those aspects of verbal art—author, text, reader, context—that previous criticism only considered fragmentarily? ... How do we account at the same level for agency, artifact, and context in human literary manifestations?"[19]

It is precisely these questions that this book aims to answer. Its purpose is to formulate a new synthesis that integrates the findings of affective neuroscience, drawing particularly on the work of Jaak Panksepp,[20] the hypotheses of post-Freudian object-relations theorists such as Joyce

McDougall and Christopher Bollas, and neuropsychoanalysts such as Allan Schore. This synthesis will account for the creative process emanating from the author-as-agent that is missing from virtually all theories of fictive representation propounded during the past half-century, the relation of this activity to the author's environmental circumstances, and the mechanisms and effects of the process of reception experienced by the reader/spectator.

The book also aims to develop a revised understanding of the process whereby readers/spectators receive and respond to a work of fiction, given that neuroscience is now able to develop a hypothesis about the affective attunement that takes place between the author and the recipient (see chapters 9 and 10). This account differs in important respects from accounts of reception that assume that this is solely a result of subjective constructions facilitated by the machineries of language.

To locate the theory I am propounding in the wide range of alternative theories, I commence this study in chapter 1 with an overview of thinking about fictive representation from earliest times to the present. From this overview, it becomes clear that the neuropsychoanalytic view I present was intuitively foreshadowed in the speculations of Aristotle and John Milton on the nature of catharsis, and that my hypothesis that the function of fiction is to procure an affective re-equilibration was foreshadowed in Sir Philip Sidney's brilliant intuition that "poesy"–that is, imaginative fiction–causes the author who invents it to "grow, in effect, into another nature."[21] In this respect, then, the synthesis formulated in this book is a professedly humanistic one in that, rather than seeing literature or cinema as a sub-branch of philosophy, it refocuses attention on the author's inventive creativity and on the effects that fiction has on a recipient at the level of embodied emotional experience that human beings–as we now know from affective neuroscience–share with all other mammals.

Having outlined the changing configurations that the theory of fiction has undergone from one period to another, I devote chapters 2 through 7 to a theoretical exposition of the mental processes that enter into the creation of fictive representations on the part of the author. I integrate the speculations of neuroscientists Joseph LeDoux, Antonio Damasio, and Jaak Panksepp with those of neuropsychoanalysts Allan Schore and David Servan-Schreiber and those of object-relations theorists D. W. Winnicott,

Joyce McDougall, and Christopher Bollas. On the basis of this synthesis, I propose that fictive representation is motivated by a desire to express primary affective experience from the precognitive levels of an author's brain in an effort to achieve emotional homeostasis. This attempt to reach some sort of personal emotional equilibrium by working through autobiographical issues in fictive form, I suggest, entails the use of images, symbolization, and other strategies of displacement to creative imaginative fantasies calibrated to address sources of perturbation, or to facilitate different types of explorative play, or to register delight at the appealing aspects of life that the world has to offer now or in the future. As human beings, we need either to create fictions or to consume them as a means of grasping the conditions of our lives in order to grow. Although this impulse sometimes arises out of pathology, this is not always the case: the urge to create often comes from the joy that can be derived from imposing order on what otherwise would be undifferentiated chaos and thus inaccessible to the sense of gaining control.

Chapters 8, 9, and 10 consider how fictive representations are received by readers and spectators and the effects that such reception induces. Again, having surveyed the conflicting theories that have been used to explain reception, I offer a neuropsychoanalytic account that suggests that the process of response involves much the same affective and emotional activity that goes into the creation of the fiction in the first place, with the reader/spectator displaying a comparable creativity in the way that he or she imaginatively adapts the representation to his or her psychic needs by re-creating a version of it with associations derived from personal memories, some of which are conscious and explicit but many of which are unconscious and implicit. In a recipient's experience of a fictive work, I suggest, there is an intersubjective exchange between the author and the respondent that involves an intentional attunement in which both exercise considerable agency.

To supplement the incidental discussions of cinematic and literary works in the earlier chapters (such as those analyzing Charlotte Brontë's *Jane Eyre*, Edmund Spenser's *The Faerie Queene*, Milton's *Samson Agonistes*, and the films of Ingmar Bergman, Bernardo Bertolucci, Jane Campion, Amos Kollek, and Alexander Payne), the final section of the book explains how the theory elaborated in earlier chapters might be applied through a series of case studies: Truffaut's acclaimed film *Jules and Jim* in chapter 10; William Shakespeare's *Hamlet*–the supreme test for any critical theory given its complexity and its status in Western consciousness–in chapter 11; and the entire oeuvre of the filmmaker François Ozon–the *enfant terrible* of contemporary French cinema–in chapter 12. These case studies illustrate the different levels at which the neuropsychoanalytic theory I propound may be applied, from consideration of a particular work to an exploration of an author's entire output. They also show how this theory directs attention back to the formal attributes of fictive representation and how these may be linked to the biographical circumstances of the author that inform a work's creation.

This book is designed primarily for scholars and students of literature and film, for whom it is meant to make neuroscientific information and psychoanalytic concepts accessible while demonstrating the integral links between them that make a neuropsychoanalytic approach to the study of fictive representation, whether through cinema or literature, so fruitful. I hope to show that such a perspective opens up a range of new possibilities and restores the legitimacy of certain aspects of fictive representation that have been badly neglected during the past few decades: the author's creative agency; the links between the author's biography and the content of the representation; the input of the emotions and their conversion into images and actions from which a symbolic configuration is formed; the psychological dimension of diverse narrative techniques; the role of the unconscious in motivating the preoccupations of a fiction and determining its content, through operations that bypass propositional logic and often remain unknown to the author until years after the work has been completed; and the ways in which intersubjective attunement between the author and the reader/spectator is solicited and achieved, and with what outcomes. All of these, as well as many other topics, open up exciting areas for future study.

Finally, I hope this book will suggest a more liberal, inclusive, humane approach to the study of fictive representation that reaffirms its relevance, once more, to the perennial, ongoing preoccupations in life that attest to our humanity. Storytelling is not just a form of entertainment, but one of the essential ways in which human beings attain an understanding of the conditions of their existence and, as the poet John Milton put it, set "their affections in right tune."[22]

1

Changing Configurations in Theories of Fictive Representation

Charting a course through the waters of theoretical speculation on the nature and function of fictive representation from earliest times to the present requires one to tack and turn to avoid shifting sandbanks. The reason for this tortuous path is that, while almost everything that has been said about fiction has been around for some time, the ways in which different schools of thought inflect these insights vary greatly, depending on whatever intellectual and ideological currents are flowing most powerfully when a particular theory is formulated. In this chapter, I provide an overview of the evolving ways in which fictive representation has been conceived in theory throughout history.

EMBODIED FICTIONS, OR FICTIONS AS SIGN? CLASSICAL PERSPECTIVES

Writing about 335 BC, Aristotle claimed that "poetry" (from Greek *poiesis*, or "making"–that is, a work of fictive invention) derives from *mimēsis*–an instinct toward representation that is "innate in human beings from childhood," through which we learn and in which we gain pleasure.[1] With respect to tragedy, which was the specific genre he was discussing, Aristotle believed that the function of the representation was to effect "through pity and fear the *catharsis* of such emotions."[2] Earlier, Simonides of Ceos (556–468 BC), according to Plutarch in his essay "De gloria

Atheniensium" (c. AD 100), had made the claim that "painting [is] inarticulate poetry and poetry articulate painting."³

These suppositions–that fictive representations have an educative purpose–work through the delight they impart, have an emotional influence, and function like a speaking picture, were reiterated as commonplaces by subsequent classical authors, most notably Horace in his *Ars Poetica* (c. 19 BC), in which he asserted: "Aut prodesse volunt, aut delectare poetae, / Aut simul et jucunda et idonea dicere vitae" (Poets aim either to benefit, or to amuse, or to utter words at once both pleasing and helpful to life),⁴ and claimed: "Omne tulit punctum qui miscuit utile dulci, lectorem delectando pariterque monendo" (The writer who has combined the pleasant with the useful wins on all points by delighting the reader while he gives advice).⁵ Following Simonides, Horace added: "Ut pictura poesis" (As a painting, so is a poem).⁶

Plato, in his *Republic* (c. 380 BC), countered this comparatively appreciative view of "poetry" by banishing poets from his ideal state on the grounds that "the imitative art is an inferior who marries an inferior, and has inferior offspring."⁷ Plato's disapproval arose not only because poetry merely produces an imitation of an imitation, and hence has "an inferior degree of truth" in relation to reality, but also because the poet "awakens and nourishes and strengthens the feelings and impairs the reason."⁸ Here, Plato, like Aristotle, identified the affective power of fictive representation, but disapproved of its influence. Because of his dualistic separation of reason and emotion, and his privileging of the former at the expense of the latter, he saw the emotion aroused by poetry as subverting reason rather than assisting or complementing it in a beneficial way.

In these early classical perspectives on poetic imitation, we can see the beginnings of a split between two conceptualizations: one, a view of fiction as embodied, integral, and operating instrumentally to achieve an emotional as well as cognitive end; the other, a sense that the literal surface of the fictive invention is illusory and therefore untrustworthy, which means that it needs to be penetrated to find the "truer" reality of which its literal sense is an imperfect manifestation achieved at several removes. Both of these perspectives persisted throughout the centuries to come. The embodied conceptualization found new life during the Renaissance, as reflected in the great works of Sir Thomas More, Sir Philip

Sidney, William Shakespeare, and John Milton. The dualistic view informed much of the literary activity of the Middle Ages. Both views are still very much with us, the former finding expression, for example, in cognitive criticism (but deprived of the affective dimension so valued during the Renaissance); the latter, in certain types of modern myth criticism (such as that of Northrup Frye) and various forms of psychoanalytic and poststructuralist criticism (such as that of Jacques Lacan).

THE EFFECTS OF CHRISTIAN CONVERSION: A MEDIEVAL BIFURCATION

Following the conversion of the Emperor Constantine, who ruled the Roman Empire from AD 306 to 337, and the rapid spread of Christianity throughout Europe, the second of the two classical perspectives on fictive representation—that is, the Platonic notion of an ideal reality of which fiction presented an imperfect shadow—took root in a method for interpreting the proper meaning of the Christian scriptures. One of the prime theorists for this method was Saint Augustine of Hippo (AD 354–430), who elaborated his theory of biblical exegesis in *De Doctrina Christiana* (On Christian Doctrine). According to Augustine, the narratives of the Bible are composed of "things" and "signs." A "thing" signifies "that which is never employed as a sign of anything else: for example, wood, stone, cattle, and other things of that kind." There is also a second category of things, those that, "though they are things, are also signs of other things." In addition, there is a third type: "those which are never employed except as signs." Accordingly, although "every sign is also a thing," the obverse is not true: "Every thing... is not also a sign."[9]

This system of biblical exegesis, which was grounded in a fundamental Platonic dualistic view of the world in relation to a transcendent "reality," was easily and quickly transferred to the interpretation of secular literature in order to present it as "Christianized." By adopting an allegorical method of interpretation, pagan subject matter, and the sensibility that accompanied it, could be considered compatible with Christian doctrine. One example of this allegorizing predisposition can be found in the late-Medieval French work *L'Ovide moralisé* (written between 1317 and 1328), which reinterprets Ovid's *Metamorphoses* by turning it into an exemplum of Christian morality. In the story of Jason and Medea (Book VII), for example, whereas Ovid did not judge Jason adversely for his desertion of Medea, in *L'Ovide moralisé* he is denounced as "li maus trichierres, / Li faus, li desloiaus, li lierres" (the evil trickster, the false, the disloyal one, the thief).[10] A similar impulse can be found in *De casibus virorum illustrium* (On the Fall of Illustrious People), written between 1355 and 1360 by Giovanni Boccaccio, which recounts the calamities befalling famous historical figures apparently favored by Fortune, such as Priam, Hannibal, Dido, Cleopatra, Cicero, and King Arthur, to point up the moral that the only sure way of overcoming misfortune is to adhere to the Christian conception of virtue.

Counterpointing this highly didactic medieval approach to literature, which was designed to underline the teaching function of fiction, was a radically contrasting form of literature that aimed solely to entertain–the existence of which attested to the extent to which Horace's mingling of *utile dulci* (profit and delight) had become unwound into two separate strands. The most colorful expression of this alternative mode of literature was the extremely scurrilous *fabliau* tradition that had arisen in France, Italy, and England, consisting of comic tales marked by sexual and scatological obscenity, anticlericalism, antifeminism, and anticourtliness. Examples of such *fabliaux* are Boccaccio's *Decameron* (1353) and several of Geoffrey Chaucer's *Canterbury Tales* (1387–1400)–for example, "The Reeve's Tale" and "The Miller's Tale"–which were themselves merely a fraction of a vast corpus of unrecorded popular forms forming a very vibrant tradition.[11]

THE RENAISSANCE HUMANIST SYNTHESIS AND ITS AFTERMATH

For about a century during the English literary renaissance, the idea of fictive representation as an embodied process working through the emotions and the view that through it one can gain access to transcendental truths were brought together again in the Christian-humanist synthesis of the later sixteenth and the early seventeenth century. This was a period in which writers sought ways of reconciling a revived classical learning inspired by ancient Greece and Rome, which privileged the pursuit of rational wisdom through the persuasive eloquence of rhetoric, with the Calvinist-inspired theology of the Reformation in England with its emphasis on spirituality.[12]

One can register the change wrought by the revival of classicism in the comments of Sir Thomas More, one of the early English humanists, on the function of images, especially in relation to interpretation of the Bible. Whereas for Saint Augustine and later medieval exegetes, the literal sense had been less important than the allegorical meaning that could be extrapolated from it, More laid much more importance on the literal meaning itself, especially as conveyed through visual imagery: "Ymages paynted / grauen / or carued / may be so well wrought and so nere to the quycke and to ye trouth / that they shall naturally / and moche more effectually represent the thynge then shall the name either spoken or wrytten."[13] To illustrate his point, More cited the visual impact of a crucifix: "There is no man I wene so good nor so well lerned / nor in medytacyon so well accustomyd / but that he fyndyth himself more mouyd to pyte and compassion / vpon the beholdynge of the holy crucyfyxe / than whan he lackyth it."[14] As Plato and Aristotle had centuries earlier, More here acknowledged the moving power of fictive representation, working through images of sight, to arouse the emotions. Unlike Plato, however, More approved of this affective influence as a good thing because of its very instrumentality; indeed, he went as far as to say, in an insight that foreshadows the invention of cinema nearly 400 years later, that "surely sauynge that men can not do it / els if it might commodiously be done / there were not in this worlde so effectuall wrytyng as were to expresse all thing in ymagery."[15]

More transferred this belief in the innate connection of meaning to the literal sense, and the emotion it arouses through visualization, to the secular sphere in his practices as a writer of fiction. Rather than construct a fictive representation that was merely a pretext for delivering an allegorical *significatio* (i.e., decoded meaning), in which the fiction could be discarded like a husk once the kernel of signification had been extracted, he employed a fully dramatized, mimetic mode in writing *Utopia* (1516) – which Sir Philip Sidney recognized as the "most absolute [way of] patterning a commonwealth" because of how it exploits "the feigned image of poesy."[16]

In defining "poesy" (i.e., fictive representation) as "an art of imitation ... that is to say, a representing, counterfeiting, or figuring forth–to speak metaphorically, a speaking picture,"[17] Sidney was drawing on what Stephen Halliwell has identified as "a second family of meanings" in the word *mimēsis* that is often ignored: the idea that fictive representation has to do with "model-building and imagination," which signifies "a 'world simulating' or 'world creating' conception of artistic representation" rather than a "world reflecting" one.[18] This mode of fiction-making was to be the lifeblood of poetic creativity in England for the next hundred years and was to eventuate in some of the greatest works ever written in the English language–or in any language, for that matter.

Sidney himself was the outstanding theoretician of this fusion of classical aesthetics with Christian spirituality in sixteenth-century England, elaborating a synthesis that survived in various forms until the twentieth century. Picking up on the classical theorists, Sidney, like More, alleged an affective power in the mimetic mode of fictive representation that is capable of moving the "poet" (and his readers) "into another nature"–with "no small argument to the incredulous of that first accursed fall of Adam: since our erected wit maketh us know what perfection is, and yet our infected will keepeth us from reaching unto it."[19] The difference between Sidney's version of these ideas and the earlier formulations of Aristotle and Plato was that, for Sidney, as for More, poetry did not merely "move," but delighted "to move men to take that goodness in hand, which without delight they would fly as from a stranger, and teach, to make them know that goodness whereunto they are moved."[20]

Although he lacked the scientific evidence that neuroscience has now supplied, Sidney intuited the processes of mind that lend peculiar force to fictive representations. Comparing philosophy and history with "poesy" (the sixteenth-century term for fictive representation) in terms of their relative effectiveness in conveying insights into how life should best be lived, Sidney concluded that the former two are inferior to the latter because, whereas philosophy prioritizes "precept" and history focuses on "example," "both, not having both, do both halt."[21] The writer of fiction, asserted Sidney, is more effective than either the philosopher or the historian, because he "yieldeth to the powers of the mind an image...."[22] As a consequence, any forms of knowledge that either philosophy or history can impart, in Sidney's view, "notwithstanding, lie dark before the imaginative and judging power, if they be not illuminated or figured forth by the speaking picture of poesy."[23]

Centuries before Freud, then, Sidney grasped the function of symbolization and the instrumentality of the emotions in the processes of mind that are necessary to the effectual conduct of life. Before the mind can know consciously what it needs to address, it needs to attach the associated emotion to an image, which in turn moves the subject into a course of action that is elected as a result of rational reflection (in Sidney's terms, the "imaginative and judging power"). All that neuroscience would subsequently discover through neurobiological experimentation is intuitively prefigured in this young man's brilliant intuition (he was only about twenty-five when he wrote *An Apology for Poetry*). This insight enabled Sidney to claim that the moving power of fictive representation, far from being reprehensible (because irrational) and something to be feared, was instrumental to a regenerative end. In this way, he was able to counter attacks by contemporary Puritan moralists who denounced "poetry" as promoting depravity. One of these was the diatribe published by Stephen Gosson in his *School of Abuse, Containing a Pleasant Invective against Poets, Pipers, Players, Jesters, and Such Like Caterpillars of a Commonwealth* (1579).[24] However, the supreme refutation of such Puritan denunciations, and perhaps the fullest exemplification of Sidney's theory of poetry during the Renaissance, was John Milton's *Paradise Lost* (1567), together with the brief epic *Paradise Regained* (1671) and his tragic drama *Samson Agonistes* (published in the same volume), which I analyze in a subsequent chapter.

NEOCLASSICISM VERSUS ROMANTICISM: A NEW DISJUNCTION

Following the vitalizing blend of Renaissance humanism and spiritual belief and of reason and emotion, which was able to dramatize the tensions in human experience without loss of complexity, successive literary periods again tended to separate out the integrated elements of this synthesis, emphasizing one or the other at the expense of the rest, and sometimes advancing one as a reaction against the other. For example, in the age of

Augustan "neoclassicism," the humanist element became rigidified into a set of assumptions that privileged reason, order, and "Nature," as in Alexander Pope's *Essay on Criticism* (1711):

> First follow nature, and your judgement frame
> By her just standard, which is still the same:
> Unerring nature, still divinely bright,
> One clear, unchang'd, and universal light,
> Life, force, and beauty, must to all impart,
> At once the source, and end, and test of art.
> Art from that fund each just supply provides;
> Works without show, and without pomp presides:
> In some fair body thus th'informing soul
> With spirits feeds, with vigour fills the whole,
> Each motion guides, and every nerve sustains;
> Itself unseen, but in th'effects, remains.
> (lines 68–79)[25]

The function of fictive representation is thus to reproduce the "order" found in Nature, and the best way of doing this is to follow "those rules of old discover'd, not devis'd," which "Are nature still, but nature methodiz'd" (lines 88–89). Hence, drama needed to conform to the classical unities of action, place, and time, and verse needed to be constrained within the order imposed by the heroic couplet. The religious element, on the other hand, grounded in an awareness of the deficiencies that entered human nature after the Fall, produced a preoccupation with satire, as in Jonathan Swift's *Gulliver's Travels* (1726), which castigated such human defects as vanity, cupidity, and base carnal desires.

Predictably, such an identification of literature with "enlightened" rationality and order soon led to a privileging of their opposites, first in the elevation of emotion and the power of the creative imagination espoused by the Romantics and then in the aestheticism of the *fin-de-siècle* writers and critics at the end of the nineteenth century, who espoused the doctrine of "art for art's sake." Representing the first tendency, the English Romantic poet William Wordsworth, commenting on the choice of subjects in his *Lyrical Ballads* (1800), reveals that

> Humble and rustic life was generally chosen, because, in that condition, the essential passions of the heart find a better soil in which they can attain

their maturity ... because in that condition of life our elementary feelings coexist in a state of greater simplicity, and, consequently, may be more accurately contemplated and more forcibly communicated.[26]

Similarly, Samuel Taylor Coleridge extolled the creative power of the imagination, which he elevated to a status above reason:

> The primary IMAGINATION I hold to be the living Power and prime Agent of all human Perception, and as a repetition in the finite mind of the eternal act of creation in the infinite I AM. The secondary Imagination I consider as an echo of the former, co-existing with the conscious will. . . . It dissolves, diffuses, dissipates, in order to re-create.[27]

Thus, rather than being constrained by a highly rigidified structure of order in both society and nature, European Romantics, in the words of Isaiah Berlin, were impelled by

> a new and restless spirit, seeking violently to burst through old and cramping forms, a nervous preoccupation with perpetually changing inner states of consciousness, a longing for the unbounded and the indefinable, for perpetual movement and change, an effort to return to the forgotten sources of life, a passionate effort at self-assertion both individual and collective, a search after means of expressing an unappeasable yearning for unattainable goals.[28]

The Romantic reaction against the neoclassical "Augustan" conception of literature reflected a major shift motivated by social and economic developments in the eighteenth century, one that promoted a further move away from a preoccupation with a rigidly hierarchized ethical and social order toward a new emphasis on the aspirations and psychological condition of the individual. In literary practice, this change of focus led to the rise of the novel;[29] in literary theory, it led to a privileging of creative originality and aesthetic experience.

DISPLACING THE LOCATIONS OF AUTHORITY: MODERNISM AND POSTMODERNISM

The forces for change set in motion by the social, economic, and intellectual developments of the eighteenth and nineteenth centuries initiated by the Industrial Revolution (which had commenced in the second half of the eighteenth century) produced still more dramatic consequences in the first half of the twentieth century. Both the horrors of the First World War (1914–1918) and the deprivations of the Great Depression generated skepticism not only about the certainties of the Enlightenment, but also about the idealism of Romanticism (including that of late Romantics, such as Matthew Arnold, who were inclined to see literature as a substitute for religion). Consequently, there soon eventuated a wholesale dismantling of the prior assumptions of the two movements that had proven so effete in the face of the realities of the industrial age.

In literary theory, this dismantling began with modernists' subversion of the authority of the author, first by replacing it with the form and structure of the work itself and then by transferring it to contextual factors such as class, ideology, and gender operating through discourses. Further dismantling was subsequently accomplished by the postmodernists, who attempted to deconstruct the possibility of determinate meaning in fictive works altogether.

As a result of these successive intellectual impulses, the twentieth century saw a wholesale rejection, in theory, of the privileging of rationality, of the primacy of ethical and social order, of poetic "sensibility" as valued by the Romantics, and of the personality of the individual. Instead, the catch-cry was "Make It New!"[30] In practice, this meant rejecting realism in favor of symbolism, surrealism, expressionism, imagism, and experiments with avant garde forms and styles; in theory, it meant rejecting the idea that literature should represent the personality of the author as creative genius and abandoning any idea that literature might express the values of a stable human and social order.

A typical reaction was that of T. S. Eliot and others who adhered to the "New Criticism," believing that poetic creation involves a process of *depersonalization*, whereby the poet engages in a "continual surrender of himself . . . a continual self-sacrifice, a continual extinction of personality."[31] In Eliot's view, "poetry is not a turning loose of emotion, but an escape from emotion; it is not the expression of personality, but an escape from personality."[32] Such overturning of prior conventional assumptions was replaced by a type of formalism that denied the relevance of meaning outside the text itself, and of any historical context. Instead, the enduring structures of great art were seen as timeless: a man writes, said Eliot, "with a feeling that the whole of the literature of Europe from Homer and within it the whole of the literature of his own country has a simultaneous existence and composes a simultaneous order."[33]

Postmodernism, which arose in the aftermath of, and as a reaction to, the Second World War (1939–1945), took this process a step further, seeing as its main target "essentialist" principles that had reached their apotheosis in the Enlightenment and were still lingering in aspects of modernism.[34] In retrospect, one can see that postmodernism was a response to the Second World War's horrific demonstration of the damage that could be done by authoritarianism and totalizing systems–specifically, how rationality could become an instrument of oppressive ideologies enforced through state apparatuses; how the elevation of the individual could produce dictators like Hitler, Mussolini, and Stalin; how the "civilizing" mission of imperialism could lead to economic exploitation and cultural/political subjugation of colonized nations–with all of those negative manifestations of the principles informing humanist idealism being expressed in global calamities of nearly unimaginable proportions.

Inevitably, in the world of the academy there was a powerful reaction against the intellectual assumptions that had delivered such an assault on human well-being. The outcome was a series of theoretical reformulations prefaced by "post" to signify an even more radical break with the past than that which modernism had attempted: "poststructuralism," "postmodernism," "postcolonialism," which collectively comprise a bundle of doctrines subsequently referred to as "critical theory."

At the heart of all these new theories was a dismantling of perceived systems of domination and authority–ethical, political, and epistemological–accomplished through the simple expedient of using the linguistic theory of Ferdinand de Saussure regarding the differential process used to assign signifieds to signifiers to undermine the possibility of stable meaning altogether, and hence the existence of any of the universals privileged by classical-humanist-Enlightenment thought. As the theorist Robert Stam has pointed out, this destabilization was achieved by re-inscribing Saussure's concept of a differential relation existing *between* signs as "a relation *within* signs, whose constitutive nature is one of constant displacement or trace." This move destroyed any possibility of determinate meaning being contained in the work itself.[35]

The effect of such an assumption can be seen in the work of Christian Metz, one of the foundational theorists of cinema, who foregrounded "the *psychoanalytic constitution of the cinematic signifier*."[36] Applying a model from Lacan's linguistically derived notion of the unconscious as being structured like a language, Metz saw representation as posing a problem: "How does the spectator effect the mental leap which alone can lead him from the perceptual *donnée*, consisting of moving visual and auditory impressions, to the constitution of a fictional universe, from an objectively real but denied signifier to an imaginary but psychologically real signified?"[37] His solution was to propose that cinema presents a representation that stimulates the senses while reminding us of the "lack of presence," so that what we perceive as not real is therefore imaginary.[38] Adopting an even more extreme version of this view, Slavoj Žižek pushes the logic of the implied answer to the question by asserting that "the subject" (in this case, the spectator), "is 'spoken' by the symbolic structure, rather than the other way round," thus extending Metz's application of Lacan's argument to a further extremity.[39]

Once this basic differential relation within signs had been asserted–as Gilles Deleuze, for example, did in proposing his "philosophy of difference,"[40] all value systems, by extension, and, indeed, our perception of empirical reality itself could be seen as inescapably relativized; all totalizing grand narratives could be considered destabilized; all objective grounds for authority could be deemed to have vanished; and psychological, social, and historical phenomena could be dismissed as manifestations merely of contingency, not of any cause and effect. And once Jacques Lacan had posited that the unconscious itself is structured like a language, the very idea of a unified human subject with agency could be dismissed, to be replaced with the notion of a "self" that is decentered, fragmented, and trapped in a space of inescapable indeterminacy.

The philosopher Frank Farrell has succinctly summed up the moves implicit in this radical epistemological shift, which occurred during the second half of the twentieth century:

The passage from modern thought to the present might be described in terms of three great reductions: first, modern thinkers dissolve the world into mind or subjectivity; the subjective or psychological as expressed in a phenomenology of the conscious self and its self-to-world relations, is dissolved into language; and third, that level of the linguistic or grammatical may be dissolved into social practices, into patterns of social power.[41]

In the domain of literary theory, the elimination of a stable sign instantly subverted the possibility of any interpretations of fictive works other than those that found in the work a confirmation of deconstructive theory—given that, in accordance with the theory, none other was possible. Similarly, the decentering of the human subject led, in Roland Barthes's famous formulation, to "the death of the author" and "the birth of the reader."[42] Both of these outcomes tended to divert attention from the intrinsic attributes of the fictive work, redirecting it instead toward the extrinsic cultural conditions deemed to have "written" it. Ultimately, the replacement of objectivity by an assumption of inescapable subjectivity destroyed the very possibility of any kind of "meaning" that could be considered authoritative, fueling a deep, pervasive skepticism.

In a complementary postmodernist dismantling of "essentialist" notions of universality, cultural theorists such as Stuart Hall argued that representations cannot escape being grounded in historically specific cultural contexts owing to the presence of discursive formations that shape their construction, and hence are instrumental in creating particular "regimes" of representation.[43] In Hall's view, a discursive approach "examines not only how language and representation produce meaning, but how the knowledge which a particular discourse produces connects with power, regulates conduct, makes up or constructs identities and subjectivities, and defines the way certain things are represented, thought about, practiced and studied."[44] Unlike pre–World War II formalist critics such as T. S. Eliot, or universalists such as the Canadian theorist Northrop Frye, both of whom detached fictive art from any authorial or historical specificity, the cultural critic assumes an inescapable imbrication of the work in time-bounded specificities that differ from one cultural context to another.

RENEWED ALLEGORICIZATIONS: PSYCHOANALYTIC THEORIES OF INTERPRETATION

At the same time as various versions of modernist and postmodernist critical theory were being formulated, another type of intellectual challenge to prior assumptions about the nature of fictive representation was being mounted, in this case by psychoanalytic literary theorists. Almost without exception, these theories were based on Sigmund Freud's model of the mind as consisting not only of rational consciousness, but also of an unconscious dimension that underlay it, generating repression of forbidden or unwanted content through psychic defenses, such as metaphoric condensation, metonymical displacement, and fantasy. More fatally, however, these theorists followed Freud's own decision to privilege the *repressed* unconscious—with its conflicted sexual and aggressive dimensions (in accordance with his theory of the libidinal and aggressive drives)–at the expense of the *receptive* unconscious, the implications of which have constituted a comprehensive concept of the unconscious that was too complex to be communicated in Freud's time, even though, as Christopher Bollas has recently demonstrated, Freud recognized this complexity.[45]

From the beginning, Freud's ideas were applied to literature, not least by Freud himself. In chapter 5 of *The Interpretation of Dreams*, for example, Freud cited Sophocles's *Oedipus Rex* and Shakespeare's *Hamlet* as exemplifying his belief that parents play a leading part in the infantile psychology of all persons who subsequently become "psychoneurotics."[46] In his reading of *Hamlet*, for instance, the reason that Hamlet hesitates to exact his revenge on the man who killed his father and took his father's place with his mother is that Claudius "shows him in realization the repressed desires of his own childhood."[47]

Scholars were quick to take up Freud's ideas in their literary analyses and to seek in literature confirmation of the truth of his theories. Ernest Jones, for example, developed Freud's observations about *Hamlet* into a book-length study published in 1949,[48] and psychoanalytic criticism, treating literary characters as case studies, soon became fixated on the Oedipus complex in literature. Freud's theory of repression and displacement became the justification for searching out and decoding symbols, with the result that the literary work, in the words of Norman Holland, was viewed "as a congress of phalluses, vaginas, and anuses, with token reverence to aesthetic mysteries."[49] This simplistic approach, as Holland observes, gave psychoanalytic criticism a very bad name. Harold Bloom, for example, dismissed Freudian literary criticism of Shakespeare as "a celestial joke."[50]

The real reason for such hostility, one suspects, was that the kind of interpretation applied by the likes of Freud and Ernest Jones involved allegorization as extreme as that practiced by the Christian exegetes of the Middle Ages. By that I mean that the literal sense of the fiction was regarded simply as a shell (in Freudian terms, a "defense,") that concealed the real, timeless inner meaning, which consisted of the universal structures of the psyche as hypothesized by Freud's drive theory; this shell could be discarded once the kernel had been extracted.

Later Freudian theorists tried to devise more subtle formulations of this interpretive framework, but their paradigms nonetheless retain the basic split between the sign and the signified on which it depends. Norman Holland has argued that the purpose of literature is to be "a *self-stimulation system*," in which "we are cycling through well-nigh instantaneous circuits of expectation, form-and-defense, content as schemas and fantasy, and finally a closure or 'making sense' that gratifies the original expectation" and thus safeguards our pleasure.[51] Unlike earlier Freudian theories, this modified Freudian approach shifts the emphasis from the psychology of the author and/or his or her characters to the process and effects of reception; nonetheless, it still depends upon an assumption that the work of fiction is to maintain defenses, involving repression, against the primary fantasies posited by Freud and later followers (such as Melanie Klein).

Another theorist who offers a nuanced account of how Freudian theory can be used to illuminate literature is Peter Brooks. Taking *Beyond the Pleasure Principle* as Freud's "masterplot," Brooks constructs another theory of representation based on Freud's drive theory. As an alternative to using Freud to study the psychogenesis of the text (the author's unconscious), the dynamics of literary response (the reader's unconscious), or the "occult motivations" of the characters, Brooks focuses on "the dynamics of temporality and reading, of the motive forces that drive the text forward, of the desires that connect narrative ends and beginnings, and make of the textual middle a highly charged force."[52] In this model, "desire" is not only "the motor force of plot," but also "the very motive of narrative" itself, being present at the beginning of a plot and showing itself ultimately to be a desire for the end.[53] Between the beginning and the end is an "inescapable middle" consisting of "repetition and return," both of which are "perverse and difficult, interrupting simple movement forward."[54] The reason for this "doubling back," according to Brooks (following Freud), is that "*the aim of all life is death*," which reflects an innate desire in all human beings to restore an early state of things. Consequently, "What operates in the text through repetition is the death instinct, the drive towards the end."[55] In Brooks's view, all narrative texts display an ambiguous dynamic:

> We have a curious situation in which two principles of forward movement [the pleasure principle and the death drive] operate upon one another so as to create retard, a dilatory space in which pleasure can come from postponement in that this—in the manner of forepleasure?—is a necessary approach to the true end.[56]

The logical outcome of such a supposition is that "plot itself stands as a kind of divergence or deviance, a postponement in the discharge which leads back to the inanimate."[57] As with Holland's elaboration of Freud, the emphasis in Brooks's model shifts from the author to the reader, resulting in the fiction itself being seen as less important than the underlying drive that it serves to mask.

A far more radical revision of Freudian ideas was accomplished by the French psychoanalyst Jacques Lacan, who, while not developing a fully fledged theory of representation, drew on literature to support his rereading of Freud so as to make Freud's tenets accord with poststructuralist belief in the agency of language in subjective constitution. Using Edgar Allan Poe's short story "The Purloined Letter" as an exemplification, Lacan asserted that "the unconscious is structured like a language,"[58] an assumption that allowed him to suppose that speech and language are beyond the subject's control, meaning that, to the contrary, the subject is written by "the Other [which] must first of all be considered a locus, the locus in which speech is constituted."[59]

These key Lacanian ideas have been taken up by one disciple in particular, Slavoj Žižek, who uses them to support an even more extreme contention with respect to fictive representation. Frequently drawing on cinema to illustrate his radical theory, Žižek argues that the very power of "the fictitious world of symbols" to tear apart "what 'naturally' belongs together," proves "*the inherent ontological nullity of what we call 'reality.'*"[60] He sees *The Matrix* (Andy Wachowski, 1999) as a paradigmatic exemplification of this supposition:

> What, then, is *The Matrix*? Simply the Lacanian "big Other," the virtual symbolic order, the network that structures reality for us. This dimension of the "big Other" is that of the constitutive alienation of the subject in the symbolic order: the big Other pulls the strings, the subject doesn't speak, he "is spoken" by the symbolic structure. In short, this "big Other" is the name for the social substance, for all that on account of which the subject never fully dominates the effects of his acts, that is on account of which the final outcome of his activity is always something else with regard to what he aimed at or anticipated.[61]

Inevitably, then, Žižek ends up where any assumption that the unconscious is structured like a language (in accordance with Lacan's unsubstantiated conjecture) must inevitably lead: to an inescapable indeterminacy in which even the possibility of an objective subject position is denied. Thus, to approach the fictive work as an object in its own right with any kind of determinate signification other than a confirmation of the veracity of the theory informing the approach is a futile enterprise from the outset.[62]

ALTERNATIVE PSYCHOANALYTIC FORMULATIONS: OBJECT-RELATIONS THEORY

A much more fruitful harnessing of psychoanalytic theory to fictive creativity, in my view, can be found in the work of scholars and clinicians who have drawn on object-relations theory as developed by Melanie Klein, Wilfred Bion, D. W. Winnicott, Joyce McDougall, and, more recently, Christopher Bollas.

One of the most important theorists who have built on their theoretical foundations is Hanna Segal, who looked to Klein for her speculations on aesthetics. According to Segal, "Every creative artist produces a world of his own. Even when he believes himself to be a complete realist and sets himself the task of faithfully reproducing the external world, he in fact only uses elements of the existing external world to create with them a reality of his own."[63] In Segal's view, based on her reading of the fiction of Marcel Proust, "an artist is compelled to create by his need to recover his lost past." The function of a work of representational art, she says, is to capture memories that would otherwise remain fleeting, elusive, and "emotionally valueless and dead" in order to give them permanent life, to integrate them with the rest of life.[64] For Segal, the creation of a fictive work of art is thus a reparative response to *mourning*–rooted in Klein's depressive position–that is designed to re-create the lost world:

> all creation is really a re-creation of a once loved and once whole, but now lost and ruined object, a ruined internal world and self. It is when the world within us is destroyed, when it is dead and loveless, when our loved ones are in fragments, and we ourselves in helpless despair–it is then that we must re-create our world anew, reassemble the pieces, infuse life into dead fragments, re-create life.[65]

Here is a version of psychoanalytic theory that sees fictive representation not primarily in terms of drives, repression, and defense mechanisms, but rather as an instrument of self-repair. Even though Segal's theory is far too narrowly circumscribed by a preoccupation with mourning as the motive for fictive creation, and is altogether too morbid to account for the full range of preoccupations that fictive creation encompasses, by emphasizing the role of memory in the construction of invented images, it does anticipate a number of the discoveries that neuroscience would make about how the brain works.

Before closing this discussion of psychoanalytic theories of fictive representation, one should acknowledge Northrop Frye's recasting of Carl Jung's theory of archetypes residing in the collective unconscious into a comprehensive theory of literature as "an order of words . . . [involving] conventional myths and metaphors."[66] Although Frye, who claimed to work empirically, did not explicitly identify his theory as psychoanalytic, like Jung he saw literature "as a complication of a relatively restricted and simple group of formulas that can be studied in primitive culture,"[67] meaning that literature can be systematized into a set of modes, symbols, and genres that transmit and diversify this inherent mythology. For Frye, as for Jung, these recurrent structures attest to structures in the mind that are just as universal and timeless as Freud's supposed libidinal and aggressive drives, along with the developmental phases they entail.

RENEWED FORMALISMS: COGNITIVE
AND EVOLUTIONARY THEORIES

By the mid-1990s, it had become apparent that theories of fictive representation grounded in poststructuralism, psychoanalysis, and social constructivism were increasingly being perceived as having exhausted their usefulness.[68] Scholars like David Bordwell, in *Post-Theory* (1996), rejected the whole project of "Grand Theory" as spurious because of its "ethereal speculations."[69] In particular, scholars were growing dissatisfied with the displacement of attention away from the form and content in the work itself to the process whereby the individual reader/spectator constructs meaning in response to it, accompanied by a further displacement of the author-as-creative-originator by larger extrinsic discursive, ideologically inflected formations that are presumed to "write" the work independently of any individual agent.

The inevitable reaction, when it came, drew on the resources of cognitive science and evolutionary biology to direct attention back to the phenomenal qualities of a fictive work, relating these to the evolved needs of human nature, which once again were seen as *essential*.[70] Evolutionary criticism and cognitive theory express themselves in literary studies as "literary Darwinism" and in film studies as "evolutionary bioculturalism,"[71] both having as their target the idea—intrinsic to postmodernist theories—that discourse "constructs" reality. In contrast, cognitivism, as F. Elizabeth Hart states, "accepts that the brain/mind is a constraining mechanism through which all human knowledge and experience must filter," which has the effect of deconstructing "the epistemological extremes of realism and relativism," substituting instead a notion of "constrained constructivism."[72]

A cognitive approach to literature drawing on social and experimental psychology has found a vociferous advocate in Patrick Colm Hogan, who, in a way that parallels (although in very different terms) the efforts of Carl Jung and Northrop Frye, has reintroduced the idea of "literary universals" in his book *The Mind and Its Stories: Narrative Universals and Human Emotion* (2003). Hogan's argument is designed to counter the particularist view held by postcolonial literary theorists that universality is "a hegemonic European critical tool."[73] In defense of his position, he asserts that "the study of literary universals is largely a subfield of cognitive research," arguing that "literary universals are to a great extent the direct outcome of specifiable cognitive structures and processes applied in particular domains and with particular purposes."[74] More recently, drawing on neural network theories, Hogan has argued in *How Authors' Minds Make Stories* (2013) that the creations of great authors "result from the same operations as our everyday counterfactual and hypothetical imaginations, which cognitive scientists refer to as simulations."[75]

Literary Darwinism is exemplified by Brian Boyd's book *On the Origin of Stories* (2009), which, as the allusion to the *Origin of the Species* suggests, draws heavily on the Darwin's evolutionary theory. Combining Darwin's ideas with certain findings of neurobiology, Boyd proposes that art is an adaptation designed to enhance the chances of human survival. He defines artistic representations as "cognitive play with pattern," surmising that "art's appeal to our preferences for pattern ensures that we expose ourselves to high concentrations of humanly appropriate information eagerly enough that over time we strengthen the neural pathways that process key patterns in open-ended ways."[76] Thus, art "serves as a stimulus and training for a flexible mind, as play does for the body and physical behavior" and becomes "a social and individual system for engendering creativity, for producing options not confined by the here and now or the immediate and given."[77] Positing the existence of "intuitive ontologies," Boyd argues that, as we track focal characters in stories, "simulation allows us to make swift inferences about their situation from goal-relevant information that we amplify by keeping it alive in working memory."[78]

Further theoretical conceptualizations in this vein can be found in the work of those who embrace the emerging fields of neuroaesthetics and psychocinematics. These include Paul. B. Armstrong's *How Literature Plays with the Brain* (2013), which explores the neuronal processes involved in aesthetic experience, and *Psychocinematics: Exploring Cognition at the Movies*, edited by Arthur P. Shimamura, which investigates the techniques filmmakers use to drive our sensations, thoughts, and feelings.[79] In my view, the limitation of these approaches is that they reduce mental events to simple brain processes that can be observed through functional magnetic resonance imaging (fMRI), leaving unexplained the more complex forms of mental activity that motivate and drive the creation and composition of fictive representations in the first place. The result is an extreme form of reductionism. Integrating neuroscience with a phenomenological approach, for example, Armstrong articulates a view similar to that of Brian Boyd:

> Literature plays with the brain through experiences of harmony and dissonance that set in motion and help to negotiate oppositions that are fundamental to the neurobiology of mental functioning–basic tensions in the operation of the brain between the drive for pattern, synthesis, and constancy versus the need for flexibility, adaptability, and openness to change.[80]

For Armstrong, as for Boyd, fictive representation is conceptualized as an adaptive tool for strengthening the effectiveness of cognitive processes designed to enhance our chances of biological survival. While this may be true, it leaves unexplained the origins and disposition of the content to be found in fictive representations and the affective impact this content induces in the reader.

In cinema, an equivalent to this literary theory of representation can be found in Torben Grodal's *Moving Pictures: A New Theory of Film Genres, Feelings, and Cognition* (1997) and *Embodied Visions: Evolution, Emotion, Culture, and Film* (2009).[81] Like Boyd's assumption of "intuitive ontologies," Grodal maintains that "aspects of the human mind have been formatted by evolution" to promote certain functions based on "innate brain-circuitry."[82] Being the product of evolutionary adaptation, the templates are unchangeable and universal, lying outside any kind of cultural specificity. In Grodal's view, "audiovisual media are the most sophisticated yet invented by man for simulating and manipulating the many ways in which we perceive, feel, think, act, memorize, associate, and socialize."[83] Filmic fictions, he says, "reflect core elements in the emotional heritage that enhanced human survival in the past," often being "based on stories and situations that activate innate emotional dispositions."[84] The purpose of fiction is to facilitate brain functions that provide "basic models for the way in which we orient ourselves in the physical and social world."[85] Ironically, by investing fiction with an instructional and educative purpose, cognitive theory has brought speculation right back to the neoclassical humanist view expressed by Sir Philip Sidney in 1580, that the function of poetry is to feign "notable images of virtues, vices, or what else."[86]

NEUROPSYCHOANALYSIS AND THE NEED FOR A NEW SYNTHESIS

Although all of the theories discussed in this overview have some valid insights to offer, none of them in itself is sufficient to account for fictive representation as a persistent phenomenon in human experience. Moreover, many of them are exaggerated in their claims or excessively reductive, given that each theory tends to seize on one or more aspects of the phenomenon and assert it as the whole. And in formulating its theories, each age, it is clear, understandably tends to define them in accordance with its own concerns, values, and ideological investments, all of which are conditioned by cultural and political circumstances prevailing at the time. The effect is to produce a constraining reflexivity that makes all of these theories seem unsatisfactory and time bound.

A further pattern can be observed: each successive age either overcorrects the extremes and excesses in the theories of the previous one, or else pushes the tendencies latent in those theories to an even more extreme formulation. As a result, theories end up being excessively partisan as well as partial. As natural as this may be, given the tendency of human beings to structure their thought in terms of binary oppositions, such partiality and exclusion is deeply unfortunate. There is no need to repudiate everything that has been said about fictive representation by one's predecessors in order to remedy oversights or introduce new insights; indeed, it seems implausible that so many observers throughout history could have been completely wrong. There *is* some imitative component that relates fiction to a reality that is neither merely discursively constructed nor apprehended purely through a relativized and relativizing process of internal differentiation. Fiction often *does* seem to mirror the real world in terms that are not solipsistically subjective, just as the classical writers and neoclassical theorists supposed. It is equally true that fiction *is* both pleasant and useful, and that the countless millions of people who have sought it out and read or viewed it have done so because it provides a source of instruction and entertainment. To acknowledge as much is not to deny that the response of readers and spectators *is* highly subjective or that texts *are* susceptible to a multitude of different readings according to whatever perspective or experience individual readers/spectators bring to it. Nor is it to deny that ideologies working through discourses *do* have a significant influence on how texts come to be written and consumed. Furthermore, it would be foolish to deny that works of fiction constitute aesthetic objects, with their own internal architecture and representational systems, that have no relationship to any cultural contexts outside the text. It would also be foolish to ignore the light that cognitive science has been able to shed on how the brain reacts to stimulation provided by the patterning found in fictive representation, reinforced by highly potent images of sight, sound, hearing, and taste presented to the reader/spectator.

In short, while all of the explanations proposed to date have something to offer, none by itself is sufficient to account for the phenomenon as a whole; moreover, many of their claims are counterintuitive. The emphasis in poststructuralist theory on the subjective response of the reader/spectator, for example, has deflected attention from the creative input of the author and from the text or film as an object in its own right, with its own intrinsic properties, form, and meaning. Manifestly, fictive representations *do* have authors, and it is worthwhile knowing what motivates those authors, how their fictions come to be created, and what purpose these fictions serve, both for the author and the reader/spectator. To study literature or film through an extrinsic approach alone—whether as a manifestation of culturally determined discursive formations, or the material circumstance of production—leads to a very impoverished reading that overlooks many elements observable in the enunciation of these fictions, along with their affective impact.

Although the cognitive theories that have been proliferating recently mark a step in the right direction by emphasizing the role of the human brain in the construction of fiction, many of them are limited by their assumption that fictive creation is exclusively a *cognitive* activity, placing an excessive emphasis on *cognition* at the expense of *emotion* and *conation* (or motivation). As a result, they deal only with the byproduct of fictive creation, ignoring its motivation and its affective function.

Predictably, such an emphasis has eventuated in a new kind of formalism, in which the main activity of criticism is to perceive patterns and deviations from them, along with the narrating strategies that draw attention to them. There is nothing inherently wrong with such an approach–indeed, it can yield highly illuminating results. But when the presentation of patterns is construed as the main purpose of fictive representation, leading to a neglect of the attributes of the work that relate to emotion and conation, then the results can be reductive and mechanistic to the point of being grotesque, especially given the complexity of human experience as revealed in works of fictive representation. To avoid the pitfalls of cognitivism, therefore, one needs a more substantial theory of mind. As the neuroscientist Joseph LeDoux says, "a purely cognitive view of the mind, one that overlooks the role of emotions, simply won't do."[87] To put it crudely, the lack in many cognitivist approaches of sufficient attention to the intersection of bottom-up and top-down mental processes, as distinct from purely cognitive ones, and to the input of the *unrepressed* unconscious, severely limits their ability to propose a persuasive theory of fiction at large, rather than simply certain cognitive aspects of it.

Advances in neurobiological research, combined with a new interest in the sources, roles, and effects of emotion evident in both the humanities and the social sciences–which is viewed by some as reflecting an "affective turn" superseding earlier "linguistic" and "cognitive" turns[88]–suggest that the time is right for a new synthesis. As far as fictive representation is concerned, this new synthesis is only possible if the findings of neuroscience are married to the insights of psychoanalysis.

In proposing a "neuropsychoanalytic" theory of fictive representation, I am responding to Eric Kandel's suggestion that, for neuroscience to make further advances, it needs to be married with psychoanalysis. Proclaiming in 1999 that psychoanalysis "still represents the most coherent and intellectually satisfying view of the mind,"[89] Kandel admitted that "we do not yet have an intellectually satisfactory biological understanding of any complex mental processes," the human mind being too complicated in its workings to be explained merely by the neurobiological processes that science has been able to observe. Kandel outlined eight areas in which biology and psychoanalysis together might make important contributions:

1) the nature of unconscious mental processes, 2) the nature of psychological causality, 3) psychological causality and psychopathology, 4) early experience and the predisposition to mental illness, 5) the preconscious, the unconscious, and the prefrontal cortex, 6) sexual orientation, 7) psychotherapy and structural changes in the brain, and 8) psychopharmacology as an adjunct to psychoanalysis.[90]

Obviously, all but the last of these eight areas are highly pertinent to the subject matter and methods of fictive representation. Wisely, however, Kandel cautions against a neurobiological approach to psychoanalytic issues that reduces psychoanalytic concepts to neurobiological ones: "Such a reduction is not simply undesirable but impossible. The agendas for psychoanalysis, cognitive psychology, and neural science overlap, but they are by no means identical. The three disciplines have different perspectives and aims and would only converge on certain critical issues."[91] The kind of reduction Kandel warns against is precisely what makes the cognitive and neobiological approaches to fiction described in this chapter fall short of being satisfying.

A number of scholars have recently begun to integrate neuroscientific and psychoanalytic approaches in the investigation of fictive representation along the lines that Kandel suggests. Updating his earlier psychoanalytic speculations, Norman Holland in *Literature and the Brain* (2009) emphasizes the input of human emotional systems, especially in their relationship to the projection and introjection involved in the reception of texts. Reading a text, he argues, is a two-way experience: "We project the work *outward* from ourselves when our brains automatically translate sensations within our bodies outward into a three-dimensional text independent of our bodies." Similarly, "We also project into that literary work 'out there,'" fleshing out the people, events, and language and filling in the gaps in a story. Conversely, "We also merge in the other direction.... We introject. We take in what we take to be the text's portrayals, so that what is 'out there' in the literary work feels as though it were happening 'in here,' in your mind or mine."[92]

Taking a similar approach, Joseph Newirth in *Between Emotion and Cognition: The Generative Unconscious* (2003) foregrounds the generative power of symbols as a means of controlling underlying primitive fantasies and integrating experience through play, as the result of "an initial experience of agency, of being in control of the inner world of relationships and not simply as pushed and pulled by inner and outer forces of an objective world.[93] Also focusing on the neurobiological origins of symbols, Erik Goodwyn follows Jung in positing "an underlying universal mechanism of symbol construction" and "multiple unconscious memory systems that are each focused on distinct and separate emotional evolutionary tasks that function independently for the conscious systems of the brain."[94]

As much as they illuminate particular aspects of fictive representation, none of these attempts to blend neuroscience with psychoanalysis has yet offered a sufficiently precise account of how the fictive work comes into being in the first place. Moreover, they depend on a number of assumptions drawn from older metapsychologies that must be accepted on faith rather than on the basis of empirical evidence. What evidence is there to suggest—as Goodwyn does, following Jung—that symbols have their origins in an underlying universal mechanism of symbol construction constituting "a collective unconscious" that has built up over time by natural selection?[95] There are other ways of accounting for why certain *mythoi*, or commonplaces, recur in literature and across cultures. Similarly, why should one assume—as Holland does following Freud—that the primary function of fictive representation is to create defense mechanisms designed to guarantee our pleasure, and that the fictive scenarios to be found in literature can all be reduced to regressive symbolizations that refer to one or another of the libidinal phases posited by Freud?[96] Although plentiful instances of regression and the symbolic expression of repressed infantile libidinal fantasies are certainly to be found in cinematic and literary fictions, it is reductive to assume that this is all that fictive representation involves. A more dynamic and flexible psychoanalytic model is called for than those developed by either Freud or Jung—in other words, a model that accommodates what is now known about the human brain and reconciles this with recent developments in psychoanalytic theory that recognize creative and receptive functions of the unconscious as well as a merely repressive one.

In this study, I argue that such a model can be constructed by combining the work of the affective neuroscientist Jaak Panksepp, of neuropsychoanalysts and neuropsychologists such as Mark Solms, Mauro Mancia, Allan Schore, and Daniel J. Siegel, and of post-Freudian/Kleinian object-relations theorists such as Joyce McDougall and Christopher Bollas. Pointing to advances made during the "decade of the brain" in the last ten years of the twentieth century, Allan Schore observes: "The ontogenesis of the human mind is now thought to involve more than the emergence of increasingly complex cognitions."[97] Rather than simply being top-down and cognitively driven, the largely nonconscious processes that regulate emotions—which are fundamental to self-regulation, according to Schore—involve a mechanism "lateralized to the right prefrontal areas" that "does not involve a verbal component."[98] This right-lateralized affect-regulating function, he says, is "dominant for coping with the stress and uncertainty that is a fundamental accompaniment of the human condition."[99]

This new understanding of affect-regulating capacities centered in the right hemisphere has led to a reformulation of Freud's concept of the unconscious. Whereas Freud hypothesized an unconscious system that operates via *repression* to bar sexual and aggressive wishes from consciousness, the current findings of neuroscientific imaging suggest that, instead of repression, the operations of the unconscious should be defined in terms of "nonconsciously mediated processes that are essential components of normal and abnormal cognition."[100] According to J. M. Davies, there exists a "relational unconscious," one that evolves out of

> an ever present, yet constantly changing, system of affective, cognitive, and physiologically based self-experience in ongoing interactive and dialogic discourse with a host of significant internally and externally derived objects.... Not one unconscious, not *the* unconscious, but multiple levels of consciousness and unconsciousness, in an ongoing state of interactive articulation as past experience infuses the present and present experience evokes state-dependent memories of formative interactive representations.[101]

Similarly, rather than prioritize the effects of innate drives as Freud does, Jaak Panksepp highlights the importance of primal emotional feelings, seeing these as "inbuilt value functions of the brain" designed to "energize and inform the rest of the mental apparatus about basic survival values" so that "secondary-process learning / memory functions and tertiary-process cognitive thinking-ruminative functions" can be activated, thus "yielding bottom-up evolutionary controls that ultimately allow top-down regulatory controls."[102] Schore agrees with Panksepp, noting that Freud's characterizations of the unconscious inner world have been transformed as a result of neuroscientific research: "Instead of a repository of archaic untamed passions and destructive wishes, the unconscious is now seen as a cohesive, active mental structure that continuously appraises life's experiences and responds according to its schemes of interpretation."[103] Solms, too, accepts that consciousness is intrinsically "evaluative," emphasizing that bottom-up activation is necessary for higher cortical processes to become conscious: "When the need-detector systems register that one of the homeostatic mechanisms they monitor has moved out of its acceptable range, they activate seeking–'appetitive'–behavior to correct it."[104]

In the complementary domain of psychoanalytic theory, Christopher Bollas, adopting a "symphonic" model of the unconscious, highlights the role of associative thinking and the importance of evocative and transformational objects.[105] To complete this triad of intellectual influences, Joyce McDougall has established the inseparable relationship between the human need to fantasize and the soma.[106] Panksepp, Schore, Solms, Bollas, and McDougall have outlined the existence of a mental process in human beings that is far less drive-driven, more exploratory and generative, and less repression-oriented than that outlined by Freud, even though in certain other respects their findings accord with Freud's basic premises about the existence of an unconscious mind and the strategies it uses in response to encounters with experiential realities.

Drawing on these theorists, I attempt to outline a new, updated model of fictive creation, treating it as a phenomenon in human life with a complexity and functional importance that are even more significant than is commonly conceded. I argue that a fictive representation may be understood as a constructed experience, composed of images drawn from autobiographical memory (which can be influenced by discourses and collective memory), that serves to bring into consciousness things that both its creator and its consumer need, or want, to know about.

The impulse that propels this desire, I argue, derives from an encounter with the environment, being motivated by the emotions that this encounter arouses. The function of the images comprising the fiction is to present to awareness what is valued, desired, and sought or feared, abhorred, and shunned for the sake of giving such values representation in conscious thought so that the differentiated elements in our lives become integrated in a way that supports the possibility of a productive future.

When such images are arranged into stories, I argue, the arrangement is shaped in accordance with fantasies that enact, at a fantasmatic level, a process whereby hopes and potential possibilities can be imaginatively explored and fears and desires resolved, with the aim of achieving, restoring, or maintaining a degree of emotional and psychic homeostasis, of experiencing the self, or of enhancing one's empathic imagination of future or alternative possibilities. Such an outcome is achievable because bottom-up representations, constructed imaginatively from the convergence of diverse systems operating unconsciously, frequently converge with top-down processes so that, in the words of LeDoux, they can be made "to direct activity back down the processing hierarchies."[107] The result is a correction of emotional dysregulation that equates to what Aristotle called "catharsis,"[108] and Milton described as the allaying of "the perturbations of the mind" and the setting of "the affections [i.e., emotions] in right tune."[109] Or, to use terms proposed by Jaak Panksepp, the effectiveness of fiction resides in its unparalleled ability to integrate the primary processes (bottom-up) and secondary processes (top-down) of the "BrainMind" (or "MindBrain") in order to bring about emotional re-equilibration, or empathically and imaginatively to project what might potentially come about in the future.[110]

In this theory, fictive representation as a phenomenon in human life emerges not only as providing entertainment and instruction, nor as an adaptive tool designed to exercise the human mind, like a body in a gym. Instead, it is an essential process in the construction of an individual self at a microcosmic level, and as a vital social tool for reinforcing the health of the society that produces it at a collective level. In short, I suggest that fictive representation plays an integral role in the negotiation of the relationship of both individuals and the collectives they form to the external environment, in all its physical, psychological, socioeconomic, and (increasingly international) reality. In the chapters that follow, my overriding aim is to demonstrate how neurobiology and psychoanalysis can be brought together to elucidate this most complex, and perhaps most necessary, of all human mental preoccupations.

2

Why Does Fictive Representation Exist?

The universal need for human beings to represent their world and explore the meaning of their experience by creating imaginative (or "imaged") stories is attested by history and confirmed in our times by the mass consumption of fiction in cinematic, televisual, and printed forms. In short, fictive representation is intrinsic to the way the human brain has evolved in response to the need to ensure biological survival. As discussed in the previous chapter, theorists since classical times have speculated on the formal and thematic attributes of fictive representation and on the effect it has on the reader/spectator. Understandably, however—because of a lack of scientific knowledge of the brain—there has yet to be a fully satisfying theoretical account of *why* fiction exists or how it comes into being, given that until recently we have not had sufficient knowledge of what takes place biologically to motivate and shape the creative process. As Eric Kandel puts it, "For biologists, the study of creativity ranks with the study of consciousness as being on the edge of the unknown."[1]

The older view held by literary theorists—that the purpose of fiction is to "teach and delight"—is true enough with respect to some works, but not all: there are plenty that seek neither to be edifying, nor to impart enjoyment. Similarly, the ancient concept of poetry as deriving from a "divine frenzy" (*furor poeticus*) experienced by the poet (or "maker" in Sir Philip Sidney's terms), extrapolated by Marsilio Ficino and others in the Renaissance, on the basis of certain Platonic notions, is no more helpful in explaining what actually transpires in the mind of the author. Following the neuroscientific revolution of the past three decades, we now know a lot more about what happens in the brain, and scholars have begun to speculate on the implications of this knowledge for an understanding of the phenomenon of fiction.

Such speculations, as outlined in chapter 1, have already eventuated in an updated "cognitivist" version of the ancient classical theory, a new view that sees art as cognitive play with pattern (producing "delight") aimed at providing the information necessary for biological survival (that is, "instruction"). The cognitivist account of fiction, however, is very reductive and limited in that "cognitive science is a science of only a part of the mind–the cognitive part–and not a science of the whole mind,"[2] as neuroscientist Joseph LeDoux has pointed out. For an account of fiction to be complete, it also needs to incorporate the other parts of the trilogy that forms the mind, which means dealing with emotion and conation (motivation) as well as cognition, together with the processes that allow human beings to bring experience into consciousness and exploit working memory to construct narrative. In other words, a comprehensive view of fictive representation requires an explanation of the *motives* of the creative process and the nature of the symbolic figuration that it produces, rather than simply an account of its structural, thematic, and functional attributes and effects.

Prominent neuroscientists like Kandel and Antonio Damasio are quick to point out that neuroscience alone, given the present state of knowledge, cannot fully account for the creative process. Damasio admits: "At the level of systems I can explain the process up to the organization of neural patterns on the basis of which mental images will arise. But I fall short of suggesting, let alone explaining, how the last steps of the image-making process are carried out."[3] Thus, while neuroscience can explain the building blocks produced in the brain, one needs to resort to psychoanalysis for an explanation of how they are "picked up–selected–assembled in a particular arrangement."[4] In a similar vein, neuroscientists Jaak Panksepp and Mark Solms have suggested that because "the human brain has an inherent capacity to generate reflexive self-reports of subjective states," it will never be possible to "understand the reflexive tertiary processes of human brains without studying experiential verbal reports."[5] The clinical experience of psychoanalysts working with analysands is obviously one source of such experiential reports, but fictive creations, as their authors in interviews make clear, are another invaluable, complementary source. Picking up on this, my purpose in this chapter is to propose an explanation for the creative process that synthesizes what affective neuroscience and the post-Freudian expansion of psychoanalytic knowledge are able to tell us about why human beings need to create and consume stories.

EMOTIONAL SYSTEMS AND THE HUMAN BRAIN

We now know from neuroscience that human beings have over time evolved a "triune" brain.[6] The earliest part to evolve was the reptilian brain, centered in the basal ganglia, which governs whole body responses to fear; the second part was the old mammalian brain, or limbic system (septum, amygdala, hypothalamus, hippocampal complex, and cingulate cortex), which regulates the social emotions (maternal acceptance and care, social bonding, separation distress, and rough-and-tumble play); the third and last part to evolve was the neomammalian brain, or the cerebral neocortex, which governs various appraisal processes in response to emotions arising from the old mammalian brain. Associated with these three parts of the brain are three distinct types of knowledge: the reptilian brain supplies us with behavioral knowledge, which is innate and relates to the basic instinctual action necessary for physical survival; the old mammalian brain furnishes us with emotional knowledge deriving from subjective feelings arising from affective responses to external events; and the neomammalian brain provides us with declarative knowledge consisting of propositional information about external events on the basis of information derived from sight, sound, and touch.[7] In simplified terms, the triune brain can be conceptualized as having two functions: those of a "cognitive brain–conscious, rational and geared towards the outside world," controlling cognition, language, and reasoning, and those of an "emotional brain"–largely unconscious, primarily concerned with survival, and above all tied to the body. Both of these "brains" are highly interconnected, and constantly striving toward balance. Often, however, rather than cooperate, they compete for the control of thinking, emotions, and behavior.[8]

In this regard, we also know from science that all organisms, from a single cell upward, seek to maintain homeostasis, which can be defined as the tendency toward a relatively stable equilibrium between interdependent elements, one that promotes healthy functioning and seeks to further its enhancement. Homeostasis is sought at all levels and in all areas of life:

> [It] begins in unicellular living creatures, such as a bacterial cell or a simple amoeba, which do not have a brain but are capable of adaptive behavior. It progresses in individuals whose behavior is managed by simple brains, as is the case with worms, and it continues its march in individuals whose brains generate both behavior and mind (insects and fish being examples).... From there on, an organized self process could develop and be added to the mind, thereby providing the beginning of elaborate conscious minds.[9]

The goal of homeostasis, according to Damasio, is "to provide a better than neutral life state, what we as thinking and affluent creatures identify as wellness and well-being."[10] This not only concerns bodily states but extends into the psychic, social, and political realms, so that "the success or failure of humanity depends in large measure on how the public and the institutions charged with the governance of public life ... [formulate] principles and policies capable of reducing human distress and enhancing human flourishing."[11]

In more complex mammals such as humans, "homeostasis needs help from drives and motivations"; in addition, humans have "sophisticated warning systems regarding future needs," which is where emotions have evolved to play a key role.[12] Owing to the research of Jaak Panksepp in affective neuroscience, we know precisely how the human brain, like all mammalian brains, is hardwired with a number of primary-process emotional systems concentrated in ancient subcortical brain regions that approximate those proposed by Darwin in 1872.[13] Panksepp uses a special capitalized nomenclature for these basic emotional systems. The "Big Seven" are SEEKING (expectancy), FEAR (anxiety), RAGE (anger), LUST (sexual excitement), CARE (nurturance), PANIC/GRIEF (sadness), and PLAY (social joy).[14] They provide a perception of the state of the subject in response to conditions in the outer world. SEEKING is an "appetitive motivational system" that serves as a generalized substrate for all other emotional processes and "energizes the many engagements with the world as individuals seek goods from the environment as well as meaning from the everyday occurrences of life."[15] It becomes activated when need-detector systems register that one of the homeostatic mechanisms they monitor has moved out of its acceptable range, setting in motion "appetitive behavior" to correct it.[16] LUST is associated with gratification and generates feelings of pleasurable delight.[17] RAGE, FEAR, and PANIC are activated when our drives are unmet and are associated with varieties of "unpleasure."[18] The RAGE system is activated when goal-directed actions are thwarted, which produces frustration and results in aggression.[19] The FEAR system is activated by dangerous situations and promotes fight or flight, and the PANIC/GRIEF system (closely related to separation distress and attachment, social bonding, and the process of parenting) is associated with both panic-anxiety and feelings of loss and sorrow.[20] Of the two remaining systems, CARE involves chemicals that influence the mother's behavior around birth so as to increase mother-infant bonding, and PLAY, according to Solms and Turnbull, seems to function "according to homeostatic principles similar to those that regulate such basic functions as sleep," having a developmental purpose.[21] Psychoanalyst D. W. Winnicott, defines playing as "an essential recurrent phase of a creative relation to the world" that extends from early childhood into the cultural experience of adulthood.[22]

As Panksepp has demonstrated, these basic emotional systems operate independently of neocortical (rational thinking) processes and are "foundational for secondary learning and memory mechanisms, which interface with tertiary-process cognitive-thoughtful functions of the BrainMind."[23] Each emotional system has its own brain circuit and neurochemical system, and imbalances in the chemical systems that generate feelings (acceptance, nurturance, love, safety, etc.) cause emotional disturbance.[24] Similarly, when thoughts, emotions, and motivations become uncoupled, "if the mental trilogy breaks down, the self is likely to begin to disintegrate and mental health to deteriorate."[25]

To avoid such imbalances and deterioration, and to maintain emotional and sociocultural homeostasis, the impulses prompted by the primitive, instinctual emotional systems need to be regulated and inhibited by higher executive systems in the prefrontal cortex so that actions arising from them remain within a zone of safety and promote well-being.[26] One problem faced by humans, however, is that conscious mental operations make up only a small fraction of what resides in the mind. Neuroscientists have confirmed that Freud was correct in hypothesizing the mind as largely nonconscious (in Freud's term, "unconscious"), internal, and unrevealed, only becoming disclosed through a narrow window of consciousness. The bulk of mind processes, of immense scope and power, take place "under the sea level of consciousness."[27]

In fact, "the vast bulk of the information we constantly need to process must be processed in the unconscious part of the mind," and scientists have hypothesized that 95 percent of our actions are unconsciously determined.[28] For the feelings aroused by emotions to become regulated, relevant information involving long-term implicit memory first needs to be brought into consciousness so that it can be placed in explicit memory, where it is integrated and processed.[29] To put this neuroscientific explanation in psychoanalytic terms, using the words of Christopher Bollas, "Before this calling forth, no mental object exists (or no set of internal objects exists) in the form necessary to the mental realization or processing of the called forth."[30]

METAPHORICAL CONCEPTUALIZATION

Here a second problem arises, given that at its current stage of evolution the human brain has an imperfect set of connections between its cognitive and emotional parts.[31] To enhance the cognitive capacities of the hominid brain, LeDoux says, our cortex was extensively "rewired" in the course of evolution to create connectivity in cortical processing networks, thus making natural language possible.[32] However, although this "rewiring" enabled complex abstract thinking, it left unresolved the problem of how to achieve connectivity between cognitive systems and the other parts of the mental trilogy—the emotional and motivational systems.[33] As the French psychiatrist and neuroscientist David Servan-Shreiber puts it, "The separation between the cognitive and the emotional brains creates an extraordinary capacity to remain unaware of the small alarm bells going off in our limbic brain."[34]

As bioimaging findings have shown, the reason for this separation is that, whereas the amygdala influences the deposition of emotional memories in various parts of the brain (hippocampus, striatum, cortex), only the hippocampus is needed to remember them. According to neurophysiologist and psychoanalyst Mauro Mancia, this means that "emotional experiences can be recalled only if they involve the hippocampus, hence the explicit memory, while if they remain in the implicit memory they cannot emerge to the surface."[35]

One of the mind's solutions to this problem was to create metaphors—that is, as the linguist George Lakoff and his associates have comprehensively demonstrated, the ability to allow "inferences in sensori-motor domains (e.g., domains of space and objects) to be used to draw inferences about other domains (e.g., domains of subjective judgment, with concepts like intimacy, emotions, justice, and so on)."[36] This conflation of inferences can occur because neural maps of retinal images formed in the visual systems of the brain and neural maps of the body "projected" to neural clusters in the motor cortex form *domains*, or "highly structured neural assemblies in different regions of the brain." These domains are connected by physical links, or "neural circuitry linking neuronal clusters called *nodes*." The long-term potentiation of neurons connected to the source and target neural ensembles that are co-active during conflation eventuates in "neural recruitment," which in turn produces a stable, conventional system of primary metaphors that are independent of language.[37]

A good example of the brain's primary conceptual metaphor-making capacity is the metaphor found in most languages, Affection is Warmth, as in "He's a *warm* person" or "She's a *block of ice,*" which arises from the universal experience of a child being held affectionately (or not) by a parent. During such an experience, neuronal activation occurs simultaneously in two parts of the brain—one devoted to emotions and one devoted to temperature—thus making the associative connection embodied in the metaphor.[38] There are many other conceptual metaphors that illustrate the mind's capacity to correlate sensations drawn from the sensorimotor domains with feelings arising from the domains of subjective impressions: Happy is Up; Sad is Down; Good is Up; Bad is Down; Bigger is Better; Much is Better; Time is a Moving Object; Love is a Journey; Ideas are Food; Significant is Big; and so on.

Not only is metaphorical thought "normal and ubiquitous in our mental life, both conscious and unconscious"[39]; it is also the very foundation of storytelling because our ability to combine simpler conceptual metaphors into more complex ones, and link these into a structure, is the basic mechanism of fantasy–that is, the construction of imaginary scenarios–on which fictive representation depends. Freud recognized this in proposing his notion of "figurability." This is the ability of the brain to convert a feeling into a symbolic equivalent that can be visualized so that its psychic investment can then be translated into a sensorial intensity, and thus provide the basis for secondary elaboration through displacement.[40] In later chapters, I give detailed demonstrations of how metaphoric condensations of diverse internal elements can be extended into larger fictional organizations to express complex emotional experiences.

IMPLICIT AND EXPLICIT MEMORY

Fictive creation is inseparably bound to the human dual memory system, involving both implicit and explicit memory.[41] *Implicit memory* refers to memories that are "not cognitively, but commonly affectively, experienced."[42] It is "managed by the amygdala,"[43] and consists of "maps" of the visual structure and sensorimotor patterns associated with an object encountered in the past, providing guidance through well-established routines that are not consciously controlled.[44] The interconnections between activated neurons that constitute implicit memory produce mental models as a result of the generalization of repeated experiences: "Implicit mental models, the schemata that we don't even know are coming from the past, can directly shape the themes of our life stories."[45]

Explicit memory, on the other hand, is controlled by the hippocampus.[46] Otherwise known as "episodic memory," it entails the conscious recollection of experiences and information that "makes it possible to leap across space and time and conjure up events and emotional states that have vanished into the past yet somehow continue to live on in our minds."[47] Panksepp defines episodic memory as "a fully formed, personally meaningful remembrance that has integrated many aspects of an event, including information about specifically *what* happened, *where* and *when* it happened, and *who* were the main people involved."[48] It is episodic, intimately autobiographical memories that "allow us to travel forward and backward in time through our experienced past—permitting us to imagine, and especially to anticipate and think about, future possibilities."[49] Whereas explicit or declarative memory is "conscious, verbalizable and recollectable," implicit memory is "neither verbalizable nor recollectable."[50] Only through some form of symbolization can this order of presymbolic, preverbal affective experience deposited in implicit memory become "verbalizable and 'thinkable,'" through a filling in of "the gap of non-representation"–as in dreams, fantasies, and fictive representation.[51]

Following Ledoux, Mauro Mancia observes that the effects of trauma and stress on the two memory systems are very significant given that "trauma of various types can make apparently extinct conditioned responses to fear re-emerge in mammals."[52] This apparent extinction does not cancel the experience, which is "stored in the implicit memory and continues to influence the emotional and cognitive aspects of a person for the rest of his or her life."[53]

The dual memory system has implications for our understanding of the "unconscious," and its role in the creation of fictive representations. Rather than merely one unconscious that is produced by repression, there is also an unrepressed unconscious stored in implicit memory comprising experiences that are preverbal and presymbolic.[54] To be brought into explicit memory, such experiences need to undergo a dynamic process that entails the operations of working memory, a higher-order cognitive function that uses a complex array of memory systems, having short- and long-term, as well as episodic, autobiographical, and semantic, components, to make cognitive acts possible.[55] We now know that it is the right hemisphere—to which the processing of visual and auditory stimuli, spatial manipulation, facial perception, and artistic ability is predominantly lateralized—that "seems to be delegated to organizing the lower level of emotions and integrating it with their higher level" through a process that can be described as "symbolopoietic."[56] The need for preverbal, unconscious, affective experience deposited in implicit memory to find expression, so that it can be cognitively processed, makes the creation of fictive representations necessary, whether unconsciously in dreams or consciously in fiction.

IMPLICATIONS FOR POSTSTRUCTURALIST CRITICAL THEORY

In the light of neuroscientific findings about the brain and its functions, there is clearly a need to revise several of the basic assumptions that have upheld attempts to extend the poststructuralist philosophy of difference into critical theory—at least as far as the generation and perception of meaning is concerned. Whereas poststructuralist theory denies the existence of identities prior to difference, assuming that perception depends on a differing/deferring process made necessary by a difference that is internal and "not exterior or superior to the thing,"[57] we now know from neuroscience that any such differential process is only one part of a much larger, more complex process of perception, given that it relates only to the cognitive processing and verbal articulation of experience involved in reflection and appraisal. Prior to that, experience of the environment is registered via several other processes that do not involve any internal relativizing differentiation. At the most primitive level, the brainstem physiologically registers threats to bodily homeostasis. At the level of the subcortical brain, the limbic system affectively registers threats to biological survival and promotes actions that enhance it. Finally, the neocortex reflectively reacts to the evidence presented to conscious awareness by the other two parts of the brain by appraising its significance as the foundation for future action. Difference is thus not prior to identification, as poststructuralism presupposes, nor is perception inescapably relativized: before the cognitive brain consciously activates a differential process using explicit memory to appraise experience, the emotional brain has already associatively identified the experience in accordance with hardwired models of affective perception that operate unconsciously. These models draw on implicit memory to match events with specific emotions that we now know humans share with all other mammals and that are activated whether cognition is involved or not.

The mistake poststructuralists make in extending the philosophy of difference into a self-sufficient critical theory is that they overlook the central role of the emotional brain in the creation (and subsequent interpretation) of fictive representation. Most fictive representations are not primarily philosophical, even though it is possible to construct fictive works that are, in the first instance, conceived cerebrally and philosophically; this is the case with many cubist paintings and certain forms of avant garde literature and experimental cinema. To the contrary, fictive representation forges a mediating bridge between what is instinctual, implicit, and unconscious and what is reflective, explicit, and conscious. As many authors/auteurs have attested, fictive inventions are simultaneously a means of self-expression and self-experience, and a means of bringing implicit knowledge into conscious awareness, especially about affective life, so that it can be mastered, harnessed, and directed toward future action. According to novelist Edmund White, "Fiction is a continual discovery of what one wants to say, what one feels, what one means..."[58]; it cannot be regarded simply as evidence of the metaphysical flux that would prevail if the machineries of language were all that governed our engagement with empirical reality.

THE FUNCTIONS OF FICTIVE REPRESENTATION

Generally, then, the purpose of fictive representation is to bring into conscious awareness what one feels in response to an encounter with environmental circumstances, with the aim of constructing models of understanding that encompass an experiential complexity that cannot be captured through any other means. This is owing to fictive representation's unique ability to integrate implicit and explicit memory under the eye of "an observing, narrating aspect of the mind"[59] through the affective and associative power of *image*. When condensed images drawn from episodic memory are arranged in meaningful sequences, the "stories" that result, as the psychologist Louis J. Cozolino explains, "serve as powerful tools for high-level neural network integration":

> The combination of a linear storyline and visual imagery woven together with verbal and nonverbal expressions of emotion activates and utilizes the dedicated circuitry of both the left and right hemispheres, cortical and subcortical networks, the various regions of the frontal lobes, and the hippocampus and amygdala.[60]

And he suggests that the effect of these cooperative and interactive processes is to sculpt and maintain "neural network integration while allowing us to combine our sensations, feelings, and behavior with conscious awareness."[61]

Neural network integration is necessary before we can accomplish the operations that are essential for mental well-being: the regulation of perturbing emotions; the actualizing of prospective memory to enable the exploration of future possibilities; the provision of a forum for imaginative play; and the dispersion and evacuation of toxic affect. In fictive works, many, if not all, of these functions coexist in varying combinations and to varying relative degrees at any one time, often resulting in a representation made up of extremely complex components.

THE CREATION OF COMPLEX MODELS OF REALITY

It now becomes clear why human beings have evolved an ancillary strategy–imaginative, symbolic figuration–for maintaining affective homeostatic regulation. Fictive representation is useful: first, because it brings unconscious mental content–both repressed and unrepressed–into consciousness through symbolization and symbolic structuration; second, because its images harness the moving power of the affects they arouse; third, because these affect-inducing images, when combined in a narrative sequence, enable environmental circumstances to be grasped in a complexity and communicated with an effectiveness that normally exceed the capacity of propositional logic alone; and fourth, because its representational mode, which integrates the cognitive processes of the left hemisphere with the sensuous procedures of the right hemisphere, eventuates in internal objects that allow emotional experience to be processed psychologically.[62] Such processing is necessary not only for the management of affective disturbances, but also for reception of "news from the self." Fictive representation has thus evolved as a means of achieving maximal integration of the complex BrainMind/MindBrain processes necessary for the restoration and enhancement of health (both psychic and sociocultural) because, as many writers and filmmakers have attested, its use of images–especially visual images–arouses "sensations that can take us into contradictions that words cannot."[63] Or, as Ingmar Bergman puts it, "We go straight to the feeling, not the intellect–thoughts come afterwards."[64]

Such insights have been confirmed by psychoanalytic theorists, as Christopher Bollas explains in commenting on the associations that follow the sight of an "evocative object":

> The "me" that thinks that way is a much more complicated "me" than the "me" that thinks consciously. When I think consciously I can think only one thought in any given moment. Yet an image ... simultaneously contains many thoughts. The image, worth a thousand words, is an unconscious organization.[65]

Because of the evocative power of images, especially when they condense multiple internal elements, fiction can transcend the limitations of linear reasoning while bridging the separation between the cognitive and the emotional brain, and between explicit and implicit memory. This helps explain fiction's universality and persistence.

Fiction is instrumental to this purpose because the integration of the neural procedures of the right hemisphere with those of the left hemisphere facilitates self-experience, which is the basis for reflection. The right hemisphere, which is associated with the retrieval of autobiographical memory, is specialized for holistic and simultaneous processing involving visual imagery, nonverbal perceptions (for example, emotions), and visuospatial information. The left hemisphere is dedicated to linear processing involving "syllogistic reasoning, looking for cause-and-effect relationships that can explain the rightness and wrongness of things."[66] Moreover, the right cortical hemisphere is "centrally involved in the processing of self-images, at least when self-images are not consciously perceived," and is also dominant "in processing unconscious negative emotion," especially emotion related to the consequences of disturbed attachment.[67] Fictive representation's unique power is that it harnesses these capacities so as to make affective content available to the analytical powers of the left side, the role of which in this integrative procedure is to organize perceptions and experiences, to control working memory, to regulate emotions, and to "anticipate, plan, and carry out complex behavior."[68] It does this by activating a dynamic interchange between explicit and implicit memory that is made possible by the *priming effect* that occurs—in which the processing of one item influences the processing of another—in the course of fictive creation.[69] The outcome is that fiction can create powerful "models of perceptual and emotional reality."[70]

The mental procedures activated in the creation of and response to fiction are much the same for the reader/spectator as they are for the author (a topic I explore at greater length in chapters 8 and 9). As Ernst Kris suggests, "The brain of the artist as a creative modeler of physical and psychic reality is paralleled by the brain of the viewer as a creative remodeler of the physical and psychic reality depicted by the artist."[71] This means that a fictive work is not a static object but one that activates a reshaping, dynamic, instrumental process. Sir Philip Sidney recognized this in the sixteenth century, when he claimed that the effect of fictive creation is such that the poet, to which one can add the receiver, "lifted up with the vigor of his own [mental] invention, doth grow, in effect, into another nature."[72] This "other nature" is no less than a new condition of awareness in a brain in which neural circuits imprinted by earlier environmental experience (which varies from individual to individual) are reshaped as a result of the convergence of bottom-up and top-down mental processes activated by the fiction. The kind of knowledge produced exceeds that which can be achieved by propositional logic alone because it requires the activation of simulated emotion to "move" the creator/receiver into the understanding it imparts, which is why the human imagination needs to be constantly fed by fiction.

Even though the role of storytelling as a tool of comprehension arises from the evolved structure of the human brain, such an insight by itself does not explain what it is that prompts the need to know in the first place. For that, it is necessary to examine what motivates the urge to create stories, a subject I explore in the next chapter.

3

The Wellsprings of Fictive Creativity

Fictive representation, while necessary as a means of facilitating communication between the emotional and cognitive parts of the brain, does not emerge out of nowhere; it is prompted by motivations that arise out of the brain's emotional systems, and is designed either to express or induce emotion(s), or both. The rich history of humans creating stories shows that the affects involved can be combined in a variety of ways that are as infinite as the subtle differences between every human being and between every human experience. Within this variety and complexity, however, a certain number of predominant motivations can be discerned, which eventuate in a range of fiction categories that we have come to identify as "genres," distinguished by the nature and manner of their preoccupations. Before the role of genres can be fully apprehended, however, their relationship to the basic affects needs to be established.

MOTIVATIONS ARISING FROM THE BASIC AFFECTS

At the heart of all impulses to create fiction is the SEEKING system that prompts humans, like all other mammals, "to search for, find, and acquire all of the resources that are needed for survival." This is an instinctual-emotional impulse, according to Panksepp, that is involved in the appetitive phases of all of the other emotional systems.[1] When the

SEEKING system aligns itself with other affects that connote perturbing emotions in the individual, such as GRIEF/PANIC (associated with separation distress), the fiction it prompts tends to be deeply personal, as are almost all auteur films as well as a great preponderance of literary fictions. When SEEKING aligns itself with CARE and adopts a social focus, a different kind of fictive work is produced, one that primarily harnesses the moving power of affect for the sake of addressing issues that have consequences for the well-being of a collectivity. One can see this kind of concern in social problem novels such as Elizabeth Gaskell's *North and South* (1855), which describes the "misery and hateful passions caused by the love of pursuing wealth as well as the egoism, thoughtlessness and insensitivity of manufacturers." It is also seen in *Uncle Tom's Cabin* (1852), Harriet Beecher Stowe's antislavery novel. Many fiction films similarly focus on social issues, such as *Days of Glory* (Rachid Bouchareb, 2006), dealing with the experience of soldiers from the Maghreb who fought for France in World War II, only to find themselves the victims of discrimination in France, and *Shame* (Steve McQueen, 2011), which addresses the phenomenon of sexual addiction, currently widespread, and the misery it can cause.

Fictive representation also draws on the hardwired human impulse to PLAY, the importance of which has been extensively theorized by psychoanalyst D. W. Winnicott, who argues that it is "in playing and only in playing that the individual child or adult is able to be creative and to use the whole personality, and it is only in being creative that the individual discovers the self."[2] Fictive representation as found in cinema and literature is fundamentally an advanced adult form of playing, and its overriding purpose is the same as that which Winnicott ascribes to the play of children:

> Into [the] play area the child gathers objects or phenomena from external reality and uses these in the service of some sample derived from inner or personal reality. Without hallucinating the child puts out a sample of dream potential and lives with this sample in a chosen setting of fragments from external reality. . . . In playing, the child manipulates external phenomena in the service of the dream and invests chosen external phenomena with dream meaning and feeling.[3]

These words serve as a description of a process that is found in every work of fiction created by an adult. In fictive works that address social issues,

PLAY often manifests itself in the construction of hypothetical imaginary scenarios showing how a problematical situation may be resolved or how future possibilities may be achieved.

In terms of the fundamental impulses that prompt fictive creation, then, one can see that fictive creativity is not merely an outcome of pathology; indeed, many works seem to be motivated by the desire to explore, play, or simply experience pleasure. Nevertheless, when one looks at the range of fictive works, it is quickly apparent that the majority do address experiences that are complex, often painful or perturbing, and in a multitude of ways problematical, suggesting that among fiction's functions, a main one is to provide a powerful instrument for processing potentially disequilibrating emotions. Insights derived from clinical psychoanalytic experience illuminate why this is so.

PSYCHOLOGICAL MOTIVATIONS AND OUTCOMES

Being human is difficult owing to the nature of the emotional "operating system" that evolved in the mammalian brain some 200 million years ago. At the heart of that system is a hardwired dependency on attachment to a caregiver that motivates an infant to seek proximity to parents in order to be soothed and protected from harm.[4] Indeed, many now see this need for attachment as a more powerful force in human behavior than the erotic libidinal drive posited by Freud.[5] As the neuropsychologist Allan Schore has shown, "the early social environment, mediated by the primary caregiver, directly influences the final wiring of the circuits in the infant brain that are responsible for the future social and emotional coping capacities of the individual."[6] Because of the intersubjective transactions that occur within an attuned mother-infant dyad during the first two years of life, the child is able to "shift from the negative affective states of hyperarousal, protest, or hypoaroused despair to a reestablished state of positive affect."[7] Commensurately, in the second year of life the child shows more intense interest in the father's emotional availability, and if the father is indeed emotionally available, "an early experience of being protected by the father and caringly loved by him becomes internalized as a lifelong sense of safety."[8] Thus, when caregiving is sensitive and "good enough" (to use Winnicott's term),⁹ the child develops an internal working model that generates "a felt sense that others are dependable and can and should be relied upon as needed." This is the foundation of *security*.¹⁰

Conversely, any failure of or interference in parental functions during early childhood–arising, for example, from parental neglect or abuse–can impair an individual's ability to regulate the intensity of affects in later life.¹¹ If interactions with a caregiver are inconsistent, intrusive, or abusive, causing the child to develop a sense that he or she cannot rely consistently on the caregiver, or if the caregiver is insufficiently attuned to the child's needs, mental models become encoded in the brain that eventuate in anxious, ambivalent, avoidant, or resistant attachments. This is the foundation of *insecurity*.¹² The ongoing perturbations that linger in adult life as the legacy of psychic insecurity provide a powerful incentive for the person suffering from this affliction to be fictively creative, as many authors/auteurs attest.

Closely associated with attachment is the human need to come to terms with "the Forbidden" (forbidden libidinal longings, such as incest and parricide), and "the Impossible" (impossible narcissistic desires that relate to universal traumata, such as the need to be one sex or the other, aging, and the inevitability of death).¹³ In childhood, prior to the world of "'Little Oedipus' . . . the much smaller Narcissus . . . must come to terms with the definitive loss of the magical breast-mother."¹⁴ In adulthood, the individual must also confront all the dangers in the external world that threaten biological survival. To successfully negotiate these experiences both psychically and physically, an individual needs to be able to distinguish himself or herself from the "not-me" environment so as to create a sense of personal identity:

> The structuring of the psyche is a creative process destined to give each individual his unique identity. It provides a bulwark against psychic loss in traumatic circumstances and, in the long run, *in man's psychic creativity may well lie an essential element of protection against his biological destruction.*¹⁵

The important role of symbolization and fantasy in psychic structuring has been established from the observation of sleeping behavior in babies. To sleep peacefully, in the earliest beginnings of fantasy life, a baby needs to develop a primitive form of activity akin to dreaming, so as to symbolically create a good internal state of being comparable to that experienced in the mother's arms. If a mother, because of her own problems (such as anxiety or depression), cannot permit her baby to create a primary identification that enables him or her to sleep without continual contact with her, the result is insomnia in the baby unless he or she is rocked continually in mother's arms. The same outcome occurs if mothers remain too remote from their babies. In either case–by being too close or too far away–when mothers fail in their function as a shield against the stream of stimuli to which their baby is subjected, the baby, "in default of a sound psychic model of one's existence as an individual in relation to others," is left with "a dangerously deficient feeling of inner safety."[16] According to McDougall:

> If the model does not contain such symbolic and fantasy construction to order, process, and contain all that is experienced, the individual will experience existence as an overwhelming phenomenon fraught with the danger of being submerged and losing his identity.[17]

The sleeping patterns of infants thus reflect the degree to which they have mobilized the capacity for symbolization: a first baby makes small sucking movements and sleeps peacefully; a second baby sleeps with his thumb planted firmly in his mouth; a third sucks frenetically and does not sleep.[18] These three infant types illustrate three distinct models of subjective relating to the external world. The first infant displays a capacity for psychic representation involving primary autoeroticism that enables some form of hallucinatory discharge of excitation. The second is dependent on an actual object in the outer world for the discharge of excitation. The third, lacking an internalized fantasmatic object as well as any material object that can stand in for the absent mother is "thrown into a perilous cycle of endless discharge."[19] These ways of dealing with affective excitation point to the most important role of fictive representation, which is to enable a processing of emotional content through the creation of fantasy, as exemplified in the behavior of the first baby.

The necessity for creative fiction arises, therefore, because even if the initial maternal environment has been "good enough," the adult individual will be faced with an ongoing need to deal with his or her frustration, excitement, fear, anxieties, and other manifestations of affective stimulation, and the best way of accomplishing this is through symbolic mediation. Symbolic mediation begins with the child's separation from the "adhesive identification" with the mother that characterizes the earliest stages of infancy, in which the primary contacts between mother and baby are tactile, resulting in "the primordial fusion of mother and nursling . . . composed of smells, sounds, and visual and tactile sensations."[20] It extends into adulthood and persists through the lifespan as an ongoing negotiation required to regulate both emotions aroused by events encountered in the external environment and those arising from the activation of unresolved childhood issues. If at any time emotional excitation is not dealt with psychologically, especially mental pain, a "psychosomatic process may take over" with serious consequences for an individual's physical health.[21]

A story functions instrumentally as a "transitional object," bridging the gap between an individual's unconscious longing for security—either derived in infancy from his or her primal adhesional fusion with the mother, or missing but longed for—and the realities of the outside world through which he or she has to negotiate a safe passage. Fiction serves this purpose in part because it operates through the same sensuous procedures that conditioned the relationship between nursling and mother in earliest infancy, being expressed through the senses just like the smells, sounds, and visual and tactile sensations experienced in the maternal dyad. Because of this autoerotic, self-soothing dimension, the fictive work can serve as a correlative of "the addictive mother of early babyhood," enabling the subject to work out, at an advanced adult imaginative level, the relationship between "me" and "not-me."[22] In neuroscientific terms, this process, whereby an experience is "digested" in order to identify the emotions, thoughts, and physical arousal that are no longer necessary after the event, may be supposed to involve activation of the same "digestion mechanism built into our brain as the 'adaptive information-processing system'" that is presumed to operate during Eye Movement Desensitization and Reprocessing (EMDR) therapy, given that fiction prompts the same kind of spontaneous "free-associating through the vast networks of related memories at different levels of consciousness."[23]

The emotional promptings that require processing through fantasy do not always arise from pathological disturbance. For example, the appetitive instincts generated by the SEEKING and LUST affective systems, together with the instinct to form substitute attachment relationships because of the prohibition against incest with a parent, promote the search for a mate or partner. Just how useful fictive representation is in providing models for behaviors to be emulated or avoided, as well as for partners who should be sought or shunned, is confirmed by the plethora of literary and cinematic romances, melodramas, and romantic comedies. Similarly, simple anxiety arising from an awareness of external threats, such as the fear of terrorism following 9/11, can serve as a powerful stimulus to fictive invention. This is apparent in the cycle of American blockbuster action/thrillers about attacks on the United States, reflecting a collective experience of FEAR that such an event could occur again.

Very often, the creation of a fictive representation arises out of, and projects, a complex nexus of emotions shaped by the author into a symbolic configuration that reflects his or her particular concerns. These, in turn, are provoked by autobiographical experience or cultural and other environmental contexts, or by an intersection of both working together. This means that fictive representations can be as variable in their complexion as the infinite possible divergences between different authorial personalities and the circumstances that produce them. The presence of recurrent genres in film and literature, however, suggests that fictive representation often concerns itself with a number of basic human preoccupations.

EMOTIONAL PERTURBATION AS A SOURCE OF CREATIVITY

Many creative artists—writers, filmmakers, dancers, and musicians—acknowledge that their creative enterprise and inspiration originate in psychological and emotional disturbances. Among filmmakers, for example, Ingmar Bergman has revealed that all of his films deal with issues from his childhood: a puritanical, repressive, disciplinarian father, in particular.[24] Bernardo Bertolucci, Woody Allen, and many others have made similar confessions (although their particular circumstances were somewhat different).

Such motives for creativity are not limited to filmmakers or writers. Even in more abstract forms of representation such as dance or music these motivations can be a powerful stimulus. The prominent contemporary street dancer Storyboard P, for instance, revealing that he was raised in a situation of extreme deprivation by a father who was a dictatorial disciplinarian and a withdrawn mother who suffered from bipolar disorder, acknowledges that his dancing "comes from hurt.... It's not ever gonna come from a good feeling."[25] Dancing, he says, is a response to the legacy of that deprivation: "Not having a lot, you're going to create.... When I got a toy, I always broke it apart, put a new arm on it, reinventing it ... not having a new toy, but knowing I can create one for myself. That's where the storytelling came from, that fantasy."[26] Like Storyboard P, many creative artists replicate the patterns of response they devised to protect the integrity of their individual self during childhood. Others invent fictions to create an alternative world for themselves. According to French filmmaker François Ozon: "For me, art is very important. I think without art life is too hard to assume and to survive, so I need art like I need movies."[27] In an exaggerated expression, Joyce McDougall summarizes the psychological impetus behind such creativity: "It is better to be mad than dead."[28]

For a whole range of reasons, then, individuals are likely to find themselves confronting what Milton called "perturbations of the mind" that must be resolved or, in Milton's terms, "allayed." As Alexander Luria said when proposing a model of complex intellectual processes, the subject "who tries to solve a problem in an organized manner must first discover its conditions, and pick out the essential elements; he creates a hypothesis or general plan (strategy) for solving the problem and selects the methods (operations) by which this may be done."[29] This is precisely what the creation of fiction on the part of the author, most often unconsciously, and the response to it on the part of the reader/spectator, for the most part unconsciously, is designed to achieve: it enables both to know the conditions of what they are confronting by highlighting the essential elements, and it devises a model of action that either shows how the problem can be resolved, or reveals the consequences of certain potential behaviors, especially undesirable ones. In this regard, Aristotle was right in identifying an instructional as well as a cathartic function in fictive representation.

THE FUNCTIONS OF STORYTELLING
FOR THE COLLECTIVITY

The striving toward attaining and maintaining homeostasis is just as relevant to the collectivity in any society as it is to the individual. There are three reasons for this. First, ethical and moral values are not built into the nervous system as birthrights, but are "epigenetic emergents of developmental landscapes"–that is, they arise from nongenetic factors that require the organism's genes to express themselves differently.[30] Second, primary-process affects and emotions need to be reconciled with "the massive culture-induced plasticity of the human brain."[31] Third, "most of the 'object relations' of emotional systems to world events have to be learned,"[32] meaning that the individual is constantly adjusting the way his or her emotions relate to the circumstances of the external environment, especially as construed by cultural influences, including ideologies and discourses that may change over time. The need for these ongoing adjustments means that fiction identifies environmental shifts, threats, and opportunities that may affect the collectivity in order to propose imaginative ways of responding to them so as to avert danger and maintain social coherence and well-being. Antonio Damasio has suggested that the arts sustain sociocultural homeostasis by serving as a means of communication; as a means of transacting factual and emotional information; as a means of inducing nourishing emotions and feelings; as a way of exploring one's own mind and the minds of others; as a way of rehearsing specific aspects of life; and as a means of exercising moral judgment and moral action.[33] The arts prevailed in evolution, Damasio adds, "because they had survival value and contributed to the notion of well-being" by helping to cement social groups, promoting social organization, and compensating for emotional imbalances caused by fear, anger, desire, and grief.[34] All of these functions can be observed in literary and cinematic representations that have a collective scope, concern sociocultural rather than personal issues, and are addressed to a broad popular audience. Considering the instrumental utility of fictive representations in maintaining both the psychic and the emotional health of the individual and the sociocultural health of the collectivity, it is not hard to see why Damasio believes that "the arts are one of the most remarkable gifts of consciousness to humans."[35]

THE PREOCCUPATIONS OF STORYTELLING

The role of fictive representation in addressing emotional excitations and promoting personal and sociocultural well-being becomes strikingly apparent if one looks at the categories into which representations can be grouped, and then the incidence of the representations within them. In the case of literary fiction, it is very difficult to do this in other than a highly subjective and impressionistic way because the field is so vast. The year 2012 alone saw a "mind-boggling" proliferation of more than 300,000 new titles.[36]

A further problem is created by the great variability in the way genres (and subgenres) are defined, not to mention confusion in the use of the term, given that it is applied to literary forms (drama, poetry, novels, pulp fiction), modes (tragedy, comedy, romance, satire, magic realism, fantasy), and subject categories (science fiction, mysteries, historical fiction, adventure novels, psychological thrillers, horror stories, crime fiction). These factors make any kind of quantitative appraisal of the distribution of book fiction across genres virtually impossible.

In the case of cinema, the situation is very different because the output is smaller, the range of generic types is less fractionated (at least in the way the industry and critics classify movies), and the form is relatively new (the making of fiction films is barely 100 years old). This means that the patterns of thematic preoccupation in cinema are much clearer than in literature, being quantifiable to a certain extent because of the existence of comprehensive databases (Allociné, the French internet cinema reference site; The Numbers, which provides detailed movie financial analysis; and the Internet Movie Database (IMDb), which provides information on films, television programs, filmmakers, and actors). Even here, though, there is considerable discrepancy in terms of how the databases assign films to generic categories, meaning that the figures they furnish must be used with caution. Nevertheless, for the purposes of this argument, I draw on the statistics listed on Allociné, using as a sample movies released between 2010 and 2013, and triangulate this information with figures supplied by IMDb and The Numbers.

Among the films listed by Allociné for 2010–2013, by far the largest group consists of dramas: 4,182, which is twice as many as in any other category. The next largest group is comedies (2,290), to which one can add movies classified as dramatic comedies, many of which could just as easily have been classified as dramas. At a considerable distance behind are thrillers (1,632), action films (1,227), horror/terror films (824), and romances (800). Finally, in a rapidly descending numerical sequence, there are adventure films (560), science fiction films (520), fantasy films (467), historical films (290), war films (147), and Westerns (61).[37]

The pattern of distribution revealed on Allociné is similar to that provided by IMDb, except that the latter places comedies first (with 615,195 entries). Closer inspection, however, reveals that IMDb classifies as comedies many films, such as *The Wolf of Wall Street* (Martin Scorsese, 2013), that are classified as dramas by Allociné. Allowing for adjustments of this sort and the reincorporation of family movies, listed separately by IMDb, the two databases are basically congruent in the drama category.

The distribution of films across these categories is significant because it indicates the subjects that filmmakers are most interested in addressing. The movies classified as dramas all tend to focus on the individual, exploring his or her interpersonal relationships, behaviors, or encounters with particular environments (familial, social, natural, and political). Almost always, the experience depicted is difficult, problematical, or disturbed. To take a random sample, the films *Anna Karenina* (Joe Wright, 2012) and *Diana* (Oliver Hirschbiegel, 2013) explore the perennial theme of passionate love affairs that cannot be socially fulfilled; *Blue Valentine* (Derek Cianfrance, 2010) and *The Place Beyond the Pines* (Derek Cianfrance, 2013) center respectively on a dysfunctional marriage and the impact on sons of fathers on both sides of the law; *Melancholia* (Lars von Trier, 2011) and *Shame* (Steve McQueen, 2011) deal with uncontrollable psychological states that cause suffering to the victim—profound depression in the former and sexual addiction in the latter; *Young & Beautiful* (François Ozon, 2012), *Tomboy* (Céline Sciamma, 2011), and *Blue Is the Warmest Color* (Abdellatif Kechiche, 2013) depict the troubled sexuality of girls and young women; *The King's Speech* (Tom Hooper, 2010) explores pathological shyness that causes stuttering in a monarch who has to perform a public role; *Pardonnez-moi* (Maïwenn, 2010) and *Polisse* (Maïwenn, 2011) deal with the traumatic consequences of child abuse. The list goes on.

In terms of the affective systems implicit in these dramas, there is an imbrication of all four of the most dominant systems identified by Panksepp: anxiety, alarm, and foreboding arising from pain and the threat of destruction, producing FEAR; loneliness, grief, and separation distress arising from social loss and the loss of relationships, producing PANIC/GRIEF; indignation and hatred arising from frustration or physical injury, producing RAGE; and desire, hope, and anticipation–at least at certain stages in the drama–reflecting the appetitive impulses of SEEKING. Almost always, the search for love is accompanied by LUST. The true value of such fictions is that they allow both the creator and the spectator to enter into an understanding of such dysfunctions and simultaneously contemplate possible ways of alleviating the distress they cause or the destructive consequences that ensue if they are not resolved.

Whereas FEAR and PANIC predominate in dramas, when we switch to the next most popular category, comedies, it is clear that these films are motivated by, and cater to, a different affective system: PLAY–even though this is blended, to varying degrees, with aspects of other affective systems. Comedy, in fact, is fundamentally a social phenomenon, and it depends on a perception of incongruity or an idea, image, text, or event that is in some sense "odd, unusual, unexpected, surprising, or out of the ordinary."[38] It generates humor, which is an expression of the positive emotion of mirth, and performs the important biosocial function of "coupling together the positive emotions of members of a group and thereby coordinating their activities."[39] The laughter a comedy produces can be a means of positively reinforcing desirable behavior in others ("laughing with") or a potent form of punishment directed at undesirable behaviors ("laughing at").[40] As a manifestation of the PLAY affective system, comedy is "an experience-expectant process" that brings participants "to the perimeter of their social knowledge, to psychic places where they must learn about what they can or cannot do to each other."[41] Its positive emotions "widen the individual's focus of attention, allowing more creative problem solving and a broader range of behavioral response options."[42] It is thus a powerful instrument for accomplishing social conditioning, by weaving subjects into their social structures, and for promoting social reform, by presenting new possibilities in a nonthreatening way.

The comedies released during the 2010–2013 period clearly display these functions. A significant number of films ironize, or mock, undesirable behaviors. *Bad Teacher* (Jake Kasdan, 2011), for example, presents an outrageous middle-school teacher who is entirely amoral and unscrupulous, curses at her students, drinks and does drugs, seduces colleagues, and fakes test results until a relationship she develops with a decent man leads her to behave in a different manner. Similarly, *Heartbreaker* (Pascal Chaumeil, 2010) depicts a heartless seducer who ends up as the biter-bit when he actually falls in love with the young woman whose impending marriage he was hired to disrupt. Just like an entire class of "slacker-striver" movies such as *Knocked Up* (Judd Apatow, 2007), these films are designed to educate young men in a sound approach to romantic relationships and their social responsibilities.

An equally large proportion of comic films deal playfully with the need to resolve contemporary social issues, particularly those involving disparities in wealth, class, and race. The runaway international hit *Intouchables* (Olivier Nakache, 2011), for example, presents a utopian image of social integration by showing the mutual benefits gained from a relationship between a rich quadriplegic and his caregiver, a black ex-criminal from the suburbs. *The Women on the 6th Floor* (Philippe le Guay, 2011) similarly shows the breaking down of prejudice between a rich bourgeois Frenchman and a group of immigrant Spanish cleaning ladies, just as *My Worst Nightmare* (Anne Fontaine, 2011) depicts the overcoming of class barriers when a wealthy Parisian art dealer develops empathy for the uncouth worker her husband has hired to undertake overdue repairs. A comparable impulse toward ameliorating social practices can be observed in romantic comedies of this period, in which a recurrent theme is the need, following the excesses of the sexual revolution, to rediscover the connection between sex and emotional intimacy, as in *No Strings Attached* (Ivan Reitman, 2011) and *Friends with Benefits* (Will Gluck, 2011).

Moving from comedies to the third most popular broad category, in which I include both thrillers and action films, one sees that these films are made almost exclusively in response to emotions arising from the FEAR system. Fear as an emotion is the natural consequence of a perceived threat, and it is significant that action/thrillers are the American genre *par excellence*. This can be seen in the statistics: whereas France, for example, produced roughly half the number of dramas and comedies made in America, for action/thrillers the proportion declines to just one-eighth.⁴³ The reason is not hard to find: the American preoccupation with action/thrillers reflects the traumatic legacy of 9/11. As theorists have pointed out, "an act of terrorism is in essence an attempt to manipulate the human fear of mortality," and terrorism, being a form of psychological warfare, "can radically distort fear perception out of proportion to the actual threat."⁴⁴ This creates what the psychiatrist Philip Zimbardo has labeled "a pre-traumatic stress syndrome," expressed as acute anticipatory fears of what is to come or what could happen.⁴⁵

American action/thrillers address this fear by constructing fantasies in which unspecified, unknown dangers are first identified and then, when the odds seem overwhelmingly stacked on the side of the enemy, the threat is overcome through the ingenuity and exceptional capacity of protagonists who are either superheroes from the outset, or ordinary people who attain heroic status through extraordinary courage and determination. Fear of the unknown can be represented as an invasive disease, as in *World War Z* (Marc Forster, 2013) and *Contagion* (Steven Soderbergh, 2011); as an attack by fearsome, powerful monsters or aliens, as in *Pacific Rim* (Guillermo del Toro, 2013) and *War of the Worlds* (Steven Spielberg, 2005); as a natural disaster, such as *Megafault* (David Michael Latt, 2009) and *2012* (Roland Emmerich, 2009); or as a literal attack by terrorists, often imperiling the president and putting the country's political institutions and safety at risk, as in *Olympus Has Fallen* (Fuqua, 2013) and *White House Down* (Roland Emmerich, 2013). The purpose of constructing these fantasies, which repeatedly recycle a number of generic motifs, is to contain this generalized, undifferentiated fear by identifying it and giving it form. As the multimedia artist Jenny Holzer has said, "Categorizing fear is calming," or, as the neuropsychoanalyst Daniel Siegel has said, "When we can 'name' it we can tame it."⁴⁶

A closely related genre in terms of the affective systems involved is the horror/terror film. The dynamic is comparable to what is found in disaster/action/thrillers, but it is usually on a different, smaller scale. However, the categories frequently overlap, as in the *Resident Evil* series (Paul W. S. Anderson, 2002, 2004, 2007, 2010, 2013) and *World War Z*. The FEAR system is similarly appealed to, but the manifest level of unreality in horror films means that high levels of tension and sensation can be simulated in a safe environment, allowing the fear to be evacuated and, in the case of slasher movies, sadistic fantasies (especially on the part of males) to be discharged.

If the figures for fiction films supplied by Allociné and IMDb are compared with those given by The Numbers for market share, a further interesting fact emerges: the number and types of films made do not entirely correlate with the market share of earnings. In 1995 the market share for drama was 28.57 percent; for comedy, 21.57 percent; for action, 19.8 percent; for adventure, 13.35 percent; and for thriller/suspense 6.22 percent. These percentages reflect the overall distribution of film types suggested by Allociné and IMDb. If one compares these percentages with those for 2013, however, a fairly dramatic shift in the order can be observed: adventure films, 25.62 percent; action films, 20.31 percent; comedy, 20.28 percent; drama, 13.60 percent; and thriller/suspense, 10.49 percent. In this reversal, one can see the twin effects of 9/11 combined with an intensification of the demographic shift in Hollywood commercial cinema audiences toward young males aged 15 to 25 that began in the 1970s. While drama remains the predominant film type that filmmakers feel moved to make worldwide, in terms of market share from theatrical release, the figures suggest that the current emotional and psychological preoccupations of audiences may have shifted in emphasis–although even here one needs to be cautious given that the figures do not take into account the dramas watched by more mature audiences, women especially, at home on television and DVD and via online streaming and downloading.

What is certain is that both factors–the ongoing desire of filmmakers to explore the personal and relational issues that characterize dramas, and the desire of (mostly youthful and male) audiences to see action films that show superheroes (idealized role models for future masculine responsibilities) confronting dangers and overcoming threats–confirm the crucially instrumental role of fictive representation in promoting psychic homeostasis–that is, the attainment of an equilibrated self-process–personally at the individual level, and collectively at the sociocultural level.

Even though the output of literary fiction is impossible to quantify in the way I have attempted to quantify cinematic output, the work of scholars who have studied popular formulaic literary genres (such as social melodrama, detective and crime, horror and science fiction, and romance) suggests that similar patterns may prevail, and for the same reasons. John G. Cawelti, for example, in his pioneering study of popular fiction, *Adventure, Mystery, and Romance: Formula Stories as Art and Popular Culture,* demonstrates how archetypal story formulas reflect the psychological needs and cultural attitudes of the period in which they are consumed,[47] mirroring the adaptation of generic formulas that can be observed in Hollywood's genre cinema. Studies of fiction to date, however, have not explicitly linked such formulas and appropriations to the basic affective systems as I am attempting to do in this book, and the situation with high-art literature is even less well defined, largely because of the influence of the poststructuralist literary theories that have dominated literary studies for the past thirty years, which tend to ignore the emotions almost entirely, and the influence of postmodern theories that assume all meaning to be discursively produced and culturally written and so ignore the input of an individual subject who has agency, whether as author or reader.

It is apparent from the previous discussion that fictive representation, both in terms of its motivating impulses and its effects, does far more than merely provide entertainment and furnish instruction, even though, as the ancients unerringly realized, these are among some of its most important functions. Fictive representations are brought into being as a creative way for the BrainMind/MindBrain to present to conscious awareness the nature and causes of emotional conditions that reside in the unconscious part of the mind so that they can be effectively processed for the sake of life management and the maintaining of psychic and social well-being, both for individuals and for larger groups that may be defined in terms of gender, class, race, ethnicity, and sexuality. Whereas earlier psychoanalytic criticism tended to assume that at the heart of all fiction are regressive infantile fantasies relating to the drives and libidinal phases posited by Freud, it is now clear that the actual dynamics animating fiction are often much more complex and multivarious, inhering in a wider range of basic emotions than aggression and libido alone. Commensurately, the functions of fictive representation are not always merely repressive and defensive (although many of the fantasies to be found in cinema and literature are); they can also involve exploration and play.

Although the motivations and outcomes of fictive representation may now be clear, the particular means by which the mind creates its fictions still need to be established. In the chapter that follows, I outline the processes involved in the formation of images; the nature of symbolization and symbolic figuration; the mechanisms of projection, introjection, and displacement; and the shaping influence of unconscious, preconscious, and conscious fantasies. Whereas previously psychoanalysis could grasp these phenomena in part in psychotherapeutic contexts, the insights into how the brain works provided by neuroscience now allow us to understand much more fully how these mental operations work in the creative process involved in invented fictions, to which I now turn.

4

The Materials of Fictive Invention

In chapters 1 and 2, I establish why fiction enacts more than merely a didactic or entertainment purpose, suggesting that it has a mind-altering function more complex than propositional logic alone can accomplish—that is, without emotional reactions having been processed into thought. I argue that fictive representation, motivated by the SEEKING system, activates areas in the right hemisphere of the brain to enable communication across, and integration between, the two hemispheres, which in turn allows material that would otherwise remain cognitively unrepresented in the unconscious mind to be brought into conscious awareness. This process itself, I suggest, depends on the "moving" power of emotions that arise from the basic affective systems with which evolution has equipped humans, along with all other mammals, as an adaptation designed to increase the chances of survival and enhance well-being.

I also argue that fictive representation accomplishes its tasks through the construction of fantasies that allow unacknowledged or disavowed affect, as well as affect consciously experienced as a result of environmental circumstances, to be processed psychologically. This is a precondition for the regulation of affective experience and hence the management of life itself. Before exploring in more detail how fantasies actually work in literary and cinematic fiction, it is necessary to examine some of the representational devices and strategies they comprise.

THE MATERIALS OF FICTIVE INVENTION 71

THE BUILDING BLOCKS OF FICTIVE CREATIVITY

The creative process is initiated when an individual confronts some experience or situation in the external world that stimulates him or her to feel that either a challenge or threat to homeostatic integrity or a positive opportunity for the enhancement of well-being is being presented. Such events and experiences can pertain to the individual or to a social, cultural, or political group as a whole. When stimuli of this nature occur, awareness of them is presented as feelings that register mentally (and somatically). This process is activated by neurons in the brain, which are sensitive to changes around them, receiving signals from the body and the outside world and sending signals to other cells.

Neurons are organized in small microscopic circuits, which combine into progressively larger circuits, which form networks or systems.[1] In Damasio's view, "Minds emerge when the activity of small circuits is organized across large networks so as to compose momentary patterns." In society, such patterns are reinforced by cultural understandings. They represent things and events located outside the brain, either in the body or in the external world, and are experienced in our minds as images (visual, auditory, visceral, tactile, olfactory, etc.) accompanied by feelings, whether registered consciously or residing unacknowledged in the unconscious.[2] Such images form the building blocks of fictive representation.

Stories come into being when an individual mind, using episodic memory and episodic foresight, combines emotion, memory, and reasoning, using the brain's provision for volition,[3] to organize images into an expressive structure that invests them with a potential meaningfulness in awareness that can be anchored in both the emotional brain and the cognitive brain. This process is not entirely automatic; rather, biological evolution has predisposed us to make "cinemalike editing choices" involving "value-stamped selections" when we draw on our unconscious or conscious memories to create such a structure.[4] These selections are "prejudiced, in the full sense of the term, by our history and beliefs,"[5] which means that we inevitably select images that are felt to be the most valuable for ongoing life management.[6]

To a large extent, our "history" comprises our transformation of the past into a story, or myth, that we can tell ourselves and that resides in the unconscious as "a deep stream of thoughts" that actually constitute "an interpretive chain."[7] However, when "vivid experiences in the here and now create lines of contact down into that flow of deep dream-thoughts,"[8] the mind also has the capacity to "restore and enhance" images and memories and combine them into new scenes that never previously existed in actuality, thus making possible exploratory or hypothetical scenarios.[9] This ability to create through imaginative invention is the foundation of fiction and the main reason for its worth and necessity: the capacity to "figure forth" (to use Sir Philip Sidney's phrase) experiences in a re-created form that never before actually existed, enabling the mind to discover what is most important to it in terms of fears, hopes, ideals, and aspirations in its search for well-being, and, through the psychic processes stimulated by fictive invention and its reception, to restore, maintain, or enhance emotional equilibrium as well as expand empathic understanding of the world we live in.

THE MONTAGE PRINCIPLE

The foundation of all forms of fictive representation is what Sergei Eisenstein calls "the montage principle," by which he understands something far more than "splicing bits of film together."[10] For Eisenstein, montage—by which he means the strategy of juxtaposing two objects—extends across all forms of fictive representation, including cinema, literature, theater, and even painting; indeed, it is what differentiates these imaginative forms of artistic expression from the informative logic of "an affidavit exposition."[11] In Eisenstein's view, montage is inseparably tied to emotion, given that "the whole fund of prelogical, sensuous thought serves as a fund of the language of form."[12] Thus, "the very principle of montage, as is the entire individuality of its formation, is the substance of *an exact copy of the language of excited emotional speech*."[13] The importance of "emotional speech," in Eisenstein's terms, to fictive representation cannot be underestimated. When we see two objects placed side by side, he writes, we draw certain conclusions almost automatically: "Take, for example, a *grave*. Imagine a weeping woman in mourning beside it. And it is almost a sure guess that you will conclude that she is a *widow*."[14] The product of juxtaposing two montage pieces is "a third something" that "is always qualitatively (that is, in dimension, or power, if you like) different from each of the components taken separately." This "third something" is what conveys the author's "theme," or expressive intent.[15]

Eisenstein describes the creative process thus:

> The author sees with his mind's eye some image, an emotional embodiment of his theme. His task is to reduce that image to two or three *partial representations* whose combination or juxtaposition shall evoke in the consciousness and feelings of the spectator the same generalized initial image which haunted the author's imagination."[16]

In other words, the author, before he or she creates the representation of a feeling or perception, first needs to associate it with a number of discrete images and then place those images in a relationship that generates an emotional signification greater than the sum of its component parts. It is this larger composite image that provides the "image" of the author's thematic intent in the depiction of a specific incident, a scene, or the work as a whole.

To illustrate what he means, Eisenstein takes an episode from Pushkin's poem "Poltava," which recounts the story of the rebel Mazepa and shows the execution of Kochubei, the heroine's father. Eisenstein observes that the emotional effect of the description of the execution is created by the juxtaposition of three discrete details:

> "Too late," someone then said to them,
> And pointed finger to the field.
> There the fatal scaffold was dismantled,
> A priest in cassock black was praying,
> And on to a wagon was lifted
> By two Cossacks an oaken coffin.[17]

Rather than present an "affidavit exposition," this description generates its affective force from the collocation of these particular images.

As a further example from a different expressive form, Eisenstein cites Leonardo da Vinci's notes on how the biblical deluge should be painted to illustrate that "an image emerges before our very eyes out of a chaos of individual details and representations." For Eisenstein, Leonardo's description could very well serve as a "shooting script":

> Beginning with a description of the heavens, the picture ends with it. In the centre is a group of humans and their experiences; the scene develops from the heavens to the humans and back through groups of animals. The most noticeable details (the close-ups) are given in the centre, at the climax of the description ("hands clenched and fingers locked together... bits that ran blood"). The elements typical of montage composition are clearly defined.[18]

The dependence of cinematic representation on montage is well known, but its fundamental role in the other fictive arts is seldom acknowledged. For Eisenstein, however, no matter how diametrically opposite these spheres of art may appear, "eventually they are bound to become interrelated and unified by the method we now perceive":

> The conclusion is that there is no contradiction between the methods employed by a poet, by an actor who *inwardly* embodies what the poet has written, by the same actor performing *within the frame of a single shot*, and by a director who, using the montage method of the exposition and construction of the film as a whole, makes the actor's performance, as well as environment and all that goes to make the film, sparkle with life. And that is because the methods used by all of them are based in equal degree on live human qualities and principles which are inherent in every human being and every vital art.[19]

As I demonstrate in the examples that follow, the juxtaposing strategies of montage, owing to their ability to activate diverse memories, associations, and perceptions simultaneously, are what make possible the complexity found in great works of art.

VISUALIZATION AND SYMBOLIZATION IN THE ENCOMPASSING OF COMPLEXITY

The human brain has evolved with a unique ability to capture complexity because of the way it assembles and re-creates images compiled from memories, and then exploits the affective associations inhering in those images–especially when brought together in meaningful collocations through montage—to access "insight" that is often hidden from the conscious mind but stored in the unconscious mind. As the philosopher turned filmmaker Bruno Dumont explains, the feelings elicited by visual images make it possible for us to grasp the truth of paradoxical experiences—when an individual experiences apparently contradictory things simultaneously, both of which are true—"beyond the natural scope and gravitational pull of our reason,"[20] which normally separates them out to order them logically. To illustrate what I mean, I will analyze two sequences, one drawn from literature and the other from cinema. Both, like all works of fiction, depend on symbolization.

At this point, it is useful to draw on American philosopher of mind and art Susanne Langer's identification of two types of symbol: "presentational symbols," which are iconic, poetic, and evocative; "discursive symbols," which are encoded in a verbal language system. Langer describes the function of these two types thus:

> The purpose of presentational symbols was to present the pattern of our emotional and experiential life in an evocative and sensual way. Their purpose was not primarily to present ideas as propositions, which was the role of discursive symbols (secondary process or rational language), but to show the nature of patterns in which we live and the experiences we have. The discursive symbolism of language, on the other hand, conveyed relations and discriminations in the world of objects through an agreed set of conventional symbols that merely referred to but did not iconically or imagistically present that which it symbolized.[21]

For Langer, "discursive symbols represent a report function of language in which information is exchanged, while presentational symbols represent a command function through which an individual organizes his/her relationships and specifies how a particular message should be experienced and received."[22] What is particularly notable in the two sequences I discuss is how presentational and discursive symbols are invoked together, in a form of montage, to create an objectified experiential moment capable of being understood in conscious awareness, even though not all of the elements of signification presented by the symbols are grasped by the subject at the time of their genesis. This exceptional ability to encompass and capture emotionally complex experiences, I believe, is fundamentally why humans have always found, and continue to find, the creation and reception of fictive representations necessary.

DISCURSIVE AND PRESENTATIONAL SYMBOLS IN SHAKESPEARE'S *ROMEO AND JULIET*

The first of my examples is from William Shakespeare's *Romeo and Juliet*, a play that in performance presents a powerful visual element but depends primarily on its poetic verbal texture to communicate meaning. In the play, Romeo, the adolescent son of the Montagues, a prominent Veronese family, falls passionately in love with Juliet, the daughter of the Capulets, a rival household. Between the Montagues and the Capulets there is a deadly enmity. Here is Romeo's speech a moment before he and his companions, in disguise, gate-crash a festivity being held by the Capulets:

BENVOLIO.
This wind, you talk of, blows us from ourselves;
Supper is done, and we shall come too late.

ROMEO.
I fear, too early: for my mind misgives
Some consequence yet hanging in the stars
Shall bitterly begin his fearful date
With this night's revels and expire the term
Of a despisèd life closed in my breast
By some vile forfeit of untimely death.
But He, that hath the steerage of my course,
Direct my sail![23]

In Romeo's words, the interaction of discursive and presentational symbols is working through microcosmic montage to articulate a condition of semi-awareness that Romeo's unconscious mind impels him to know. Stated baldly in propositional language, this interchange indicates that Romeo fears that something bad will happen (e.g., something intervening from the outside like the blowing of a wind) if he enters the house of the Capulets. He decides to do so nevertheless.

Presentational symbols implicit in the condensed metaphors of Romeo's speech, however, tell a different story, revealing a more complex representation of the thoughts and emotions involved. The possible outcomes of Romeo's incursion are imaged as an indefinable abstraction ("some consequence") that is nevertheless likened to a dangerous physical object (implied by the word "hanging"), which is then personified in human terms (by the use of the pronoun "his"). This personified presence, who is given a metaphysical dimension by being imagined as residing in the stars (infinite in scope and associated with fate and hence death), is then imagined as someone who, like Romeo, is going to attend the Capulet revels and thus "keep a date," suggesting that this will be something that has been preordained. The presence of this feared guest will be bitter, metaphorically associating the outcome of his visit sensuously with a sour taste, something that one would ordinarily avoid. In Romeo's perturbed imagination, the metaphorical consequence will be that his "lease" (on life) will be foreclosed by some "vile forfeit"; in other words, he will die prematurely as the penalty for some transgression of the lease he has been granted in order to secure his bargain. Despite his apprehension of such an outcome, he confesses that his life is in any case "despisèd" because, in typical adolescent fashion, he feels imprisoned in an existence ("closed in my breast") that he does not want (we know from earlier in the play that another girl he has been wooing, Rosalind, does not requite his love). Feeling defiant, he decides to press on by transgressively attending the festivity being held by his enemies, invoking another personified force ("He"–ambiguously either Cupid or God) to determine what happens to him (imaged as a boat sailing a particular course).

This brief passage is dense with images that appeal to various senses (sight, taste, sound), and one notes how each metaphoric reference merges seamlessly into another, creating a complex overlay of experiential associations. In neuropsychoanalytic terms, we see how images drawn from explicit memory combine with images conjured by episodic foresight (ostensibly by Romeo the character but, by extension, by Shakespeare, his creator). This combination is simultaneously intensified by a tertiary process of abstract reflection in order to represent the multiple, conflicting considerations that constitute Romeo's state of mind at this point. On the one hand, the hero knows at some level that what he is about to do is wrong: the "consequence yet hanging in the stars" is personified as "He" and imaged as a severe authority figure (with suggestions of a severe father) who is going to punish a transgressor in terms that evoke the codes of law that bind society. This implies Romeo's sense of guilt as well as his fear. However, his self-pity prepares him to be reckless, to cast discretion to the winds, by abrogating to some power beyond himself the responsibility for what will happen, taking it out of his control. In this way, the passage captures the paradoxical mixture of antithetical emotional impulses that propel Romeo into the fateful meeting with Juliet, leading to the tragedy that unfolds and the immensely complex array of emotions and insights conveyed to the sensitively reflexive reader or spectator.

The movement of thought in this brief passage bears out Freud's description of the psychic form of a line of thought: "The logical chain corresponds not only to a zig-zag, twisted line, but rather to a ramifying system of lines and more particularly to a converging one. It contains nodal points at which two or more threads meet and thereafter proceed as one."[24] Without the symbolization made possible by this collocation of sensuous images drawn from episodic memory and combined in a montage reinforced by a consciously directed logic of sequence, only a small portion of this meaning could have been conveyed. The dense signifying complexity in just eight lines of one scene is a tiny fraction of what Shakespeare accomplishes in the play as a whole through this representational strategy.

VISUAL AND VERBAL INTERPLAY IN ALEXANDER PAYNE'S "14ᴱ ARRONDISSEMENT"

My second example, from cinema, is the highly esteemed short film by Alexander Payne, "14ᵉ Arrondissement," the final segment of the anthology film *Paris, je t'aime* (various directors, 2006). I have chosen this sequence for analysis because–apart from the interaction between discursive and presentational symbols–it illustrates the interplay between the visual, verbal, and, in this case, aural elements of fictive representation. It shows how such interplay can expose latent awarenesses that have been disavowed and relegated to the unconscious–in this case by the story's protagonist.

The sequence concerns a middle-aged American woman, Carol (Margot Martindale), a postal carrier from Denver, who is recording for her French class a description, in French, of her impressions of Paris, which she has recently visited on her first trip to Europe. As we hear her reading in heavily accented, frequently ungrammatical French, we see shots of her in various locations in the 14ᵉ arrondissement while English subtitles juxtapose the translation of her description against the images being shown. This complicated narrative procedure generates a representation in which Carol's conscious self-report is offset by an unconscious scenario revealed to us, the spectators, through the implied import of these visual images.

Carol's manner of composing and enunciating her French lets us know that she is a fairly naïve, unsophisticated, simple woman, an impression underlined by the ironic relationship of what she says to the shots that appear on the screen. The juxtaposition of her report with these images creates an irony arising from the discrepancy between Carol's lack of self-awareness and the greater insight offered to the informed spectator. At the moment when Carol confesses that "the food wasn't as good as I'd thought," for example, we see on the screen—in a classic use of montage in which a sound image is juxtaposed with a visual image—a plate of half-eaten hamburger and chips and a bottle of Diet Coke, revealing that the kind of food she ordered was American, not French. Similarly, when Carol says that the reason she has been learning French for two years is to have "a genuine foreign adventure," the image track shows her asking a French woman, in French, where she can find a good restaurant in the area; in response, the French woman, recoiling at the crudity of Carol's French, condescendingly replies in English. When the woman discovers that Carol is indiscriminate in her choice of cuisine, she directs the latter to a Chinese restaurant, which she presumes, again condescendingly, is more to Carol's tastes.

The irony in both scenes reveals the extent to which Carol is imprisoned by her cultural conditioning and at the same time exposes her lack of awareness of her own limited perspectives, which deprive her of the authentic experience she is seeking—a state of being for which she is not responsible, and which thus elicits the spectator's empathic compassion and, potentially, identification.

At the heart of this short movie, however, is the revelation of Carol's unacknowledged loneliness and her longing for love, which is depicted in a highly affective manner. At the level of Carol's narration, she emphasizes her self-sufficiency and independence. As we hear her say, "I had considered going with a tour group, but I am a very independent person," we see her wandering alone through the streets of Paris. Just prior to this, we have seen shots of her looking wistfully out of her hotel window, filmed in a blue light that conveys sadness, and have heard her admit that she had wanted to go for two weeks but shortened this to six days because she "couldn't leave her dogs, Lady and Bumper, for so long." This suggests a need for attachment that is itself a displacement for a relationship with a partner that is lacking in her life. As the film proceeds, the ache of this lack becomes more and more apparent. When her voiceover narrative remarks that Paris is where people go "to find something new in their lives.... They say it is where you can find love," we see Carol sitting alone, eating her meal at an isolated table in the corner of a restaurant.

By degrees, Carol's encounter with Paris induces her to reflect on her life in a way that allows her unacknowledged longings to surface into semiconscious awareness. When she visits the cemetery at Montparnasse, she sees the grave of two famous lovers, Jean-Paul Sartre and Simone de Beauvoir (whom, with comic irony, she confuses with Símon Bolívar, the Venezuelan political leader). Their togetherness, even in death, puts her in mind of her aloneness—her sister died young and her mother recently died of cancer—and the inevitability of her own eventual death. She tries to resist these feelings by asserting that she is "not a sad person" but a "happy person with many friends." Nevertheless, as we see her at the top of the Montparnasse Tower looking over the expanse of Paris below, her voiceover admits that it would be good to have someone with whom to share such beauty, but there is no one. Her ex-boyfriend Dave, to whom she has not spoken for eleven years, is now married with three children (an awareness that implies Carol's regret for the children she has not had). Finally, in "a pretty little park," as she sits on a bench gazing at children playing, young lovers, and an older couple engaged in animated conversation to the accompaniment of plangent elegiac music, Carol experiences a moment of epiphany:

THE MATERIALS OF FICTIVE INVENTION   81

Sitting there, alone in a foreign country, far from my job, and everyone
I know, a feeling came over me. It was like remembering something I'd
never known before, or had always been waiting for, but I didn't know
what. Maybe it was something I'd forgotten, or something I've been missing all my life. All I can say is that I felt, at the same time, joy and sadness.
But not too much sadness, because I felt alive. Yes, alive. That was the moment I fell in love with Paris. And I felt Paris fall in love with me.

The interplay of showing and telling that Payne uses in this sequence
allows him to capture the paradoxicality (or in Bruno Dumont's terms,
"contradictions") of the emotional experience that makes us human. At
the same time, it exemplifies, in the depiction of Carol's engagement with
Paris, the process in fictive representation itself whereby things that lie
concealed in the unconscious mind are brought into cognitive awareness through associations aroused by images, which are then often (but
not always) processed through rational discourse. The two processes—
emotional arousal and cognitive reflection—progressively interact with,
and reciprocally influence, one another. It is small wonder that Payne has
confessed his pride in having made "14ᵉ Arrondissement," which lasts a
mere six minutes and forty-six seconds.[25]

The two episodes just examined, one literary and the other cinematic,
illustrate the building blocks of fictive representation—associative collocations that are combined, through montage, into multilayered networks of
interrelationships for the purpose of constructing symbolic figurations of
specific states of feeling or awareness. When such building blocks are assembled and arranged to form complex narrative structures, as can be seen
microcosmically in "14ᵉ Arrondissement," fictive representation functions
as an instrument for emotional repair and restitution among other outcomes that depend upon the activation of affect.

METAPHOR AND VITALITY AFFECTS

Another important element in fictive representation is what the psychiatrist Daniel Stern has called "vitality affects," or "forms of vitality,"
which invest the experiences depicted with affective force.[26] Vitality

affects make up a fundamental dynamic pentad (movement, time, force, space, and intention/directionality) that gives "a temporal and intensity contour to the content" of a representation and hence evokes "a dynamic experience."[27] Vitality affects include mental movement as well as physical action (a thought can "rush" onto the mental stage, "swell," "race" ahead, "linger," or quietly "fade"), and in fictive representation they tend to be manifest in devices that engage the senses.

Vitality affects are inevitably imbricated in metaphors, which, as the linguist George Lakoff has argued, are not merely arbitrary mappings from one conceptual domain to another but patterns of thinking that have a basis in our interactions in the physical environment and our social and cultural experience.[28] Through repeated encounters, Lakoff says, metaphorical maps become part of our brains:

> Whenever a domain of subjective experience or judgment is coactivated regularly with a sensorimotor domain, permanent neural connections are established via synaptic weight changes. Those connections, which you have unconsciously formed by the thousands, provide inferential structure and qualitative experience activated in the sensorimotor system to the subjective domains they are associated with.[29]

Because of the mind's predisposition to engage in cross-domain mappings, we "speak metaphorically whether we want to or not."[30] This innate predisposition is reflected in the ubiquity of a system of primary metaphors in which Knowing is Seeing, Understanding is Grasping, Importance is Big, More is Up, Happy is Up and Sad is Down, Similarity is Closeness, States are Locations, Relationships are Enclosures, Purposes are Destinations, Affection is Warmth, Difficulties are Burdens, and so on.[31] Metaphors are not always expressed in the words of a language; as cinematic representation amply demonstrates, nonlinguistic metaphors can be manifested in gestures, actions, and rituals.

In fictive representations, the marriage of metaphor with vitality affects generates a very powerful emotional, sensuous, and somatic experience, which is further intensified by other expressive devices such as rhythm and sound effects, not to mention syntactical patternings. This is what Alexander Pope meant when he said of poetry: "The sound must seem an echo to the sense," illustrating his precept with a virtuoso display of different metrical feet used in combination with other sound effects (alliteration, assonance):

> Soft is the strain when Zephyr gently blows,
> And the smooth stream in smoother numbers flows;
> But when loud surges lash the sounding shore,
> The hoarse, rough verse should like the torrent roar.
> When Ajax strives some rock's vast weight to throw,
> The line too labours, and the words move slow;
> Not so, when swift Camilla scours the plain,
> Flies o'er th'unbending corn, and skims along the main.[32]

As Stern points out, vitality affects color the experience of the content, which can be "an emotion or shifts in emotion, a train of thoughts, physical or mental movements, a memory, a phantasy, a means-end action, a sequence of dance steps, or a shot in a film," and are colored by it as well.[33] They are generated by arousal systems associated with the basic affects discussed in the previous chapter and "ascend to the cortex, to the centers of perception, emotion, movement, and cognition, and almost all parts of the brain where they adjust sensitivity to stimulus, motoric activity, emotional responsivity, and cognitive activity." Thus, they become part of episodic memory[34] and can be used to communicate experiences depicted in fictive constructions that draw on such memories.

The way vitality affects work with metaphor and other expressive devices in figurative representation is strikingly apparent, for example, in Sonnet 129 of Shakespeare's *Sonnets*, in which the poet describes the power of desire that drives men to engage in sexual intercourse and the shame that follows orgasm:

> Th'expense of spirit in a waste of shame
> Is lust in action; and, till action, lust
> Is perjured, murd'rous, bloody, full of blame,
> Savage, extreme, rude, cruel, not to trust;
> Enjoyed no sooner but despised straight;
> Past reason hunted, and no sooner had,
> Past reason hated as a swallowed bait
> On purpose laid to make the taker mad.[35]

The effectiveness of this passage derives not merely from the fact that the sound, in Pope's terms, "echoes the sense" but also from the way in which the vitality affects, working through changes in rhythm, provide an added layer of signification to what is ostensibly said in the words themselves. In the first quatrain, there is an extreme contrast between the halting rhythms of the first two lines, which first describe in rationally articulated terms the spasms of ejaculation and then describe an orgasmic climax. The next two lines simulate the accelerating thrusting of copulation, which produces the orgasm. Whereas the placement of "spirit" (i.e., semen) and "shame" in line 1 identify sex as shameful, and the words accompanying the copulatory rhythms of lines 3 and 4 denounce it in terms that equate it with the basest, least desirable aspects of human nature, the rhythms themselves evoke the visceral excitement and mounting pleasure of the sexual act, and thus work against the negation being asserted. What is intimated in the representation taken as a whole, therefore, is a split within the psyche of the speaker himself: on the one hand, he is possessed by an encultured moral conviction that what he is doing is sinful (it leads him to hell), reflecting (to use Panksepp's capitalized nomenclature) FEAR; on the other hand, his visceral being, moved by LUST, propels him to SEEK an alternative outcome. The split within the self depicted here is not dissimilar to the split represented in Romeo's speech discussed earlier, suggesting at the very least a generalized problem experienced by members of Shakespeare's society, and at most a personal difficulty with sexuality in the poet himself, reflected in his recurrent preoccupation with such issues in the *Sonnets* and elsewhere (for example, *Hamlet*).[36]

In the example just analyzed, vitality affects operate through rhythm. In literature, they can equally deploy through the duration of sounds, which can be harnessed to the accentuation of specific elements in the representation that are felt to have particular significance. This can be seen in the passage from *Romeo and Juliet* I quoted, in which the pattern of long vowels ties together certain ideas and their attendant emotions. If one momentarily uses quantitative rather than stress-based scansion, the following parings of words become highlighted and linked through an arrangement of long vowels subtly enhanced by alliteration: "my mind" (– –), "misgives" (– –), "some consequence" (– – ᴗ ᴗ), "yet hanging" (– – ᴗ), "bitterly begin" (– ᴗ ᴗ ᴗ –), "fearful date" (– ᴗ –), ("this night's revels" (– – – ˘), "expire the term" (˘ – ˘ –), "despisèd life" (˘ – ˘ –), "my breast" (– –), "some vile forfeit" (– – – ˘), "my course" (– –), "my sail" (– –). A symbolic equivalency is enacted here: duration of sound is equated with significance in conjunction with metaphoric evocations–all at a level arising from emotional awareness that, at this early stage, cannot yet be articulated at a rational level following the completion of reflective processing. (Indeed, neither Romeo nor Juliet lives long enough to attain this state of reflective awareness, which in Shakespeare's vision is one of the things that make their tragic experience so pitiful.)

VITALITY AFFECTS IN CINEMATIC REPRESENTATIONS

Just as in literary enunciation, in cinematic enunciation the operation of vitality affects is equally apparent–possibly more so because, as Stern says, cinema, being the ultimate mixed art form, "can create vitality forms through its own unique means as well as, simultaneously, through any of the other art forms that operate under its roof."[37] One only needs to think of the variation in the duration of shots in cinematic representation, such as the fast cutting that generates the visceral excitement of action sequences and the long takes that promote reflection; the use of hard or soft lighting to create shadows and intimate emotional tonalities; the movement of the camera in the frame and the various focal lengths; the spatial arrangement of elements in the frame; and the use of colors and music in combination with all of these techniques. While most filmmakers use these techniques intuitively, some are able to describe the link between their use and the filmmakers' unconscious preoccupations. Bernardo Bertolucci, for example, who candidly admits that he makes films because "I find that I must live through the relationships that a film creates in a direct way, without logical or rational references,"[38] collaborates with his preferred cinematographer, Vittorio Storaro, to exploit vitality affects for this purpose. Storaro, describing this collaboration, acknowledges the importance of the chiaroscuro lighting frequently used in Bertolucci's films. These chiaroscuro effects imitate Caravaggio's paintings, which involve "subjects transfixed in a bright beam of light that falls quickly into shadow and increasingly intensifies detail and facial expression." In Storaro's lighting, images are "steeped in chiaroscuro, the radiant and color-rich cinematography offset by swaths of deep shadow" in order to evoke a sense of mystery, of "the unconscious and the unknown intruding into otherwise recognizable worlds."[39] Such effects are integrated with Bertolucci's exploitation of the language of the camera to explore ideas that "are extremely hidden, buried, never at the level of conscious thought."[40] As I argue in chapter 5, vitality affects are what alert us to a polysemic potential in an image that indicates a concealed, informing fantasy.

To illustrate how cinema can exploit moving images to harness vitality affects to the purposes of representation, I take two contrasting instances from films made by Jean Renoir. The first, *La Fille de l'eau* (*The Whirlpool of Fate*), is a silent film made in 1924 that concerns a lonely girl, Virginia (Catherine Hessling), who, after the tragic drowning of her father in a storm, is delivered into the clutches of her abusive uncle, Jef (Pierre Lestringuez). Jef dissipates her inheritance and attempts to rape her. Eventually, after various adventures, Virginia is rescued by Georges Raynal (Harold Levingston), the handsome son of a local landowner, who has fallen in love with her, and the film ends with the pair leaving for Algeria in search of a more promising future. In the course of the film, Virginia has a dream in which her hopes and fears present themselves in contrasting surrealistic images. One is of her being swept away to safety by her lover on his white horse. The other is of her coming across Uncle Jef hanging from a tree; far from being dead, however, Jef descends and makes leering advances toward her; as he removes the rope from around his neck, it turns into a writhing serpent, which he presents to her fascinated gaze before she turns and runs away.

The effectiveness of these juxtaposed dream episodes (followed by others) derives from a combination of vitality affects with the symbolic associations inherent in the images they realize, and the stark contrast presented between the two. At a symbolic level, the white stallion on which Georges carries away Virginia is a conventional romantic motif, but when the pair gallop spectrally across trees and clouds, the movement of the horse, which is swift, agitated, forward moving, and linear, enhances the sensation of flight away from danger. In contrast, the rope around Jef's neck that mutates into a snake in his hands evokes an opposite and more equivocal effect. As a hangman's noose, it is associated with death; as a snake, it is associated with temptation, seduction, the serpent in the Garden of Eden, and a fall involving phallic sexuality (a fall that is literally enacted later in the dream sequence when Virginia drops earthward through the clouds). Again, vitality affects reinforce somatically the registering of these associations. The writhing of the snake is sinuous and slow, evoking not only horror but sliding slickness, with sexual overtones that are made obvious when Jef thrusts the snake at Virginia in a way that suggests an erect phallus.

The contrast between the vitality affects and their attendant symbols in this dream sequence (white horse + direct, swift, forward movement, versus snake + slow, winding, encircling movement) replicates a symbolic collocation that is frequently found in literature–for example, in George Herbert's poem "A Wreath":

> A wreathed garland of deserved praise,
> Of praise deserved, unto thee I give,
> I give to thee, who knowest all my wayes,
> My crooked winding wayes, wherein I live,
> Wherein I die, not live: for life is straight,
> Straight as a line, and ever tends to thee, . . .[41]

This poem depends on the same juxtaposition of two forms of movement: on the one hand, the "crooked winding wayes" that are the ingenious lines Herbert is ostensibly weaving into a poetic garland in praise of Christ; on the other hand, the straightness of the unswerving line that actually leads to Christ, an awareness of which exposes to the poet the sinful pride that motivates what he is actually doing (seeking praise for himself because of his creative ingenuity). Vitality affects are brought into play through the movement of the syntax and the concatenating repetition of key words from one line to the next, suggesting a sinuous writhing/wreathing that is the equivalent of Renoir's rope/snake, whereas the straight line is the equivalent of the regular forward movement of Renoir's horse. In both cases, the effect is to generate a problematic ambivalence arising from the presence of contradictory impulses.

Renoir denied that *La Fille de l'eau* had any significant thematic content, asserting that it had been designed simply to display the photogenic qualities of Catherine Hessling, at that time his wife: "We were doing battle with the attitude of the intellectuals, who give first priority to the theme and consider the content more important than the container."[42] The presence of vitality affects, however, shows that we need not believe him. Whether he knew it consciously or not, Renoir at a fantasmatic level was depicting a romantic ideal that was raced toward but with an element of flight from something feared. The thing that is feared is deadly, but it is also seductive and attractive and associated with sex. In *La Fille de l'eau* these ambivalent feelings are placed in Virginia, but the casting of Catherine Hessling (who had seduced both Renoir senior and his son) as Virginia may suggest that the film is staging Renoir's own complex feelings about his relationship with his wife–a likelihood reinforced by his decision to adapt Émile Zola's eponymous novel *Nana* as his next film (*Nana*, 1926), in which he cast Catherine Hessling as an actress of humble origins who uses her charms to rise to wealth and status, but in the process brings both herself and the men who pursue her to ruin.

A second example of Renoir's use of vitality affects is the lengthy sequence in his first color film, *The River* (1951), set in India, in which scenes along the river are seen from a drifting boat. What is striking about this sequence is the constant sensation of evenly paced, floating movement, which is nonetheless varied through the intercutting of shots of people and activities in close-up, of other boats moving on the river in medium shots, and of temples and steps leading down to the water in long shots. Despite the variety of focal object and type of shot, a unified impression is imparted by the fact that all of the shots are traveling shots: it is the subject that remains fixed, not the camera, which moves at the pace of the flowing river, creating a powerful somatic sensation of floating down the river on the part of the spectator. While the effect is beautiful–being induced by the amodal qualities of regularity, evenness, and unbroken forward, level movement–it carries a still deeper burden of signification that is imparted with no recourse to rational discourse. In his memoir, Renoir wrote:

> A thing that has unquestionably influenced my development as a creator of films is water. I cannot conceive of cinema without water. There is an inescapable quality in the movement of a film which relates it to the ripple of streams and the flow of rivers. That is a clumsy way of describing a feeling. The truth is that the affinity between the film and the river is the more strong and subtle because it cannot be explained.[43]

Renoir was fascinated by India and fell in love with it—the steps from the temples leading down to the water, the graceful bearing of the women in their saris, the music and dancing, and the colors—which coincided with his longstanding desire to make a film in color.[44] In the sequence shot from the river, therefore, the somatic sensation induced by the vitality affects informing Renoir's shooting style constitute much more than an ethnographic study: he conveys nothing less than the sum total of his love for film, his fascination with India, and his happiness at making a movie in color—all through the association in his imaginary of the experience of cinema (making it and watching it) and the flowing waters of the river itself.

These examples show how, as Stern explains, dynamic forms of vitality provide access to "non-conscious past experience, including memories, dissociated experiences, phenomenological experience, past experience known implicitly and never verbalized, and in particular 'implicit relational knowing.'"[45] Vitality affects cooperate with other signifying devices to give expression to feelings inhering in the object or situation being depicted that may, or may not, be available to the conscious awareness of the author/ auteur. Their ability to convert feelings and emotions latent in the mind of the author/spectator into a perceptible form is what invests fiction with its communicative power. It is in the nature of fictive evocation that vitality forms are always at work in one guise or another; moreover, they can never be separated from the emotions that give them their expressive force because the former arise, like metaphors, from primary experiences in the environment in which human beings have to thrive and survive. As I explain in a later chapter, they also condition the response of the reader/spectator, thus constituting a crucial component in the intersubjective relationship between author and recipient via the mediating form of the fiction.

EVOCATIVE OBJECTS, NETWORKS OF ASSOCIATION, AND THE UNCONSCIOUS

Before considering how these basic tools of fictive representation are used in the construction of actual narratives, one more essential element in the creation of fiction needs to be identified: evocative objects and their role in the operations of the unconscious. As the psychoanalyst

Christopher Bollas has explained, "We are forever finding objects that disperse the objectifying self into elaborating subjectivities."[46] These objects can be anything that the mind selects to summon "news" from within through the evocation, or calling forth, that the object facilitates because of associations that become attached to it. It is this identification of evocative objects that makes possible symbolic elaboration of implicit self-experience that would otherwise remain stored in the unconscious.[47] In turn, symbolic elaboration is the very foundation of fictive representation, the prime purpose of which is to facilitate it. Once an object has been chosen to serve this function, it can be summoned recurrently to assist in bringing any subsequent self-experience into conscious awareness, and this is precisely what one sees in the repeated use of recurrent images, metaphors, and motifs in the work of a writer or filmmaker. It should be noted, too, that "some self experience arises out of the thing's play on the subject as much as from the subject's use of the object" (through introjective as well as projective subjectification), and that any pathology of mind "biases the subject toward the selection of objects that are congruent with unconscious illness."[48]

Subjective objects of this sort function in unconscious mental life, in which we move associatively from one thing to another "in an endless sequelae of thoughts."[49] This is because complex mental processes depend on widely distributed regions of the brain being linked together in order to work as a functional whole.[50] Considering the complexity in this network of interconnections, Bollas has likened the unconscious to a symphonic score in which a vertical axis consists of different categories of unconscious presentation, or representation, each of which has its own line of movement, with different lines often converging to create "nodal points."[51] Categories on this vertical axis might include (1) the semantic/phonemic, (2) the sonic, (3) the use of objects, (4) transference, (5) projective identification, and so on. According to Bollas, we can imagine these categories as symbolic musical instruments that play at different times, sometimes in unison, sometimes alone, in accordance with some form of "orchestration."[52] He proposes that this unconscious symphony comprises "a vast network of creative combinations" constituting a "received unconscious" (as distinct from a "repressed unconscious") in which aggregated impressions are stored and organized in what forms the matrix of creativity.⁵³ Bollas's multimodal conception of the unconscious finds an equivalent in the cognitive neuroscientific notion of the brain as "a de-centered, parallel-processing network consisting of reciprocal top-down, bottom-up connections among its interacting parts."⁵⁴ (The parallel between Bollas's psychoanalytic conception of the unconscious and a computer should not be pushed too far, however; Jaak Panksepp has argued that this metaphor is highly misleading because of its implication that mentation is purely cognitive, which thus ignores the inseparable interrelation between cognition and emotions.)⁵⁵

To illustrate the multilayered, multimodal way in which the unconscious works, Bollas explores the range of associations that can be unpacked from one word, "helicopter," as used by a patient in an analytic session. If one imagines this word traveling along a line in the phonemic category, below the line might be all of the signifiers that can be extracted from the word: "hell," "I," "cop," "copt," and "her." Above the line might be the corresponding cultural signifieds that the signifiers suggest: images of war, of a chopper, of it flying, of transgression and its consequences, and many other potential associations.⁵⁶ The image of the helicopter might thus associate to marital discord, to a transgressive affair, or a number of other experiential things being unconsciously evoked. Inevitably, the presentation of such an image with multiple, complex associations is intensified by the vitality affects, which unconsciously draw the reader/listener/spectator's attention to overdetermination in the image.

This kind of activity is constantly at work in fictive representations. Sometimes the evocative objects that appear in fictions have an overtly symbolic signification. In Maurice Gee's *Plumb Trilogy*–*Plumb* (1978), *Meg* (1981), and *Sole Survivor* (1983)–which deals with the psychological impacts of the puritanism of the Presbyterian minister George Plumb and the dysfunctional intergenerational family relationships it generates, one encounters the recurrent image of eels in a creek, as when Plumb sees an eel rising with its "dead mouth" and "snake's body" from a dark hole in the slime of the creek that runs through Peach Haven, the family's orchard, which has connotations redolent of the Book of Genesis, the serpent, original sin, and the Fall of man in the garden of Eden.⁵⁷ This is an autobiographical memory from Gee's childhood in Henderson Creek, near Auckland, New Zealand, where, in his own words, he got his "first sight of death,"[58] but it also serves as a symbol for evil, a topic with which Gee has professed himself to be obsessed.[59]

Another example of an evocative object used for its direct symbolic pertinence can be found in Alan Duff's autobiographical novel *Both Sides of the Moon* (1998), in which frequent reference is made to the hot springs in which Jimmy, the youthful protagonist, likes to bathe. This recurrent image derives from Duff's own boyhood in the thermal town of Rotorua, and its use in the novel is associated with the longing for a maternal love of which Duff, like his fictional avatar, felt deprived. The spouting geyser Duff describes associates not only to the literal geysers for which Rotorua is famous, but also to Duff's awareness of, and feelings toward, his mother's promiscuity, recounted in the novel as an episode in which the concealed boy watches his mother masturbate a lover to orgasm in "the marital home" while her husband, unaware, is in an adjacent room.[60]

More often than not, however, evocative objects are incorporated into the texture of a fiction simply for the associations they have, and the feelings that attend them, in the mind of the writer or filmmaker. Examples abound. Ingmar Bergman, in an interview recorded late in his life, revealed that whenever he wanted to sleep he would remember the objects in his maternal grandmother's apartment, and that he had made much use of these objects in the mise-en-scène of *Fanny and Alexander* (1982).[61] These objects include lace curtains over the windows and ice on the inside of the window panes (over which Alexander's hand passes as it had earlier passed over the face of a woman projected on a screen in *Persona* [Ingmar Bergman, 1966]); a gilt statuette of a cherub clashing cymbals; a clock (which frequently appears in Bergman's films); a white statue of a nude woman that comes to life (in his imagination); and many more (lighted candlesticks, a piano, paintings). As the camera follows Alexander's gaze ranging over these things, the tinkling of a music box is heard, supplying a sound object to accompany the visual objects. These objects have no direct allegorical or metaphorical significance, but in the rhythm of the film, as a result of the autobiographical memory of the filmmaker, they evoke the happiness associated with a loving and beloved grandmother who stands in contrast to the harsh, judgmental, disciplinarian stepfather who soon makes Alexander's life a living hell. The closeness of such feelings to those Bergman experienced in real life undoubtedly explains why he used them recurrently, not only in this film but intermittently in others. As Bergman put it, these are objects that retained "a magic significance and importance" for him, even at that late stage in his life.[62]

Comparable cinematic examples can be found in the films of Jane Campion, who recurrently incorporates in her mise-en-scène a variety of evocative objects that associate to her childhood and her relationships with her parents, particularly her mother. One set of objects is horses. Both Kay in *Sweetie* (1989) and Fanny in *Bright Star* (2009) have a collection of toy horses, as does the teenage girl who is the main character in *The Water Diary* (2006). Edith Campion, Jane's mother, was a keen horsewoman, as was the adolescent Jane, meaning that horses as an object evoke a happy dimension of a time that was in many other respects highly disturbing for the filmmaker, leaving her feeling very miserable and insecure.[63] Another recurrent object is cats, also associated with her mother, who had a particular enthusiasm for them.[64] Cats appear at significant moments in almost all of Campion's films: Janet is surrounded by cats when she brings Bernard his breakfast as their love relationship develops in *An Angel at My Table* (1990), Madame Merle holds a cat in her arms in *The Portrait of a Lady* (1996), Frannie feeds a cat in *In the Cut* (2003), Keats holds a cat on his lap in *Bright Star*, and so on. How the camera directs our attention toward the cats (through framing and focal length) lets us know that their appearance is not casual. A key to their associative meaning for the filmmaker may reside in a poem written by her mother, who suffered from suicidal depression, in which she describes the comfort she gained from cats, affirming that even were she to go to Hell her cat would be loyally waiting for her.[65]

Other evocative objects associated with Campion's childhood and youth abound in her films: the gumboots Janet wears in *An Angel at My Table* evoke the family's move to the country when Campion was 13 years old: whenever she puts on gumboots, Campion reveals, 'it is like a physical memory, an extraordinary sensation. . . . I don't know whether Janet [Frame] actually had them, but I wanted her to wear them."[66] Another object of this sort is the caravan in which she shows Janet writing at the end of the film. Campion has revealed that this has associations with a caravan her father won in a raffle and in which she had "so many happy and important times."[67] There are many more such subjective objects, which is one of the reasons Campion's films are felt to have such a rich and dense emotional texture.

All writers and filmmakers use evocative objects in their fictions. Reader/spectators do not know, and usually have no way of knowing, the specific autobiographical associations inhering in such objects, but they feel their signifying relevance in the context of the representation as a whole, usually as a result of the accompanying vitality affects that the artist exploits. This is because, as Lakoff has demonstrated, the nature of the metaphoric system means that "one person's dreams [or fantasies] can have powerful meanings for other people"[68] and that the vitality affects that the creator has invested in evocative objects and metaphors at the moment of creation elicit a commensurate dynamic in the mind of the reader/spectator, often accompanied by a somatic sensation that in turn communicates an affective import at an unconscious level. In terms of neurobiology, this response results from the mirror neurons in the brain activating sensori-affective systems so that a "feeling" is generated in response to the representation (a topic to which I return in chapter 9).

In the creation of imaginative fiction, the elements that I have described as the building blocks of fictive representation—visual images, symbols, metaphors, evocative objects, networks of associations, montage juxtapositions, and vitality affects—play an essential role, but are not the whole story. A fictive work acquires its ability to induce a cathartic or restorative outcome only when these elements serve an informing fantasy, as I demonstrate in the next chapter.

5

The Informing Role of Fantasy

As suggested in the previous chapter, the resources of fictive representation that I have identified so far—visualization, symbolization, metaphor, vitality affects, and so on—are normally not used merely as ends in themselves (although they can be, as in haiku poetry) but are harnessed in the service of a "fantasy." By "fantasy," I mean the underlying thought, usually unconscious, prompted by the affective impulse that constitutes the motivating force behind the creation of the fiction. In popular usage, a "fantasy" has come to mean any imagined situation that is not real. In psychology, however, the nature of fantasy has been successively elaborated in psychoanalytic theory by figures such as Sigmund Freud, Melanie Klein, and Jacques Lacan, all of whom, following Freud, saw the primary role of fantasies as that of a defense mechanism. Recent neuroscientific discoveries, in my view, argue for a broader and more inclusive definition that needs to be established before the full range of functions of fictive representations can be understood—although this is not to deny that earlier psychoanalytic conceptualizations may have been valid with respect to particular works.

THE NATURE OF FANTASY

The problem with earlier psychoanalytic definitions of fantasy is that they tended to be too narrow and restrictive. Because Freud based his view of fantasy on his assumption of the existence of libidinal and death drives, based mainly on his investigation of dreams, he concluded that fantasies are a defense mechanism. A dream, he argued, consists of dream thoughts (composed of memories) and psychic material that has already undergone a process of selection and ordering in response to psychological imperatives that generate a wish: "The wishful purpose that is at work in their production has mixed up the material of which they are built, has rearranged it and formed it into a new whole," thus constructing a fantasy.[1] So far so good, but Freud saw these new arrangements as conditioned by the libidinal and aggressive drives he believed underlay all psychic life, which, because the full expression of the drives themselves needed to be controlled, requires the compensatory construction of fantasies *as a defense mechanism* to keep reality at bay, doing so by expressing wishes in an imaginative scenario that subordinates reality to the pleasure principle.[2]

Similarly, Melanie Klein saw "phantasies" as originating in infancy as a defense mechanism involving projective identification, whereby a baby splits off and evacuates bad parts of the self in response to oral-sadistic impulses and cannabalistic desires.[3] These phantasies, Klein believed, continue throughout life as "the mental expression of the activity of both the life and death instincts," eventuating in "a world of good and bad objects" that are "the source of internal persecution as well as of internal riches and stability."[4] In adult life, these objects, through projection and introjection, became the basis for fantasy life in accordance with Freud's idea of hallucinatory wish fulfillment.

In recent years, especially in the light of empirical research relating to attachment theory, Klein's view of fantasies has been severely critiqued. Morris N. Eagle, for example, has objected to her presumption of innate destructive impulses in the infant—including "phantasied attacks on the mother's body" through "urethral and anal sadism," in which "excreta are transformed into dangerous weapons: wetting is regarded as cutting, stabbing, burning, drowning, while the faecal mass is equated with weapons and missiles"—on the grounds that such elaborate and complex fantasies seem much beyond the young infant's capability.[5] In Eagle's view, the assumption in Freudian and Kleinian psychoanalysis of "fantasied pleasures and the dreaded retributions" in the childish mind unnecessarily drew attention away from the impact of actual biographical events on the child's development.[6]

The discovery of the basic affective systems in the mammalian brain supports Eagle's position: something much more grounded in reality is at work in the formation of the fantasies that compose fiction. While it is certainly true that some fantasies give expression to repressed wishes, especially relating to things forbidden or impossible, many others do much more. One of their main functions is to provide a vehicle for an imaginative registration of the meaning of things: aspects of experience that reside as memory traces from the past; things that represent an actuality in the present; or things that might potentially exist in the future. I therefore propose that, for the purpose of appraising the nature and operations of fantasy in fiction, one redefine "fantasy" as *an imaginative scenario, involving a serial logic, that serves as a vehicle for the processing of emotions and memories through associations that are activated by the structure in which the components of the fantasy are arranged.* The process by which a fantasy is generated involves the conversion of an individual's experience into an explanatory myth that reflects assumptions that he or she has formed about the meaning of his or her place in the world. In response to affective pressures generated by the individual's encounter with the environment, this personal myth prompts and informs the construction of an imaginative scenario that performs any number of functions beyond simple repression or the evacuation of unwanted parts of the self: they can offer substitute gratification or consolation for what is missing in life; they may express denials aimed at countering unconscious impulses; they can be contrived to heal or undo past defects, wounds, or former conflicts; they can express hopes for the future; they can outline a template for life choices and serve as a rehearsal for future action; they can be an elaboration of childhood play; they can function as an evacuation of sadistic strivings and a discharge of aggression; and they can provide a theater in which we can preview the possible scenarios of our life to come.[7] The goals of fantasy, in this revised conceptualization, are not so much to guarantee pleasure by defending against repressed wishes as to provide the basis for an emotional and cognitive understanding that enables decision making by integrating memory, emotion, motivation, and cognition.

THE MECHANISMS OF FANTASY

Even though Freud's meta-understanding of the aims of fantasy may need to be modified, the mechanisms he identified whereby fantasies are constructed remain as true today as they were in his time. The mind, according to Freud, exploits metaphoric condensation to form new unities–composite persons, mixed images, and words treated as things that undergo the same combinations as do the ideas of things. In doing this, the mind also exploits displacement as a strategy to strip the elements of dream material of "the high psychic value of their intensity" and, "by means of overdetermination," creates "new values from elements of slight value."[8] Freud described the process of altering dream material for the purpose of dream formation as *Darstellbarkeit*, which is usually translated into English as *representability*, but is translated into French as *figurabilité*. The latter has been carried over into English by Sára and César Botella as *figurability*, a term which, in my view, is preferable because it more accurately reflects the fact that "what is irrepresentable cannot be psychically apprehended by the same processes that allow representation to be understood. The modes of intelligibility ... are different."[9]

All works of fiction, to varying degrees, express fantasies constructed through this process of figurability. For Freud–with whose view I disagree–fantasies are invariably regressive, being based on the impressions of childish experience and impelled by two categories of drive: *libido* and *aggression*. He believed that dream anxiety, for example, has its origin in sexual life, "corresponding to libido which has been diverted from its purpose and has found no employment."[10] Similarly, he saw masochistic dreams, in which the subject is humiliated or chastised, as the result of an aggressive or sadistic component that has been converted into its opposite, thus constituting "a counter-wish dream."[11]

Despite any disagreement one might have with Freud's reductive account of the purpose of fantasies, his account of how material drawn from experience, often unconscious, is converted, mixed together, rearranged, and fit together to create a new whole in fantasy, is absolutely crucial to any viable theory of fictive representation. First, fiction uses the same mechanisms of metaphoric condensation and metonymical displacement, and involves a similar process of figurability, even though the semiotic formalization that shapes the representation is determined, at least in part, by a degree of cooperation between the conscious and the unconscious parts of the author's mind. Moreover, storytelling lends itself to the construction of fantasies because of its ability to present otherwise unrepresentable emotions and feelings through symbolic figuration at various levels, from the individual image to the story arc as a whole. The strategies and techniques of fictive representation, working together, have the power to move the mind into a condition of awareness that would be difficult to attain through propositional logic alone, whether because of the sheer difficulty of apprehending certain states of abstraction, or because of active censorship enforced by unconscious repression or disavowal.

FANTASIES AND THE AFFECTIVE SYSTEMS

A revision of Freud's view of fantasy opens up new possibilities. As Panksepp has pointed out, the affective wishes that can be ascribed to the two drives posited by Freud are "considerably more limited than those produced by the seven affective systems that have since been revealed by neuroscientific research."[12] Furthermore, "it is difficult to reconcile Freud's views on anxiety . . . as well as his views on lust in relation to attachment and affectionate bonds, and much else besides, with the knowledge we have derived from rigorous neuroscientific investigation."[13] This investigation shows, in fact, that apart from the SEEKING system that underlies all of the other affective systems, GRIEF "may be the most powerful affective network of the human brain" given that sadness 'lights up' our brain more spectacularly than any other emotion."[14] Neuroscience has found that the general anatomy of human GRIEF is the same as that of the system that mediates separation calls, as mapped in animals, and that "this key system for feeling the sting of social isolation appears to have arisen evolutionarily from brain systems that mediate the affective intensity of physical pain."[15] It is not surprising, then, that many of the fantasies informing cinematic and literary fictions engage with the threat or consequences of separation distress rather than primarily defend against libido or aggression. This is owing to the hardwired mammalian need to bond with others for emotional and biological security, starting with the attachment between mother and infant prompted by the CARE system and extending into the love relationships and dynamic social interactions formed in later life under the influence of the PLAY system, which "may help stitch individuals into the stratified social fabric that will be the staging ground for their lives."[16]

Thus, even though some fictive fantasies are regressive in the way that Freud supposed, serving as defenses against libidinal or aggressive desires, many others arise as more direct expressions of the emotions that prompt them—such as the FEAR symbolically figured in action/thrillers involving incursions by terrorists or aliens, or the SEEKING blended with LUST that motivates romances, or the desire for PLAY that produces many comedies and farces. Moreover, in the case of many works of popular fiction, hack writers and filmmakers who act merely as *metteur en scène* rather than as auteur can take over a pre-existing fantasy, such as might be found in the stereotypical plots and conventions of popular fiction and films (crime stories, thrillers, romances, horror stories, etc.), and simply create a fiction that invests these stereotypes with as much affective force as they can contrive. Even in these instances, however, there is likely to be some fantasizing work taking place by vicarious substitution as the writer or *metteur en scène* draws on his or her own store of autobiographical memories in order to stage the fiction.

Rather than try in all instances to decode the symbolism in fictive fantasies in order to find the libidinal or aggressive drive that lies underneath, along with its attendant primitive developmental phase (oral, anal, phallic, and oedipal), if one approaches fantasies as imaginative reconstitutions of elements drawn from the author's prior experience in response to the promptings of all seven basic affective systems, the stories they constitute can be allowed to retain the specificities of their representation. There is, in fact, no need to try to "decode" the fantasies in fiction: their primary work inheres in the sensations that the emotions they arouse deliver to awareness so that experiential phenomena arousing perturbation or other forms of dysregulation can be apprehended in consciousness.

THE FUNCTIONS OF FANTASIES

When fantasies are viewed in relation to the affects that motivate them, it becomes obvious that they are created to perform, as I suggested earlier, a very wide range of functions. In terms of motivations, they can express a desire to gratify erotic or aggressive impulses; a desire to feel good about oneself; a desire to maintain a sense of safety by containing fears and denying unpleasant realities; and a desire to regulate emotion and undo the effects of trauma.[17] Often, they are indeed motivated by a wish arising from unconscious wishes, as Freud supposed, but not always: they can equally be the visualized materialization of something that is perceived as a cause of dread. Even when they are conscious, fantasies are normally hidden from others, and often "their deeper meanings remain hidden from the fantasizer as well,"[18] having their roots are in the personal myth residing at a deep level in the unconscious part of the mind, the informing presence of which is revealed in recurring metaphors and paradigmatic actions and in the logic of sequence into which these elements are arranged. Invariably, fantasies are composed of elements that issue from many different levels of the mind, consequently forming "a multilayered meshing of images."[19]

MECHANISMS OF DISPLACEMENT

The fantasmic displacement underpinning many fictive scenarios is often very great indeed, remaining hidden from the author at the time of creation. At the heart of all fantasies is the strategy of projective identification, which is a process whereby feelings (for example, unwanted feelings) are psychologically relocated into others. In the case of fiction, these feelings are relocated into characters that the author or filmmaker creates. Fictive creation also provides for the obverse process, introjective identification, which occurs when an author creates a character with aspects that are desired for the self that can then be "taken in," in fantasy, to correct defects or supply missing attributes.[20]

Another device that frequently accompanies projective and introjective identification is splitting, which is used in fantasies to materialize divided identifications.[21] In fictive representation, splitting is manifest in the creation of two or more characters who embody different parts of the author's self. Such a fantasmatic strategy can serve a number of purposes. Splitting is often used to address unwanted emotions (such as rage, hatred, or envy) that the subject fears could eventuate in unacceptable actions (such as violence or murder). In these cases, the undesirable aspects of the self, which are usually repressed in real life, are gathered together and embodied in one or more characters (representing the feared "shadow" in Jungian terms) who are then contained within the fantasy–usually by being disabled or neutralized in various ways or even literally killed off. In literature, a classic example of this is found in Charlotte Brontë's *Jane Eyre* (1847), in which the feared impulses latent in the author–partially reflected in real life in Charlotte Brontë's intense and sexually charged (but unrequited) passion for Constantin Heger, a married man[22]–are distributed between the gothic hero Rochester, a would-be adulterer and bigamist, and his mad wife Bertha, who is concealed (symbolically) in the attic. These characters respectively embody the temptation to surrender to a compulsive passion and the insanity that constitutes such an irrational act. The fantasy works to contain these impulses symbolically by having Bertha die in a conflagration and rendering Rochester docile by maiming and blinding him. This simultaneously figures forth not only the author's awareness of her need to curtail her passion, but also the personal cost to her of having to do so. Significantly, Charlotte Brontë feared going blind in real life, which illustrates how images deriving from autobiographical experience can become worked into invented fantasies in the service of projection. Additionally, insofar as Rochester is a stand-in, in fantasy, for the beloved (Heger) who is married to another woman, his mutilation and blinding are a fantasmatic punishment inflicted on the object desired in real life for not requiting the author's love. The outcome of the novel, in which Jane marries Rochester and has a son, expresses a hope that, despite the containment that the fiction has enacted, all may yet be well, and it prefigures Charlotte Brontë's actual marriage to Arthur Bell Nicholls, her father's curate, a few years later in 1854. Ironically, this real-life eventuality inverted the scenario that had prompted the writing of *Jane Eyre* in the first place in that Nicholls was the pursuer and Charlotte the pursued, rather than the other way around. The reciprocal imbrication of life and art in this instance illustrates the functional potency of fiction as an instrument for promoting a re-equilibration of the self that can eventuate in real-life action.

A comparable cinematic example of projective identification and splitting can be found in Jane Campion's *Sweetie* (1989), which, like *Jane Eyre*, has its roots in autobiography.[23] The film revolves around two sisters, Kay and Dawn, who are presented as antithetical doubles: Kay is austere and self-contained to the point of suffering sexual aversion, while Dawn is anarchic, violent, and sexually aggressive. Although the relationship between these two bears a shadowy resemblance to the real-life relationship between Jane Campion and her sister Anna in certain respects, notably in their sibling rivalry, Campion insists that Dawn is not to be identified with Anna; rather, both characters are likely to represent parts of the filmmaker herself. Campion is explicit in admitting her relationship to Kay: "an alter ego part of me is Kay–a very extreme version of a part of me."[24] Implicitly, Dawn represents the other part, the part that Campion associates with the rebellious and wild side that she expressed in her youth in a curiosity that "has always been on those margins of what's acceptable... what we as wild creatures really are, as distinct from what society wants us to buy into."[25] Thus, in Campion's own words, Dawn "has this access to her animal self, if you will–the stuff that Kay is too frightened to contact."[26] In the fantasy presented through the film, therefore, this latent potential, which is feared as being destructive, has to be literally killed off–Dawn ("Sweetie") dies when her tree house collapses to the earth. At the same time that this feared shadow side is contained, residual envy and resentment arising from the real-life sibling rivalry between the sisters are evacuated through an act of displaced symbolic violence, thus fortifying psychic equilibrium.

Splitting combined with projection can also serve the purpose of actualizing divided identifications, especially when the author is seeking to understand or resolve them. One of the most striking examples of this is Sir Thomas More's *Utopia* (1516), written when More, full of humanist idealist hope, but fearful at the possibility of an impending monarchical tyranny, was trying to decide whether or not to accept an invitation to enter the service of King Henry VIII. To explore this dilemma, More objectified his ambivalence by creating two separate characters who represented his contradictory inclinations. He then put these two characters, "Thomas More" and "Raphael Hythloday," in dialogue with one another in the context of a traveler's tale providing an exemplum of an "ideal" commonwealth that each of them sees as confirming his view, without the reader being able to decide which of them, if either, is right or, if they are both right, what that ultimately means in terms of resolving the initial issue. The effect of this imaginative procedure is to create a milieu in which trial identifications can occur in a framework that facilitates speculation at a metaphysical level as to why the human situation presents one with such a dilemma. The fiction thus constitutes a highly serious form of play designed to assuage anxiety without denying the very real grounds for it. This assuagement is achieved as a result of the reassurance generated by a perception of the providential purposefulness underlying the existence of the dilemma itself–a perception that can only be attained via the experience of the dilemma that the fictional representation induces in both the author and the reader.

Another example from cinema concerning projection through splitting and displacement is Bernardo Bertolucci's *Last Tango in Paris* (1972). By his own admission, Bertolucci, the son of a famous Italian poet, Attilio Bertolucci, makes films as a way of managing the acute anxiety, panic, and depression from which he habitually suffers.[27] Indeed, for him a symbiotic relationship exists between filmmaking and psychoanalysis: when he entered personal analysis in 1969, he made a "great discovery ... [that] psychoanalysis was like adding a new lens, a new objective to my camera."[28] Adding that "the therapeutical effect of psychoanalysis on me came also through my movies," Bertolucci acknowledges that in his movies he has been "obsessed with the father, the father, the father.... What is very strange is that in many of my movies there is the murder of the father or the attempted murder of the father."[29] For example, *The Spider's Stratagem* (1970), set in Fascist Italy during the 1930s, is about a man who investigates the truth about his father; *The Conformist* (1970) is about a young man, this time an Italian fascist plagued by guilt over his homosexual feelings, who goes to France to kill his teacher; *The Dreamers* (2003) has a father–like Attilio Bertolucci, a poet–whose authority is ostentatiously discarded by his children (twins who happen to be enjoying an incestuous relationship). At first sight, *Last Tango in Paris*, notorious at the time of its release for its depiction of explicit sex, might seem far removed from such manifestly oedipal concerns, but Bertolucci has revealed that this is not the case.

Last Tango in Paris tells the story of Paul (Marlon Brando), a middle-aged American in Paris tormented by the recent suicide of his wife, who meets Jeanne (Maria Schneider), a young bride to be, in an empty apartment and has a series of torrid sexual encounters with her without knowing who she is. Finally, when Paul starts to feel an emotional connection with Jeanne, she shoots him dead. As John W. Whitehead points out, the anonymous sexual encounters serve as a form of purgation for Paul, who "retaliates against the hypocrisy of cultural institutions such as the family, church and state through the medium of Jeanne's body," with sex used both as a weapon and as a symbolic cure.[30]

At a fantasmatic level, much more is going on. Maria Schneider claims that Bertolucci cast her as Jeanne "because I had the body of a man and a woman," which is congruent with Ingmar Bergman's intuition that *Last Tango in Paris* is really a film about two homosexuals: "If you see it as being about a man who loves a boy, you can understand it. It all makes sense this way."[31] Bertolucci has partially confirmed this surmise: "In *Last Tango in Paris*, Brando, the father, is confronted by a bisexual and bifocal character represented by Maria Schneider and Jean-Pierre Léaud."[32] However, Marlon Brando has revealed that Bertolucci said to him, "You are the embodiment, or reincarnation . . . you are the . . . symbol of my prick."[33] Taken together, these statements point to what the representation enacts at the level of fantasy. The filmmaker, "obsessed" with his father, has projected different parts of his fantasmatic inclinations into three separate characters. Paul, the father figure embodies a potency from which the creator of the fantasy wants to secure his masculinity (symbolized in Paul's sexual domination of Jeanne). Paul is also identified with the filmmaker himself, as indicated in the admission to Brando, but, concomitantly, Jeanne and her fiancé Tom, acted by Jean-Paul Léaud, also represent the split-off and personified components of a latent bisexuality in the filmmaker that is presented as an unresolved problematic. As Bertolucci has pointed out, "Léaud, instead of making love to Maria, films her,"[34] which, in a *mise-en-abyme*, replicates the ambiguity generated in the surrounding film.

Bertolucci's strategy in this film demonstrates the imaginative practice to which Jane Campion has also attested, which is a tendency to "mix and match" elements drawn from autobiographical memory in order to reallocate them across several invented characters.[35] Altogether, *Last Tango in Paris* shows how fictive invention enables Bertolucci to represent, unconsciously, a complexity in his own psychic life that would have been very difficult to encompass and articulate in any other way–and certainly not before it had been presented for apperception through the images and action of this film-as-fantasy. One can see why Bertolucci, as he confesses, takes his films as material to discuss in therapeutic sessions with his psychoanalyst.[36]

The final strategy of displacement I will discuss is that of *reversal*, which is well illustrated by Amos Kollek's remarkable trilogy of films about desperate, lonely women on the margins of society in New York looking for someone who will pay attention to, and love, them: *Sue* (1997), *Fiona* (1998), and *Bridget* (2002). At first sight, these fictions might seem a world away from the filmmaker's own experience. Kollek, the son of a famous mayor of Jerusalem, Teddy Kollek, and university educated, has never lived on the margins of society. Nevertheless, as he reveals in a number of interviews, he recognizes that a large degree of personal projection has gone into the creation of these heroines:

> I don't know where my interest comes from, but, to a certain extent, I have the impression that I am projecting myself in these characters. I have always lived with the feeling of being a stranger, in all of the societies in which I have found myself. I don't know where that comes from, because I have never lived on the edge, being born into a well-to-do Israeli family; but even so, I felt like a fish out of water [my translation].[37]

Even after migrating to New York, where most of his films have been made, Kollek still feels isolated, telling his interviewer: "In New York, I do not fit into the mold of those who are seeking success–I identify strongly with the feeling of being a stranger, someone who does not really live in society and does not function very effectively."[38] As the interview proceeds, he comes to realize that the isolation he shows these women suffering is a symbolic projection of his own isolation, embodied in the marginalized figures with whom he identifies even if they are removed from him in terms of gender and class. His reason for doing this through women characters, he tells us, is that "to put it simply, women interest me in a bare and 'purist' way–that is to say, without all the habits, values, goals, rules, and masks imposed by society and culture. I am interested in the essentials" [my translation].[39]

This displaced identification is reinforced by the conjunction of two motifs that recur in Kollek's work: the child who is abandoned and the prostitute. In *Fiona*, for instance, the heroine's prostitute mother abandoned her on a New York street at the age of six months. The eponymous heroine of *Bridget* has lost her son, having had him taken away from her because of her alcohol addiction. Again, Kollek's own comments allow us to infer the process of symbolic figuration involving metonymic displacement that has taken place. Referring to the motif of an abandoned child, he says:

> Two things come into play here. First, my own childhood, even though it was very different. My father was an eminent figure in political life in Israel, being Mayor of Jerusalem for 28 years. As a child, I scarcely ever saw him, even if I would not go as far as to label him an absent father. He was there, but seldom available.... For a long time, I felt resentment towards my father, believing that he didn't pay enough attention to me, but devoted it, instead, to the State of Israel.[40]

Following Kollek's hints, one can surmise that at a fantasmatic level the "addicted mother" in *Bridget* and the mother who "prostitutes" herself in *Fiona* are stand-ins, through a process of reversal, for the parent who pays insufficient attention to the emotional needs of his child, leaving the child feeling emotionally abandoned and hungry for love, just like Sue in *Sue* or any of Kollek's other heroines. In the case of this feminine trilogy, the filmmaker has composed his female protagonists from elements drawn from his actual observation of "criminals, the homeless, and the desperate" in the East Village[41] in order to create a symbolic correlative capable of figuring his own emotional perturbations.

FANTASY AND VISUAL POLYSEMIA

The effect of an informing fantasy is thus to create a form of visual polysemia in which two types of narrative coexist simultaneously: an ostensible narrative consisting of the literal storyline and a hidden narrative deriving from a fantasmatic scenario arising out of the author's prior affective experience and the unconscious legacy it has left behind in the structure of his or her personality. This double procedure, in my view, is very similar to how Raúl Ruiz, the esteemed and prolific Chilean experimental filmmaker, describes his theory of the cinematic unconscious. When we watch a film, Ruiz says, we encounter not only an "apparent narrative logic" that inheres in the storyline but also "wanderings, cracks, and zigzag trails . . . [that] can be explained by a secret plan." This "secret plan" intimates the presence of an "unexplicit film whose strong points are found in the weak points of the apparent one."[42] In Ruiz's view, both the apparent and the unexplicit film "function together according to a secret structure," which is "neither subject matter nor enigma, but rather an arbitrary although coherent plan, like the genetic code that is said to determine a person's character."[43] The images in the fiction thus serve "as a matrix for two potential sequences whose final coherence is guaranteed by the secret plan."[44] This can occur, Ruiz says, because of the capacity of the image to perform a dual role: "Evocation, invocation: the two functions of the moving image can be complementary."[45] As the literary examples I have discussed confirm, what Ruiz says about cinematic narratives pertains equally well to literary narratives.

Ruiz's view of the coexistence of an unexplicit narrative concealed within an apparent one, in accordance with a "secret plan" that functions like a genetic code, is very similar to Christopher Bollas's view that the image is an unconscious organization informed by the factors in an individual's experience that have come to exert an influence on his or her way of seeing the world. The difference is that Ruiz does not attach this double signifying capacity to the underlying structures of psychic identity in the way that I am trying to do here. I nevertheless argue that the myriad examples in which one can see the presence of these informing models of perception, including those I have just cited, suggest that many if not all authors compose fictions precisely because of the ability of the image, owing to its polysemic capacity, to give expression to the fantasies that those models of perception promote.

What this account of the creative process underpinning fictive representation suggests is that the role of the brain's affective systems as an evolutionary tool for survival is far more decisively instrumental than earlier theories have fully allowed. Our new understanding of how feelings generated by the emotions become stored as memories, which can then be summoned for the purpose of translating them through symbolic figuration into images that are fitted together to form stories, restores the idea of an originating author who exercises agency in the construction of fiction. The neuroscientific understanding of homeostasis also lets us see how the purpose of fictive representation, frequently unconscious, is to achieve the re-equilibration of troubled emotions, to enhance well-being through the exploration of potential scenarios, or simply to furnish enjoyment through playful recreation.

Before exploring more fully the effects of fictive recreation both for the author who creates it and for the reader/spectator who experiences it, it is worthwhile to look more closely at the way fictive scenarios are shaped so as to actualize the affective force of the representational strategies described in this chapter, while conveying the motivating fantasy that determines their use. This is the topic of the next chapter.

6

The Shaping of Fictive Scenarios by the Author: Motivations, Strategies, and Outcomes

The ways in which narratives are shaped has received much attention under the twin influences of structuralism and psychoanalysis. Narratologists have examined the semiotic formalization of actions that constitute a story (the effects of sequence: narrative tension, suspense, curiosity, and surprise), and the devices used to direct the reader/spectator's attention during the telling (narrative perspective, focalization, voice, rhythm, and frequency) in literary fiction.[1] Film theorists have done the same for cinematic representation, identifying the distinguishing features of film narrative (mise-en scène, framing, types and duration of shots, editing, and film sound).[2] As well, psychoanalytic critics have examined literary and cinematic narrative through the lens of Freudian psychology, emphasizing the relationship between shaping motivations and temporal dynamics (the play of desire in time),[3] or they have applied the theory of the unconscious posited by Jacques Lacan, positing an inferred similarity between the structures of a film and the structure of language.[4]

In several key respects, the model of narrative presentation I outline in this chapter differs from these earlier accounts—chiefly by according a much more central role to the emotions arising from the affective systems identified in earlier chapters. In my view, narratological theories informed by structuralism, although valuable in terms of describing the mechanics of narration, have been severely limited by an implicit assumption that narrative activity is exclusively a cognitive process. This has placed a disproportionate emphasis on purely formal elements, as, for example, in David Bordwell's cognitivist approach to film narrative, which enforces a separation between form as representation and form as narration, or in Rick Altman's otherwise excellent account of literary plot structures in *A Theory of Narrative*.[5] My aim in this chapter is not to present a model that supplants these cognitively oriented accounts but to complement them by showing how affective motivation determines the formal structures and enunciatory practices that narratological theories describe.

The psychoanalytic theories of narrative formulated to date also need to be modified, in my view. Despite the fact that psychoanalytic theorists have acknowledged some of the strategies that cognitive theory overlooks—such as devices used to register unconscious content (for example, splitting, projection, reversal, symbolization, and schemas)[6]—they tend to locate these primarily in the reader/spectator, not the author/auteur, which reflects, perhaps, a coyness about speculating on the creative process because of assertions about an "intentional fallacy," Roland Barthes's proclamation of the "death of the author," and the disapprobation in which old-fashioned Freudian psychobiography is now held. This has resulted in views that tend to exclude the author and underestimate his or her role in generating content. Norman Holland, for example, insists that "the literary work does not deliver 'content.' We construct 'content.'"[7] Peter Brooks similarly believes that "plot" is "best conceived as an activity, a structuring operation elicited in the reader trying to make sense of meanings that develop only through textual and temporal succession."[8] In my view, to diminish the role of the author in the creative process in this way flies in the face of all that we now know about the brain and its procedures. Equally, when it is assumed that the function of a text is merely to erect defenses to guarantee one's pleasure as reader (Holland) or to stand "as a kind of divergence or deviance, a postponement in the discharge which leads back to the inanimate" (Brooks),[9] the author's creative inventiveness in producing the work is vastly underestimated and underappreciated.

An understanding of brain processes from a neuropsychoanalytic perspective restores the author to his or her proper place. If we take into account the structure of the brain, the location and function of the basic affective systems, and their role in the bottom-up and top-down reciprocal interactions of the BrainMind, the activity whereby authors shape fictions emerges from the shadows into its full glory—an exhilarating form of creativity that most of us intuitively feel exists.

DETERMINANTS OF FORM

A fictive representation can be viewed as an extended form of metaphoric thought in which one condition of experience (affective) is structured in terms of another (visualized material drawn from autobiographical memory) to create what the psychoanalyst Christopher Bollas has described as a "transubstantial object," which enables internal psychic reality to be transferred to another realm.[10] This process of "transubstantiation" inevitably involves a conversation with the self that needs to be given some form of structural coherence for any messages from the self, or to the self, to be delivered.

The means whereby this symbolic figuration of a fiction is given coherence are those that structure any other form of conversation: *participants* (in the form of characters whose actions define the conversation); *parts* (played by the characters, whose participation is put together in a certain fashion); *stages* (minimally including a beginning, a central part, and an end); *linear sequence* (to avoid an incoherent jumble of communicative elements); *causation* (the prompting of one element in a conversation by another); and *purpose* (the reason the conversation is taking place).[11] The shape of a fictive scenario is determined by the combined effect of these dimensions working together. What has not been adequately appreciated, however, is the extent to which *causation* and *purpose*, which influence the configuration of the *stages,* depend on a conjunction of the prompting emotion(s) that have moved the author to create his or her fiction and the particular homeostatic effect(s) that the fiction is instrumentally designed to achieve.

It would be convenient and neat if different types of fiction could be categorically assigned to specific emotions, but more often than not a complex range of intersecting emotions are blended in any particular work, both in terms of the affects that motivate it and the emotions that the representation itself generates—as, for example, in the case of François Truffaut's film *Jules and Jim* (discussed in chapter 10). Nevertheless, even though the affective complexity of fiction in this respect mirrors the complexity of life itself, it is usual for one of the primary emotions to predominate, especially when an author opts to exploit the conventions of a particular genre to construct his or her fantasy. In comedy, for example, PLAY predominates but is often blended with CARE. In tragedy, FEAR predominates but is often blended with PANIC/GRIEF and sometimes RAGE. In melodrama a wider range of emotions are often more evenly distributed across the work–for example, SEEKING, PANIC/GRIEF, LUST, and CARE; in romantic comedy SEEKING and LUST predominate, conditioned by the threat of PANIC/GRIEF; in social problem fiction, CARE predominates in response to FEAR. In all instances, the ways in which these emotions are deployed have a direct influence on the shape and components of the structure of the work.

Often, the affective mental condition that motivates an author to create his or her fiction is veiled by the metonymical displacements and metaphoric condensations that have produced the fiction; nevertheless, it is always implicit in the emotional effects that the work generates. Moreover, authors are increasingly open in talking about their motivations. In the case of film, this occurs particularly in interviews given as part of the marketing of the film–for example, in director's commentaries included on DVD releases. With literary authors, biographies and autobiographies provide a rich source of information, along with metacommentaries attached to the works themselves, in addition to interviews. Where sufficient information exists, as either direct comments or contextual evidence concerning the author's autobiographical circumstances, the process whereby affective motivations become converted into a fictive representation can usually be inferred. I now look at several instances where the relationship between affective motivation and the shaping of the resulting representation is readily apparent.

CONVERSION OF METAPHOR INTO PLOT: PRESTON'S *PERFECT STRANGERS;* SPENSER'S *FAERIE QUEENE*

The extension of the process of metaphor formation that lies at the heart of all story making is strikingly apparent in *Perfect Strangers* (Gaylene

Preston, 2003), which the filmmaker has described as her "most personal film."[12] Set on the wild and remote West Coast of the South Island of New Zealand–a setting that serves as the correlative to a disturbed emotional state–the film tells how the heroine, Melanie (Rachael Blake), picks up a suave stranger (Sam Neil) in a Greymouth bar and agrees to go home with him, only to discover that she has been kidnapped. In a remote cabin, the stranger romances her, to which she responds appreciatively until she realizes he will not let her go. When her romantic fantasy turns into fear, she impulsively stabs him in the stomach as he tries to prevent her from leaving. The wound is not instantly fatal, and Melanie remains to nurse him, her affection growing for him, until he eventually dies, following which she conceals his body in a freezer. Subsequently, a former lover, Bill (Joel Tolbeck), a rough, simple bushman in whose "bach" (the New Zealand term for a small weekend holiday house) the stranger has been living in Bill's absence, returns to the bach, finds Melanie there, helps her dispose of the body, and then takes her back to civilization, where the two marry. Melanie nevertheless continues to be haunted by the stranger, recurrently hallucinating his presence, and the film ends with a fantasy sequence in which she dances alternately with her husband and with the fantasmatic stranger.

At first sight, it is hard to see how this story–a "monster genre bender," in Preston's words, mingling the conventions of romance, thriller, fantasy, and crime fiction, in which the predator and victim exchange roles–could be Preston's "most personal film," and it is significant that she herself only came to realize what she had done after the film had been released:

> I was standing on the stage of the London Film Festival at the Odeon Theatre in Leicester Square [during a Q and A] . . . and I realized as the questions came that I was born to make this film because I grew up in a marriage that had a third person in the metaphorical freezer. I was thinking, "Yes, my mother was in love with another man before my father came back from the war." I was the little golden-haired girl who was born to bring the marriage back together again. My father was a kind, generous man, a milkman who owned a fish and chips shop. He was always thoughtful, but plainspoken and never appeared debonair or romantic, and my mother was in love with a handsome stranger she had rejected to save the marriage. I hadn't realized until then that in the film I had unconsciously

painted this portrait of the world I lived in as a three-year-old. Quite a moment to be realizing this, I must say.[13]

Only relatively late in life did Preston learn the truth about her mother's wartime lover–when she interviewed her mother, Tui Preston, along with a number of other women of her generation, during the making of her documentary *War Stories Our Mothers Never Told Us* (Gaylene Preston, 1995). Significantly, the making of this nonfiction documentary, which renders the details of the affair explicit, had not been sufficient by itself to liberate Preston from the mental perturbation that her unconscious awareness as a child had caused her throughout her life. An intermediating process was necessary for the emotions inhering in this knowledge to be processed psychologically, which was why she had needed to follow her nonfiction documentary film with a full-length fiction feature. In creating her fiction, Preston had unconsciously constructed a fantasy in which the feelings inherent in her implicit memories–affectively experienced but not at the level of rational thought–had become symbolically converted into a metaphoric form that made it possible for her to consciously apprehend them, even though there was a time lag before this apprehension could be fully registered in her conscious awareness.

The process of conversion is instructive in that it reveals some of the strategies the unconscious uses to shape fictive narratives. Both the participants and the general outline of the story mirror the real-life people and events they shadow: Melanie is the filmmaker's mother; the suave stranger is the lover she takes while her husband is overseas during World War II (a stranger because he is unknown to the filmmaker-daughter); Bill, crude but good-natured, is the husband who returns to his home (the bach that the stranger has occupied in his absence) after the War; the setting is converted into a fantasy island to signify the separation of the affair from mundane time and place; and the killing of the stranger symbolizes the mother's need to give up her lover in order to remain in her marriage, which is enacted at the end of the movie in Melanie's marriage to Bill but with the phantom of the stranger looking on.

In the imaginative construction of these metaphoric equivalents, it is interesting to observe how elements derived from unconscious autobiographical knowledge are conflated with fantasmatic elements derived from preexisting genres: the stranger is the hero of romance but also the sinister villain of gothic fiction; Melanie is similarly a Cinderella type drawn from fairy stories, but also the *femme fatale* of *film noir*; Bill has attributes of the archetypal, stoical, self-contained Man Alone who is a ubiquitous figure in New Zealand fiction. The realization of the fiction thus captures the kind of paradoxical double-sidedness that, as I will show, is so obvious in the fictions of Bruno Dumont. Viewed solely in terms of its generic components and from a strictly rational perspective, *Perfect Strangers* might seem an incoherent farrago, but experienced imaginatively in terms of its metaphoricized and dramatically enacted affective components, it makes compelling sense, capturing as it does the paradoxicality of the feelings generated by the affair in the mother with whom the filmmaker identifies.

In literature one finds the same kind of metaphoric conversion shaping a fiction in Edmund Spenser's great epic poem *The Faerie Queene* (1590–1596)–with the difference that the process takes place on a much more massive scale and within the constraints of a powerful, external, ideological structure. To illustrate how this transmutation of metaphor into plot works, I will examine just one of the seven extant books of the poem–book 1, "Contayning The Legende of the Knight of the Red Crosse, or Of Holinesse."[14]

The shape of book 1 is determined by the superimposition of a number of governing metaphorical ideas, which together constitute a multilayered, complex whole. The first of these master metaphors is the idea that holiness comprises a *rise* and eventuates in a happy victory after *battle*. The complementary master metaphor is the idea is that sinfulness involves a *fall*, eventuating in imprisonment and despair. The instrumental process in generating both outcomes is conceptualized as a series of encounters: on the one hand, with enemies who must be engaged in combat; on the other hand, with benevolent female figures who nurture, comfort, and heal one in preparation for a climactic trial of strength and fortitude.

Within the compass of these dominant master metaphors, secondary metaphors show the same kind of metaphoric conversion of abstract elements into visible, material forms. Among the enemies whom the Red Cross Knight must fight, duplicity is a beautiful, ostentatiously dressed woman who is a treacherous witch, intending him harm (Duessa); the negative impulses deriving from his own dysregulated emotions are personified as three Saracen soldiers–Sansfoy (faithlessness), Sansjoy (depression), and Sansloy (lawlessness, or the enactment of unrestrained impulses); and temptation is an evil magician (Archimago). On the other side, truth is a beautiful, simply dressed, loving woman who is unfailingly loyal (Una); the positive mental dispositions that can assist the Red Cross Knight in fulfilling his quest and the felicity that attends it are three beautiful sisters–Fidessa (faith), Speranza (hope), and Charissa (charity, or love); and the divine grace that, in Spenser's Protestant belief system, makes salvation possible, is a glorious prince (Arthur).

The signifying interrelationship of these key elements is intimated through an intricate system of metaphorical mapping, consisting for the most part of doubling for the sake of establishing parallels and contrasts: the Red Cross Knight has a choice between two female companions, one loyal (Una) and one unfaithful (Duessa); he visits two houses, one with rich trappings inhabited by a vainglorious queen (Lucifera) and courtiers in "gorgeous array" (the House of Pride), and the other one an "auncient" edifice devoted to "pure unspotted life" presided over by "a matron grave and hore" (Dame Caelia), and inhabited by the theological virtues and their officers.[15] These antithetical edifices are complemented by the "brazen towre" in which Una's parents (Adam and Eve) are kept imprisoned by their fear of a huge dragon (the devil)–the tower being a symbol of phallic tumescence that signifies the entrapment of human beings in their appetitive impulses because of defects in their nature caused by original sin.[16] Symbolic mapping extends even into the landscape and topography, with the Red Cross Knight entering a dark wood when he encounters error, being thrown into a subterranean dungeon when he is imprisoned by pride (Orgoglio), traversing a sterile, rocky, barren landscape when he is tempted by despair, and being led up a high mountain by contemplation to be shown a vision of the New Jerusalem.

Through this extension of metaphorical thought into the structuring fabric of the fiction, Spenser externalizes a psychological process whereby he imaginatively fashions the affective being of his hero so that it is aligned with a frame of reference imposed by the imperatives of the cultural belief system prevailing in his time. Unlike Gaylene Preston, whose exercise of this extension of metaphor into the shaping of plot is entirely unconscious, as we have seen, Spenser appears to be highly conscious of what he is doing, drawing attention to it by using names that serve as cyphers and through the direct comments he offers as narrator. The basic procedures, nevertheless, remain the same.

SYMBOLIC MAPPING: THE FILMS OF JANE CAMPION

In the absence of a widely shared belief system requiring conformity, like Spenser's Protestantism, most contemporary authors exercise greater freedom in the way they convert affective experience into fictive representations via metaphor. However, they instinctively draw on the same mechanisms of metaphor-making and metaphor-mapping when they create their stories, as is very apparent in the next author I discuss, the filmmaker Jane Campion, who has been unusually forthright in revealing her motivations and how they relate to her creative process.

For Campion, as she acknowledges in her director's commentary on *In the Cut* (2003), "One of the responsibilities of drama is working out the psychic fears."[17] The problem she finds she needs to overcome, however, is that for her this responsibility is accompanied by an urge to protect herself against having to confront those fears:

> I can't let myself know things in a direct way, so I've always understood and known more than I can know directly through metaphor. Like, it's the same as going to see a psychic–part of me already knows something's doomed, but I can only read it in signs . . . . all the good ideas just arrive, you don't figure them out, they just arrive. You don't know how they come. A lot of the time you're trying to block that instinct because it's more than you want to know about.[18]

The construction of fiction, then, is how Campion overcomes unconscious defense mechanisms: "to find out what you think yourself that you can't know you think because you're blocking it." This, she confesses, was the purpose of *Sweetie* (1989), the film that brought her to prominence at Cannes.[19] In creating it, having learned early on that she was prone to writer's block because of her reluctance to encounter the "unthought known" (to use Christopher Bollas's term), she learned how to cooperate with her subconscious:

At the age of 25, I began to work in a very particular way, by developing a relationship with my subconscious. It was when I was writing my first film. After three pages, I came to an end, I could not go any further. Then, I passed the baton to my subconscious. But in order for this process to work, it is necessary to believe that responses [from the subconscious] are possible.[20]

Her means of accomplishing this release into knowledge, she says, is by allowing images to "arise from the unconscious." This is because she thinks that "people understand the world in terms of symbols. Things are rarely what they seem. They are metaphors of what is or what could be. And that also goes for our interior torments."[21] Very often, she says, she is "not conscious of [her] choices."[22]

This creative procedure results in a structure in Campion's films that comprises, in addition to the manifest plot, which is usually quite simple, a network of symbolic markers (images, actions, motifs, and movements) that are organized into a metaphorical system. Her images, including settings, frequently enact a symbolic and metonymic purpose, as in the case of the New Zealand bush setting in *The Piano* (1993), which for Campion "carried secrets and hidden things" relating to sexuality.[23] Consequently, her plots often display a symbolic movement between locations. This movement can be geographical–as when Janet in *An Angel at My Table* and Ada in *The Piano* move between Europe and New Zealand, or when Ruth in *Holy Smoke* (1999) moves between India and the desert in Australia in search of liberation from emotional suffocation. Or it can be local–as when Ada, Janet, and Fanny in *Bright Star* (2009) move out of confining interiors into the natural world, a move that brings with it an emotional expansion. Campion's movies are replete with symbolic motifs–physical elements (water, air, earth and fire), sites, objects, and colors–that are arranged in patterns that recur at significant intervals, constituting a psychic "map." One thinks of the water in *The Piano*, which, as a raging sea at the beginning, delivers Ada to her encounter with primitive passion and, as a placid ocean at the end, symbolizes her temptation to suicide–a motif repeated later in *Top of the Lake* (2013), in which Tui and Robin wade into the freezing lake that is associated variously with secrets and a depressed and despairing state of mind. One thinks, too, of the dark underground places in Campion's movies associated with transgression, such as the catacombs in *The Portrait of a Lady* or the cellar in *In the Cut;* of the symbolic use of color: red, associated with sexuality (in *In the Cut*), blue autochrome tones associated with depression (in *The Piano*), and golden light associated with emotional and sensual expansiveness (also in *The Piano*). Structure in Campion's films, therefore, consists of more than just syntagmatic sequencing: the metaphorical maps created by the deployment of symbolic elements bring into being a form of preverbal consciousness of states of feeling and intuitive knowledge that Campion finds she ordinarily blocks, for the sake of achieving psychic self-awareness and self-repair.[24]

DICHOTOMIZATION: THE FILMS OF BRUNO DUMONT

The influence of affective motivation on the determination of form is equally apparent in the fictive creations of the esteemed French director Bruno Dumont, a teacher of philosophy turned filmmaker. Dumont professes himself to be concerned above all with emotional "expression." To achieve this, he invents "a story where individuals meet." The plot, however, which he regards as "banal or indifferent," is not important as an end in itself in the overall scheme of things but is merely a device for creating a movement that requires the characters to interact and thus reveal themselves.[25] Whereas "the story is the skeleton," "the flesh and blood" is provided by "poetry," which for Dumont consists of images designed to arouse *sensations*. The goal of this arousal is an awareness involving "the passage into oneself. It means releasing oneself to oneself."[26] Unifying the whole is an overarching thematic concern: "I look for something, I have principles, I have a set of images ... I have a lot of elements that I try to tie together through a dogma."[27]

While Dumont's intent and method are similar to those of Campion in that his films are composed of symbolic images that render "interior states that remain invisible" (especially through his use of landscapes),[28] his affective motivation differs from hers, translating into a different deployment of "poetic" materials. Rather than seek what lies hidden in his unconscious, as Campion does, Dumont seeks to give expression to the contradictory impulses that he recognizes as arising from his own nature as a human being in order to bring them under control. All films, Dumont believes, talk about evil and love, which spring from a duality in human nature, as he asserts when reflecting on his film *Hadewijch* (2009):

> In fact, our soul is double. We're capable of being a saint and a bastard... quite clearly. And it's this ambiguity that must be resolved by our moral code. But to resolve it, it must be represented. That means that the viewer has to take a journey. The soul has to be shaken up a bit. It's what we call catharsis. It's inscribed in the fundamental purpose of a work of art. Its function is to purify... to cleanse, if you like, our dark side.[29]

Thus, instead of creating a tapestry of evocative symbols and metaphors, as Campion does, Dumont constructs scenarios in which opposites are starkly juxtaposed.

Dumont's oppositions are to be found both within and between characters: Hadewijch can simultaneously devote herself to an intense love of God and set off a terrorist bomb in the Paris Metro; Freddy in *The Life of Jesus* (1997) can be both lover and assassin; in the Bailleul of *Humanité* (1999), both the saintly Pharaon De Winter and the murderous Joseph can coexist as friends. It is the paradoxical coexistence of these opposites, along with the sensations they arouse, that in Dumont's view can take us beyond contradictions in a way that words alone cannot: "Sensation can simultaneously combine the desire for sainthood and the desire to be a bastard. Thought can't do that—it has to choose. So in cinema you can get into zones of contradiction, very human, very interesting."[30]

In all of Dumont's films, the minimal elements of plot exist only to marshal these contraries so that they can be directed toward violent outcomes, usually in the form of rape, murder, or psychic torture, as in *Camille Claudel 1915* (2013). These grim scenarios point to the psychological function of fictive creation for Dumont, which he expects it will be for the audience when they watch his films: to evacuate feared or unwanted impulses in the self by identifying them projectively with fictive characters and by then having those characters vicariously act out the impulse:

> She [Hadewijch] sets this bomb that we all want to set. She sets it for us in a film. And that relieves us of the dark side within us [which is reflected in the fact that] people are still fascinated by New York's twin towers. This

fascination must be killed. It must be killed. That's what the film does....
Through art we can awaken ourselves by going through difficult and dark
times.... We can be relieved by accompanying a terrorist and making
them into a hero.[31]

Cinema thus allows the primitive parts of our nature to be experienced
safely: "In order to be civilized, you have to have the experience of barbarism in the cinema. There's no danger there." Dumont takes care to add,
however, that "you have to be civilized when you come out!"[32]

SYMBOLIC SPATIALIZATION: TRUFFAUT'S *THE LAST METRO*; PANARELLO'S *ONE HUNDRED STROKES*

Given our universal, hardwired impulse to form attachments with
those who care for us and those for whom we care, it is not surprising to
find that some of the most powerful literary and cinematic fictions eventuate as a response to the emotional legacy of attachment relationships
that have been disrupted, dysfunctional, absent, or lost. As Jaak Panksepp has noted, "Anything that hints at shunning or even milder forms
of social exclusion is experienced as psychologically painful." With the
developmental programming of the neocortex, he continues, "we become
profoundly intersubjective creatures who care deeply about the quality of
our social networks."[33] This is particularly the case with the relationship
between the child and his or her parents, but it also pertains to any close
attachments formed in later life–for example, between marriage partners
or between members of a close-knit group.

Cinema and literature are full of works depicting the pain of disturbed
attachments along with a search for self-repair. In such works, it is common to find different types of space exploited as a metaphoric equivalent
for an interior mental journey that the author traverses while creating the
fiction, usually accompanied by a fictive alter ego who, in the diegesis, is
shown to achieve a comparable movement.

A very striking example of this imaginative shaping is François Truffaut's *The Last Metro* (1980), one of his most popular films, which is set in
Paris during the German Occupation between 1940 and 1944–the Paris
of Truffaut's childhood–and depicts the efforts of actress Marion Steiner

(Catherine Deneuve) to manage a theater while keeping her Jewish husband Lucas Steiner (Heinz Bennent) hidden from the Nazis in the cellar of the theater. Concurrently, a young actor, Bernard (Gérard Depardieu), tries to seduce Marion and eventually succeeds. At the end of the opening night performance of the play, the concealed husband emerges from the shadows to take a bow along with Marion and Bernard, with all three hand in hand.

While the film is usually interpreted as an exploration of the relations between life and art, it is also deeply autobiographical, enacting a fantasy of which not even Truffaut himself was aware at the time he made it–its roots extend deeply into the filmmaker's childhood. Truffaut was the illegitimate son of an unknown Jewish father and a mother who was emotionally remote and indifferent to him, putting him in the care of various nannies and sending him to live with his grandmother until he was ten. It was only by accident, when he was twelve, that Truffaut discovered that Roland Truffaut, whom he had believed to be his father, was not his real father at all–an event that is depicted in *The 400 Blows* (1959), which fairly closely follows the course of Truffaut's life as a young adolescent.

At the time *The Last Metro* was made, no one but Truffaut himself knew that the man who had raised him was not his real father. He had not known who his biological father was until 1979, when, during the shooting of *Stolen Kisses* (a film in which, significantly, the hero works at a detective agency), he hired a detective to find out the truth of his origins, thus reflecting the fiction in real life. This sleuth informed him that his father was a Jewish dentist living in eastern France. Truffaut never contacted his father, but is purported to have made a trip to observe him secretly at night.

Soon after *The Last Metro* was released, film scholar Anne Gillain wrote an article about it.[34] Even though she knew nothing of Truffaut's discovery, by following the network of repetitions, in particular the images of hands, forbidden spaces, and the recurring theme of undisclosed secrets, she concluded that the whole film was a vast metaphor evoking a hidden father inside the mysterious maternal body represented by the theater. When she sent this interpretation to Truffaut and asked him what he thought about it, he replied, "J'ai été estomaqué" ("I felt stunned"). The reason Truffaut was "estomaqué" was that the article had made him realize that in *The Last Metro* he had unwittingly staged the central mystery of his life: the unknown Jewish father concealed in his mother's memory. Without consciously knowing it, by setting the action of the film in his childhood (wartime Paris), and by representing a young hero, Bernard (Gérard Depardieu), seeking to attract the attention of a remote female figure whose loyalty lay elsewhere, he had recreated a displaced expression of the psychic drama that had haunted him throughout much of his life. An inducer image from autobiographical memory appears in a very striking way in the form of a black-and-white clip from Georges Franju's *La Première Nuit* (1958), used as a supra-diegetical insert to evoke the Paris Metro of Truffaut's childhood, in which he, as a lonely child who felt unloved, would sneak off and spend the night. The focal center of this clip shows a young boy of Truffaut's age at the time and the labyrinthine corridors of the Metro, which mirror those of the theater in which the action of the film takes place. Another autobiographical memory is condensed into the image of Marion Steiner, who is the seductive but remote and unfaithful mother of Truffaut's childhood (as depicted in the more directly autobiographical *400 Blows*) and Truffaut's former lover in real life, Catherine Deneuve, in whom he fantasmatically had sought in actuality, and was still seeking in the fiction of his film, to find a replacement for his indifferent mother.

Examples of the symbolic figuration of inner psychic states of preconscious awareness translated into visual images abound in this film. The hidden Lucas Steiner secretly directing proceedings on the stage above, through a hole in the broken plumbing, is a brilliant symbolization – represented spatially – of Truffaut's implicit sense of the impact on him of the absent father in a family that is dysfunctional at a deep level. Similarly, the sight of Lucas emerging from the shadows of the wings at the end of the performance enacts the successful attainment of the goal of the representation itself, which is, in the fantasy of this film, to restore the love of the indifferent mother (signified in Bertrand's seduction of Marion, the mother stand-in) and to gain the love and approval of the father who had abandoned him. Symbolically, this is figured forth when all three join hands to take their bows and acknowledge the applause at the end. At a fantasmatic level, the theater itself thus expresses, through a visual configuration of symbolic space, an unconscious drama being performed in the mental theater of the filmmaker himself, unconsciously designed to objectify and repair the emotional damage imprinted in his psychic structure. To put it another way, the spatial structure in this work is metaphorically coterminous with the fantasy that motivates it, in which an emotionally deprived boy is restored to the love of his mother and the approval of his true father, the concealed Jew, who emerges, metaphorically as well as literally, on the stage to joins hands with his wife and son.

A comparable example from literature of the use of space to structure a fantasy of self-repair can be found in Melissa Panarello's *Cento colpi di spazzola prima di andare a dormire* (2003), published in English as *One Hundred Strokes of the Brush before Bed*. This is the fictionalized memoir of a Sicilian teenager who recounts her sexual behavior during two years from the time she was fifteen, comprising loveless encounters with a series of men, group sex, a lesbian affair, and a sadomasochistic episode with a married man.[35]

At the beginning of the story, Panarello presents her fictionalized self, "Melissa," as having no internal peace: "It's as if a mouse were gnawing away at my soul, so gently that it even seems sweet. I'm not ill, but I'm not quite well; what's worrying is that 'I'm not.'"[36] The only way she can "find" herself is to fix her gaze on her reflection in the mirror. In this action, we see the fragility of Melissa's feeling of narcissistic integrity and self-esteem: she feels as if she has no real existence because of an emptiness caused by the neglect and indifference of her parents: "My mother says I'm a zombie .... My father knows zilch about how my days unfold.... Love is what I'm missing, an affectionate caress is what I want, a sincere look is what I desire."[37]

According to psychoanalytic theory, individuals who must struggle to maintain their "narcissistic homeostasis" attempt this in two ways: by keeping a distance from others or, at the opposite extreme, by grasping at others, "displaying an unquenchable need of the person chosen to reflect the image that is missing in the inner psychic world." Often, a sexual partner is asked to fulfill this function.[38] Initially, Melissa responds to her inner emptiness simply by adopting the first solution – closing herself off from the outer world as if in "a bell jar of the most delicate glass." She tries to find the missing image in her own reflection: "As I look into my eyes, I'm filled with a feeling of love and admiration for myself.... The only thing that really makes me feel good is the image I behold and love; everything else is make-believe."³⁹ On entering puberty, however, she finds that this narcissistic strategy no longer works, which prompts her to switch to the second solution—first by seeking what is missing in a sexual partner to "experience a pleasure produced by someone other than me."⁴⁰ When that too fails—upon her discovery that her lover, Daniele, merely wants sex, not love, displaying "only indifference, insults, irritating laughter,"⁴¹—she turns to addictive, masochistic, promiscuous sex, which eventually leads Melissa into the "dark labyrinth" of a living hell.⁴²

Like Truffaut, Panarello exploits spatialization in constructing a fiction that allows her to achieve a form of self-repair. In this case, it involves the creation of a symbolic topography that mirrors that found in Dante Alighieri's *La Divina Commedia*, on which Panarello draws as an intertext to provide a symbolic commentary on her heroine's experience. Allusions to the *Inferno* suggest how Melissa's descent into compulsive promiscuity amounts emotionally to a descent into hell. As she begins her recovery, she begins an ascent that takes her through a form of purgatory. During this phase, she needs to evade "an arrogant angel and his devils and behind them an ogre with a bellyful of babies' bodies, and farther on an androgynous monster followed by young sodomites"—in other words, the metaphoric incarnations of the lovers she has taken in the course of the novel.⁴³ Eventually, she attains the fulfillment of her quest by attaining the earthly paradise, which takes the form of the gaze of a "gentle and sweet man," Claudio, who, in affirming an undying commitment to her, allows her to know true joy and happiness—"something I've sought in so many beds, in so many men, even in a woman, something I've sought in myself and then forfeited."⁴⁴ The effect on her of Claudio's genuine love is transformative: "When I returned home I saw that my hair was still shining and my makeup intact. A princess, as my mother always says, so beautiful that even dreams want to steal her away."⁴⁵

The fact that by this point the narrative has turned into a wish fulfillment fantasy is deeply instructive because it shows how Panarello's fictive design serves a therapeutic function—to process, through symbolic mediation, the pain of emotional deprivation arising from a disturbed parental attachment in such a way as to provide a template for future aspiration. Panarello herself has acknowledged this function of her fiction: "The process has been extremely painful.... But the fact of exteriorizing my own suffering, of talking about the violation I have undergone, has been a form of therapy, and has freed me from a kind of drug."[46] Thus, although the degree of displacement is less extreme than in *The Last Metro*, the fantasy in *One Hundred Strokes*, via a symbolic topography, has been structured so as to achieve a very similar psychological outcome.

What these examples show is that the way fictive representations are shaped does not depend solely on a cognitive linear arrangement of the events in a narrative, although the nature of that arrangement does indeed make an important contribution. In addition, the mind makes use of its ability to convert emotions and sensations into a metaphoric equivalent, which can then be presented in the visual or spatial dispositions of the text. In some instances, such as Gaylene Preston's *Perfect Strangers*, the metaphor itself can be literalized to provide the components of the action.

In some of the examples I have discussed, it will be observed that the author exploits the preexistent thematic elements of one or more intertexts–Ariosto's *Orlando furioso* and the Bible in the case of Spenser, Dante's *Divina Commedia* in the case of Panarello–as well as the formal elements of various genres. That is a topic in its own right, which I explore in the next chapter.

7

The Exploitation of Generic Templates and Intertexts as Vehicles for Affect Regulation

So far, the majority of fictions I have examined involve highly original scenarios that draw on the metaphorical and symbolic mechanisms out of which fantasies are constructed. I now turn to several examples of another, very commonly used, distinct shaping strategy: a generic template, often accompanied by a structuring intertext (as seen in Spenser's *Faerie Queene* and Melissa Panarello's novel, discussed in chapter 6), for the representation of an emotional condition or complex psychological experience.

THE NATURE AND FUNCTION OF GENRES AND INTERTEXTS

A "genre," in the sense in which I am using the term, may be defined as a conjunction of "semantic" (thematic) and "syntactic" (structural) elements that are configured into a pattern with a recognizable narrative shape combined with a preestablished set of thematic expectations.[1] Genres come into being because of their fitness-to-mean; in other words, they embody shared models of understanding for the interpretation of various aspects of human reality. Their repeated use means that they have been confirmed as useful for the expressive purposes of the author, and as satisfying for the reader/spectator through the feedback loops provided by the reader/spectator's response. As the Chilean filmmaker and film theorist Raúl Ruiz puts it with reference to cinema, the codes that are embedded in genres presuppose "an international community of connoisseurs and a shared set of rules for the game of social life."[2] The same applies to literature, especially with genres that are found across diverse cultures and have been confirmed through the passage of time.

In fictive creation, the use of genres is often tied to the complementary use of an intertext, or source, that powerfully embodies the semantic-syntactic configuration in a particular genre. Intertexts are useful not only because they evoke this configuration, with its established, preexisting capacity to signify what the author has chosen it to express, but also because they are an effective means of displacement, and thus function like metaphoric configurations. In addition, they allow projective and introjective identification by the author that facilitates the imaginative articulation of what he or she wishes to express.

To demonstrate the utility of generic templates, I pursue three case studies that make explicit use of source intertexts. The first, drawn from literature, is John Milton's *Samson Agonistes* (1671), which is based on the biblical account in Judges 23–31 and imitated from Greek tragedy; the second is the wave of contemporary American blockbuster films presenting alien invasions or attacks by terrorists, which combine elements of action/thrillers and often science fiction or horror; the third is François Ozon's *Une nouvelle amie* (*The New Girlfriend*, 2014), which is based on a story by the British crime writer Ruth Rendell and converts it into a comedy/drama. These case studies show how genres and intertexts can serve the same function as an actual autobiographical event or as a set of circumstances in terms of providing a stimulus and pretext for creative invention.

TRIUMPH THROUGH TRAGEDY:
JOHN MILTON'S *SAMSON AGONISTES*

Some time after the restoration of the English monarchy in 1660, John Milton composed a closet drama in verse, *Samson Agonistes*, which he published together with his short epic *Paradise Regained* in 1671, soon after his monumental epic *Paradise Lost*, which had first been published in 1667.[3] It is illuminating to analyze this work because it shows how Milton exploits the affective pattern inherent in the genre of tragedy to objectify an extremely perturbed emotional condition in order to overcome it, using the displacement made available through the use of a source text.

In the 1660s, Milton had good reason to be perturbed. From the time he was a youth, he had a very strong sense of his vocation as a divinely inspired poet with a contribution to make to his country in the service of the reformed religion to which he felt "time" and "the will of Heav'n" were leading him.[4] When the Civil War broke out, Milton returned in July 1639 from his scholar's sojourn in Italy to throw himself as a polemicist into the assertion of liberty, spending the next twenty years writing prose pamphlets defending the Puritan revolution.[5] Among his more radical pamphlets was *The Tenure of Kings and Magistrates*, written just before the execution of King Charles I on January 30, 1649, and published on February 13, 1649, which argues that power resides in the people and that it is lawful to call to account a tyrant or wicked king and, after due trial and conviction, put him death. A month later, the Council of State appointed Milton Secretary for Foreign Tongues.[6] As holder of this office, he wrote *Eikonoklastes* (October 1649) to confute *Eikon Basilike,* a proroyalist work published soon after Charles's execution that portrayed the king as a model of piety; he also defended the regicide in both *Defensio pro populo Anglicano* (February 1651) and *Defensio Secunda* (1654) against the outcry from royalist sympathizers on the continent as well as in England. As late as February 1660, only two months before Charles II was restored to the throne, Milton was still publishing tracts in defense of the revolution with *The Ready and Easy Way to Establish a Free Commonwealth,* in which he highlighted "the inconveniences and dangers of readmitting kingship in this nation."

It was small wonder that when the restoration of Charles II was proclaimed on May 8, 1660, Milton went into hiding in the house of a friend in Bartholomew Close. The seriousness of his position was reflected in an order for his arrest, and on August 27, 1660, the public executioner burned copies of his books at the Old Bailey. Milton's life, in fact, hung in the balance until the Act of Free and General Pardon, Indemnity and Oblivion was proclaimed on August 29, 1660, and his name was not among its exceptions. However, although he had escaped the death penalty, he was still liable to arrest and was indeed arrested and imprisoned in the Tower of London until December 15, 1660.[7]

Milton's experience in politics was thus deeply traumatic. Not only had the political cause to which he had committed himself failed catastrophically, but in his personal life he had been suffering from blindness since 1655; these afflictions left him with a profound sense of failure and a fear of God's abandonment both of the nation and of himself. Faced with a need to respond to the negative emotions ("passions") aroused by this situation ("the perturbations of the mind," to use Milton's expression), he turned to fictive representation as a means of seeking "to temper and reduce them to just measure with a kind of delight," paraphrasing Aristotle's notion of catharsis, in the preface to *Samson Agonistes*.[8]

To address the failure of the Puritan revolution at a general level, Milton turned to the genre of classical epic with *Paradise Lost*, in which his aim was to "assert Eternal Providence, / and justify the ways of God to men" (book 1, lines 24–25). While the epic form, with its cosmic perspective and universal compass, may have been appropriate to address a nation, the rhetorical distance required between the narrator and the action hardly qualified it to be consoling or sustaining at a personal level. For that, a more intimate genre was required, and Milton, having complemented *Paradise Lost* with the brief epic *Paradise Regained*–which laid out a paradigmatic exemplum of complete obedience to divine will on the part of the unfallen redeemer of mankind, the incarnate Son of God–found such a genre in tragedy.

Tragedy was an appropriate generic vehicle for the psychological processing of Milton's personal predicament because, as well as pity, it addresses *metus* (in the Latin version of Aristotle's definition that Milton gives as an epigraph to *Samson Agonistes*), which translates as "fear," "dread," "apprehension," "anxiety"–emotions from which one can imagine Milton had been suffering. Tragedy acknowledges these emotions by representing them through an action that leads the hero to catastrophe–like the one Milton had recently experienced. The story of Samson's tragedy, drawn from a brief passage in the Old Testament (Judges 16: 21–31) was particularly apposite because of the scope it provided for Milton to identify with him.

Milton's identification with Samson is starkly apparent. Like Samson, he was blind and has been delivered into the hands of his enemies. Like Samson, too, he had a wife who aligned herself with his enemies–in Spring

1642, the Powells, his wife's family, had declared for the King, and in August of that year Milton's wife Mary had left him to return to her family. As the play begins, we see that just as Milton was convinced he had a divine calling, Samson believes he had been "Design'd for great exploits"– exploits he is no longer able to accomplish because he is "Betray'd, Captiv'd, and both my Eyes put out" (32–33).

Through the displacement that the fictive invention allows, Milton gives expression to the "restless thoughts, that like a deadly swarm / Of Hornets arm'd" rush upon him and present "times past, what once I was, and what am now" (20–22):

> My griefs not only pain me
> As a ling'ring disease,
> But finding no redress, ferment and rage,
> Nor less than wounds immedicable
> Rankle, and fester, and gangrene,
> To black mortification.
> Thoughts my Tormentors arm'd with deadly stings
> Mangle my apprehensive tenderest parts,
> Exasperate, exulcerate, and raise
> Dire inflammation which no cooling herb
> Or med'cinal liquor can assuage,
> Nor breath of Vernal Air from snowy *Alp*.
> Sleep hath forsook and giv'n me o'er
> To death's benumbing Opium as my only cure.
> Thence faintings, swoonings of despair,
> And sense of Heav'n's desertion. (616–632)

To achieve the affective retuning he is seeking, then, Milton, through his identification with Samson, must find a way of rescuing Samson from this state of toxic negativity–or, in theological terms, despair.

Milton accomplishes Samson's recovery by leading him through a rising movement of spiritual regeneration eventuating in a positive state of mind that means that his death, paradoxically, is turned into a triumph instead of a confirmation of his failure. The instrument of Samson's regeneration, which in itself manifests God's providence, is a triple temptation that mirrors in its structure the sequence of temptations Christ undergoes in *Paradise Regained* at the hands of Satan, whom Milton calls "the Adversary." Samson's first temptation is to accept his father Manoa's efforts to secure his ransom—in other words, to be delivered from the punishment that is coming to him because of his uxoriousness. Samson resists this temptation by acknowledging his guilt and expressing deep penitence. The second temptation is presented by Dalila, who similarly offers to intercede with Samson's enemies in order to procure his release into her care. Samson rejects this offer on the grounds that it would require him to "live uxorious" by her will, thus reenacting his original fault. The third temptation comes in the form of Harapha, the Giant of Gath—a figure invented by Milton—who tempts Samson to feel daunted and intimidated. However, perceiving that Harapha is a windy braggart, Samson realizes that "My trust is in the living God" (1140), which leads him to have faith that God will support him to a degree that Harapha's god, Dagon, will be unable to match. At this point in the action, by subjecting his painful memories to reflection, Samson is now able to remind himself of God's mercy and grace, which pulls him out of his despair:

> All these indignities, for such they are
> From thine, these evils I deserve and more,
> Acknowledge them from God inflicted on me
> Justly, yet despair not of his final pardon
> Whose ear is ever open; and his eye
> Gracious to re-admit the suppliant;
> In confidence whereof I once again
> Defy thee to the trial of mortal fight,
> By combat to decide whose god is God,
> Thine or whom I with Israel's Sons adore. (1168–1177)

It does not require much of a stretch of the imagination to detect a thinly veiled reference to the "god" of the restored Anglicans and the "God" of the Puritans, with Milton/Samson realizing that he can shake off his abjection and still issue a challenge "with plain Heroic magnitude of mind / And celestial vigor arm'd" (1279–1280) on behalf of his God, whom the adversaries (figured in Harapha) will be unable to withstand.

The outcome of this emotional and spiritual recovery becomes evident at the crisis of the play, when Samson is summoned to display some proof of his amazing strength at a solemn feast honoring Dagon, the god of his enemies (an event that shadows the requirement under the Clarendon Code, following the restoration of Anglicanism, that all municipal officials attend Anglican services as a gesture of uniformity). This summons seems to present Samson with an impossible dilemma given that, as an *Ebrew*, he is forbidden to participate in idolatrous rites—just like the dilemma in which Satan puts the Son at the climax of *Paradise Regained*, when he places Christ on the top of a pinnacle and dares him to "stand, if thou wilt stand . . . if not to stand, / Cast thyself down; safely if Son of God," which would be a betrayal of his humanity and hence subvert his redemptive mission (*Paradise Regained*, book 4, lines 551–555). Like the Son, who answers Satan: "Tempt not the Lord thy God . . . and stood" (*Paradise Regained*, book 4: 561), Samson vanquishes temptation by being obedient to the "rousing motions" he starts to feel, confident that whatever happens will be "nothing dishonorable, impure, unworthy / Our God, our Law, my Nation, or myself" (*Samson Agonistes*, 1424–1425). When Samson pulls down the pillars of Dagon's temple and slays all the assembled Philistians, like Christ he not only pays a ransom (for sin), but also secures a triumph out of apparent defeat (his own death), paradoxically meaning that he does indeed accomplish the great work for which he was "foretold": "With God not parted from him, as was fear'd, / But favoring and assisting to the end" (1717–1718). Samson thus restores justice (by exacting his revenge) at the same time that God, through the exemplum Samson furnishes, provides reassurance for the remaining Danites:

> His servants he with new acquist
> Of true experience from this great event
> With peace and consolation hath dismist,
> And calm of mind, all passion spent. (1755–1778)

Symbolically, through his identification with Samson, Milton uses the tragic mode to construct a fantasy in which he simultaneously restores his emotional equilibrium, reassures himself of the divine purposefulness of his experience, justifies himself, and fulfills his vocation as a poet whose mission is to be "doctrinal and exemplary to a nation," as Sophocles and Euripides had been–a mission he had foreshadowed twenty years earlier in *The Reason of Church Government* (1642).[9] In my view, by publishing *Samson Agonistes* with *Paradise Regained* in 1671, especially in the context of the publication of the first version of *Paradise Lost* in 1667 and the revised twelve-book version of 1674, Milton was signaling the function of that tripartite enterprise: namely, to "pull down the temple," metaphorically speaking, of the idolators (Anglicans and royalists), like Samson, even while seeming to be servile and abject in the midst of his enemies. By writing and publishing those great works, he was making himself the proof of the merit of his own exemplum, reassuring others at the same time as he was reassuring himself–a feat that had been made possible by his use of a tragic generic paradigm as an instrument for the activation of a triumphant emotional restoration. Milton's creative adaptation of his biblical intertext bears out the truth of Paul Valéry's saying: "Tout ce que tu dis parle de toi: singulièrement quand tu parles d'un autre" (Everything you say speaks about yourself, especially when you are talking about someone else).[10]

CONTAINING ANXIETY AND EVACUATING FEAR: CONTEMPORARY AMERICAN BLOCKBUSTERS

It might seem like passing from the sublime to the ridiculous to move from Milton's profoundly tragic poem to contemporary Hollywood blockbusters, but popular films of this sort can illuminate how a generic template can contribute to the shaping of a fantasy that answers to external conditions. This is nowhere more apparent than in the superhero movies, the political action/thrillers, and the alien invasion movies that have proliferated since the 9/11 terrorist attacks that traumatized America, unleashing a determination to exact revenge in the so-called War on Terror.

Among the superhero movies, all of which reproduce the imagery of buildings under attack and falling in flames that stunned viewers on TV screens on 9/11, may be numbered the reboot of the *Batman* franchise–*Batman Begins* (Christopher Nolan, 2005), *The Dark Knight* (Christopher Nolan, 2008), *The Dark Knight Rises* (Christopher Nolan, 2013); those in the *Iron Man* franchise–*Iron Man* (Jon Favreau, 2008), *Iron Man 2* (Jon Favreau, 2010), *The Avengers* (Joss Whedon, 2012), and *Iron Man 3* (Shane Black, 2013); the reboot of the *Captain America* franchise–*Captain America: The First Avenger* (Joe Johnston, 2011); and the reboot of the *Superman* franchise–*Man of Steel* (Zack Snyder, 2013). Complementing these science fiction fantasies are two strikingly similar action/thrillers, both involving attacks on the White House and the presidency: *White House Down* (Roland Emmerich, 2013), and *Olympus Has Fallen* (Antoine Fuqua, 2013). Among the many alien invasion movies, *War of the Worlds* (Steven Spielberg, 2005) stands out as drawing on the same post-9/11 apocalyptic imagery—attacks from the sky, scenes of destruction, buildings falling, people running in panic, and conflagrations.

The explosion of films in these categories is not coincidental. The original superheroes were created in the 1930s—*Superman* in 1933 (by Jerry Siegel and Joe Shuster) and *Batman* in 1939 (by Bob Kane and Bill Finger). In each case, the inventors of the characters were the children of Jewish immigrants, leading the French psychoanalyst Serge Tisseron to link their creation to the rise of Nazism in Europe: "The creation of superheroes saving innocents was a way for them to try and imagine a fantasmatic solution to the growing dangers, in default of being able to imagine a real solution [my translation]."[11] Steven Spielberg, the director of *War of the Worlds*, makes a similar connection between anxiety aroused by perturbing political situations and alien invasion movies such as his own, which is based on H. G. Wells's novel of the same name written between 1895 and 1897. Admitting that he would probably not have adapted the novel had 9/11 not occurred, he points out that earlier adaptations were also prompted by political fear:

> Wells' novel has been made into a film several times, notably always in times of international crisis: World War II had just begun when Orson Welles terrified millions of Americans with his legendary radio play version, the headlines were dominated by reports on Hitler's invasion of Poland and Hungary. When the first screen version came into the movie theatres in 1953, the Americans were very afraid of a nuclear attack by the Soviet Union. And our version also comes at a time when Americans feel deeply vulnerable.[12]

According to Spielberg, in an interview with *Reader's Digest*, the film delivers "a wakeup call to face our fears as we confront a force intent on destroying our way of life."[13]

The causative link between fear generated by political circumstances and the choice of these closely related genres points to the latter's usefulness in providing preestablished templates for the containment of anxiety. They can serve such a function because they depend on a number of paradigmatic plot structures showing a threat being successfully neutralized despite fearful odds. The first of these paradigms is a hero with superhuman capacities who, working on the side of justice, triumphs over evil by frustrating the destructive intent of attacking enemies—as in the *Superman* movies. The second is an imperfect man of humble status—usually estranged from members of his family or experiencing difficulties in his relations with them—who, in the face of a dire threat (usually terrorists or attacking aliens), discovers an untapped source of courage and fortitude, and through his ingenuity either overcomes the attackers (as in *White House Down* and *Olympus Has Fallen*), or evades them, saving his family in the process (as in *War of the Worlds*). A third model is a man—regularly a wealthy philanthropist—who exploits technology to give himself an invincible advantage (as in the *Batman* and *Iron Man* films). Different elements from these paradigms can overlap or be blended in various ways.

Obviously, there is a considerable degree of symbolic troping taking place in these paradigmatic structures. Superman may be regarded as a personification of America itself, in terms of its status as a superpower in the role of policing the world to protect it from villainy, which in turn emblematizes any threat to American values or the American way of life. The fact that the more ordinary heroes of the political action/thrillers are estranged in various ways from families that have become dysfunctional symbolically figures the need for restored unity and reconciliation in the nation's "family" in order to combat the threat posed by vicious enemies intent on destruction. Finally, the exploitation of super-advanced technology in the third category of films delivers a symbolic, reassuring reminder of America's technological advantage as the world's richest nation-signaled in billionaires Batman and Iron Man—and hence its ability to fund the resources necessary to win the war against terror.

One can infer the effects of these stereotypes, which furnish a vehicle for the activation of multilayered fantasies. At the simplest level, they objectify and categorize what is feared by giving it a visual appearance. This involves the summoning and incorporation of many traumatic memories, such as the sight of the U.S. Capitol falling in on itself in *White House Down*, which evokes the image of the Twin Towers collapsing, or the sight of horrified citizens gazing upward in disbelief during the airborne attacks that occur in these movies. It also "speaks" the need for resistance, with a sense of what an effective response might require from individuals. In that regard, the films offer an idealized image of masculine courage and prowess with which, in fantasy, young men are invited to identify in preparation for the role that society might in due course expect them to play.

At another level, the representation of these fearful events allows the anxiety prompting the creation of the fiction to be brought under control. This affective containment does not result simply from the fact that these films deliver a fantasy in which their heroes triumph over America's enemies; it also springs from the feeling that comes from the very act of arranging events in a formal order to create a fictive representation, as Steven Spielberg acknowledged in 2007 when explaining the reason he started making films:

> I was infatuated with the control that movies gave me in creating a sequence of events, or a feeling, or a train wreck with two final trains that I could then repeat and see over and over again, and I think it was just a realization that I could change the way I perceive life through a funnel or another medium to make it come out better for me.[14]

Without specifying how such control leads to a change in the way life is perceived, Spielberg accurately acknowledges the transformative effect that fictive structuration can achieve.

At a still deeper level, the exploitation of these generic stereotypes allows for a fantasmatic enactment of revenge–as is reflected in the title of one of the *Iron Man* spin-offs, *The Avengers* (2012), in which four of the major American superheroes–Iron Man, Captain America, the Hulk, and Thor–join together under Nick Fury, the aptly named director of an espionage agency called S.H.I.E.L.D., to stop Thor's evil brother Loki from subjugating Earth. It is even possible that the violence and destruction marking these movies, heightened by the use of spectacular CGI special effects, provide a vicarious means of evacuating frustration and anger at the world generally on the part of frightened citizens who feel powerless and vulnerable in the face of an invisible, unknown enemy who can strike at any moment.

It should be obvious by now that the choice of superhero, action/thriller, and alien invasion genres in these instances is not motivated simply by a desire to exploit the opportunities they present for entertainment in the form of rip-roaring action and spectacle—two of the biggest draws for the young males who constitute the largest audience group for these male-oriented blockbusters. Rather, the prime raison d'être comes from the need of those for whom they are intended, as in the case of John Milton several centuries earlier, to allay their mental perturbations in order to gear themselves up, emotionally, for whatever contribution that unknown events in the future might require of them.

In light of the functions I have identified, the juxtaposition of Milton's *Samson Agonistes* with American blockbusters turns out not to be as arbitrary as might have at first appeared—indeed, Jerry Siegel revealed that in envisioning Superman as a hero, Samson (along with Hercules) was one of the mythic characters on which he modeled him.[15] Milton's tragic play and the blockbusters, although separated by more than three centuries, do in fact share much in common: both address psychic fears aroused by a dangerous political situation threatening the safety and values of the author and his society; both draw on the conventions of existing genres to give form to their feelings; and both depict a triumph achieved against apparently impossible odds. Thus, in their own separate ways, they demonstrate how genres can be used instrumentally in the shaping of fictive scenarios to induce a form of psycho-affective processing that eventuates in a tempering and reduction of dysregulated emotions (to echo Milton), leading to reassurance and consolation at both an individual and a collective level.

ENACTING A FANTASY OF RESTITUTION: FRANÇOIS OZON'S *THE NEW GIRLFRIEND*

As I intimate in chapter 6 with respect to Spenser's *Faerie Queene* and Panarello's *One Hundred Strokes*, one of the most effective ways in which an author shapes the creation of a fiction is to take an existing text and adapt it to his or her purposes. The utility of this strategy is nowhere more apparent than in the latest film by the enfant terrible of French cinema, François Ozon.

Ozon's *The New Girlfriend* (*Une nouvelle amie*, 2014) is based on a psychological suspense short story by the British crime writer Ruth Rendell in which a woman discovers that her friend's husband is a closet cross-dresser. Ozon was attracted to the story, he says, because of a long-standing personal interest in cross-dressing; in fact, he had first come across the story much earlier, at the time he was making his short film *Une robe d'été* [A Summer Dress] (1996)–another film in which the male protagonist puts on a dress (having lost his bathing suit)–and had even prepared an adaptation of the Rendell story but could not secure financing or find the right cast.[16]

What is interesting about *The New Girlfriend* in terms of generic templates is that when Ozon finally did make his adaptation twenty years later, he completely changed the genre of the original. The source text is a suspense thriller in which the female protagonist kills her friend's husband when he declares his love and tries to have sex with her, in the manner of the TV series *Alfred Hitchcock Presents*.[17] In contrast to this brutal outcome, Ozon allows a fully-fledged romance to develop between Claire (Anaïs Demoustier), the protagonist, and her friend's husband David (Romain Duris) in his identity as a woman named Virginia. He makes another significant change by having Claire's friend Laura (Isild Le Besco) die of an illness soon after the death of her child, which leaves her husband in a state of grief, mourning her loss while looking after their baby. Ozon also changes Claire's reaction to David's cross-dressing from one of initial revulsion to one of self-liberating acceptance. The process of adaptation thus results in a transformation of the genre, unsettling the spectator's expectations so that Ozon can register his personal perspective on the matter and convert it to his own purpose, which is to explore a fantasy relating to his own sexual identity as a gay man. In Ozon's words, the audience "can't say: it's a comedy, it's a drama ... it's difficult to define."[18] Most Internet sites identify the film as a "drama," but it is also a comedy with respect to David's pleasure in cross-dressing[19] and a romantic comedy in that it involves the progressive education of both Claire and David into a more tolerant understanding of sexual identity and their own sexual feelings, eventuating in the formation of a couple, celebrated by a happy ending.[20]

What, then, constitutes the fantasy that this genre-bending transformation of an intertext expresses? Ozon is candid in admitting that the fantasy is his own and that he chose the source story because it provided him with a means of imaginative displacement: "It's easier for me to project myself in a woman because I am a man. I have more distance.... I think I speak about myself but you are not really able to see, 'Oh, that's him.' I am hiding myself."[21] This is a strategy used by many male filmmakers and writers both heterosexual and gay, such as Amos Kollek in his trilogy consisting of *Sue, Fiona, and Bridget*. In Ozon's case, a clue to the fantasy being projected is his introduction into the story of a child and the death of a mother, which activates the idea of a maternal absence. When Claire accidentally discovers David dressed in his dead wife's clothes as Virginia, he explains that he is doing it as a way of filling the maternal void from which his baby daughter is suffering – it is a means of bringing the mother back. Laura's absence, Ozon observes, also "creates a void in which Claire and Virginia will find each other."[22] Fantasmatically, therefore, the reworked story allows the projection of a longing for the restitution of a bonded closeness with a woman, a mother, who is now inaccessible. Furthermore, compensation for the loss of that relationship is provided in the form of a same-sex relationship in which the partner becomes a stand-in for the absent mother.

The significance of the substitution is underlined by three successive iterations: in the lifelong bond between Claire and Laura from the time they were children; in the relationship that develops between the adult Claire and David-as-Virginia, in which she sees the absent mother in the gender-converted man; and in a brief fantasy Claire has when she voyeuristically (and symbolically) sneaks into a men's changing room, where she has a vision of her husband Gilles (Raphaël Personnaz) making love to David in a shower.

This latter glimpse of a gay male encounter signals the deep-seated preoccupation that animates the film as a whole. Viewed as an extended metaphor, it literalizes the capacity of an individual to see the unattainable mother in the feminine potential of another man, who is then chosen to serve as a stand-in for the missing fusional bond for which the subject unconsciously longs. Thus, through projection, reversal, and displacement, the fictive representation allows the author to explore the origin and nature of his own sexual and emotional impulses at a level that transcends mere rational comprehension, but allows the expression and contemplation of feelings that are partially, if not largely, unconsciously driven.

Ozon has said that he wanted to make a film where the audience could "identify with the characters and enjoy the transvestism without guilt or discomfort."[23] At the same time, and for himself, he recreated a representation that allows him to get in touch with the deeper determinants of his own sexual identity.

GENERAL INFERENCES

As far as the author who creates a fictive representation is concerned, it is clear from the various examples discussed in the last two chapters that emotions play a much larger role in the shaping process than is commonly recognized. On the one hand, the affects that prompt the impulse to create in the first place inform the selection of genres and intertexts that mold the fiction in combination with images summoned from autobiographical memory. On the other hand, the shape given to a representation through the integration of these elements, along with the affective response they elicit in the reader/spectator as well as in the author/auteur, stimulate a mental activity that enables the processing of affects that give rise to perturbations so that emotional equilibrium can be recovered.

In shaping fictive scenarios through these strategies, the mind makes use of the basic mechanisms involved in the formation of metaphor; in other words, material from the domains of subjective feelings and apperceptions is converted into material drawn from the sensorimotor domains in order to create a displaced symbolic equivalent that allows subjective feelings and apperceptions to be registered in conscious awareness, based on affective correlations registered via the senses. The plot patterns and other structuring strategies, such as metaphorical mapping and spatialization for symbolic purposes, amount to a figurative extension of this basic metaphor-making process, thus allowing the construction of fit-for-purpose fantasies that are then available for metabolization by the reader/spectator for the sake of a re-equilibrating outcome similar to that which the author has already gained in composing and enunciating the work. This is not to say that all the structuring and narrative procedures identified by narratologists and semioticians are unimportant; rather, they are subservient to, and informed by, the kinds of affective motivations that I have outlined.

So much for the authoring stage of the creative process; it now remains to explore the equally creative and complex activities that take place in the process of reception on the part of readers in the case of literary fiction and spectators in the case of cinematic representations.

8

Theories of Reception in the Twentieth and Twenty-First Centuries

When one surveys the history of efforts to explain how a fictive work produces an effect in a reader/spectator, several things become apparent. First, the diachronic sequence of theories of reception shows the same pattern or reaction and counter-reaction that one sees in the history of conceptualizations of the nature of fiction itself–in other words, a pendulum swing between antithetical possibilities. Second, the way theorists construe the dynamics and outcomes of reception have depended on their assumptions about three crucial components intrinsically involved in it: the nature of the human self, the way the mind works, and the status of a text with regard to meaning. In this chapter, after tracing the evolution of theories of reception to the present day, I propose that recent findings concerning the neurological functioning of the brain require us to rethink certain tenets that have held sway during the past fifty years: specifically, the view that meaning is wholly a subjective construction by the reader/spectator; the view that the text exists independently of the author, together with the idea that authorial intention is a "fallacy"; the view that the recipient's perception of meaning is largely, if not exclusively, the outcome of a cognitive act; and a recent assumption that reception involves a form of hypnosis induced by the fictive representation whereby a recipient is manipulated, without independent agency, by the materiality of the specific form of representation. What is needed, I argue, is a more inclusive sense of the multiple emotional, psychological, and material factors involved in reception, without limiting reception to the confines posited by any one of the schools of thought that have tried to explain the phenomenon during the past few decades.

READER-RESPONSE THEORY VERSUS
THE NEW CRITICISM

The modern debate about the nature of reception kicked off when Louise Rosenblatt proposed in *Literature as Exploration* (1938) that "the reading of any work of literature is, of necessity, an individual and unique occurrence involving the mind and emotions of a particular reader."[1] This view was elaborated in *The Reader, the Text, the Poem: The Transactional Theory of the Literary Work* (1978),[2] in which she argued that "a text, once it leaves its author's hands, is simply paper and ink until a reader evokes from it a literary work."[3] Rosenblatt's view that meanings derive from a transactional exchange between text and reader was soon countered by the view propagated by post-war New Critics such as William K. Wimsatt in *The Verbal Icon* (1954): that both the intention of the author ("The Intentional Fallacy") and the response of the reader ("The Affective Fallacy") are irrelevant in the analysis and evaluation of a literary work, given that the work exists independently of both, and that any emotions it contains are correlative to the fictive objects it presents.[4] Within twenty years, then, the pendulum had swung from an assumption that meaning comes into being only when a subjective process is activated to the view that referential meaning has an objective existence independent of the reader, along with a rejection of affective criticism.

Since then, theories of reception have tended to align themselves with one or the other of these mid-twentieth-century positions: on the one hand, a belief that no immanent textual meaning exists until it is invested in the work by a reader/spectator;[5] on the other hand, a belief that meaning is innately encoded in the formal structures of a work of fiction, or else induced by the materiality of their form.[6] For reader-response theorists, textual interpretation has very little place in reception studies; instead, textual interpretations are of interest only in so far as they are produced historically, especially through discourses that are bound by time and place.[7] For cognitivists, textual analyses, especially involving the tracing of formal patterns and cognitive architecture, are virtually all that is important, and little attention paid to the reader's subjective experience on the grounds that the "simulation" generated by these features is sufficient for the reader to make swift inferences from "goal-relevant information" embodied in the text.[8]

Such polarizations point to issues of readership and spectatorship that need to be resolved. Is the reader (or spectator) merely a passive recipient of meaning already "objectively correlated" in the work? Or is he or she the prime generator of meaning? Or is there some other relationship between the two? If the receiver is the generator of meaning, is he or she influenced in the production of his or her subjective constructions primarily by the unconscious processes identified by psychoanalysis, or primarily by the discursive, ideologically inflected processes prioritized by cultural studies?

VERSIONS OF READER-RESPONSE THEORY

Theoretical speculations since the 1960s and 1970s have variously encompassed all of these possibilities. For proponents of reader-response theory, literature exists and signifies only when it is read. Wolfgang Iser, for example, believing that the reading process "might be described as the reader's transformation of signals sent out by the text," argues that any "meaning" that is "apparently independent of every realization of the text, is in itself nothing more than an individual reading experience that has now simply been identified with the text itself."[9] He goes even further, asserting that "indeterminacy embodies an elementary condition for readers' reactions."[10] Another reader-response theorist, Stanley Fish, slightly modifies this extreme position by proposing that reading activity takes place in "interpretive communities"; meaning, however, although constrained by the internalized understanding of language shared by these communities, retains an entirely subjective status in this formulation.[11]

Turning to the other main issue—the question of what induces or produces this subjective response in the reader/spectator—one finds that theorists espouse either a psychoanalytic or a cultural materialist explanation. A group of scholars, mainly based in Europe, has promoted the idea that fictive representations generate a form of hypnosis whereby the recipient is rendered into a condition similar to that of a subject who has been hypnotized.

PSYCHOANALYTIC ACCOUNTS OF RECEPTION

Scholars propounding a psychoanalytic theory of reception divide into those who adopt a Freudian framework and those who invoke Lacan's linguistically derived model of self-formation and the unconscious. Prominent among the first group is Norman Holland, who in *The Dynamics of Literary Response* (1968), invoked Freud's drive theory in proposing that the reader's response is motivated by deep-seated psychological needs evoked in response to primal fantasies, which the reader then controls through the experience of reading that the fiction invites, with the fiction performing a function equivalent to that of a dream:

> In effect, the literary work dreams a dream for us. It embodies and evokes in us a central fantasy; then it manages that fantasy by devices that were they in mind, we would call defenses, but being on a page, we call "form." And the having of the fantasy and feeling it managed give us pleasure.[12]

In a later work, written after conducting an experiment with a group of readers responding to a selection of shared texts, Holland came to the view that "the text as such almost vanishes in the astonishing variability of different readers' recreation of it"[13] and concluded that "texts do not structure content–people do."[14]

With regard to cinema spectatorship, Christian Metz, one of its foundational theorists, adopted a Lacanian framework, marrying it to certain ideas drawn from semiotic theory to propose (in rather abstruse terms) that in the cinematic experience the spectator himself is "the place where this really perceived imaginary [i.e., the objects in the film] accedes to the symbolic by its inauguration as the signifier of a certain type of institutionalized social activity called the 'cinema.'" In other words, "the spectator *identifies with himself*, with himself as pure perception (as wakefulness, alertness): as the condition of possibility of the perceived and hence as a kind of transcendental subject, which comes before every *there is*."[15]

Rather than regard the reception of a fictive representation as a strategy of self-defense, Metz conceived of it in ontological terms as a mechanism for locating oneself, which, like Lacan, he saw as a process of inescapable specularity in which "the perceived is not really the object, it is its shade, its phantom, it double, its *replica* in a new kind of mirror:"

> A strange mirror, then, very like that of childhood, and very different. Very like, as Jean-Louis Baudry has emphasized, because during the showing we are, like the child again, in a sub-motor and hyper-perceptive state; because, like the child again, we are prey to the imaginary, the double, and are so paradoxically through a real perception. Very different, because this mirror returns us everything but ourselves, because we are wholly outside it, whereas the child is both in it and in front of it.[16]

As with all theories of reception that focus on the reader or viewer as "subject," the author as agent of any kind of meaning communicated to the receiver disappears along with, more radically, the idea of any kind of agency in the subject because of Metz's application of Lacan's idea that subjectification depends on the machineries of language and that the unconscious is structured like a language. These assumptions, as I will argue shortly, can no longer be sustained in the light of what is now known about the brain and its procedures.

CULTURAL AND HISTORICAL MATERIALIST PERSPECTIVES

Those who adopt cultural or historical materialist perspectives express a very different view of how meaning comes to be registered in the reader/spectator, focusing on the effects of discourse and other external, historically situated, contextual factors rather than internal psychological factors. Stuart Hall, for instance, has argued that "production" constructs the message through meaning-producing practices, and that "codes" implicit in a representation "contract relations for the sign with the larger universe of ideologies in a society."[17] He identifies a "circuit of culture" in which meaning depends on the "frameworks of interpretation" we bring to the representation of things and by how we use such representations or integrate them into our everyday practices.[18] For Hall, in short, "meaning and representation seem to belong irrevocably to the interpretative side of the human and cultural sciences," which in turn means that the reader/ spectator's response is governed by "discourses."[19]

Hall's constructionist/discursive theory is matched in cinema studies by the historical materialist approach propounded by film scholars such as Janet Staiger, who believes that "contextual factors, more than textual ones, account for the experiences that spectators have watching films and television, and for the uses to which those experiences are put in navigating our everyday lives."[20] These contexts involve intertextual knowledges, personal psychologies, sociological dynamics, and specific historical situations, which, along with the socially constructed identities that individuals have, "intersect to produce groups of responses that may be linked to broader dynamics of class, race and ethnicity, generation, gender and sexuality identities."[21] As with all receiver-focused theories surveyed thus far, Staiger's theory separates meaning from the text itself.

COGNITIVIST THEORIES OF RECEPTION

Reader-response theories of reception, especially once harnessed to the poststructuralist assumption of an inescapable differential relativism, posited a response so completely subjective that it deprives a text of any inherent meaning. In contrast, the accounts of postmodern cultural theorists, which privileged the operation of locally and historically specific discourses that "write" the subject as well as the text, deprive the reader/ spectator of any independent agency. Inevitably, these extreme formulations, which deflect attention from the author on the one hand and the text on the other to refocus it on the reader and specific cultural contexts, generated a counter-reaction.

The strongest challenge came from scholars who sought to rethink the nature of literature and cinema in the light of developments in cognitive science by refocusing attention on to the text, which was assumed to constitute an evolutionary adaptation, and then on the author who creates it. These scholars argued, variously, that the purpose of art is to arrange inputs in "a single organizing frame" so that "the shared frame gives the inputs an analogical relation."[22] This makes it possible to construct "models of others (and themselves)" that can then be used to "tune into what others are thinking and feeling."[23] According to the cognitivist theorist Keith Oatley, "The understanding of relationships in fictional simulation is less like a wristwatch and more like a weather forecast. When we read, hear, or watch a weather forecast, it comes from the output of a computer simulation."[24]

The analogy Oatley draws between reading or watching a fictive representation and computer processing points to the main assumption in cognitivist theories of reception: reception is a cognitive act, with the mind itself functioning *like* a computer. In Oatley's view, when we read a story, a relationship is built between narrator and reader that prompt us to make inferences "about what the narrator is intending, thinking and feeling."[25] Other cognitivist theorists go further, linking the reception of fiction to "goal-relevant" concerns. According to Patrick Colm Hogan, "Our emotional experience of a literary work is a function of junctural evaluation of narrative events in relation to our own goals–specifically our preferred final outcome, a goal that need not be the same as that of the protagonist."[26] Brian Boyd specifies the process involved more specifically:

> Experiments show that in understanding stories our minds keep extraordinarily close track of agents, especially of a principal agent, and especially of his or her active goals. We simulate the focal agent's situation, taking what psychologists call either an observer (outside) or field (inside) position, as we can in our own memories and dreams. As we track focal characters, simulation allows us to make swift inferences about their situation from goal-relevant information that we amplify by keeping it alive in working memory.[27]

Once again, the underlying metaphor implicit in this assumption is that the experience of reading or watching a story involves *information processing*, with the brain functioning like a computer.

Indeed, cognitivist theorists have hypothesized that reception, as in the case of music, depends on "three basic cognitive capacities– categorization, cross-domain mapping, and the use of conceptual models" to make sense of complex and multidimensional patterning sequences.[28] In the case of fictive stories, during the course of this operation "emotions are elicited not by events as such but evaluations of events relevant to goals."[29] Or, as Hogan puts it, emotion "results from a type of evaluation in which one judges the implications of a certain situation for oneself. One implicitly weighs the possible consequences of the situation in terms of their likelihood and the degree of positive or negative consequence."[30] In this account, therefore, emotion is not a source of fictive creativity, as I have been arguing, but a consequence: the main driver of the entire process of response in this theory is the cognitive, analytical part of the brain, which sifts and sorts all the data presented to it so as to be able to make a rational, evaluative decision at the end of the process, following an incredibly complex exercise in mental computation. Increasingly, theorists have become dissatisfied with such a mechanistic account of a process that seems to involve much more than merely cerebral computation.

EMBODIED SIMULATION AND THE "EXPERIENTIAL TURN"

The first decade and a half of the twenty-first century have seen the beginnings of a major revision of the prevailing orthodoxies that dominated the second half of the twentieth century. Predictably, the pendulum has swung in the opposite direction: instead of a reader/spectator whose response is solely subjectively determined according to the imperatives deriving from the processes of meaning assignment inherent in the differentiating mechanisms on which all verbal languages depend, or according to the hegemonic influence of cultural discourses arising from particular historical contexts, theorists now assign to various media an independent power of psychic and affective operation that inheres in the medium itself. Similarly, instead of a reader/spectator whose response is largely governed by cognitive rationality, new theories emphasize the role of the respondent's animal nature, positing a mode of reception that, to a large extent, is induced independently of any input from rational volition. Especially in Europe, film and media scholars who have been keeping pace with the findings of neuroscience regarding the brain and its cognitive processes are increasingly unhappy with the hermeticism of earlier theories and their detachment from observable human experience.[31]

An eloquent spokesman for this revised perspective is the Italian media scholar Ruggero Eugeni, who objects to the way that conventional semiotics has tended to detach the fictive text from actual, lived experience. Eugeni summarizes his objections to the customary semiotic approach on the following grounds. First, it focuses on "the text" as its main object of study, construing it "as a simple 'effect of sense' produced by cultural conventions within media experiences."[32] Second, semiotic approaches consider media experience as primarily cognitive and rational, reflecting a failure to acknowledge the "sensitive, emotional, affective aspects of media experience." Third, in these approaches there is a separation of theory and analysis from the phenomena being observed, which leaves the subject in "a meta-dimension and detached from the textual phenomena observed."[33]

To counter these misplaced emphases (as he supposes), Eugeni posits that the object of study is not the text "but the design of the experience conveyed by the sensory materials provided by media studies." In short, he advocates a shifting of critical attention away from media semiotics toward a "theory of media experience." In fact, he proposes that we recognize the advent of what he calls an "experiential turn" resulting from the dialogue generated between the humanities and the hardcore sciences, especially neuroscience.[34] Promoting what he terms "Neurofilmology," Eugeni advocates a research program restricted not to a model of the "viewer as mind" or to a model of the "viewer-as-body," but rather to a model of the "viewer-as-organism."[35]

As far as fictive representation is concerned, this "experiential turn" has shifted attention away from the indeterminacy posited by poststructuralist theories of how language works to an emphasis on an "embodied mind," in which bodily and mental data are intimately–and even inseparably–interrelated. It also marks a departure from the primacy that cognitive theories have accorded to cognitive analytical rationality. In film studies, the implications of this new conceptualization have been articulated in pioneering fashion by Gilles Deleuze, who promotes the idea that the film image has qualities that modulate the spectator's sensitivity and emotions through its materiality.[36] Complementing this assumption is the proposition that the film viewer also has a body, and thus constitutes an "embodied subject," as argued by Vivian Sobchack.[37]

HYPNOSIS, ANIMALITY, AND THE "BODY OF CINEMA"

For the past 30 years, Raymond Bellour has been the chief exponent of the idea that fictive representation—specifically in cinema—involves a modified form of consciousness determined by the effects of the medium, most recently in his magisterial work, *Le Corps du cinéma* (2009).[38] Contrary to his mentor Christian Metz, who saw spectatorship as an intrapsychic process, Bellour, as Hilary Radner notes in a succinct summary, posits a "primal relationship between the cinematic state and the animal state," in which "cinema serves as the catalyst that activates the qualities that the human subject (the child who sleeps) shares with animals."[39] According to Bellour, following Henri Bergson, there is "an instinctual component that extends from the animal body into the hypnotic relationship itself."[40] Moreover, "animality thus embodies the inner element of hypnosis that is intrinsic to the emotional body—in line with animal hypnosis—through an influence operating from body to body."[41] As far as the cinema spectator is concerned, the "body of cinema"—in other words, the material qualities of its mode of representation—induces a light form of hypnosis conditioned by "the mass of varied emotions that the film arouses." Being "polymorphous and perpetually moving," these emotions are deployed via a *dispositif* designed to intensify and disseminate their captivating power.[42] (All Bellour quotations are my translations.)

Deeply influenced by the work of the American psychiatrist Daniel Stern, Bellour sees an analogy between the experience of the cinema spectator and that of the very small infant in its intersubjective exchanges with the mother, which involve a "visual-haptic transference" operating primarily through amodal forms and intensities (what Stern calls "vitality affects") that are inseparably linked with emotions.[43] This means, according to Bellour, that there is an intrinsic element of regression involved in the spectator's experience of a cinematic representation: "There is always in the adult who thinks about cinema a thought addressed to the cinema-infant within him . . . possessed by 'the fascination with the image.'"[44] The end result of the spectator's experience of cinema is that he or she is constantly subjected to multiple identifications, "changing, modulated, graduated, diversified, stratified, mixed, and very often in the process of mutating."[45]

As Mireille Berton astutely observes in a review article, "Cinéma et hypnose," Bellour's theory of the "body of cinema" implicitly rejects two fields of knowledge that are hostile to hypnosis—psychoanalysis and cognitivism—and repudiates key tenets of structuralist and poststructuralist theory. Indeed, Berton sees Bellour as having distanced himself from his earlier alignment with thinkers in these schools. In particular, she notes, Bellour opposes all approaches that submit the spectator to the primacy of "narrative intellection," involving a rationally determined decoding of the meaning of a film.[46] Instead, he substitutes hypnosis for the psychoanalytic-oneiric model often invoked in film studies, and, instead of a spectator "who is supposed to decipher the filmic text as if it were a puzzle," postulates a spectator who is "a complex organic entity who combines competencies that are simultaneously affective, physiological, mental, and cognitive [my translation]."[47] It is too soon to gauge the impact of this radical shift in the theory of reception on scholarly thinking, but it certainly marks a sharp turning away from the most basic assumptions of the rival schools of thought that preceded it.

SHORTCOMINGS IN CONTEMPORARY THEORIES TO DATE

What becomes strikingly apparent from this overview of contemporary theories of reception is that they have swung from one extreme to the other, as if scholars feel a biological compulsion to define their position in opposition to the one that preceded or competes with it. Within several decades, theorists have ranged from the idea that meaning is determined wholly subjectively by the reader/spectator at an intrapsychic level, through a view that the reader/spectator's response is almost wholly cognitively driven, to a view that rational cognitive processes have very little influence on a reader/spectator's response, which is induced primarily through somatic, embodied processes or results from cultural discourses that write both the text and the subject.

Among the scholars who, since the turn of the twenty-first century, have been growing increasingly dissatisfied with the stand-off between the entrenched oppositional stances of the dominant schools of thought—poststructuralists and subjective constructionists in one corner and cognitivist formalists in the other—is Michele Aaron, who in *Spectatorship: The Power of Looking On* (2007) proposes a synthesis that restores agency to the receiver (in this case, the spectator) comparable to the sort accorded to the reader in cognitivist theory. Acknowledging a distinction between the "viewer" construed in cultural studies as a living, breathing, actual audience member situated in a specific sociohistorical context, and the "spectator" as conceived by poststructuralist film theory of the 1970s, Aaron seeks to reconcile previously conflicted elements by exploring "the interaction of textual practices, psychological processes and social context."[48] Although a step in the right direction, Aaron's synthesis leaves unexplained the actual mental processes that make possible the interactions she is seeking to describe and hence the agency she ascribes to the spectator, and she ignores altogether the implications of the embodied simulation posited by theorists who align themselves with the experiential school.

In short, all varieties of theory about reader response and spectatorship, while most offer partial glimpses of aspects of the overall phenomenon of reception, have blind spots and push their claims too far. Poststructuralist and reader-response theories have two main weaknesses. On the one hand, they treat fictive representations as if their meaning were only determined according to the differential processes that determine the relationship between signifiers and signifieds in verbal language. Such an assumption overlooks the input of the embodied mind and the emotions, which exert at least as much influence on the reader/spectator's perception of meaning and, in most cases, considerably more. On the other hand, they depend on a model of subject formation that assumes that the unconscious is structured like a language, which seems more and more unlikely as neuroscience advances in its discoveries about the human brain.

Cognitivism, for its part, underestimates the role of the emotions in determining a reader's response and overemphasizes the role of rational analysis (or "computation"). Although cognitivist theory accords a role to metaphor as enabling the mind to engage in cross-domain mapping in support of analysis, it pays almost no attention to symbolization and other mechanisms of displacement, let alone the role they play in the operations of the unconscious, working through displacement via projection, introjection, and fantasy. The virtue of cognitivist theory is that it readmits both an author and a reader with agency, but its vice is that it reduces that agency to the mechanical computations of a reasoning machine, with the emotions allowed into the process merely to assist with the evaluation, not to generate the creation of the fiction itself or the reader's response.

For those who favor the "experiential turn" or the "affective turn," focusing on the material manifestations of the somatic responses induced by fictive representations, the animal nature of man and its subservience to embodied visceral processes is substituted for the purely rational, cognitive processes of the cognitivists. Although experiential and embodiment theories acknowledge the corporeal and affective vectors that contribute to reception, they fall short in accounting for the motivations that guide the recipient in his or her response, and so once again deprive the reader/spectator of much of his or her agency. Such theories also tend to reduce the communicative interchange between author and respondent that takes place in the experience of a fictive work to a one-way direction—in which the reader/spectator, because of the somatic effects induced by the embodied simulation, together with the hypnosis presumed to be involved, is rendered a relatively passive recipient of what the representation compels him or her to feel.

All of these theoretical positions, it seems to me, lack one crucial thing: a sufficiently nuanced account of what actually transpires in the *intersubjective transfer* that takes place in reception. I believe further that such an account is impossible to achieve in the absence of an adequate explanation of the role of the unconscious and the creative procedures it uses, involving memory, to make contact with the cognitive part of the brain via the facilitating medium of imaginative invention. There is no need to suppose an antagonism between the embodied affective response induced by the experience of fiction and the ratiocinative response produced by cognitive reflection; rather, the findings of neuroscience, when married to the findings of post-Freudian psychoanalysis, suggest that one of the primary functions of fictive representations of whatever kind is to generate a *dialogue* between embodied, affective experience, which is nonpropositional, and cognitive reflection, which does indeed invoke the capacities and techniques of propositional logic.

In short, what one needs is a more inclusive, more comprehensive theory that integrates the perspectives of a variety of disciplines and aligns the findings of subjects that are primarily aesthetic and philosophical with those grounded in the hard sciences, neuroscience in particular. The purpose of this book is to do precisely that, and in the chapter that follows, I suggest ways in which recent findings on the brain and its processes can be reconciled with the various, and apparently mutually exclusive, perspectives of theorists of reception to date.

9

A Neuropsychoanalytic Theory of Reception

As suggested in the previous chapter, there is a gaping hole in theories of reception precisely where both the self of the author and the self of the reader/spectator should be, together with an understanding of the kind of agency that is exercised by each in intersubjective transfer. All of the theoretical formulations I have outlined account for partial aspects of the overall phenomenon: the reader/spectator is indeed a crucial determinant of meaning owing to the subjective nature of his or her response, but it is also true that meaning is innately encoded in the formal structures and fictive material already embodied in the work because of the subjective description of objects, and the objective description of subjects, fueled by emotions that are transmitted to the recipient. Similarly, while internal unconscious psychological processes in the receiver do influence his or her response, he or she is also influenced by external contextual factors and the operations of discourse and cultural conditioning. Furthermore, even though few would now maintain that responses to fiction are purely rational and cognitive, it is going too far to claim that they are wholly somatic, involuntary, and embodied, given the capacity of human beings to invoke memories selectively and voluntarily as well as automatically, unconsciously, and involuntarily. It is thus becoming increasingly clear that each of the theories outlined in the previous chapter excessively prioritizes one or more of these dimensions of the phenomenon at the expense of seeing the complexity of the process of reception as a whole.

In this chapter, I attempt to formulate a theory that enables the opposed viewpoints of the past fifty years to be reconciled on a harmonious continuum. To do that, however, requires a revision of prevailing postmodern views on the subject, as well as the operations of the mind, and indeed the very nature of consciousness itself and the role that the arts play in it.

THE NATURE OF THE SUBJECT AND SELF-FORMATION

Poststructuralist theories that privilege the reader as the producer of meaning have been heavily influenced by Lacan's view that the self is formed through a process in which the "I" is formed in a mirror, meaning that it is a fantasy, an unreal image that only seems real, so "the ego exists for us only in the illusory identifications the imaginary offers, while our 'authentic being' is found in the absent world of signifiers, constituted by the other, over which we have no control."[1] Such an assumption is bound to put the emphasis on the reader/spectator's efforts to construct these illusory identifications. In contradistinction, researchers working from the new perspective of an *embodied* mind rather than a perspective that maintains a separation between body and mind, as poststructuralist theory does, have found evidence of a primary consciousness accompanied by input from the body, including internal sensations, "momentary states of arousal, activation, tonicity, levels of motivational activation or satiety ... and well-being."[2] Antonio Damasio, a neurobiologist, has proposed that the self is unified and embodied, being built in stages that comprise the "protoself," the "core self," and the "autobiographical self."[3] The psychiatrist and psychoanalytic theorist Daniel Stern has elaborated a more refined notion of a unified self by identifying six developmental stages in its evolution: "the sense of an emergent self," "the sense of a core self," "the sense of core self-with-another," "the sense of an intersubjective self," "the verbal self," and "the narrative self (selves)."[4]

The importance of this radically different notion of the self to an understanding of the reception of fictive representations is that it focuses attention back on a degree of *agency* exercised by both the creator of the fiction and the reader/spectator who responds to it. When this is combined with new knowledge of brain processes as they relate to the production of stories, a completely different picture of reception emerges–one in which the reader/spectator responds to a meaning already implanted in the text, having been placed there by the author through imaginative invention, but a meaning that nonetheless induces respondents[5] to construct their own meaning by "metabolizing" the fantasy already immanent in the work. Thus, a very complex transactional, intersubjective process takes place between the self of the author and the self of the reader/spectator via the text as an object that is both the outcome of a creative process (on the part of the author) and the stimulus to a further creative process (on the part of the respondent). I now explain in greater detail how this transaction takes place.

MIRROR NEURONS

In recent years, the deficiencies of earlier assumptions about representation and reception have been highlighted by the groundbreaking discovery of a type of neuron in the mammalian brain that not only enables affective experience to be transmitted from one subject to another but also enables the *intention* of that communication to be transmitted in a way that can be inferred by the recipient.

Mirror neurons were discovered accidentally in 1990 by a group of Italian neurophysiologists at the University of Parma while studying a macaque monkey. They found that certain neurons in the monkey's premotor cortex fired both when the animal performed an action and when it saw another perform the action. Since then, it has been established conclusively that human beings also possess a mirror system that involves several brain regions, including the premotor cortex, the posterior parietal lobe, and the visual cortex of the temporal lobe.[6]

The function of mirror neurons is to receive excitatory inputs from visual regions of the brain and "translate" the visual language into motor language.[7] Because of this, *seeing* an action activates our own body. Since the initial discovery, neuroscientists have found that mirror neurons respond not merely to the sight of an action but also to the *sound* of an action and the *imagination* of an action.[8] Just as important, a similar system exists outside the domain of actions, in which "both the premotor cortex and the insula are involved in neural circuits that allow us to vicariously share the actions and emotions of other individuals."[9] The insula is an arena in which "our own actual emotions come together with those of others and those we read about and imagine" as the result of "a rich mosaic of neural activity" that we share with the observed individual.[10] In Christian Keysers's view, "What the mirror system really does is not so much mirror the neural state of [those] whom we observe as *translate* and *reinterpret* what we see into the language of what we would have done or felt in that situation."[11] In this way, the mirror system builds a bridge between the minds of two people, even when those people are imaginary, as in the case of invented characters, allowing for the construction of a co-created narrative and a shared emotional field.[12]

The existence of this mirror system explains why fictive representation has such an affective power. It means that understanding the actions of others does not inevitably require mentalizing; instead, an intuitive, embodied apperception can be accessed directly through the emotions, which in turn lays the foundations for fantasmatic engagement with the fictive work in order to adapt the fantasy it contains to the emotional needs and purposes of the respondent–an adaptation achieved through a hijacking of the affective force of the original fantasy. As experiments have shown, so powerful is the effect of the mirror system that the mirror in our brain even responds to the actions of robots.[13] This was recently confirmed in my own experience when, while watching *Real Steel* (Shawn Levy, 2011), I found myself empathizing strongly with robots being beaten by other robots!

EMBODIED SIMULATION, AGENCY,
AND INTENTIONAL ATTUNEMENT

One of the Italian neuroscientists who discovered mirror neurons is Vittorio Gallese, whose speculations on the function of mirror neurons is so important to any sound understanding of the reception of fictive representations that I discuss them here at some length. Because the action of mirror neurons is to generate an "implicit form of 'experiential understanding'" in which we model the behavior of other individuals as "intentional experiences on the basis of the equivalence between what the others do and feel and what we do and feel," the eventual result is an "embodied simulation" capable of leading to "intentional attunement" with "the other."[14] This intentional attunement "allows us to experience others as *directed* to certain target states or objects, similarly to how we experience ourselves when doing so."[15] Thus, intentional attunement is the foundation of empathy and constitutes a *"shared manifold of intersubjectivity"* that enables us "to decode the emotions and sensations" that others experience.[16] This form of embodied simulation—which mirror neurons allow fictive representations to emulate—involves "a mandatory nonpropositional, functional mechanism" that is "not necessarily the result of a willed and conscious cognitive effort, aimed at interpreting the intentions hidden in the overt behavior of others, but rather a basic functional mechanism of our brain."[17] To this extent, therefore, the existence of mirror neurons supports the emphasis that Bellour and others place on the embodied nature of reception. Nevertheless, according to Gallese, "this simulation process establishes a direct link between agent and observer, in that both are mapped in neural fashion."[18] Even though awareness of an agential action is activated in the onlooker, however, its "filler, which is indeterminate," is not specified:[19]

> Mirror neurons constitutively map an agentive relation; the mere observation of an object not acted upon does not evoke any response. It is just the agentive relational specification to trigger mirror neurons' response. The fact that a *specific agent* is not mapped does not entail that an agentive relation is not mapped, but simply that the agent parameter can be either oneself or the other.[20]

Put another way, while reader-response theorists are wrong in assuming that authorial intention is irrelevant, they are right in asserting that the ways in which the reader/spectator responds are in no way absolutely predetermined according to a constraint of necessity. In fact, recipients are free, in response to the intentional solicitations of the author, either to react in accordance with the author's invitations, or to invest in their response their own idiosyncratic concerns. That does not mean that authorial intention is absent, or that it is incapable of being perceived by a sufficiently attuned recipient; it only means that the process is liable to be conditioned by the recipient's overriding preoccupations, which result in projections that adapt the representation to his or her immediate purposes.

THE INTERSUBJECTIVE TRANSACTION BETWEEN THE AUTHOR AND RESPONDENT

We are presented, then, with a situation in which an array of possibilities may potentially be activated, without that fact negating an intention on the part of the author-as-agent that is capable of being picked up by the reader/spectator, depending on the strength and nature of his or her personal investment. What cannot be ignored, however, is the existence of an intersubjective transaction that occurs between the author and recipient in any response to a work of fictive representation.

"Intersubjectivity" may be defined as "a deliberately sought sharing of experiences about events and things,"[21] which operates on the basis of "some shared framework of meaning and means of communication."[22] What is at stake in the experience of intersubjectivity is "nothing less than discovering what part of the private world of inner experience is shareable."[23] For the purposes of this discussion, it becomes startlingly apparent that the intersubjective process outlined by Stern can be generalized to fictive representation itself because of the comparability of what is shared and how it is shared.

During any intersubjective experience, what is shared is (1) attention, (2) intentions, and (3) affective states. I would suggest that the reception of fictive representations involves the sharing of exactly these elements. In the relationship between a mother and child, *sharing of the focus of attention* is achieved through "the gesture of pointing and the act of following another's line of vision," thus permitting inferences to be made.[24] In literary and cinematic representations, the equivalent of pointing occurs in the selection and arrangement of plot elements and in strategies of enunciation such as narrative perspective, framing, control of distance, and timing. Similarly, the *sharing of intentions* within the mother/child dyad consists of "signaling behavior," indicating that the sender is aware of the effect that the signal is having on the listener. Again, the strategies whereby such signaling is conveyed find their correlatives in fictive representation: alternations in eye gaze contact between the goal and the intended listener are replicated in the shifts of focalization characteristically found in narratives; augmentations, additions, and substitution of signals find their equivalents in such devices as voiceovers and supra-diegetic inserts in cinema or direct intrusions by the implied author in literature; and changes in the signal toward abbreviated and/or exaggerated patterns are matched in representations by techniques of structural and metaphorical mapping.[25] Finally, the *sharing of affective states* is achieved in fictional narratives through conceptual metaphor, the arrangement of montage elements, the construction of plot shape, and the use of tone, especially as these inhere in the intrinsic affective structures of genres—all of which work together to create "interaffectivity."[26]

All of these strategies working together mean, as Sergei Eisenstein recognized, that "the spectator is made to traverse the road of creation which the author traversed in creating the image."[27] This co-creation is induced by the "emotional speech" that results from the montage principle operant in all forms of fictive representation: "The spectator not only sees those elements of the work which are capable of being seen but also experiences the dynamic process of the emergence and formation of the image just as it was experienced by the author."[28] Such co-creation in the receptive process imposes a constraint on the response of the spectator without definitively determining its precise outline, "just as the personality of a great actor fuses with that of a great playwright in the process of creating a classical image on the stage."[29] Eisenstein offers a succinct summary of this guided reception:

> Each spectator creates an image along the representation guidance suggested by the author, leading him unswervingly towards knowing and experiencing the theme in accordance with his own personality, in his own individual way, proceeding from his own experience, from his own imagination, from the texture of his associations, from the features of his own character, temper, and social status. The image is at one and the same time the creation of the author and the spectator.[30]

The intersubjective transfer that takes place in the co-creation shared by the author and the reader/spectator is what allows the author's unconscious investments to be detected by the recipient through a process of "projective transidentification."[31] It also allows the recipient to convert them to his or her own purposes to the extent that these investments "concatenate" with the recipient's personal history at the point of interaction.[32]

THE ROLE OF "INTERFANTASY"

According to Stern, many thinkers in France believe that intersubjectivity ultimately involves "interfantasy," eventuating in the fact that "the fantasies of the parent come to influence the infant's behavior, and ultimately to shape the infant's own fantasies."[33] Exactly the same is true, I suggest, in fictive representation. Because of the affective attunement achieved through effects induced in the respondent by the categorical and vitality affects immanent in the text of the fictive work, the reader/spectator is brought into contact with the fantasy/fantasies of the author—but because any form of intersubjective experience involves the coexistence of "core-relatedness" as well as "intersubjective relatedness" in the self-sense of the reader/spectator, the interaction of these two forms of self-experience, in which each domain affects the experience of the other,[34] means that a new fantasy is constructed; the fantasy of the respondent himself or herself, which may remain close to that of the author, or diverge significantly to a greater or lesser degree, depending on the contextual factors and affective motivations influencing the respondent at the time of reception.

What has become undeniable since the emergence of attachment theory as developed by the pioneering research of John Bowlby and his associates, is that any response on the part of an individual subject to a work of fictive representation is likely to be influenced by the "internal working models" that the subject as a child has developed in relation to his or her attachment figures as a means of interpreting the external world and better predicting potential negative or threatening environmental experiences.[35] According to Bowlby, a child in infancy forms internalized representations of the attachment figures based on his or her experiences with them, which then prompt patterns of reaction that are resistant to change, given that they have a power to assimilate new experiences into the existing interpretive schemes now hardwired in the subject's brain.[36] Invariably, these attachment patterns serve an adaptive function, which can nevertheless have maladaptive consequences depending on the extent to which the individual has resolved his or her personal issues. Bowlby in fact proposes four main attachment classifications: (1) securely attached, (2) avoidant-dismissive, (3) anxious-ambivalent, and (4) disorganized-disoriented.[37] I would suggest that subjective individual responses to fictive representations are likely to group themselves in accordance with these categories and that they are likely to be motivated by the same defensive strategies that each of these attachment styles promotes.

THE "METABOLIZING" OF FICTIVE FANTASIES BY THE RESPONDENT

The effect of attachment styles is nowhere more apparent than in the manifest responses of individuals to works of fictive representation. As Norman Holland discovered when he conducted an experiment with a group of actual readers, readers "re-create the original literary creation in terms of their own personalities" (which, as I have suggested, are fundamentally built around the internal working models that are constructed as a result of attachment styles).[38] This re-creation in the mind and emotions of the respondent lies at the heart of the process whereby fictive fantasies become "metabolized." I now explore specifically how this metabolizing is executed.

The interfantasy work that takes place in the reception of a fictive work involves the twin operations of *projection* and *introjection*. As Holland puts it, we project into the literary work "out there" by fleshing out the characters, events, and language. In addition, "we fill in gaps in a story. We infer the inner thoughts of characters or the parts of an environment that we cannot see."[39] In the other direction, we introject: "We take in what we take to be the text's portrayals, so that what is 'out there' in the literature work feels as though it were happening 'in here,' in your mind or mine."[40]

The process of response, however, extends further than this by also drawing on *projective identification*, using the same strategy that authors often use in the creation of the original fiction. Projective identification differs from simple projection in that feeling states corresponding to the unconscious fantasies of the reader/spectator are imagined to be processed by another person—in this case, a fictive character. In this way, the fiction can be used to experience and contain an aspect of the projector (that is, the reader/spectator). To put it another way, a kind of "transference" takes place during reception, in which the reader/spectator either places parts of the self that are experienced as intrinsically dangerous into the work, or places valued parts of the self into the work for safekeeping. As in the transference that occurs during a psychoanalytic session, this can involve "a splitting of the ego that allows the good parts of the self to survive the bad parts of the self."[41] *Introjective identification* can also be involved, whereby the respondent, through identifying with certain characters, tries out various self-states simply to experience them to find out what "feels right" as an expression of his or her inner reality. This process can be used to evoke new inner experiences and to facilitate new object formation.[42]

Evidence for these processes can be found in the observations of filmmakers and writers involved in cinematic adaptations of literary works. In a conversation between Clark Gregg, the actor/director who made the film *Choke* (2008), and Chuck Palahniuk, the writer of the novel *Choke* (2001) on which the film was closely based, Palahniuk, who co-wrote the script, reveals to Gregg that "unless it reflected something for you, unless it was an expression of something unresolved or unexpressed in your life, you would not have the passion to do this thing, that there's no point in reproducing what someone else has done unless it expresses and sort of exhausts something of your own."[43] For his part, Gregg confesses that he found it "tremendously cathartic" to engage with Palahniuk's depiction of "really painful ideas and moments," especially in the flashbacks in which Victor, the hero of the story, is shown with "a mother who simply can't respond to his needs":

> I found it really painful, and the sexual dysfunction, and the emotional hopelessness; if you kind of describe what goes on for the people, it makes you want to put a bullet in your head, yet when you read it, it's screamingly funny, and ... there's something very cathartic about going in to those places and finding the humor in it, that you're able to look at those things

in a way that doesn't make you give up hope, but which allows you to absorb something in a way that perhaps is digestible and meaningful.[44]

Here, then, is a classic instance of the fantasy in an existing work being appropriated and metabolized in a way that converts it to the purposes and needs of the person responding to it – in this case, the filmmaker who, in constructing his own version of the story, visibly reproduces the same adaptive process that takes place whenever any reader/spectator engages with a fictive representation.

Because of the opportunities a fictive work offers for projection and introjection, it can serve as what Christopher Bollas calls "a transformational object" owing to its ability to perform a function that is similar to the mother's and the father's facilitative handling of the infant self.[45] In childhood, the mother's role is to help integrate the instinctual, cognitive, affective, and environmental dimensions of the infant's being. Because of this, she is experienced as "a process of transformation," a feature of early existence that, in Bollas's view, lives on in certain forms of object seeking in adult life, when the object is sought for its function as a signifier of transformation:

> Thus, in adult life, the quest is not to possess the object; rather the object is pursued in order to surrender to it as a medium that alters the self, where the subject-as-supplicant now feels himself to be the recipient of envirosomatic caring, identified with metamorphoses of the self.[46]

In adulthood, I hypothesize, memories of this early, facilitated experiencing of the self can be reactivated by the intense affective responses that fictive representations elicit, kindling a perceptual identification of the fictive work as a transformational object – one that promotes a reinvestment and reshaping of one's emotional predispositions – with the difference that the transformation has now been displaced from the relationship with the mother and repositioned in a relationship with the work itself.

MOTIVATIONS FOR THE RESPONDENT'S ENGAGEMENT WITH A FICTIVE REPRESENTATION

When a reader/spectator engages with a fictive work, the reason that the fantasy or fantasies it contains become metabolized during the response is that the effects induced by the mirror system interact with the effects of the activation of other brain areas. A similar activity in somatosensory areas can thus lead to very different feelings depending on the activity in other brain regions.[47] This is why contextual factors enter so powerfully into the equation: autobiographical memories relating to the individual's personal experience, idiosyncratic wishes, the need to maintain self-protective psychic mechanisms, cultural conditioning, and the effect of discourses can all influence the way different readers/spectators respond to a representation, as well as the ways in which they convert it to their own use. To illustrate the power of contextual circumstances, one only needs to think of the difference in the affective response elicited from seeing a knife cut through a loaf of bread as compared with seeing it cut through a human hand: the action is the same, but the context is different, leading to a different effect.[48] It is also the case that certain brain areas, notably in the frontal lobe, can become activated to prevent us from acting out the actions we only want to be internally simulated.[49] This operation becomes significant when a respondent wishes to activate defense mechanisms or enable disavowal or denial.

The end result of these processes is that the original fantasy in the fictive work is converted into a personal fantasy serving any number of purposes. Such a fantasy can be made to provide a substitute gratification for what is lacking in one's own life or offer consolation for this lack.[50] It may be designed to heal or undo past defects, wounds, and old conflicts, promote emotional regulation, or provide a form of self-soothing. When directed toward the future, the fantasy can act as a rehearsal for future action or furnish a template for life choices by serving as "a theater in which we preview the possible scenarios of our life to come."[51] At the simplest level, the fantasy so constructed can function as a straightforward expression of a wish, or simply as a way to nullify anxiety by allowing one to feel strong in circumstances that generate anxiety, as in the case of vigilante fantasies.[52] It can be designed to expand one's imaginative, empathic experience of personalities and situations that one is never likely to encounter in real life.

In all instances, though, the adopted/adapted fantasy is multilayered, incorporating elements drawn from the readers/spectators' autobiographical memories of events in their own lives as well as those presented in the stories of the fictional characters to which they are responding. In this way, the material of the original fantasy is altered so as to accord with the receiver's personal motivations.

EVIDENCE DERIVED FROM SELF-REPORTS

What evidence exists to support these claims? Given that the reception of fictive representations is so highly subjective, it is difficult at this stage to gather evidence beyond self-reports by readers and spectators of their actual experience and their observations of the responses of others. To illustrate the kind of evidence such observations can furnish, I describe instances when I personally witnessed the dynamics of response as they occurred in individuals with whom I was sharing a viewing experience.

The first of these occasions took place in Oxford when a colleague and I were being entertained at the home of a don from one of the Oxford colleges. Fairly late in the evening, all three of us, along with the don's wife, settled in to watch a wartime Hollywood-style short musical, *I'm the Proudest Girl in the World!* (Julian Roffman, 1944), which features a chorus from the Canadian Women's Army Corps in uniform, singing the song that supplies the film's title, with the aim of encouraging women to enlist. To our astonishment, before this brief film–which is barely two minutes long–had finished, my colleague burst into tears and between sobs repeatedly uttered, "It's not fair, it's not fair . . ." This inexplicable outburst swiftly brought the evening to a close, with embarrassment all around. When I discreetly asked my colleague the next day what had happened, it turned out that this jingoistic wartime propaganda piece had triggered a release of a flood of emotion in him that had been pent up since his father's premature death twenty years earlier–a tragic event that my friend had never properly grieved. Why had this happened? The film had presented the fantasy of fresh-faced, smiling young women eager to go off to war to support their men, convinced of the inevitability of victory (summed up in the words "YOU + YOU = **V**" [for victory] that briefly flash across the screen). The sight of the chorus leader in her army uniform had activated my friend's memory of a photograph of his father, who had fought in North Africa and Italy during World War II, in a similar-looking uniform. That had been enough to impress on him an unconscious awareness of the grotesque contrast between the myth being propagated in the film and the tragic reality of his father's experience of war, whose premature death could be attributed to the emotional and physical damage he had suffered. My friend had unconsciously converted an optimistic fantasy inherent in the original representation into a tragic one, which released blocked emotion without his knowing why. Here we have, then, a striking example of the dynamics of a response to fictive representation, together with a demonstration of how swiftly that response can work its transformative effects through interfantasy.

My second example derives from my experience of observing two young sisters, who had lost their father at a very early age, having powerful responses when watching movies. I had had contact with these two girls for a number of years, ever since their father had died.

The first instance was when the elder of the two, Jessica, then aged eight, saw *The Chronicles of Narnia: The Lion, the Witch and the Wardrobe* (Andrew Adamson, 2005). Completely absorbed by the story, this young child, like my colleague in Oxford, burst into uncontrollable weeping not during the film itself but later, after we had left the theater. It was not the killing of Aslan the lion on the Stone Table (symbolizing Christ's sacrifice and the atonement in C. S. Lewis's original story) that had triggered this flood of affect in Jessica, but the fact that, after Aslan has been restored to life, has revived the petrified Narnians, and has installed the four child protagonists of the story as the kings and queens of Narnia, he walks out along the beach and just slips away. In converting the fantasy of the movie into her own, Jessica had made it serve as the catalyst for a release of grief for the loss of her father, a grief that had remained incompletely processed since she was four years old.

Jessica's younger sister, Isobel, who had only been two when their father died, had a different experience when watching a movie, although this, too, revolved around the loss of her paternal figure. Isobel, by this time aged thirteen, was constantly entreating her stepfather to buy a DVD copy of *Real Steel*, the 2011 American futuristic science fiction drama depicting technologically advanced robots that engage in boxing contests. She insisted that this was her favorite movie and that she had already watched it five times–even so, she wanted to see it again and again ... The story is about a former boxer, Charlie Kenton (Hugh Jackman) who is down on his luck and owes an unscrupulous villain a great deal of money. When his ex-girlfriend dies, meaning that arrangements need to be made for the future of their son Max (Dakota Goyo), Charlie agrees to let Max's aunt Debra (Hope Davis) and her wealthy husband (James Rebhorn) have full custody of Max in exchange for a payment of $50,000, half of which is to be received in advance. In effect, Charlie "sells" his son. During a grace period in which Charlie is required to look after Max for three months before handing him over, Max becomes Charlie's savior by discovering a derelict robot that he restores, modifying it out of his child's optimistic determination and inventiveness to the point where it can successfully survive an encounter with a seemingly unbeatable super-robot, thus allowing Charlie to win a $100,000 bet. Now no longer feckless and impoverished, and having developed a true love for his son, Charlie declines to accept the remaining $50,000, returns the advance he took from the adopting couple, and decides to keep the boy with him, the implication being that father and son will continue as a close-knit team. The reason for Isobel's passionate fixation on this movie was that, without realizing it, she was unconsciously converting the fantasy it contained–of the redemptive child who is capable of magically healing his father's wounds and repairing the parent's apparent indifference to him–into her own restorative fantasy of being reunited with her lost father, who was thus, symbolically, restored to life through the nature of her response. In this instance, rather than a catalyst for the release of grief as it had been for Jessica, the process of reception had functioned as an instrument of compensatory comfort and self-repair for her younger sister.

What, then, can one conclude on the basis of these inferences? Clearly, neither the author nor the reader/spectator is solely responsible for determining the meaning of a text, whether a book or a film. Rather, meaning arises from a shared transaction in which both the author and the recipient participate. What is at issue is the author's process of creation in which affective motivation is converted through fictive shaping into a story that answers to his or her psychological investments. That creative outcome provides the stimulus for a re-creative process in the reader/spectator activated during reception. This re-creation replicates the creation of the fiction in the first place and would not exist without the representation that ensued from it; rather, it constitutes a rewriting, or translation, of it into terms that answer to the recipient's own needs.

None of the existing theories of fictive representation are sufficient by themselves to explain the complexities of this overall operation. Formalism, whether of the New Critical variety or the more recent cognitive variety, cannot account for the affective dimensions of a work of fiction and leads to a gross underestimation of the author's contribution to the generation of the effects derived from the work by the respondent. Poststructuralist and cultural studies approaches similarly detach the representation from its creator and, by focusing almost exclusively on linguistic mechanisms and cultural discourses, presumed to be the determinants of signification, deprive both the author and the reader/spectator of any agency in the creation of meaning. Cultural materialist approaches fare little better owing to their assumption that neither the author nor the recipient has agency, meaning that they overlook the most influential of all contextual factors, the autobiographical circumstances that prompt and condition both the creative input of the author and the re-creative dimension of the response of the reader/spectator. Earlier psychoanalytic theories, because they adhere too closely to Freud's dual-drive theory or Lacan's deconstructive theory of the unconscious, either end up being excessively reductive and mechanistic, or construe both the author and the reader as trapped in an inescapable indeterminacy–in both cases resulting in a neglect of the myriad motivations and creative strategies that make fictive representation such a vitalizing, transformative medium. Furthermore, to the extent that neuroscience has been invoked as a framework for understanding fiction, its application ends up explaining merely aspects of the neurophysiology of response because it restricts itself to cognition without any consideration of the affective motivations that determine the shape and texture of the work, and which function instrumentally to elicit the response of the reader/spectator. In short, while all of these approaches can illuminate particular aspects of the fictive process, it is impossible to understand the overall workings of the phenomenon without a psychoanalytic perspective and without taking into account the all-important role of the emotions in fictive creation and response.

It now remains to speculate what implications these conclusions might have for the way we approach the study of literature or cinema, a subject to which I turn in the following chapter.

10

Intersubjective Attunement, Filiation, and the Re-creative Process: *Jules and Jim*—from Henri-Pierre Roché to François Truffaut

My purpose in this chapter, following the theoretical exposition in chapter 9, is to show how the intersubjective attunement made possible by the combined operation of neurological and psychological processes involved in reception generates a response that is not merely passively receptive, but also actively re-creative. To a large extent, the processes involved are invisible and unconscious, but their presence can be detected through their outward signs: namely, in patterns of unconscious filiation that can be traced from one author to the next and in the evidence of imitation and reconstitution provided by the cinematic adaptation of literary works. Neuroscience has, as yet, been unable to track empirically the neurological ways in which these intersubjective/re-creative processes are effectuated at this stage in scientific research—the human brain is far too complex for that—but enough evidence exists, in forms that are accessible to critical and historical analysis, to enable scholars to make informed surmises.

Through a detailed examination of the relations between Henri-Pierre Roché's novel *Jules et Jim* (1953) and François Truffaut's famous cinematic adaptation of it, *Jules and Jim* (1962),[1] I propose that an analysis of the strategies and outcomes of the cinematic adaptation of literary sources reveals, in externalized form, the process involved in the reception of fiction of whatever sort. Even when the response to a work of fiction does not result in a new fictive representation, the dynamics involved are much the same, constituting a form of creativity in their own right that is an essential part of the human response to the experiential realities that life requires them to confront.

UNCONSCIOUS ATTRACTION
AND NETWORKS OF FILIATION

One striking outcome of intersubjective attunement is that readers and spectators seem to be drawn ineluctably to representations created by artists whose psychic economy is similar to their own. How is this compatibility communicated and perceived? Through the recipient's sensitivity to a subjective feeling that inheres, as Jean-Luc Godard has averred, in "the subjective description of subjects" and "the subjective description of objects."[2] This subjective feeling is conveyed through the symbolic configuration of the representation and the manner in which its enunciation "nudges" the recipient,[3] reflected in devices such as the manipulation of narrative perspective; focalization; length, choice, and arrangement of shots; the insertion of overdetermined images; and so on. Combined with the effects that mirror neurons cause to be replicated experientially in the response of the recipient, the subjective feelings that such strategies communicate in turn reflect, and activate, the emotions that inhere in the psychic predispositions of the author. Thus, without the recipient necessarily realizing it, he or she is being brought into contact with the author's innermost structures of personality, while the specific emotions engendered in the work itself, relative to the situations in which they occur, are coordinates that point indirectly to the environmental circumstances in the author's life that are likely to have been responsible for those structures.

Another phenomenon can also be observed: when responding to a work of fiction, the reader/spectator tends to understand the actions, sensations, emotions, and experiences of fictive characters by evoking aspects of his or her own experience, which then enter the mental image that he or she forms of the source work.[4] The process is similar to that which takes place in an analytic interchange as described by psychoanalyst Lawrence Brown: "a shared emotional field is created through a unique blending of conscious, preconscious and unconscious experiences."[5] According to Brown, "The co-created narrative ... not only owes its lineage to the psychic issues of each partner activated at the moment, but also contains, in part, a highly distilled historical record of each individual's family history."[6]

Very often, this gravitational pull, or what the French might call *attirance* (attraction), relates to a similarity in experience with attachment figures and the extent to which that experience has informed the symbolic figuration of the representation by the author and informs the response of the reader/spectator at the time of reading or viewing the work. Sometimes, it arises from the shared experience of traumas of other sorts.

Evidence for this unconscious attraction can be found in patterns of relationship that emerge when one compares the biographical circumstances of creative artists to the circumstances of writers or filmmakers who have influenced them, or are influenced by them. The correspondences in these relationships tend to be too marked to be coincidental, especially when the underlying experience with attachment figures has been disturbed or traumatic owing to a caregiver's inconsistent, neglectful, or abusive behaviors, or a rupture in the parents' relationship, both of which can lead to narcissistic deprivation during the child's formative early years. This is precisely the phenomenon that one can identify in the personal backgrounds of the creative antecedents of the French filmmaker François Truffaut and of those who have subsequently admitted to being influenced by him.

An indication of the intricate network of affiliation surrounding Truffaut occurs in an interview in which he reveals that his reading of Jean Genet's *The Thief's Journal* was so important to him in his youth that it prompted him to desert from the army.[7] Genet and André Bazin, Truffaut says, did more for him than his own father (in actuality his adoptive father). Investigation shows that Genet himself had been similarly drawn to the poetry of Arthur Rimbaud, and, further, that when Genet fell foul of the French courts on account of his thievery, and faced the prospect of a lengthy jail sentence, his cause was taken up by the writer and filmmaker Jean Cocteau–another figure who would become one of Truffaut's heroes. Looking more closely at Truffaut's creative affiliations, one finds that among the artistic antecedents he most enthusiastically espouses, apart from Genet and Cocteau, are the French novelists Henri-Pierre

Roché and Honoré de Balzac, and the Anglo-American filmmaker Alfred Hitchcock.

Comparison of the early backgrounds of these creative artists reveals startling parallels. Truffaut himself was born of an unknown father, only learning of this fact accidentally when he was a teenager. His mother, besides being promiscuous and adulterous, was physically and emotionally abusive, abandoning her son to foster care until he was eight years old and then treating him with indifference when he rejoined the family. As a young adolescent, Truffaut was delinquent and was sent to reform school after having been expelled from a number of regular schools. As an adult, he engaged compulsively in sexual adventures, visiting prostitutes, pursuing multiple affairs, especially with the actresses in his films, and committing adultery during his marriage.[8]

The biographies of Truffaut's artistic heroes display many of the same elements. Jean Genet was similarly born of an unknown father, and his mother was a prostitute. Genet himself, like Truffaut, was abandoned to foster care at the age of seven months, and in adolescence became delinquent and was sent to reform school. As a young adult, he became a homosexual prostitute and as an adult, like Truffaut, engaged compulsively in sexual encounters. Similar familial circumstances reappear in the life of Arthur Rimbaud. His father abandoned the family when the boy was seven, and his mother was cold and remote but tyrannically invested in him. These combined factors generated a disturbed and anxious attachment. In his teenage years, Rimbaud began an infamous homosexual relationship with the poet Paul Verlaine and, like Genet, traveled widely in foreign places. Jean Cocteau, for his part, was similarly deprived of a father, his own having committed suicide when he was nine, after which Cocteau, following the pattern outlined, became delinquent as a teenager, was expelled from high school, and left the family at the age of fifteen.

The other line of Truffaut's artistic genealogy displays comparable patterns of disturbance. Henri-Pierre Roché's father died before the boy's first birthday, leaving his son entrapped in a fusional relationship with an overinvested mother, comparable to that which existed between Rimbaud and his mother.[9] Like Truffaut and Genet, Roché in adulthood engaged compulsively in affairs (as detailed in exhaustive detail in his *Carnets*). Also, like Rimbaud and Cocteau, he had intense male friendships. It is not known whether or not these were actually homosexual, or merely emotionally homoerotic relationships–a situation replicated in Truffaut's extremely close relationship with Robert Lachenay and a rumored homosexual relationship with Jean Genet, his mentor.[10] This possibility receives some support from Janine Truffaut's disparaging accusation regarding her son's relationship with Robert Lachenay: "According to her, not only had Robert taken François to prostitutes but the two boys had had a homosexual relationship at the elder's initiative," even though Truffaut strongly denied this.[11]

Alfred Hitchcock, like Truffaut, Genet, Rimbaud, and Cocteau, had a distant relationship with his father, a cold and austere man who had his son imprisoned in a police cell at the age of five to "teach him a lesson." Hitchcock appears to have compensated for the terror his authoritarian father instilled in him by forming a fusional relationship with his mother, like that of Roché–generating a fantasy that he would seek to replicate in many of his films in the archetypal "Hitchcockian blond." Replicating this basic paradigm of disturbed relationships with attachment figures, Honoré de Balzac was fostered to a wet nurse (just as Truffaut and Genet were raised by surrogates), then sent to boarding school (like Genet, Cocteau, and Truffaut), and had a mother, like Truffaut's, who was adulterous. Balzac, like Truffaut, was suicidal, attempting suicide at the age of fifteen (as Truffaut would attempt suicide several times in his late adolescence and twenties).

If one now looks at the line of artistic descent from Truffaut, similar patterns repeat themselves in the biographical circumstances of filmmakers who profess Truffaut's influence on them. The Malaysian-Taiwanese director Tsai Ming-Liang, for example, uses a younger actor, Lee Kang-sheng, as an avatar in the way Truffaut used Jean-Pierre Léaud, and his films frequently allude to those of Truffaut. Ming-Liang, too, had a distant relationship with his father, having been raised by his grandparents like Truffaut, and confesses to suffering from "existential loneliness."[12] Similarly, Christophe Honoré, whose film *Dans Paris* (2006) owes a huge debt to Truffaut's Antoine Doinel series, reveals that he lost his father when he was fifteen: "That's when the fact that I was unable to express grief was channeled into my writing" and, subsequently, his filmmaking.[13]

The similarities of background are even more marked in the case of the young French-Canadian filmmaker Xavier Dolan, whose film *Mommy* (2014) was celebrated at the Cannes Festival. Dolan has explicitly professed his preference for Truffaut over Godard, and his debut film, *I Killed My Mother* (2009), is so redolent of Truffaut's *The 400 Blows* (1959) that it could almost be viewed as a reworked version of the earlier film. Dolan grew up in a single-parent family (like most of Truffaut's mentors) following the divorce of his parents; became violent and delinquent, being sent to boarding school when he was in elementary school and again when he was in high school; and had an extremely difficult relationship with his mother, which fuels an obsession in most of his films with the mother-figure.[14] All of Truffaut's artistic descendants are homosexual and mirror the pattern evident in Rimbaud, Genet, and Cocteau, who were also gay. This suggests the possibility of some correlation of the disrupted familial circumstances they share with their sexual orientation.

What all of these instances have in common is disruption in primary attachment relationships that eventuated in various forms of emotional deprivation. The absence of a dependable father figure, or else the presence of a father who is cold and distant, tends to result in unconscious father-hunger that expresses itself in the search for substitutes: either in the form of homosexual or pseudo-homosexual relationships, or in the adoption of surrogate fathers. Conversely, emotional deprivation arising from either an unloving mother, or an overly invested one who uses the child to satisfy her unmet narcissistic needs results in an anxious attachment to the mother, or a fusional relationship with her. In adulthood, such relationships often motivate a compulsive need to seduce, in a search for mother-surrogates, with seduction ratified by orgasm functioning as a self-enhancing, mood-altering drug.[15] The parallels between the early experiences of these creative artists would therefore suggest, first, that they share a similar psychic economy; second, that the fiction they create innately conveys the elements of this psychic economy; and, third, that the act of fictive (re-)creation serves as a strategy for managing perturbations that arise from the legacy of these disrupted early attachment relationships. In all cases, such management is achieved through either or all of the following strategies:

- evacuating unwanted feelings consciously or unconsciously harbored toward the agents of the disturbance
- providing substitute gratifications, even if these are primarily imaginary
- providing images of a condition of relationship and affective contentment that is imaginatively felt to be highly desired
- identifying, through imaginative symbolization, aspects of the external environment, real or imagined, that are felt to pose threats to happiness and equilibrium

In many instances, a number of these motivations operate together in a fictive representation simultaneously, with any one of them liable to be dominant to a greater or lesser degree depending on the immediate preoccupations of the author.

I will now explore in detail how the dynamics of reception and response work in a specific example: Truffaut's *Jules and Jim*, which was adapted from the novel of the same name by one of Truffaut's father-figures, with whom he felt a particularly close affinity, Henri-Pierre Roché.

TRUFFAUT'S ENCOUNTER WITH ROCHÉ'S NOVEL

Henri-Pierre Roché's novel *Jules et Jim* (1953), and the film by Truffaut that made it famous, provide a classic example of how a reader, in this instance Truffaut, can intuitively detect in a fiction, through intersubjective attunement, a psychic economy in the author that mirrors his own, and, further, how he can then unconsciously invest the components of a fiction with associations deriving from his own memories so as to adapt the symbolic figuration in the source fiction to his own needs. The procedure externalized in Truffaut's adaptation, I hypothesize, is comparable to that which takes place in the response of any reader/spectator.

Roché's *Jules et Jim* tells the story of a romantic triangle based on the real-life ménage à trois involving Roché, his close friend, the German-Jewish writer Franz Hessel, and Hessel's wife, Helen Hessel (née Grund), during the 1920s.[16] Roché recorded intimate details of this triangular relationship—for example, how the three of them would sleep in the same bed, watching each other make love—in private journals he kept through most of his life.[17] During the course of this affair, both Roché and Helen Hessel took other lovers, a fact that is dramatized in the fictive version of these events in Roché's novel and alluded to in Truffaut's film.[18] In a major departure from the real-life story, Roché in the fictive version has Kate (alias Helen Hessel) kill both Jim and herself by driving a car off a bridge into the river Seine—an event that Truffaut replicates in the film.

Truffaut tells us that he came across this novel in a bookstore in the Place du Palais-Royal in 1955 and that, when he read it, it struck him like "*un coup de foudre*" (a bolt of lightning).[19] It is easy to see why, at a superficial level, Truffaut was attracted to it: by 1955, he was already pursuing a very active sex life involving a succession of affairs and repeated visits to brothels (as a result of which he contracted syphilis on several occasions).[20] It is likely that he saw Roché's *Jules et Jim* as providing an idealistic justification for the kind of sexual liberty he was practicing. Given his disinclination to be confined in a monogamous relationship, it is small wonder that Truffaut was enthralled by the fact he had found, as he put it, "an example of something the cinema had never managed to achieve: to show two men who love the same woman, without the public being obliged to make an affective choice between the characters, since it has been led to love all three equally"[21]—a sentiment which, in his wishful imagination, might apply equally well to a man who loves two (or more) women simultaneously while being married. In real life, Henri-Pierre Roché maintained precisely such a regime, simultaneously being married to Germaine Bonnard, secretly having a son with Denise Renard, and sustaining his relationship with Helen Hessel. He managed this feat by seeing Helen on Wednesdays and Saturdays, Germaine on Thursdays and Sundays, and Denise on Mondays and Tuesdays—without his mistress being aware of the existence of the child and its mother.[22]

Although his self-justificatory parallel between himself and Roché may have been the chief reason Truffaut gave himself and others for his fascination with the older man's novel, the real cause of his extraordinary response to it lay deeper, in his unconscious, as he revealed in an interview given in 1978: "I am never conscious of the whole meaning of a subject when I choose it and when I tackle it. Usually, I only come to understand it long after I have made the film."[23] By 1975, Truffaut had come to realize that the real reason he had wanted to make *Jules and Jim* so badly was that "the subject matter had deeply hidden roots in my own childhood, and that it would allow me to highlight all the things around me that I had felt were abnormal during the period of the Occupation when I was living at Pigalle."[24] To understand this belated admission, and why Roché's novel had the power to unleash those associations, it is necessary to consider the parallels in the childhood experiences of Roché and Truffaut with their parents during the crucial years of their development.

CLARA ROCHÉ: A "JOCASTA" MOTHER[25]

As Catherine Du Toit has painstakingly detailed in her doctoral thesis on Roché, drawing on the journals and letters of Roché and those of certain figures in his circle, Roché's childhood was indelibly marked by the absence of a father and by a very troubled relationship with his mother.[26] That trouble began from the moment of Henri's birth, when his mother Clara refused to assist in his delivery because she disliked the tone with which the doctor urged her to "push," thus prolonging the agonies of her labor. She then refused to see the infant once he was born on the grounds that he had "made her suffer too much [my translation]."[27] Very soon after, his young father died, at the age of only 28, having fallen from a balcony in a state of confusion after a bout of meningitis, thus removing the only person who could have mediated between the boy and the emotional disturbances of his mother.

After her husband's death, Clara Roché suffered deeply from narcissistic deprivation, recording in a two-part collection of aphorisms, *Profondeurs* and *Sur l'Éducation* (published at her own cost in 1926) that "it is necessary that I am loved, or else I will die. Hostility and coldness would kill me as surely as the best firearm in the world [my translation]."[28] As Catherine Du Toit puts it, "Despite the apparent forcefulness of her personality, Mme Roché seems to have considered herself the victim of unjust suffering," just as Truffaut's mother, as he perceived her, would have liked "a more brilliant career."[29] To find some form of compensation, Clara looked to her son to fulfill her hunger for affection, subjecting him to a relentless and cruel form of emotional manipulation by telling him that she had originally rejected him because he had made her "suffer so much." In so doing, she not only made him "uniquely responsible for her suffering" but also left him with a feeling of guilt, inseparably linked to his very existence."[30] According to Du Toit, "The automatic impulse to gratify the needs of his mother so as not to be deprived of the only 'maternal' love he knew did not lessen his thirst for a genuine motherly love."[31] When Henri-Pierre had his own child, the sight of the tender affection that existed between his son and his mother made him aware of the extent of his own emotional deprivation; in an entry in his diary, he notes that Denise (his wife) "observes and understands his [his son's] gestures, his apparent caprices, and makes sure she understands the cause. I recall that, when I was a baby, I had need of a nurse or a mother like that."[32] Significantly, after the death of her husband, Clara compelled her son to take his place, as Roché records in his diary entry for May 4, 1907: "Even after he [his father] was dead, for a long time she was more my wife than my mother."[33] This cross-generational spousification was signaled explicitly in a change of name: whereas Roché had been baptized Henri-Pierre, after the death of his father his mother referred to him only by the name of her husband, Pierre.

Here, then, are all the ingredients of what would now be clinically identified as an "anxious attachment," whereby a son is emotionally bound into a dependent relationship with his mother in which he is required to ensure her continuing affection by supplying her narcissistic needs. Such narcissistic hunger on the mother's part leaves little space for encouragement of the son's independent identity, leaving him with a lack in his emotional life that prompts him to seek what is missing internally in the form of an external object. Indeed, the degree to which Clara Roché had subsumed her son into a co-dependent relationship paradoxically filled Henri-Pierre with a resentment that counterpointed his devotion to her.

In dramatizing his relationship with his mother in his second novel, *Two English Girls and the Continent* (1956), Roché, in the person of his fictional avatar Claude, describes the desire of his adult self to break free of this suffocating emotional enslavement: "Although I still had filial affection, I was seized with a fierce independence: to find a woman, the opposite of Claire [Clara], but who resembled her."[34] This need to find a substitute, but one who resembled his mother, propelled Roché, as it would propel Truffaut, to seek it through sexual seduction, resulting in an insatiable Don Juanism that needed to repeat endlessly the act of seduction. Concurrently, father-hunger led him to develop intense male friendships that were homoerotic at the least, if not actually homosexual. Curiously, the heterosexual adventures Roché shared with his male friend Franz Hessel seem to have served as a displacement for the homosexual love making he denied himself; as Roché confessed in a letter to Hessel, "Making love with [Helen] is a little like making love with you."[35]

Research on attachment styles has ascertained that disturbances in the relationship of a child to parental figures like those suffered by Roché tend to result in mental models that govern the child's way of perceiving and responding to the world. This is exactly what one sees in Roché's novel *Jules et Jim*. The relationship between Jim (Roché) and Jules (Franz Hessel), apart from reflecting their real-life friendship, symbolically figures Jim's yearning for a relationship that can substitute for that with the missing father. Jim's relationship with Kate, on the other hand, simultaneously reflects his real-life ménage à trois and, at a symbolic level, signifies the spousified relationship of the author with his mother, shared originally with the father. It also signifies the author's unquenchable search for female affection, which is nevertheless accompanied by a fear of its death-dealing potential, derived from his experience with his mother and with her surrogate, the female lover (in real life, Helen Hessel), who, like the former, is narcissistic, demanding, inconsistent, and dangerous.

JANINE TRUFFAUT:
THE QUEEN OF INDIFFERENCE

In contrast to Clara Roché, who bound her son Henri-Pierre into an anxious dependency, Janine de Monferrand's narcissism led her to display a callous indifference to her son and his emotional and physical needs that propelled him into an unending search for compensatory assurance of feminine acceptance and affection. As soon as her baby was born, secretly, from an unknown father and out of wedlock, Janine placed the infant with a wet nurse; he did not live with his mother, now married to Roland Truffaut, until he was eight years old, and only then because his grandmother, who had been raising him, died.³⁶ Once he rejoined the Truffaut household, the young François perceived his mother to be resentful of his presence and even his very existence. In an interview, summing up his life with his parents, Truffaut said, "The underlying thought, which they didn't even bother to hide from me, was always–'How can we get rid of him?'"³⁷

This treatment left the young Truffaut in a constant state of anxiety: "I lived with my mother, who couldn't stand noise, and who would force me to sit motionless, without moving, without speaking, for hours and hours. And so, I read–it was the only thing I could do without getting on her nerves."³⁸ Janine Truffaut's abusive behavior toward her son was not just emotional. Truffaut records an occasion during the occupation when she kicked him on the ground because, in the context of wartime rationing, he had brought back only a box of biscuits after standing in a queue for two hours. This expression of frustration and hostility, he says, left him living with "falsehood and fear" and a belief that she hated him: "The family ambiance was such that I was almost sure of a secret concerning my birth; Mom hated me so much that, for a year, I thought she wasn't my real mother."³⁹

Although Janine's coldness toward François left him feeling completely unloved, she presented herself to him as a highly eroticized feminine object. Truffaut dramatized his memory of her behavior in *The Man Who Loved Women* (1977)–another film based on the writings of Roché, this time his *Carnets*–in which the young Bertrand is shown reading while his mother strolls past him in a state of undress that allows her silk-clad legs to be seen: "My mother was in the habit of walking semi-naked in front of me–not to arouse me, obviously, but rather, I suspect, to confirm to herself that I didn't exist."⁴⁰

In short, Truffaut's experience of his mother left him with contradictory feelings toward her. On one hand, as he wrote in a letter to Jean-Louis Bory in 1974, he hated her: "You adore your mother, I hate mine, even dead."⁴¹ On the other hand, she represented an eroticized ideal–reflected in the repeated fetishization in Truffaut's films of women's stocking-clad legs–that became conflated with his longing to be the object of the maternal, feminine love she denied him. Through an inversion of the situation he had experienced with his mother, being sexually aroused by a woman seems to have been equated in Truffaut's adult imaginary with confirmation that he indeed existed, which may explain his compulsive sexual activity.

Just as Henri-Pierre Roché's experience of an overinvested, emotionally incestuous mother had left him in an acute state of narcissistic deprivation, so too did Truffaut's experience of an indifferent, abusive yet seductive mother leave him with a painful sense of something lacking. In both cases, the narcissistic deprivation that their mothers' respective behaviors implanted in them left the two men with a gaping hole in their emotional being—one that they sought to fill through sexual adventures, which, because they functioned like a drug, could have no lasting effect but rather necessitated an endless repetition of the need to seduce.

Underneath the ostensible parallel Truffaut found in Roché's *Jules et Jim* between his erotic life and that of his author, in other words, there lay this deeper syndrome of ambiguous and conflicted feelings: on one hand, the need, at an unconscious level, to secure an equivalent to the mother's love through sexual conquest and, on the other hand, a fear of the psychic danger inherent in such a relationship, whether because of a dread of being absorbed to the point of extinction of identity on account of the woman's possessiveness (as with Roché), or because of a fear of the woman's changeability (Roché and Truffaut), or a guilty fear of punishment for infidelity imaged in the woman as avenging *femme fatale* (Roché and Truffaut). The end result was an inability or, at the least, certainly an unwillingness to remain within a committed, monogamous relationship. As one of Roché's characters asserts:

> "Love is not a passion for only one person; but rather, a feeling that has its own will.... It may be sated and decline, and find itself again with another person.... Is love necessarily singular? No. Is it a sexual fantasy? No! It's an experience that lasts as long as it was intended to."[42]

Another of his characters confesses, "What crushes me is to need you without truly wanting you."[43] This is the dilemma that both Roché and Truffaut seem to have shared as a result of an abnormal relationship with the mother: to need the compensatory objects of desire without truly wanting them, which is why none of the relationships so formed could last very long.

It now remains to explore how Truffaut's unconscious recognition of the equivalence of his own psychic condition and that of Roché translated into a response that, in turn, illustrates how the intersubjective transaction between an author and a reader can promote an imaginative recreation aimed at converting the reader/spectator's experience of the source into one that answers to his or her own needs.

MULTIPLE IDENTIFICATIONS, MEMORIES,
AND EMOTIONS IN TRUFFAUT'S *JULES AND JIM*

As outlined in the previous chapter, the neuroscientist Vittorio Gallese has argued that, even though the simulation process made possible by mirror neurons activates an "agentive relation" in the onlooker, the "specific filler" in the interchange is left indeterminate, creating a situation in which "the agent parameter can be either oneself or the other."[44] In the case of Truffaut's adaptation of Roché's *Jules et Jim*, even though Truffaut adheres very closely to the main outline of the novel, his handling of the mise-en-scène illustrates exactly the kind of subjective "filling" that Gallese hypothesizes. Evidence of personalized "fillers" can be found at a number of concentric levels, ranging from the superficial and conscious to the deeply embedded and unconscious, which results in multiple identifications inhering in the images and plot configurations that operate simultaneously. I will now extrapolate these, moving from the superficial level, conscious on Truffaut's part, to the most deeply embedded level, almost certainly unconscious.

At the most conscious level, the film maps Truffaut's current love life onto Roché's original story. In 1957, Truffaut married Madeleine Morgenstern, but by the time he actually shot his adaptation of the novel in 1961, he had entered into a relationship with the actress Jeanne Moreau, who, in her words, "made François discover Henry James and drink champagne."[45] The screenplay of the film explicitly alludes to this relationship when Jules informs Jim that Catherine's father is French but she has an English mother–a detail that is not in the source but does reflect Jeanne Moreau's real-life Anglo-Saxon origins. Commensurately, the lighthearted tone of much of the film owes a great deal to the influence of Moreau's vivacious personality—a woman of whom Truffaut wrote, "With trembling lips, wild hair, she ignores what others call 'morals' and lives by and for love"—just as Helen Hessel had.[46] While working on the script, Truffaut stayed with Moreau at her house at La Garde-Freinet, where he also met her former husband, the actor Jean-Louis Richard, with whom he formed a close friendship—made possible by the fact that "Jeanne Moreau's relationship with her former husband was one of friendship and great tenderness."[47] One can see a parallel here between the ménage à trois in the film and the one that Truffaut had entered at the time of the film's genesis. Both triangular relationships involve two men who had become friends and love the same woman, around whom their activities revolve. In Truffaut's real life, there was another triangular relationship that the film reflects: even though by now he was married to Madeleine Morgenstern, he was conducting an affair with Liliane David—thus replicating the situation in the film in which Jim maintains a relationship with Gilberte while he is conducting his affair with Catherine.[48]

The next level of identification infused into the source story concerns a level of "filling" of which Truffaut was not conscious at the time he made *Jules and Jim* but of which he became aware some years after the film's release. Having realized that the film had roots extending deep into his childhood during the German occupation, Truffaut arrived at a further realization: that *Jules and Jim* had really been about his mother:

> I had a very difficult relationship with my family, particularly with my mother, and I only understood several years after making *Jules and Jim* that I had made it to please her and gain her approval. Love affairs played a big role in her life, and given that *The 400 Blows* had been like a knife stabbed in her back, I made *Jules and Jim* in the hope of showing her that I understood her [my translation].[49]

The main event to which he is referring is his mother's real-life infidelity during World War II and her husband's tolerance of it, which Truffaut had depicted negatively in *The 400 Blows*, in the scene where Antoine sees his mother and her lover in the Place de Clichy.[50] Eventually, this adulterous affair would lead to Janine Truffaut's divorcing Roland Truffaut, after which she married the lover who had been fictively represented in *The 400 Blows*. While Truffaut may indeed have thought, belatedly, that he had made *Jules and Jim* to gain his mother's approval, one suspects that he was being dishonest with himself in suggesting that he had come to "understand her," which implies forgiveness. Elsewhere in his correspondence, although he praises the acting of Jeanne Moreau, he labels the character she plays, Catherine, as a "poule" (whore), implying a lingering bitterness that centers on his fictional heroine.[51] There is, in fact, a profound ambiguity in Truffaut's presentation of Catherine—just as there is in Roché's own novel—that relates, in both cases, to a deeper unconscious fantasy regarding the respective sons' desires to secure and assure themselves of their mother's love in fantasy, at the same time registering their fear of the unreliability and inconsistency of that love—reflected in an inability to enter into a committed, monogamous relationship, even when that relationship seems to hold the promise of fulfilling what, fantasmatically, they are seeking.

Certain aspects of the mise-en-scène, in fact, intimate the presence of memories drawn from childhood that suggest how Truffaut, in the realization of the film, invests Roché's story with the infantile longings and fears that had entered the formation of the mental models that shaped his adult personality.

One such example is the scene in which the trio, on a seaside holiday, go to the beach. The sight of Jules and Jim in their one-piece bathing suits recalls Truffaut's own excursions to the beach as a young child with his mother and foster father. Indeed, a photo survives of François as a very young boy, in the sea, being lifted on high by Roland Truffaut, who is also in a one-piece bathing suit.[52] The importance of this episode in the boy's imaginary is underlined by the action of Catherine in gathering the bathing suits of Jules and Jim off the clothesline—for which there is no hint in the source novel. To reinforce the potency of this implicit memory of childhood, on several occasions Truffaut has Catherine refer to Jules and Jim as "les enfants" (children), thus casting them in the role that he himself occupied with respect to his mother on earlier holidays, which are here remembered as moments of atypical happiness.

A further sign of the intrusion of personal memories is the screenplay's reduction of the wide range of characters that appear in Roché's novel. Whereas Roché devotes separate chapters to Jim's (and, in the earlier stages of their story, Jules's) lovers—Lucie, Magda, Odile, and

Gilberte—and gives detailed descriptions of Kate's (Catherine's) lovers—Harold, Albert, and others—Truffaut and Gruault, his screenwriter, reduce them to one apiece. The other women to whom Jim turns while in his relationship with Catherine are reduced to Gilberte, the others being conflated in Catherine herself, who becomes all the more unpredictable, capricious, and vengeful as a result. Commensurately, while Catherine's numerous infidelities during her marriage to Jules are narratively reported, only one of these lovers, Albert, is shown on screen. The effect is to focus attention on the central triangle, in which Catherine herself is the central force. This strengthens the identification between her and the ancient statue Jules and Jim visit in Greece, which ends up symbolizing the contradictory aspects of womanhood itself. As Roché describes it in his novel, this statue has an "archaic smile": "a floating presence, powerful, youthful, thirsty for kisses and perhaps for blood."[53] In his filmic adaptation, Truffaut visually emphasizes this ambiguous smile in Catherine, most notably when she is on the bridge at the end, conducting Jim to his and her death. For both Truffaut and Roché, owing to their contradictory experience of their mothers, femininity entailed both irresistible attraction and a fear of their death-dealing potential, psychologically speaking, which in the novel, as well as in the film, is figured symbolically in a literal murder of the beloved object (in fantasy, the son, who is imaginatively recreating them at a displaced remove in the fiction).

What this points to, in fact, is what Anne Gillain has brilliantly identified in her analysis of Truffaut's films: always in Truffaut's movies, there is a fantasmatic scenario that resides within the ostensible scenario.[54] His procedure may be summarized thus:

> His films, like dreams, say more than he intended, and ceaselessly decode, without him knowing it, the elements comprising the maternal enigma. Each of them is susceptible to a double interpretation, and projects simultaneously two stories: the first one is realistic, shaped in accordance with the ordering logic of a classical narrative sequence ... the second one is fantasmal, the projection of a personal lived experience in which the son tries to comprehend his relationship with his mother and to restore the possibility of having a relationship and communication with her.[55]

In Truffaut's version of the story, the presence of this fantasmatic scenario is even more marked than it is in Roché's source novel.

THE FANTASMATIC SCENARIO OF
TRUFFAUT'S *JULES AND JIM*

At the heart of *Jules and Jim* is an idealized vision of the mother as seen through the eyes of a child.[56] Catherine, the embodiment of this vision, has two aspects: in her positive aspect, she appears as seductively feminine, as when she meets Jim in her diaphanous nightgown; in her negative aspect, however, she is narcissistic and tyrannical, prone to mood swings and unpredictable changes of mind, which show her to be a woman who, in Gillain's words, "dominates without any trace of paternal mediation."[57]

In response to this figure, Jules and Jim themselves can be seen as representing two sides of the same personality: Jules figures the son who survives by accommodating himself to the demands and caprices of this woman; Jim is the son who eventually wants to break away to find something better through a relationship with a woman who can give him a child. Catherine, however, will not allow this separation to occur–as Jules explains to Jim, "She always comes back"–and when Jim finally declares his desire to separate from her, this mother figure literally and symbolically kills him rather than allow him his independence–thereby signifying the destructive consequences of this fusional, but ultimately unrealizable, bond.

The paradigmatic nature of the fantasmatic scenario at the heart of *Jules and Jim* is visible in its variants, which Truffaut obsessively repeated in the films that would follow. In *The Soft Skin* (1964), for example, the destructive, death-dealing aspect of the mother-figure is presented in the avenging wife, Franca, who punishes her unfaithful husband for his infidelity with death, just as Catherine punishes Jim. In *The Last Metro,* on the other hand, the child's vision of the mother as embodying an idealized femininity and his desire to share her with the father are represented in the triangular relationship between Bernard, Marion Steiner, and the concealed husband, Lucas Steiner, which eventuates in a happy union of all three–much like the happy ménage à trois in *Jules and Jim* before things turn sour.

Two other movies present a fetishistic adoration of the idealized maternal feminine.[58] The first, *The Man Who Loved Women* (1977), based on Henri-Pierre's Roché's account of his amorous conquests in *Carnets*, his intimate diaries, focuses on stocking-clad legs as a part-object symbolizing the erotic appeal of the mother, and depicts the compulsive nature of the hero's search to attain, through endless sexual encounters, the elusive vision they signify—a quest animated by an intensity of need that eventually kills him. The second film, *The Green Room* (1978), presents the fetishization of the idealized maternal figure as a religious cult in which, for the hero, Davenne, time itself is frozen because of his pathological obsession with the lost object—here imaged as an "exquisite corpse"—and his unwillingness to move on from the past to embrace what the future might potentially offer him.

All of these dimensions of Truffaut's complex response to the legacy of his disturbed relationship with his mother—the primary attachment figure in his life—are present in *Jules and Jim,* and their simultaneous co-activation is what gives the film its remarkable richness. Truffaut captures both the sweetness and the bitterness generated by this troubled relationship, together with an incredible yearning after something that can never be attained but nevertheless becomes the stimulus for an artistic creativity that is somehow able to palliate the loss through an imaginative recreation of it.

What this example of creative imitation in response to a work of fictive representation shows is that the intuitions of those who have speculated on the function of fiction over the centuries, from Aristotle, through Philip Sidney and Milton, to Matthew Arnold and beyond, have not been wrong: fiction does have a cathartic effect for the reader/spectator that helps him or her grapple with, if not entirely resolve, the emotional pressures that are a source of perturbation. More specifically, Truffaut's response to Roché shows that the urge to create often arises from emotional perturbations grounded in the legacy of disturbed attachment relationships. Fictive creation, in fact, is one of the prime strategies that human beings have evolved to address and manage the sources of perturbation as well as to contemplate the possibility of a happier, better life. What is true for the author who creates a work of fiction is also true for the reader/spectator who responds to it: the processes involved in imaginative creation and re-creation are virtually the same, and in both cases they are generated by the emotions that are activated in response to real events.

11

The Conversion of Autobiographical Emotion into Symbolic Figuration: William Shakespeare's *Hamlet*

In the case of François Truffaut's *Jules and Jim*, discussed in chapter 10, sufficient biographical information exists to allow one to infer Truffaut's motivations by comparing his early attachment relationships with those of the author of his source, Henri-Pierre Roché, and then by triangulating both with their respective representations. In many instances, however, an equivalent amount of biographical information does not exist, meaning that one needs to infer the psychological dynamic of a fictive work from intrinsic rather than extrinsic evidence. The purpose of this chapter is to demonstrate how, even when very little biographical information about an author survives, the process of converting affective impulses into a fictive representation can be deduced by examining the emotions expressed in the work, the situations that give rise to them, and the strategies used to make them perceptible. Through this method, one can identify the symbolic figuration that has occurred during the creation of the work and, on the basis of that, speculate on the author's purpose for its composition.

Shakespeare's *Hamlet* (1600–1601), one of the most complex of all works of fictive art, is a particularly useful subject for this exercise given that it is one of the defining expressions of Western consciousness as well one of the most enigmatic. Viewed in the light of the neuropsychoanalytic theory I have been developing, however, it can be seen to have a close family resemblance to other works I have been discussing, in terms of both substance and method. Indeed, many of the intergenerational tensions discernible in *Jules and Jim* surface in Shakespeare's play–arising from the loss of a father and manifest in an intense need for male friendship, a fusional attachment between mother and son, and a fear of the betrayal to which female sexuality may lead–suggesting that emotional complexities deriving from disturbed attachments may be one of the most powerful of all inducements to fictive creation.

Significantly, after several centuries of critical commentary that has underestimated attachment disturbance as a major preoccupation in *Hamlet,* the advent of cognitive literary studies has allowed its centrality at last to be recognized. The first scholar to discern the importance of attachment disturbance was Joseph Carroll, who, in an article published in 2010, argued that "the core of symbolic meaning in *Hamlet* is Hamlet's corrupted emotional bond with his mother," replacing "the false Freudian concept of the Oedipal complex with Bowlby's evolutionary concept of attachment."[1] Carroll was soon followed by another cognitivist literary scholar, Patrick Colm Hogan, who used *Hamlet* as a case study to illustrate a neurobiological account of grief in which he argued: "*Hamlet* is a play about the loss of attachment relations and the attempt to repair that loss through new attachments."[2] However, although Hogan convincingly demonstrated that Hamlet's anger occurs when "acts and expectations of forming a substitute attachment relation, something to take the place of what he has lost," are blocked,[3] he leaves unexplained the interrelations that exist between the author, the text, the reader, and the context that gave rise to the play's creation.

My contention in this chapter is that these interrelations can be reconstructed–but only once the processes of symbolic figuration by which Shakespeare shaped the play have been identified, and that requires a close examination of not only the text itself, but also Shakespeare's transformation of his source materials and the links between the representation and his own autobiographical circumstances at the time he created it.

THE VEHICLE FOR FANTASMATIC CONVERSION: BELLEFOREST'S ACCOUNT OF AMLETH

Shakespeare's version of *Hamlet* is based on the legend of Amleth recorded in the twelfth-century Danish *Lejrekrøniken* (Chronicle of the

Kings of Lejre) and transmitted to a wider European audience in Latin by Saxo Grammaticus in the third and fourth books of his *Gesta Danorum* (Deeds of the Danes) written in the thirteenth century. The story was translated into the vernacular again in the sixteenth century by François Belleforest, who included it as the fifth story in the fifth tome of his *Histoires tragiques* (1572), the version in which Shakespeare read it.

Belleforest tells how Horvvendille, the Governor of Jutland and Amleth's father, is murdered on his return from a Viking mission, during which he slew the King of Norway, by his brother Fengon, who marries Horvvendille's widow, Geruthe. Geruthe's son Amleth, fearing for his own life, counterfeits madness to deceive Fengon, who in turn contrives two ruses to test Amleth's sanity using women (Geruthe and a young woman). During the encounter with his mother, Amleth kills a counselor who is spying on them, delivers a harangue upbraiding her, and then disposes of the body. This persuades Fengon that Amleth's madness is feigned, and he arranges to have Amleth killed by sending him to England with secret instructions for the English king to put him to death. Amleth intercepts the instructions, however, and alters them so that the bearers are killed instead. After returning to Denmark a year later, having prearranged with Geruthe for a funeral feast to be held to celebrate his supposed death, Amleth finds the members of the court drunk and exacts his revenge by setting fire to the palace after pinning down the revelers with woolen hangings torn from the walls and by beheading Fengon with the latter's own sword. Revenge is thus achieved "many yeeres after the act committed," which leaves "men of wisdom" wondering "which was more commendable in him, his constancy or magnanimitie, or his wisdom in ordering his affaires, according to the premeditable determination he had conceaved." Amleth is then proclaimed ruler, returns to England to reclaim his wife, and has a series of adventures and misadventures. As a result of these experiences, and after killing the King of England, he is betrayed by his second wife, Hermethrude, and slain by his enemy, Wiglerus, whom Hermethrude then marries, ironically replicating the situation that Amleth avenged in the first place.[4]

What arrested Shakespeare's attention about this story? To his contemporaries, as we know from the preface to the 1608 English translation of Belleforest's French version, the moral was self-apparent:

If the iniquitie of a brother caused his brother to loose his life, yet that vengeance was not long after delayed; to the end that traitors may know, although the punishment of their trespasses committed be stayed for awhile, yet that they may assure themselves that, without all doubt, they shal never escape the puissant and revenging hand of God; who being slow to anger, yet in the ende doth not faile to shew some signes and evident tokens of his fearefull judgement upon such as, forgetting their duties, shed innocent blood, and betray their rules, whom they ought chiefly to honour, serve, and reverence.[5]

While implicitly replicating this moral in the poetic justice administered in the play's punishments, however, Shakespeare seems to have been more impressed by something else in Belleforest's account that appeared to have eluded the 1608 editor's notice: Belleforest's observation that Amleth would have been wholly admirable but for one thing:

si vne seule tache n'eust obscurcy vne bonne partie de ses louanges. D'autant que la plus grande victoire, que l'homme peut acquerir, est celle qui le faict seigneur; & dompteur de ses affections, & laquelle chastie les efforts desreiglez du sens afolé en ses conuoirises: car l'homme à beau estre fort & sape, que si les chatouillemens de la chair le surmontent, il s'auillira, & arrestera après des beautez, & deuiendra fol, & insensé à la poursuitte des femmes.[6]

(if one onely spotte had not blemished and darkened a good part of his prayses. For that the greatest victorie that a man can obtaine is to make himself victorious and lord over his owne affections, and that restraineth the unbridled desires of his concupiscence; for if a man be never so princely, valiant, and wise, if the desires and inticements of his flesh prevaile, and have the upper hand, hee will imbase his create, and gasing after strange beauties, become a foole, and (as it were) incensed, dote on the presence of women.)[7]

In offering his summative judgment, Belleforest was thinking of the lust that caused Amleth to succumb to the seduction of the untrustworthy Hermethrude, the Queen of Scotland, rather than being content with his beautiful young English wife. This was a tragic weakness that led to his death, just as it had led Samson and Hercules to theirs. Nevertheless, it was not the timeworn commonplace of men's susceptibility to feminine seduction that caught Shakespeare's attention, but the notion of needing to master one's "affections" (that is, emotions), and the difficulty of doing so. To understand the importance of this idea to his conversion of Belleforest's story to serve his own purposes, one needs to begin by tracing the major changes Shakespeare made to the source material.

SHAKESPEARE'S ALTERATIONS TO THE SOURCE

Here one encounters a further problem in that Shakespeare's *Hamlet* has come down to us not in one but in three versions: the First Quarto (Q1) published in 1603; the much longer Second Quarto (Q2), published in 1604; and a variant version of Q2 published in the First Folio (F1) of 1623.[8] To complicate matters, there was a Senecan-style play about Hamlet in existence in England as early as 1589.[9]

Allowing for the inevitable variants in the three versions ascribed to Shakespeare, several major changes to the source are immediately apparent. Chief among them is the addition of the ghost of Hamlet's dead father. A further major change is the addition of a second father figure, Polonious (called Corambis in Q1), who replaces the anonymous counselor who spies on Hamlet from behind the arras during Hamlet's encounter with Gertrude. There is also the addition of a second son, Laertes—compounded by the inclusion of a third son, Fortinbras, the son of the King of Norway, whom Horvendile (Old Hamlet in Shakespeare's play) had killed during his foray into that country, thus intensifying the focus on father-son relationships.

The additional father figures are complemented by the addition of a number of close friends of Hamlet. The "friend" in Belleforest's original who warns Hamlet of the first of Fengon's strategies (to test whether Hamlet is really insane by exposing him to a sexually available young woman) is developed into Horatio, a student of philosophy at the University of Wittenberg, who epitomizes rationality and common sense. Shakespeare also develops the two "faithful ministers," who in Belleforest's version accompany Hamlet to England as Fengon's henchmen, into Rosencrantz and Guildenstern, portrayed as Hamlet's friends since childhood. Further changes revolve around a band of visiting players, the leader of which, in response to a request from Hamlet, declaims a speech in which another avenger (Pyrrhus) kills a king who is a father (Priam), thus creating a second bereaved widow (Hecuba). Finally, the duel between Hamlet and Laertes has no precedent in Belleforest; nor does the manner in which the victims of the ensuing mishaps die. Why did Shakespeare make these very substantive changes? The structural patterns they enabled him to construct suggest a reason.

THE STRUCTURAL SHAPING OF THE REPRESENTATION

As Geoffrey Bullough has detailed, *Hamlet*, at the most obvious level, is shaped according to the conventions of the Senecan tragedy made popular by plays like Kyd's *The Spanish Tragedy:* a ghost who repeatedly calls for revenge; a secret crime revealed that needs verification; the assumption of madness in the avenger, who uses dissimulation, as do his enemies; reproaches over delay; suicidal thoughts; a play-within-the-play; and so on.[10] The choice of the Senecan revenge genre was obvious and appropriate as a vehicle for a dramatization of Belleforest's story of Amleth, especially given its popularity as attested by the rash of such plays from *Gorboduc* (1561) onward. This was not lost on a playwright concerned with box-office returns.

Within this broad conventional configuration, however, the changes Shakespeare made to his source material enabled him to construct an elaborate system of parallels and contrasts that focus attention on issues that assume a far greater prominence in the affective structure of the play than the ostensible theme of revenge.

The addition of the Ghost and of Polonius, another father who would be murdered in the course of the play, allowed Shakespeare to develop a parallel between two fathers who spy on their sons and attempt to control them from a distance. At the same time, Polonius allowed him to double the number of sons, creating a parallel between Hamlet and Laertes as sons who must avenge the murder of their fathers, but who differ in their mode of action (or inaction) and their attitude toward murder, with Hamlet paralyzed by conscience and Laertes perfectly prepared to become complicit in treachery to accomplish his revenge.

These basic doublings are further amplified by the addition of a band of traveling players who arrive at Elsinore and a plot involving Fortinbras, yet another son whose father has been slain (by Hamlet's father). The arrival of the players presents Hamlet with a further friend in the form of one actor whom he knew as a boy (the actor's face is now "valanced," that is, fringed with a beard). Meeting this actor gives Hamlet the pretext for asking him to deliver a speech about the slaughter of Priam at the sack of Troy that generates further parallels and contrasts: a parallel between Pyrrhus and Hamlet as would-be killers of a king (also containing a contrast in that Pyrrhus violently enacts murder, whereas Hamlet refrains from it when he has the opportunity) and a contrast between Hecuba, Priam's queen, and Gertrude in terms of the extreme grief of the former and the forgetful indifference of the latter. The players allow Hamlet to stage the play-within-the-play, in which the Player King and Player Queen represent an idealized image of Hamlet's parents, but in which, through an ironic twist, the presentation of the murderer as Lucianus, the king's nephew, implicitly identifies Lucianus as Hamlet in his relationship with his uncle Claudius, thus issuing the real king a public threat.

As if this complex network of prismatic parallels and contrasts were not enough, Shakespeare also exploits these new elements to create symmetry between the rising and falling action of the play by generating a series of ironic reversals. If one regards the revelation of Claudius's guilt in his reaction to "The Mousetrap" as the climax of the play, the rising action shows three sons seeking to avenge slain fathers and three parallel quests to discover the truth (Hamlet's to discover whether Claudius is guilty; Claudius's to discover how much Hamlet knows; and Polonius's to discover how his son is behaving in Paris, which parallels the Ghost's surveillance of Hamlet's behavior). The falling action then inverts this in a number of significant ways. Hamlet has exchanged roles with Claudius by killing a father (ironically foreshadowed by Lucianus in the play-within-the-play) and, as a result, has become the hunted, not the hunter. Ophelia has moved into the role of Hamlet, having become mad with grief and suicidal at the loss of a father–with the difference that her madness is real, and that she actually kills herself, rather than just engage in suicidal ideation. Similarly, her brother Laertes is now in the role of Hamlet-as-avenger, having become determined to seek revenge for the killing of Polonius.

What we see, then, is a very deliberate structural design involving the intersection of two family triangles, which, apart from generating ironies, focuses attention on the nature and dynamics of family relationships, especially attachments and whether they are strong, weak, or missing. In this regard, the action of the play is made to unfold as if a kaleidoscope is being shaken, creating shifting patterns that give the play multiple perspectives. In addition, the mutating roles that the characters find themselves assuming underline the words of the Player King: "Our wills and fates do so contrary run / That our devices still are overthrown/ Our thoughts are ours, their ends none of our own." This statement raises questions about how free human actors are to determine their own destinies or even control the outcomes of their actions.[11] As the emotional impact of these new considerations that Shakespeare has implanted in the play begin to be felt, it becomes increasingly clear that the main issue has shifted from simple revenge. A concern with revenge is still present—especially with its morality—but far more important now is what one is to do in a world that subjects one to psychic shocks delivered by tragic events that induce unbearable pain. It thus remains to examine the ways in which the images Shakespeare summons in the language of the play cooperate with the structural patterns to reinforce this preoccupation.

NETWORKS OF ASSOCIATIVE METAPHORS

As I suggest in previous chapters, the formation of sense images summoned from implicit and autobiographical memory is one of the primary strategies the human brain uses to make emotional feelings perceptible to conscious awareness—an elementary form of metaphorical troping. When such images are arranged into recurring networks of metaphors with a particular set of associations, as almost always occurs in fictive representation, tracing the metaphorical maps constituted by such associative networks is a very effective way of getting to the heart of an author's motivation in his or her creative activity. Caroline Spurgeon, in her groundbreaking study of Shakespeare's imagery, astutely points to the disease imagery that extends throughout *Hamlet* and the way it is counteracted by another class of images evoking "sheer beauty."[12] This is true enough, and the images of disease are everywhere apparent, from the Ghost's description of the "tetter barked about / Most lazarlike with vile and loathsome crust" that afflicted his "smooth body" as a result of Claudius's poison, to Hamlet's warning to his mother that persuading herself that he is mad "will but skin and film the ulcerous place / Whiles rank corruption, mining all within, / Infects unseen."[13] Yet there are other equally important image clusters, which Spurgeon tends to underestimate in her discussion.

The opening scene, for example, emphasizes how "cold" it is, and Francisco associates this coldness with a sickness of emotion: "'Tis bitter cold, / And I am sick at heart."[14] This in turn links with images of ice and snow, as in Horatio's reference to how Hamlet's father, "in an angry parle ... smote the sledded Polacks on the ice"[15] or Hamlet's wish "that this too too sullied flesh would melt, / Thaw, and resolve itself into a dew"[16] or, yet again, his bitter warning to Ophelia that should she marry: "Be thou as chaste as ice, as pure as snow, thou shalt not escape calumny."[17]

These images of coldness associate to a deep state of depression in which Hamlet has come to view the world as "an unweeded garden / That grows to seed," leaving him feeling that his engagement with it is merely "weary, stale, flat, and unprofitable."[18] In his great soliloquy (act 3, scene 1), Hamlet complements these images with images that conjure up the world's vicissitudes–an awareness of which, in his state of depression, has come to dominate his mind: "The slings and arrows of outrageous fortune" that one must "suffer," the "sea of troubles" against which one must take arms, the "thousand natural shocks / That flesh is heir to," and the need to bear

> ... the whips and scorns of time,
> The 'oppressor's wrong, the proud man's contumely,
> The pangs of despised love, the law's delay,
> The insolence of office, and the spurns
> That patient merit of th'unworthy takes.[19]

Such images show that Hamlet is troubled by far more than the need to exact revenge: the death of his father and the remarriage of his mother have delivered a shock to his emotional equilibrium so profound that he has lost his ability to see the world in its full complexion; instead, he sees only its negative aspect. Whether in a state of heightened excitation or melancholic lethargy, Hamlet has become a very different man from the exemplary figure he was:

> The courtier's, soldier's, scholar's, eye, tongue, sword,
> The'expectancy and rose of the fair state,
> The glass of fashion, and the mold of form,
> Th'observed of all observers...[20]

Spurgeon comes close to identifying what is at issue in Hamlet's transformation:

> To Shakespeare's pictorial imagination... the problem in *Hamlet* is not predominantly that of will and reason, of a mind too philosophic or a nature temperamentally unfitted to act quickly; he sees it pictorially not as the problem of an individual at all, but as something greater and even more mysterious, as a condition for which the individual himself is apparently not responsible, any more than the sick man is to blame for the infection which strikes and devours him, but which, nevertheless, in its course and development, impartially and relentlessly annihilates him and others, innocent and guilty alike. That is the tragedy of Hamlet, as it is perhaps the chief tragic mystery of life.[21]

She is right to identify a feeling in Hamlet that he is not responsible for the inner emotional sickness from which he knows he is suffering—the fact that his "wit's diseased," as he only half jokingly informs Rosencrantz.[22] However, because she focuses only on the imagery without relating it to other features in the structural shaping of the play, Spurgeon does not recognize the extent to which Shakespeare's realization of the drama implicitly supplies a great deal of information as to the source of Hamlet's profoundly disturbed state of mind.

REVELATION OF THE PLAY'S AFFECTIVE LOGIC

Within the overall structure of the play, with its rising and falling action and elaborate system of repetitions, parallels, and contrasts, there is an implicit affective pattern that is revealed in a succession of events showing Hamlet losing the ability to maintain his emotional equilibrium. The first of these events occurs when he sees the Ghost for the first time.

Addressing the Ghost in very emotive, wholly eulogistic terms as "Hamlet, / King, father, royal Dane," Hamlet becomes so determined to follow it that when his companions, fearing it might be evil, attempt to prevent him from doing so, he draws his weapon against them, which prompts Horatio to exclaim: "He waxes desperate with imagination."[23] This disequilibrium intensifies once Hamlet hears the Ghost's account of his murder and has been enjoined by him to avenge his death–without tainting his mind or harming his mother. The revelation combined with the injunction leave Hamlet so overpowered by grief and rage in "this distracted globe" that he reverses his former reverence for the Ghost and begins to treat it disrespectfully, as if it were a devil, when he hears its voice crying "Swear" from under the stage:

> HAMLET.
> Ha, ha, boy, say'st thou so? Art thou there, truepenny?
> Come on. You hear this fellow in the cellarage.
> . . . .
> HAMLET.
> Well said, old mole! Canst work I' th'earth so fast?
> A worthy pioneer![24]

His inversion of reverence into mockery is a self-defensive mechanism to alleviate the pressure of emotion that is so powerful it would otherwise be unbearable.

Hamlet displays a comparable flood of emotion when the Ghost reappears during Hamlet's tirade against his mother following the confirmation of Claudius's guilt, an effusion that prompts Gertrude to exclaim: "Alas, he's mad." This time, the emotion that overwhelms Hamlet in response to the Ghost is not the mixture of awe, respect, and affection he displayed at the latter's first appearance, but fear that the Ghost has come to "chide" his "tardy son" for not having carried out his "dread command," as if Hamlet were a delinquent boy. Significantly, on this occasion it is only Hamlet who can see the Ghost, which leads his mother to observe: "This is the very coinage of your brain," suggesting a hallucination prompted by the pressure of his emotion.[25]

The other significant occasions when Hamlet loses his emotional equilibrium both occur in relation to the important women in his life,

Gertrude, his mother, and Ophelia, his beloved. To underline the importance of Hamlet's relationship with these women, Shakespeare focuses attention on the prince's encounters with them by placing each one structurally in an equivalent position on either side of the crisis (the presentation of the play-within-the play and its confirmation of Claudius's guilt), so that the symmetry of the parallel between the two occasions can be fully registered.

The first encounter occurs in act 3, scene 1, when Hamlet comes across Ophelia, who has been set up by Claudius and Polonius to find out whether Hamlet's madness is a consequence of frustrated love. One is struck by the extreme, rapid change in Hamlet's mood from one of loving approbation when he first sees her, expressed in imagery that associates her with holiness ("Soft you now, / The fair Ophelia!–Nymph, in thy orisons / Be all my sins remembered"), to one of violent, contemptuous vituperation as he accuses her, along with all women, of sexual corruptibility:

> HAMLET.
> I have heard of your paintings, well enough. God hath given you one face, and you make yourselves another. You jig and amble, and you lisp; you nickname God's creatures and make your wantonness your ignorance. Go to, I'll no more on't; it hath made me mad. I say we will have no more marriage. Those that are married already–all but one–shall live. The rest shall keep as they are. To a nunnery, go.[26]

What has caused this extreme mood swing? A clue is given in the words Hamlet utters in response to Ophelia's greeting:

> OPHELIA.
> Good my lord,
> How does your honor for this many a day?
>
> HAMLET.
> I humbly thank you; well, well, well.

Hamlet's words "well, well, well" carry a double sense, one literal and one ironic. Claudius and Polonius are observing the scene from behind the arras at the rear of the stage, and Hamlet's exclamation implies that he has become aware of them–an awareness that is reflected again in his pointed questions to Ophelia:

HAMLET.
Ha, ha! Are you honest?
....
Where's your father?

Hamlet's rage is unleashed because of his belief that Ophelia, like his mother, the other woman in his life, has betrayed him out of allegiance to someone else, thus depriving him of a source of emotional security.[27] In a certain sense, then, at this moment Ophelia is a stand-in for his mother in Hamlet's eyes, and the tirade she receives is really aimed at Gertrude. This becomes all the more apparent in the encounter with Gertrude herself in act 3, scene 4, during which Hamlet once again loses control of his emotions as he conjures up images of his mother engaged in sex with Claudius, becoming more and more incensed:

HAMLET.
Nay, but to live
In the rank sweat of an enseamèd bed,
Stewed in corruption, honeying and making love
Over the nasty sty–[28]

As in his earlier encounter with Ophelia, Hamlet's rage is fueled by his sense that his mother has betrayed him by transferring her allegiance elsewhere. The fact that this betrayal is experienced not simply as a betrayal of his father, but also of himself is reinforced by the parallel with his rage at Ophelia in the earlier scene, which is further underlined in the staging by the fact that Hamlet again realizes that someone is spying from behind the arras, and that the woman in front of him is complicit in this subterfuge.

The final occasion on which Hamlet experiences an explosion of heightened emotion occurs after his return from England, in act 5, scene 1, when he discovers that Ophelia is dead and the sight of Laertes's gesture of bravado in expressing his grief for his sister causes Hamlet to leap impulsively into the grave in "a tow'ring passion."[29] The emotion that prompts this impulsive act, which once again exposes Hamlet to Claudius's murderous intent, arises from a depth of love (and need), of which the vehemence displayed earlier toward Ophelia was merely the obverse. Moreover, the burial of Ophelia occurs at a point near the end of the play that balances it with the Ghost's account of his death near the beginning and thus reinforces a sense of loss and bereavement through the structural parallel. What Hamlet's encounters with the Ghost and his encounters with Ophelia and Gertrude attest to, therefore, is the emotional effect on him of the disruption of an intensely fused family bond: the loss of his father on one hand and the loss of his mother on the other, compounded by the loss of the beloved, who might have acted as a surrogate, through a death that also links her loss with the loss of his father. It is the cumulative impact of these progressive losses–which generate a sense of abandonment–that is responsible for Hamlet's depression, his rage, his procrastination, and his emotional instability.

THE INFORMING FANTASY

It is now time to speculate, in the light of the neuropsychoanalytic theory that I have been developing, on the fantasy being projected through this drama.[30] Freud, I think, shot wide of the mark in trying to make *Hamlet* accord with his theory of a universal Oedipus complex by arguing that Hamlet, because of an incestuous attachment to his mother, cannot kill Claudius because his uncle has done in actuality what Hamlet in fantasy would like to be able to do. There is nothing in the imagery or formal patterning of the text to support this idea. What both the affective burden of the imagery and the mapping of affective states apparent in the structuring of the drama do suggest, however, is that Hamlet is experiencing an intense form of separation distress at the disruption of his bonds of attachment resulting from the death of his father, the remarriage of his mother, the supposed disloyalty of his beloved, and the betrayal by his former friends, Rosencrantz and Guildenstern, which mirror, as he thinks, Ophelia's betrayal. The picture Shakespeare paints is consistent with what we now know from neuroscience about the role of the PANIC/GRIEF system in the emotional processes related to attachment. Panksepp has shown that, especially in intense forms such as grief, separation anxiety is "accompanied by feelings of weakness and depressive lassitude"[31]–precisely the feelings to which Hamlet confesses himself prey. At the same time, fear of being abandoned can promote rage directed at those whom the individual fears are abandoning him–another reaction, as we have seen, that intermittently grips Hamlet. Indeed, Shakespeare shows Hamlet oscillating between the depressive lassitude of grief and the hyperarousal of panic, with both reactions constituting a state of emotional dysregulation, of which Hamlet is aware, but cannot explain even to himself.

Bearing in mind that a fantasy is an imagined scenario created to project hopes, wishes, fears, or anxieties in a displaced form so that they can be apprehended, one can infer the nature of the fantasy that informs *Hamlet* and which the play tropes through the appropriation and adaptation of a revenge-tragedy generic template. Fantasmatically, the play dramatizes Hamlet's grief at the loss of a paternal authority figure and a maternal nurturing figure, both of which, whether actual or internally introjected, are essential for a sense of personal security in order to express a fear of the difficulty of being able to cope emotionally with the vicissitudes of the external environment–here presented as premature deaths–which leaves the protagonist alternately paralyzed, or else prone to anxious overreactions, both of which make his situation worse.

Had Shakespeare concluded the play at this point, it would have been grim to the point of nihilism, but the remaining part of the fantasy shows him contriving a resolution for Hamlet's dilemma. One of the vicissitudes Hamlet faces is that events show how little power human beings have to control the outcomes of their actions or to determine their own destiny, despite the responsibilities placed on them–here metaphorically emblematized in the injunctions of the Ghost. Hamlet fears that the responsibilities he bears as a result of obligations inhering in his familial relationships exceed his ability to achieve them ("O cursed spite, / That ever I was born to set it right!").[32] This fear is intensified by his discovery that every time he tries to act he not only harms others, but places himself in greater jeopardy.

The fantasy of the play shows him attaining a condition of mind in which he is prepared to relinquish the idea that he must be responsible through the agency of his own predeterminate will. This is reflected in a radical change of mood and mode of action that are described in act

5, scene 2, when Hamlet recounts to Horatio the series of providential accidents that led him to discover, and counter, the plot against his life, leaving him convinced that "there's a divinity that shapes our ends, / Rough-hew them how we will."[33] By the time he engages in a fencing bout with Laertes, by the king's invitation, even though he has a premonition of foul play, Hamlet is prepared to discard his habit "of thinking too precisely on th'event" in order to commit himself to this providence:

HAMLET.
... we defy augury. There is special providence in the fall of a sparrow. If it be now, 'tis not to come; if it be not to come, it will be now; if it be not now, yet it will come. The readiness is all. Since no man of aught he leaves knows, what is't to leave betimes? Let be.

The willingness to relinquish the feeling that he must be solely responsible for controlling things in advance of any potential eventualities is also a way of freeing himself from existential panic, leaving him in a new state of calm and a reformed state of mind, as reflected in his expression of remorse to Laertes over the killing of Polonius.[34] In this way, the play, as well as embodying a fantasy of fear, is enacting a fantasy of self-repair as a means of overcoming that fear in order to recover a state of emotional equilibrium. That Hamlet himself ironically becomes a victim of the bloody carnage of the play's denouement, along with all of the other characters who have transgressed, does not lessen the stability of his newfound equanimity, which is mirrored in the outer, larger world by the restoration of order with the foreshadowed election of Fortinbras as ruler.

In summary, at the level of fantasy the play enacts a psychological movement whereby sources of perturbation and emotional disequilibrium are fictively objectified so that calm can be regained through a retuning of the emotions, which in turn requires that an individual accept his own human limitations and trust that the world is governed by a larger purpose than the rational mind has the power to discern. This fantasy does not negate or supersede the surface story, but at a deeper level it does constitute the basic affective condition of the playwright that is seeking expression. Once we feel this, we can see how Shakespeare appropriated the Amleth legend as a vehicle through which he could liberate these emotions in displaced, objectified form.

THE LINK TO SHAKESPEARE'S BIOGRAPHY

Is there any circumstance in Shakespeare's biography to which one can link his urge to externalize an internal psychodrama of this sort through fictive displacement? Along with several recent scholars, I believe there is. On August 11, 1596, William Shakespeare's only son Hamnet died. The boy and his twin sister Judith had probably been named after friends of their parents, Hamnet Sadler, who witnessed Shakespeare's will, and his Judith, his wife.[35] However, Shakespeare, who had left to pursue his career as a dramatist in London when Hamnet was four years old, was a largely absentee father.

Although some scholars have argued against any link between the death of Hamnet and the writing of *Hamlet*, it stretches credulity to suppose that there was no connection between the grief any father would feel at the loss of a child and the intense grief arising from the bereavement expressed in the play. This is doubly unlikely given the associative link between the boy and the protagonist of the play: allowing for the vagaries of Elizabethan spelling, "Hamnet" and "Hamlet" are the same name, as confirmed by Shakespeare's will, in which he left 26 shillings, 8 pence to "Hamlett Sadler . . . to buy him a ringe."[36] As Stephen Greenblatt has pointed out, writing a play about Hamlet may not have been Shakespeare's idea: "Someone in the Lord Chamberlain's Men, with an eye on revenues, may simply have suggested to Shakespeare that the time might be ripe for a new, improved version of the Hamlet story."[37] Be that as it may, as soon as Shakespeare decided to write the play, the identification of the name of the protagonist of the old revenge play with the name of his recently dead son triggered a whole range of new associative identifications.

If one bears this possibility in mind, one can see that many of the changes Shakespeare made to Belleforest's source material in Belleforest were designed to provide him with opportunities to work through his own complex feelings about his relationship to his son and the impact of the boy's tragic death. As clinical experience in psychoanalysis has established, one of the most powerful unconscious defense mechanisms against painful affect or anxiety is *reversal,* or a form of projection in which the feelings of the projector are relocated into the person who is the object of those feelings. One can see this taking place in *Hamlet* in the reduplication of father-son relationships in which the death of one arouses acute grief and bereavement in the other. Reverse the reversals, and the griever can just as well be the father as the son.

Once the possibility of unconscious displacement is allowed, further instances of projective reversal become apparent. There is nothing in the source material to suggest that Amleth is living away from home when Fengon murders his father, but Shakespeare not only presents Hamlet as being summoned from Wittenberg, where he has been living as a student, but replicates this separation between a son and his father by having Laertes arrive from Paris. Again, if one recognizes the unconscious reversal, one can perceive in these introduced details a figurative parallel to Shakespeare's residing in London while his family remained in Stratford. If this is indeed the case, then the re-creation of the story in the play is also working through emotions of grief, or even guilt, arising from that separation through distance–which adds extra poignancy to Polonius's desire to find out what his son is up to in Paris (for which, fantasmatically, read London), especially given the possibility of promiscuous sexual behavior to which both *The Sonnets* and various rumors attest–such as John Manningham's diary note in 1602 that Shakespeare had had a brief sexual encounter with a woman during a performance of *Richard III*.[38]

Once the contextual relevance of *Hamlet* to the biography of its author is recognized, one can see that–apart from appealing to the London audience's taste for Senecan revenge tragedy–the play served as an instrument for achieving affective re-attunement and restoration following an experience of emotional turbulence that left the playwright doubtful of his psychic well-being. The patterning of the affective components in the play shows that this restoration was brought about by the objectification of perturbations so that they could be controlled by self-regulation, as reflected in Hamlet's new state of calm at the end of the play, even though it is achieved only at the price of his own death. In Ella Freeman Sharpe's apt phrasing, "Hamlet is what he [Shakespeare] might have been if he had not written the play of *Hamlet*."[39]

THE CENTRALITY OF *HAMLET* IN SHAKESPEARE'S PERSONAL MYTH

When *Hamlet* is considered in terms of its implicit affective structure, it can be seen that it replicates some of the key elements that Shakespeare repeated from one work to the next. As I suggest in chapter 12, these recurrent elements point to what Charles Mauron has labeled a "personal myth": that is, a symbolic configuration comprising internal objects, images, and recurring actors who project components of the self that are then arranged into combinations characteristic of the strategies the author has adopted to structure his or her response to experience. In *Hamlet*, the placing of two parallel scenes involving the two women in Hamlet's life on either side of the central climax points to one of the most potent of his obsessive preoccupations: a woman whose inconstancy is feared, with the fear of betrayal causing an affective reaction so extreme that it destabilizes the hero's emotional equilibrium.

In the nontragic plays, this motif is presented in farcical form in the romantic comedy *A Midsummer Night's Dream* (1595–1596) in the capricious switching of affection between the members of the quartet of young lovers under the influence of the Puck's magic potion. It is also found in a more latently ominous form in the tragicomic *Much Ado About Nothing* (1598–1599) in Claudio's willingness to believe Hero's infidelity–that, like Gertrude, "She knows the heat of a luxurious bed."[40] Finally, it is found in the late romance *The Winter's Tale* (1610–1611), in which Leontes becomes similarly distempered when he convinces himself that his wife Hermione is unfaithful with Polixenes, causing him, in a disease image that also recalls *Hamlet*, "infection of my brains."[41]

In the tragedies, this pathological syndrome is explored in greater depth, and both its causes and consequences are anatomized in detail. As I have suggested, the basic paradigm for this syndrome is laid down in the twin relationship Hamlet has with Ophelia on one hand, representing erotic love, and with Gertrude on the other hand, representing a mother/son attachment bond. His fears pertaining to the latter are transferred to the former through vicarious imputation. The hero's fear of being betrayed (or deserted) by each type of complementary female figure is reproduced again and again in successive plays, variously, in either form. With respect to fear of betrayal as inflected in an erotic relationship with a lover/wife figure, Hamlet's fear of Ophelia's sexual corruptibility is replicated in Othello's even more powerful conviction that Desdemona has been corrupted, which leads him to murder her rather than be "discarded thence" where "either I must live or bear no life."[42] In *Troilus and Cressida* (1601–1602), written at the time of *Hamlet*, the infidelity of the beloved presented in *Othello* as purely imaginary is depicted more cynically in Cressida's actual defection from Troilus to Diomedes, which similarly involves the transfer of a token important to the hero (for Othello a handkerchief, for Troilus a sleeve) given as a pledge of eternal constancy.

The other side of the coin – the deep dependency of the hero on the relationship he has with the woman who is closest to him – is displayed in *Macbeth* (1605–1606), which shows that such a relationship has the same power to cause destruction as does the hero's fear of its removal. We see this in the crucial moment in act 1, scene 7, when the wife figure, Lady Macbeth, persuades Macbeth to continue with their plan to murder King Duncan even when Macbeth's better nature has persuaded him to "proceed no further in this business."[43] The power of the woman to subvert the male closest to her, arising from the hero's relationship of dependency, appears again in *Antony and Cleopatra* (1606–1607), in a less sinister but equally destructive form, when Antony flees the battle against Octavius at Actium, believing that "this foul Egyptian hath betrayed me."[44]

One of the last of Shakespeare's plays that centrally address emotional dependency combined with fear of betrayal is *Coriolanus* (1607–1608). It is almost as if Shakespeare chose the Roman legend of Caius Marcius Coriolanus as a vehicle for exploring the psychological genesis and structure of such dependency. The main events of Shakespeare's plot are drawn straight from the source, Sir Thomas North's translation of Plutarch's *Lives of the Noble Grecians and Romans* (1579). However, Shakespeare invented a number of scenes involving Volumnia, Coriolanus's mother, that show how her influence determines the personality that leads to his downfall.

According to Shakespeare, Volumnia has raised Coriolanus to believe that his worth resides in the honor of heroic achievements rather than the effects of love: "If my son were my husband, I should freelier rejoice in that absence wherein he won honor than in the embracements of his bed where he would show most love."[45] The analogy she draws between her son and a husband suggests emotional spousification; certainly, the young Coriolanus has been deprived of the nurturance that should come from affectionate maternal care because his mother, like Lady Macbeth, has emptied herself of all softer feelings, as reflected in her contemptuous dismissal of the dismay expressed by Coriolanus's wife Virgilia at the thought of him bleeding from his wounds:

> VOLUMNIA.
> Away, you fool! It more becomes a man
> Than gilt his trophy. The breasts of Hecuba,
> When she did suckle Hector, looked not lovelier
> Than Hector's forehead when it spit forth blood
> At Grecian sword, contemning.[46]

The effect on Coriolanus is a dependency on his mother's approval, as one of the citizens observes when commenting on his services for his country: "Though soft-conscienced men can be content to say it was for his country, he did it to please his mother and to be partly proud."[47] This grandiose pride that comes from such approbation leaves him acutely sensitive to any lack of appreciation of the merit and stature he has gained through his heroic exploits. We see this in his fury at the thought that a Volscian army does not fear him: "They do disdain us much beyond our thoughts, / Which makes me sweat with wrath."[48] Unsurprisingly, then, when he is about to be elected Consul, but must first display humility by exhibiting his wounds to the plebeians, he is unable to bring himself to do so, causing them to mutiny against him. His first psychic shock is to discover that Volumnia, who has groomed him into his patrician's contempt for the populace, yet is ambitious for him to gain the consulship, reverses her attitude in trying to persuade him to simulate humility to appease them. Coriolanus, musing that his mother "does not approve me further," refuses to placate the people, and when Volumnia herself comes on the scene, he expresses his consternation: "Why did you wish me milder? Would you have me / False to my nature?"[49]

Volumnia's betrayal is made complete when Coriolanus, having been banished from Rome, returns with a Volscian army to exact his revenge, but is persuaded to relinquish this quest as a result of Volumnia's intercession and her emotional manipulation. Her betrayal amounts to far more than the disloyalty betrayed in sexual infidelity; it involves the destruction of the very sense of identity she has induced him to craft for himself, as Coriolanus himself, at some level, recognizes:

> CORIOLANUS.
> O mother, mother!
> What have you done? Behold, the heavens do ope,
> The gods look down, and this unnatural scene
> They laugh at. O my mother, mother! O!
> You have won a happy victory to Rome;
> But for your son—believe it, O believe it!—
> Most dangerously you have with him prevailed,
> If not most mortal to him. But let it come.[50]

And come it does, with Coriolanus's bodily assassination shortly following this psychic one.

One is now in a position, I think, to appreciate the psychic structure of the personality expressed in the recurrent symbolic figurations expressing fear of a woman's actual or imagined betrayal. Each configuration of this fear is different, but the underlying dynamic is the same, just as it is in Shakespeare's sonnets. For reasons we cannot know at this distance in history, the poet repeatedly gives his fictive heroes a fear of the destructive consequences of a dependency resulting from an intense but disturbed maternal attachment—one that is experienced as dangerous owing to its ability to destabilize his fictive heroes whenever events trigger the vulnerabilities arising from it. The writing of the plays themselves would appear to be an attempt to intercept the potential for these reactions to occur uncontrollably, by subjecting them to rational scrutiny following an act of imaginative representation that makes them available for apprehension and comprehension. Shakespeare's great achievement in *Hamlet* is in finding a strategy of symbolic figuration that allows this syndrome to be troped more comprehensively, and on a larger scale, with all of its interconnected ramifications in other domains, than he had ever achieved previously, or would achieve again.

12

Tracking a Personal Myth through an Oeuvre: The Films of François Ozon

Just as a neuropsychoanalytic perspective can assist in analyzing the internal workings of an invented fiction, so too can an understanding of the brain's procedures in the creation of stories, combined with a psychoanalytic understanding of the nature and function of fantasies, sensitize one to the presence of recurring metaphors and symbolic configurations of action across the span of an author's works. Charles Mauron, in his book *Des métaphores obsédantes au mythe personnel: Introduction à la psychocritique* (1963), has labeled these recurring motifs a "personal myth," outlining a "psychocritical" model for identifying its presence in an author's work. Although Mauron's theory has been largely overlooked in Anglo-American scholarship—with the notable exception of Linda Hutcheon[1]—it remains valuable, especially given that Mauron's notion of how fictions are constituted is consistent with what we now know about the procedures of the human brain.

CHARLES MAURON AND PSYCHOCRITICISM: THE THEORY OF PERSONAL MYTH

Mauron's model depends on a theory of fantasy derived from Freud but modified in light of object-relations theory to account for the complexity and variety of fantasies in fictive representations without becoming reductive. Mauron agrees with Freud that "the earliest fantasies seem to constitute hallucinatory satisfactions of desire," and that these fantasies construct our future psyche,[2] but he also insists that fantasies play a decisive role in inhibiting and controlling impulses, as well as in expressing desires for repair, by facilitating "developmental creation, adaptation, restoration, dynamic representation of internal events, conflicts, and projected solutions."[3] In particular, fantasies are the means by which "the personality is able to achieve a discharge of repressed excitation and to master the experience of it" in response to the legacy of experiences that have left a traumatic imprint.[4]

In Mauron's view, fantasies of this sort are revealed in fictive works in unconscious "networks of obsessive associations," in which the metaphors that serve as vectors for these associations "constitute a mode of preconscious thought."[5] This mode of preconscious mentalization is closely bound up with emotion:

> the more primitive thought is, the more verbal images obey an affective logic and an internal reality; the fields of unconscious forces determine them and intercept them, and are expressed through them. At a slightly deeper level still, that is to say, preverbal, the same type of process no longer organizes words, but sensory, motivating images.[6]

When structuring a fantasy out of these associations, an author creates "a small number of dramatic scenes in which the action is just as much characteristic of the author as the actors," and "the grouping of them together composes a personal myth."[7] To create these actors, an author tends to "structure the self into components," including split or composite figures, and then arrange these components into a "practically infinite" number of combinations in successive works.[8] The figures in this personal myth, which represent "internal objects," can be constituted in a number of ways:

> An external object is internalized, becomes a person within the person; conversely, groups of internal images, loaded with love or fear, are projected on to reality. An incessant stream of exchanges thus populates the internal world, the kernel of personality, which are then assimilated, to a greater or lesser degree, and integrated into a total structuration.[9]

In addition, the creative imagination of the author is fed by linked "affective memories" that reach back into his or her past, "providing material for which a fantasy serves as the proper means of expression."[10]

In propounding this theory, Mauron takes care to emphasize that the identification of a personal myth in a work of fiction does not explain the whole work. Even though a personal myth may be persistently present in a work, beneath consciousness, for the most part it remains "in the background of the normal thought that is often uppermost."[11] This is why Mauron's psychocritical approach is much less reductive than almost any other method of psychoanalytic criticism; as he puts it, the "order" of a personal myth "has nothing timeless, abstract, or metaphysical about it," but, aiming to describe "the constancy and structured coherence of a certain group of unconscious processes," it is meaningful "only in relation to a lived-life and the processes themselves."[12] In other words, the fantasy that constitutes the myth is embodied in the fiction itself, and both are fully imbricated in the real, lived life of the author.

A "BULIMIC" FILMMAKER: FRANÇOIS OZON

Such processes are precisely what one can observe in the films of the contemporary French filmmaker François Ozon, who is perhaps the most prominent representative, internationally, of the so-called Young French Cinema. Describing himself as a "bulimic" filmmaker,[13] Ozon, since his first full-length feature film in 1998, has made fourteen features, averaging one per year, which puts him in the same category as other prolific filmmakers such as Ingmar Bergman, Rainer Werner Fassbinder, and Woody Allen, who are candid in professing that the making of fiction films is a necessity for their psychic survival. Ozon's oeuvre therefore forms a body of work that is ideal for examining why such creative activity might be necessary for the creator and, just as important, how the brain makes use of its capacity for fictive (re-)creativity to address psychic pressures that arise from an individual's emotional reaction to the circumstances of his or her developmental history or present environment.

Ozon, in interviews, has been fairly open about his reasons for making films so compulsively. The appeal of filmmaking for him is that "by telling stories, I could say many things about myself... while remaining hidden [my translation]."[14] Further illumination of the motivations behind Ozon's creative endeavor is provided by Charlotte Rampling, an actress with whom he has worked closely on a number of occasions. In an interview on *Swimming Pool*, one of Ozon's most personal films, she made the following observation:

> A director chooses characters, chooses people, either because he wants to get to know those characters, or because he knows somewhere inside himself those people are living in him, and he's not actually going to be able to, he's not going to really be those persons other than creating them through an actor and through his talent for filmmaking. I mean, he wouldn't have chosen the subject if somewhere inside himself, and perhaps he doesn't even know why, he decided that these people were going to vehicle with him something that he perhaps would find out at the end of the film.[15]

In Mauron's terms, then, the characters that Ozon invents are a means of protecting his psychic equilibrium by intercepting and controlling impulses that he fears he might be capable of, and of achieving some form of self-repair.

Ozon himself has contributed further insights into the personal dimension of the motivations that drive him. Acknowledging the emotional complexities he carries with him as a result of his family background, he observes that, in one his very first short films, *Photo de famille* (1988), he "even killed [his] parents": "They agreed to play dead people, saying to me: 'It will be a very good form of therapy. That way, you won't have to do it in reality.'" He learned, he says, that "works of art are always about one's parents, and one always needs to put into them whatever exists in the depth of oneself [my translation]."[16] "Without art," he says, "life is too hard to assume and to survive, so I need art like I need movies."[17]

Using the method outlined by Mauron, I will now identify the main strategies Ozon uses to convert his emotional life into an objectified form, showing how he constructs a personal myth in the process.

RECURRING IMAGES AND METAPHORS

One of the most striking features of Ozon's films is the "obsessive metaphors" that recur from one film to the next. Most of these images are already present in his early short films,[18] but in his feature films they are repeated over and over again in the form of symbolic locations, recurrent animal images, pairings and doublings, and other symbolic figurations.

Settings are always significant, having emblematic evocativeness. The action in Ozon's films often commences or ends at a beach or alongside a river or a lake. Even when these settings are not visible at the outset, important encounters later occur at them. In part, these recurrent images derive from an autobiographical memory of childhood occasions when Ozon's parents took the family on holidays to the Landes area of Southwest France. On one such occasion, when Ozon was nine or ten years old, he witnessed a tragedy when the husband of a couple in their sixties went for a swim and did not come back—an event that left a lasting impression on the filmmaker. This episode, which in its most elaborated form provides the whole framework for *Under the Sand* (2000), supplies the central image of the beach in the early films *A Summer Dress* (1996) and *See the Sea* (1997), and it occupies an important place in *5x2* (2004), *Time to Leave* (2005), and *Hideaway* (2009). Variants of Ozon's obsession with water—signaled when the camera lingers on a shot of the water's surface—can be found, for example, when the young pair in *Criminal Lovers* (1999) first cross (symbolically) a river and then swim in a crystal clear stream before the final disaster; at the opening of *Under the Sand*, with a shot of the Seine; and at the opening of *Swimming Pool* (2003), with a shot of the Thames. On a smaller scale, the action centers on a lake, as in *Ricky* (2009), where Katie (Alexandra Lamy) eventually goes to drown herself, or around a swimming pool, as, most notably, in *Swimming Pool* and *Sitcom* (1998). As Ozon explains, these recurrent water images are prompted by two alternative, interrelated associations: "I have often filmed water, usually the ocean which is associated in my mind with shedding one's inhibitions, or with a certain sense of fear."[19] We see this, for example, in *See the Sea*, when Sasha (Sasha Hails) leaves her sleeping baby on the beach to go into the woods, where she has anonymous sex with a stranger, or in *5x2*, when Marion (Valeria Bruni Tedeschi) warns Gilles (Stéphane Freiss), who suggests that they go for a swim when they first meet (significantly, at a beach), that "there are strong currents at this beach ... it's dangerous to swim there." Metaphorically speaking, this proves to be very true, as the marriage to which their romance then leads moves relentlessly toward train wreck and divorce. In later films, the beach is also the site where Romain (Melvil Poupaud) confronts his impending death in *Time to Leave*, as the sun sets, and where Isabelle (Marine Vacth) in *Young & Beautiful* (2013) loses her virginity to a German boy (Lucas Prisor), an event that leads her into a furtive career as a teenage prostitute. The beach, then, is a site that is symbolically associated with a significant personal transformation, almost always involving transgression of some sort. With Ozon's rivers and lakes, their surfaces, often shot at night, whether turbulent with a fast-moving current or placid, suggest the presence of hidden dangers underneath: dangers that the protagonists will encounter in the course of the action, most often in the form of latent capacities within themselves that they did not know existed prior to the experience depicted in the film.

Swimming pools, on the other hand, are associated with the stripping away of inhibitions, as is most clearly represented in the movie *Swimming Pool*, when Sarah Morton (Charlotte Rampling), an English crime writer, arrives at the country house of her publisher in the Luberon for an extended stay, during which she hopes to find inspiration for her next book. The pool is covered at first, suggesting her own repression. By degrees, it is cleared of dead leaves when a promiscuous, ebullient young woman Julie (Ludivine Sagnier) arrives and swims in it. Finally, Sarah changes places with Julie when she herself enters the pool, now pristine, which symbolizes her newfound emotional and sexual liberation.

Animals supply another class of symbolic images, suggesting either psychic states or qualities of action. One of the most striking examples occurs in *Sitcom* (1998), in which the father (François Marthouret) brings home a rat in a cage as a present. Ozon uses this rat to provide a symbolic commentary on almost all of the other members of the family in the course of the film. Whereas the mother (Évelyne Dandry) is disgusted by the rat, the son, Nicolas (Adrien de Van), is fascinated by it and takes it out of the cage. When his mother orders him to put it back into the case and wash his hands, he disobeys her by deliberately not washing his hands afterward. Soon after, when Nicolas has shocked the family by announcing at the dinner table that he is gay and the mother sends Abdu (Jules-Emmanuel Eyoum Deido), his sister's boyfriend, up to Nicolas' room to see if he can help her son, the rat bites Abdu's finger, after which Nicolas and Abdu have homosexual sex. By this point, we realize that the rat is a symbol of transgression–transgressive sex, in particular–reflected in the fact that the rat escapes from its cage as Nicolas's gay adventures escalate. After the rat is recaptured, and the mother has accused her husband of being "nothing but a rat," she herself advances on the cage, takes out the rat, strokes and then cuddles it (suggesting that it now represents what she is not getting out of her marriage) before entering Nicolas's bedroom. Finding him naked there, she masturbates him in an act of incest.

The final appearances of the rat occur near the end of the film when, in fantasy, the father takes out a pistol and shoots all of the other members of the family. After he has arranged the bodies alongside one another (recalling the similar action of the son in the early short *Photo de famille*), the rat crawls among the bodies, suggesting how the father, too, has now surrendered to a repressed transgressive impulse–which is aborted when he wakes up with the rat on his nude torso and puts it back in the cage. When the phone rings, and it turns out to be his wife calling from a therapy session saying that the rat has to be gotten rid of because it is the cause of the family's problems, the husband/father takes the rat out of the cage, microwaves it, eats the cooked carcass, and becomes transformed into a giant rat who attacks the wife when she returns, only to be stabbed to death by the daughter, Sophie (Marina de Van).

Clearly, the rat in *Sitcom* "figures forth" Ozon's sense of how the son's homosexual inclinations are regarded: as disgusting, dirty, disease-ridden, and transgressive. It also suggests the real feelings that lie repressed beneath the surface bourgeois gentility of every member of the family, underlining a degree of hypocrisy and dishonesty in the family's conventional respectability and hence the conditions of existence in his background that the filmmaker realizes he needs to grapple with.

Another highly significant animal image is a rabbit, which recurs repeatedly in Ozon's films. The most striking instance is in *Criminal Lovers*, in which a teenage pair kill an Arab boy, Saïd (Salim Kechiouche), to whom Alice (Natacha Régnier), the young heroine, is attracted, at her instigation. Her true, but disguised, feelings are revealed when, in their flight, her accomplice, Luc (Jérémie Renier), drives the car over a rabbit, which causes her distress and leads her to insist that they bury it (as they are going to bury Saïd). Then, as Luc wanders through the forest where they have buried Saïd's body, he finds a rabbit caught in a trap and frees it—just before he comes across a woodsman's hut and, spying, sees a naked older man bathing. After the woodsman (Predrag Manjlovic) has trapped the young pair and made them his prisoners, he explicitly likens Luc to "my little rabbit" and takes him outside, where he shoots a trapped rabbit and peels back the rabbit's skin so that its body looks naked. Soon after, the woodsman undresses Luc, masturbates him, and later has anal intercourse with him. Finally, after the two adolescents have escaped and gendarmes are hunting them, Luc trips, his foot caught in a rabbit trap. Thereafter, even though Alice frees him, he says he cannot go on, leaving her to escape on her own.

As with the rat image, there is much figurative work taking place in this image of the rabbit. The contexts in which it occurs in the action allow us to infer that it associates to Luc's latent but unacknowledged homosexuality. Like the rabbit, he is trapped by it: in killing Saïd, he was trying to kill off a part of himself that he did not want to acknowledge—an act that is replicated in his running over the rabbit. By exposing Luc's responsiveness to his erotic approaches, the woodsman is metaphorically, as well as literally, "stripping him bare," just as he pulls back the skin of the rabbit; and by refusing to continue on his flight with Alice, Luc, caught metaphorically in a "rabbit trap," is choosing to abide by the sexual orientation he had by then acknowledged.

Later films pick up this very evocative symbol, activating similar associations. In *Time to Leave,* a gay man, Romain (Melvil Poupaud), is informed that he is terminally ill. In an attempt to come to terms with this tragic inevitability, he conducts a literal and metaphorical detour through the archaic by visiting his childhood haunts, including the house of his grandmother (Jeanne Moreau). At night, when he is wandering in the nearby forest, where as a boy he played with his sister, he experiences a flashback memory in which he and his father find a sick rabbit. "There is no point taking him home," says the father, because "you might catch a disease." Here, again, is a powerful trope suggesting the protagonist's awareness of the way his sexual orientation would be regarded by the members of his family: as something ruinous and ultimately death-dealing, associated with disease. Ozon has acknowledged that "*Time to Leave* is . . . marked by the anxiety that my generation has experienced with regard to AIDS. Our sexual awakening came hand in hand with an acute awareness of illness and death."[20] Ozon concedes the personal relevance of this anxiety as a motivation for making the film, by revealing that he himself had had a health scare:

> When I did the test–my medical test. I think it happens very often when you're afraid of something in your life. And when it happened, I figured I had nothing, but during the time, I was waiting for the result.... during the time you are waiting for the results you think about your life, and you ask the good questions, and the things–the kind of questions you try to escape everyday in your life, you know? Suddenly, you're in front of yourself. And you have to know exactly what you want to do–who is important, what is important for you, who are important for you.... But one day, maybe I will have some bad results.[21]

Once again, Ozon's real-life remarks illustrate the imaginative signifying seriousness that underlies what might appear to be merely casual incidents or images in his fictive creations.

In a lighter vein, Ozon's rabbit reappears at the beginning of his popular comedy *Potiche* (2010), but without the high seriousness that is manifest in *Criminal Lovers* and *Time to Leave*. Like Ozon's earlier comic-noir-thriller-musical *8 Women* (2002), *Potiche*, an adaptation of a popular stage play, gives the impression of having been made to "get money by giving the public what they want," as another of his heroines, Angel (Romola Garai) cynically declares to be her intention in writing future novels, in the costume drama *Angel* (2007). Ozon has let it be known that he hoped *Potiche*, like *8 Women* (which grossed $42,426,583 worldwide), would be similarly successful so that he could "do many other things later on"–in other words, make his personal films.[22]

In keeping with its fairly cynical purpose, therefore, *Potiche* uses a camp style with a high level of contrived sentimentality and affected artifice, which seems designed to subvert and therefore apologize for the choice of such a hackneyed and conventional topic–amusing as it is, given the skill displayed in the direction by Ozon, who functions as an extremely competent *metteur en scène*. The sentimentality inherent in bourgeois affectations is displayed in the opening sequence showing Suzanne Pujol (Catherine Deneuve) jogging through the woodland of a park. Pausing for a breath, she sees a spotted fawn, a dove, and a squirrel (presented in images that recall Disney's sentimental animal films), which she registers as subjects for the banal poetry she writes. In the midst of this moment of bourgeois sentiment, however, her gaze swings to a rabbit that has mounted another and is vigorously copulating. Thus, even in the midst of what some might think is, like Angel's money-making writing, an act of bad faith, Ozon can still summon a variant of one of his favorite personal images to deliver a *clin d'oeil* (wink), perhaps to remind the spectator that he is still, beneath it all, the transgressive enfant terrible that he had earlier been reputed to be.

PAIRINGS AND DOUBLINGS IN SYMBOLIC CONFIGURATIONS

Another arresting strategy Ozon adopts is to take different parts of a single personality and project them as separate characters who are paired or doubled to establish a parallel, or contrast, or sometimes both. This kind of splitting can be expressed in a relationship between antithetical characters of the same sex, between a brother and sister, between a pair of lovers of the same age, or between an older figure and a younger figure.

The most notable doubling of the first sort—members of the same sex—occurs in *See the Sea*, in which Sasha (Sasha Sails) represents the good mother and Tatiana (Marina de Van) represents the bad, destructive mother, exemplifying between them the dual aspects of the maternal relationship in terms of the potential impact of a mother on her child. Whereas Sasha is shown cradling and nurturing her baby and changing its soiled diaper, Tatiana has had her own baby aborted and malevolently dips Sasha's toothbrush, a symbol of cleanliness, into a toilet bowl filled with unflushed excrement. The life-giving potential of the former is literally destroyed by the death-dealing potential of the latter, who kills Sasha in advance of her husband's return and sews up her vagina. These antithetical images—the one nurturing and comforting, the other castrating and destructive—reflect themes that Ozon explores obsessively in almost all of his subsequent movies.[23] Other examples of doubling between members of the same sex occur in *Time to Leave* (between Romain and his lover, who have been friends since childhood, committing transgressions together as when they pee into the holy water in a church), *Hideaway* (between Louis and his half-brother [Louis-Ronan Choisy]–a configuration that is replicated in *Potiche* in the relationship between Laurent [Jérémie Renier] and his half-brother Flavien [Noam Charlier]), and *In the House* (2012) (between Claude [Ernst Umhauer] and his heteronormative young friend Rapha [Bastien Ughetto]). In each case, the purpose of the doubling is to illustrate alternative possibilities available to the central character concerning potential states of being and courses of action.

The second kind of doubling–involving splitting between a brother and a sister–can be found in *Sitcom,* in which two siblings in real life play two fictional siblings, Nicolas (Adrien de Van) and Sophie (Marina de Van), both of whom transgress the family's norms: Nicolas by coming out as gay and Sophie, who burns her arms with cigarettes and entertains suicidal fantasies, by being a dominatrix. As their mother observes when trying to gain the attention of their detached and indifferent father, the latter has not even noticed that he has "a son who is a raging homosexual and a daughter who is a practicing sadomasochist." These designations suggest that the two siblings have been included in the fiction to designate two forms of dysfunction generated by the family dynamic in terms of the parents' idiom of care–or lack of it, in the father's case.

An alternative to this brother-sister doubling is a young pair presented as lovers, as in *Criminal Lovers,* in which Luc and Alice, both of whom are sexually attracted to Saïd, begin by being complicit in his murder, but end up opting for different paths, with Alice attempting to kill the woodsman and Luc preventing her from doing so. Symbolically, these two lovers represent alternative ways in which the hero can potentially react to his dilemma: either by seeking to kill the object of attraction, as Alice does, or by accepting the homosexual desire that the object elicits. Again, one senses that these are rival impulses within the one personality.

Finally, from time to time, Ozon doubles an older character with a younger version of his or her self, or future potential self. We see this in *Swimming Pool,* in which the outgoing, sexually liberated, and life-loving Julie is the self that Sarah Morton can potentially be. Similarly, in *Time to Leave* Romain repeatedly meets himself as a boy, as when he looks in a mirror and sees a reflection of his boy's face, or, climactically, on the beach at the end of the film, when he returns a runaway ball to himself-as-a-boy. Commenting on this pairing, Ozon says, "Perhaps the childhood images that haunt Romain are helping him to accept the child within him, so that he can let go, hand it over."[24]

An antithetical configuration of this type of doubling occurs near the end of *Young & Beautiful,* when Isabelle, after she has renounced her prostitution, meets up with Alice (Charlotte Rampling), the wife of a former client, in the room where the assignations took place, which Alice has hired for the purpose. Confessing to Isabelle that she herself wished she had been "more courageous, less timid" because she would have liked to have been paid to make love, Alice asks Isabelle to lie on the bed beside her. Having fallen asleep, Isabelle, when she wakes up, finds that Alice has gone. The purpose of this enigmatic episode is suggested by the image of the two women lying side by side, the one near the beginning of her life and the other near the end of hers: Alice is the regretful self that Isabelle can potentially be and vice versa, thus rendering paradoxical and ambiguous the perspective that the film generates on the young heroine's sexual behavior—which displays a compulsive eroticism that the earlier films anticipate, especially in their foregrounding of frequent scenes of masturbation.

"CINEGRAMS" AND REPETITIONS IN THE ACTION

Just as the recurring overdetermined images and character pairings in Ozon's films indicate a personal myth, so too does the reiteration of what one might call "cinegrams"—on the model of the "theatergrams" to be found in early modern drama[25]—that is, units of action, plot modules, topoi, character systems, and framing devices that help to shape the narrative.

The most dominant of these cinegrams are episodes in which a younger protagonist has a sexual encounter with one or more older figures. This can take the form of a threesome, or a seduction of a younger by an older character, or vice versa. The first time we see this configuration is in the early short *Victor* (1993), in which the eponymous hero, who, having shot his parents, was earlier seen in bed lying between their dead bodies, is instructed in eroticism by the maid and her lover during a threesome that provides a corrective mirror reflection of the earlier scene. Ozon later replicated this image of the hero inserting himself into the lovemaking of a couple in *Time to Leave*, when Romain inseminates Jany (Valeria Bruni Tedeschi) while her husband is making love to her. The association of this fantasy with parents is made explicit in *In the House* when the young hero, Claude, who spies on a sleeping couple, imagining them making love, says, "When it's stormy outside, don't all children dream of slipping in bed in between their parents?"

The next variant of this configuration first surfaces in the short *Une rose entre nous* (1994), in which the protagonist, Paul (Rodolphe Lesage), a young hairdresser (resembling Ozon himself), goes clubbing with a girl he has met, Rose (Sasha Hails) and attracts the attention of an older man, Yves (Francis Arnaud). Through the mediation of Rose, Paul has sex with the older man. When they are in bed together, Yves tosses aside a soft animal toy Paul has with him, which the camera afterward lingers on–significantly, a rabbit, another of Ozon's recurrent symbols–as it lies on the floor next to a used condom, suggesting a loss of childhood innocence. Thereafter, at the instigation of Rose, who pimps for him, Paul regularly prostitutes himself, always, as with her, "with old guys." Most recently, Ozon has replicated the paradigm outlined by this short film in *Young & Beautiful*, in which the seventeen-year-old Isabelle similarly prostitutes herself with older men.

The obverse situation, in which an older figure initiates a sexual encounter with a younger one, occurs in two variants: one in which the seducer is a man and the other in which the seducer is a woman. The first of these situations appears in *Criminal Lovers* when the woodsman first forces the teenaged Luc to lie with him on a bed, where he eroticizes the boy and then forceably rapes him through anal intercourse. Luc's attraction to the older man is obliquely indicated by his earlier fixation on the woodsman's naked body as he, Luc, voyeuristically watches him bathing (a scene that is replicated in *In the House,* in which Claude similarly imagines (erotically) his friend Rapha's companionable, hypermasculine father lathering up in the shower). In contrast to his inability to become aroused when his girlfriend Alice tries to have sex with him, Luc experiences orgasm with the woodsman, prompting Alice to observe bitterly, "You liked it, when he fucked you."

A less violent repetition of this configuration occurs in *Water Drops on Burning Rocks* (2000), a film based on an unpublished, unperformed play by Rainer Werner Fassbinder, in which an older man, Léopold (Bernard Giraudeau), who is fifty, brings home a youth, Franz (Malik Zidi), who is twenty, seduces him, and persuades him to move in with him. As in *Criminal Lovers,* this transfer of erotic commitment to a man entails the breakup of a heterosexual relationship between Franz and a girl of his own age, Anna (Ludivine Sagnier). Unlike in *Criminal Lovers,* however, the shift in sexual orientation does not lead to a liberation, but rather to its opposite, as Ozon has observed in commenting on the film: "Franz enters Léopold's desire and loses his identity, while the Pygmalion Léopold constantly reproduces the same schema.... Once the certainty of his power to dominate has been established, he becomes bored."[26] The destructive effect on Franz of Léopold's growing indifference to him, reflected in Léopold's seduction of Anna and his engagement of her in a threesome with his former transvestite lover Véra (Anna Thomson), prompts Franz, at the end of the film, to commit suicide in a final act of despair.

As well as these older male lover figures, Ozon's films repeatedly show his young heroes entering into sexual relations with older women. This repeated fixation begins in *Sitcom,* with the incestuous invasion of Nicolas's bedroom by his mother, where she makes love to her son in order to "help [him] find a cure" for his homosexuality. An even more striking instance of the attraction Ozon's youthful heroes feel toward older mother-figures occurs in *In the House,* in which Claude not only seduces Esther (Emmanuelle Seigner), the mother of his friend Rapha, but sleeps with Jeanne (Kristin Scott Thomas), the wife of Germain (Fabrice Luchini), his teacher, who is mentoring him to develop his skill as a writer. The most extreme variant of this particular cinegram occurs in *Time to Leave,* in the central scene in which Romain visits Laura (Jeanne Moreau), his grandmother. During the night he stays at her house, Romain (in a reversal of the comparable scene between mother and son in *Sitcom*) enters her bedroom, finds his grandmother naked in bed, and asks if he can sleep with her. Although no sexual act takes place, the incestuous overtones of this episode are suggested by the words he expresses to her: "I wish we'd met sooner, and I would have married you." Ozon has let it be known that for him, "the scene between Romain and his grandmother is the heart of the film."[27]

FANTASMATIC CONSTRUCTIONS

When all of these recurring elements are put together and viewed in terms of the interconnecting patterns they form, it becomes apparent that all of Ozon's films present displaced fantasmatic constructions dealing with a single problematic: the consequences—as in the case of many other authors discussed in this book—of narcissistic deprivation deriving from disturbed attachment bonds, together with the protagonist's attempts to find a way of responding to the legacy of the perturbations they entail. Between them, these films explore the full spectrum of possibilities relating to such a syndrome in an effort to identify the sources of the problem and to effect its repair—or at least to find a way of managing the perturbing emotions that linger as its legacy.

The problematic at the heart of Ozon's films is manifest in a number of recurrent preoccupations, the basic paradigm for which is laid out in his first full-length feature, *Sitcom*. As the film opens, the first focus of attention is the father, who, in a flash-forward, arrives home and (offscreen) shoots the members of his family. Near the end of the film, this episode is replayed, and this time we not only see him take out a pistol and fire at them, but also see his arranging of their bodies alongside one another. As it turns out, his actions have merely taken place in a dream: the father wakes up when he hears the phone ringing and finds it is a call from his wife, who has been attending a therapy session, suggesting that his dream was merely a wish fulfillment fantasy. Viewed from his perspective, this fantasmatic episode might suggest that the father is simply frustrated at the banality of his bourgeois existence. If the perspective is changed to that of the family, however, the homicidal violence of the dream material can equally suggest the effect that the father has on the other family members. As the movie proceeds, we see that he is remote and neglectful. He is indifferent to his son's homosexuality and his daughter's sadomasochism, saying to his distressed wife, "It'll pass," without even looking up from his newspaper. His lack of investment in his children is troped in the image that follows of him putting on a blindfold before going to sleep, metaphorically suggesting his willful blindness to the difficulties they are experiencing. The father has, in fact, washed his hands of any responsibility for parenting his children: "I'm no longer involved in their upbringing–they're free adults," to which the wife replies, "You never were involved.... You're nothing but... a rat!" To make matters worse, he is constantly uttering philosophical platitudes–as when, for example, in reacting to Nicolas's excitement about some new clothes the youth has bought on sale, he kills his son's pleasure by saying, "Remember Nicolas, 'Clothes don't make the man.'" The effect of the father's parenting on Nicolas is to fill the latter with a fear that he is unloved: "Dad, do you love me?... You seem ashamed of me. Maybe I'm not the son you wanted. You're disappointed." The father's tepid reassurances do nothing to allay the son's anxieties, and for good reason, because soon after, when Sophie asks her father whether he knows about the incest taking place between Nicolas and his mother, the father answers, "Of course," adding, "I don't think incest will solve the problems of western civilization," which once again demonstrates his indifference and affective detachment.

In Ozon's subsequent movies, it is as if his youthful heroes are constantly reacting to the sense of emotional deprivation with which the absence of paternal interest and affection fills them. In many of the films, the father of the protagonist is quite literally absent, or only briefly present (for example, in *Water Drops on Burning Rocks, 8 Women, Swimming Pool, Angel,* and *In the House*). However, his presence is constantly sought in the form of the older lovers with whom these characters seek sexual encounters.

At the midpoint of *Criminal Lovers,* Ozon's next film after *Sitcom,* Arthur Rimbaud's prose poem "Nuit en enfer" is recited in flashback to provide a symbolic commentary on the suffering that parental failings inflict on children:

> I have swallowed quite a mouthful of poison....–My entrails burn. The violence of the venom twists my limbs, deforms me, throws me to the ground. I'm dying of thirst. I am suffocating, I can't cry out. This is hell, eternal punishment. See how the flames rise. I'm burning as I should. Go, demon!... I believe I'm in hell, so I am. The catechism is at work. I am slave to my baptism. *Parents, you made my misfortune* [my italics] and you made your own. Poor innocent!–Hell cannot attack pagans.–I'm still alive! Later, damnation's delights will be more profound. Quick, a crime, so that I may fall into the void, by human law [my translation].[28]

One notes that it is not just the father who is blamed but "parents"–a joint responsibility that also finds expression in Ozon's films in the form of a corresponding overinvestment on the part of the mother that is also a source of perturbation, as much as the closeness and security it represents is sought avidly, as one sees in *Sitcom* and *In the House,* in the incestuous relationship Nicolas forms with his mother in the former and the sexual liaisons Claude undertakes with older women in the latter.

In one remarkable film, however, *Ricky* (2009), Ozon fantasmatically presents a son, this time a baby, who succeeds, through magic, in escaping from an overinvested relationship with the mother. In typical fashion, Ozon splits the elements at issue in this syndrome between two characters: Lisa (Mélusine Mayance), Ricky's older half sister, and Ricky (Arthur Peyret), the baby himself. Whereas the emotional deprivation seen in other of Ozon's young heroes is projected through Lisa, a remedy for that deprivation is depicted through Ricky and what his experience represents. Lisa has an absent father, who lives in the South and will not see his daughter. When her new male companion, Paco (Sergi López), asks Lisa's mother Katie (Alexandra Lamy) whether her daughter misses "having a dad," Katie answers: "No, I don't think so. We're a team," thus revealing the existence of a cross-generational bond in which the child takes the place of the spouse who is missing from what should be the marital relationship. This bond is deepened when Katie expels Paco from the house, believing that he has been physically abusing the baby, and Katie and Lisa comfort each other. After the baby has sprouted wings, the bond is extended to him, who in turn becomes a substitute for Paco: "I don't think of Paco now Ricky has wings," confesses Katie.

This overinvestment in Ricky has unfortunate consequences. Fearful of Ricky's being seen by others, because "he is different" once he is capable of flying, Katie and Lisa pin a blanket over the top of his crib to prevent him from getting out, thus turning it literally and symbolically into a barred "cage." As Ozon has said in an interview, Katie's "maternal instinct tends to be selfish, claustrophobic and a little bit castrating." Just as he illustrated two facets of the maternal instinct in *See the Sea*–"the good mother and the monstrous mother"–by embodying them in two very different women, in *Ricky,* he says, "these two aspects are present in the same mother, Katie."[29] To escape the monstrous aspect, Ricky needs to get away from her, which he does by literally flying away, leaving Katie so depressed that she is on the verge of committing suicide (by drowning herself in the lake) and is only saved by Ricky's temporary return before he flies away once again. Manifestly, then, in this film Ozon is presenting a need for separation as one remedy for the legacy of emotional pain that can arise from disruptions to healthy bonds of attachment. Only once Katie has let go of Ricky, accepting that she cannot keep him with her forever, is she able to become reunited with Paco and her daughter, and that the family unit can again be happy, symbolized in the fact that Katie is once again pregnant as the film ends.

STRATEGIES OF DISPLACEMENT

It can now be seen that filmmaking, for Ozon, allows him to address different aspects of a personal problematic through the imaginative displacement that fictive creativity entails. Ozon has been candid about his need to maintain a degree of distance between himself and his fictive creations, even when they are projecting dimensions of his own experience, as is the case with *Time to Leave*, one of his most personal films:

> I realized how it was difficult for me to do a film with a male character. Because sometimes I had the feeling to be in front of a mirror. And I realized, as a director, I need to have distance with the characters. In fact, to work with a woman is so much easier for me. Because you know, the character [Romain] is younger than me but he could be me. So sometimes I didn't like the character, because it was too close. So it was a real challenge for me to do the film.[30]

It is therefore not surprising to find that both prior to *Time to Leave* and since, Ozon has chosen to address his concerns through female characters who are, in fact, projections of parts of himself. In *Swimming Pool*, for example, the younger figure, Julie, is not merely a younger double for Sarah Morton but also a variant of Ozon's earlier rebellious and transgressive male avatars such as Nicolas in *Sitcom* and Luc in *Criminal Lovers*—an identification that is confirmed by the fact that, according to Ozon, "originally Ludivine's part [Julie] was going to be a boy's," which demonstrates how the genders of his protagonists are entirely interchangeable in Ozon's imaginary.[31] Furthermore, Ozon admits that the character of Sarah Morton herself is equally a projection of himself: "It occurred to me that the best way of answering these questions [about the sources of his inspiration] might be to project myself into the character of a female English novelist, rather than offering an analysis of myself as a filmmaker."[32] This highly conscious reversal of genders is a device through which Ozon projects himself again in *Angel*, another story depicting the creative process and fantasy world of an artist.[33] One also suspects that Isabelle in *Young & Beautiful* is one of Ozon's personal fantasmatic projections given that he used the same scenario, of a teenager selling his body to older men for cash, in one of his early films, *Une rose entre nous*, with the difference that in this instance the teenage prostitute was a male. Ozon indirectly says as much during an interview in which he was asked whether it had been a challenge to write from the perspective of a seventeen-year-old girl: "I was a teenager, a long time ago! I have many memories. Even if I wasn't a girl, it's the same thing. The discovery of sexuality, the violence of relationships with parents, it's always the same story."[34]

Splitting, gender reversal, and projection are not the only strategies Ozon uses to displace his personal concerns. The adaptation of preexisting literary sources also allows him the distance he needs, but in each case the changes he makes to the source text reveal the presence of his personal investment. In *Angel*, for example, although most of the details of the plot are taken directly from Elizabeth Taylor's novel of the same name, Ozon adds an important new element that is wholly of his own invention–the issue of having a child and being childless. Once her literary career has taken flight, Angel informs her disappointed mother: "I don't have time for a child ... I have my work." Her attitude contrasts with that of Esmé, her husband, who is desperate to have a child–so desperate, in fact, that when Angel miscarries while he is overseas on military service during World War I, she does not inform him, fearing that he won't come home if he finds out. Later, when he does finally return, after conducting a secret affair with a mistress, he attempts to rape Angel in a drunken stupor "to give her a baby, a little baby boy." Finally, after Esmé has hanged himself and Angel has become impoverished and semideranged, she asks her friend Nora: "Do you think that if I had had a baby, Esmé would still be alive?" None of these details are in the source, but they do link up with a recurrent preoccupation in Ozon's films with the childlessness of gay men and the question of how a gay man can propagate a child and leave a legacy. Nicolas in *Sitcom*, after he announces that he is gay, wryly observes to his parents that they will never have grandchildren; in *5x2*, Christophe (Antoine Chappey), the hero's brother, discusses with his gay lover the possibility of supplying sperm for artificial insemination; and in *Time to Leave*, Romain actually impregnates a woman with a baby to whom he bequeaths his possessions. For Ozon, then, a source can be adapted in such a way as to turn it into a vehicle for the exploration of issues that the reiteration of such motifs suggests are of personal importance to him.

THE PURPOSES OF OZON'S CINEMATIC FANTASIES

The purposes that the fantasies constructed in Ozon's films serve become obvious if one appraises the outcomes to which the actions of the protagonists lead, correlating these with the basic emotions discussed earlier in this book.

In one way or another, allowing for Ozon's characteristic strategies of displacement, virtually all of his films are about family relationships. *Sitcom* gives expression to RAGE at the combined impact of a father's remoteness and a mother's excessive closeness, eventuating in a fantasmatic assassination of the father, converted metaphorically into a gigantic rat. *Under the Sand* mourns the absence of the longed for father by displacing it into the ineradicable GRIEF experienced by a woman at the disappearance of her husband, while *Time to Leave* deepens that grief by extending it into the hero's sense of his almost total isolation when he has to confront the imminence of his own death. *Ricky*, on the other hand, dramatizes a fantasy of escape in which a child self, imaged as a baby with wings, simply flies away from the family that threatens to imprison him.

Many of Ozon's films explore the father-hunger that arises from the emotional deprivation inflicted by an uninvolved father, especially as this relates to sexual identity and modes of sexual behavior. *Criminal Lovers*, at a symbolic level, provides the most paradigmatic expression of what this father-hunger means for the protagonist. After having his sexual inclinations exposed by the woodsman's advances, just as the body of the rabbit is revealed when the woodsman skins it, Luc seeks to escape his imprisonment in the woodsman's hut. To do so, he peels back a sheet from the sleeping woodsman, takes the key from around his neck, and frees Alice, who is trapped in the cellar. Here is another example of an emotional awareness being symbolically troped in the action: even though Luc wants to leave the realm of the woodsman, it is the key around his neck–in other words, his sexual orientation–that is literally and metaphorically the key that can release the repressed version of his self from imprisonment. Luc's preventing Alice from killing the woodsman shows that what he represents must "live on" even once the hero has escaped into the wider world. Once he is there, however, after a brief idyll with Alice, Luc is captured, Alice is shot dead, and the woodsman is taken prisoner, suggesting that the real world does not readily accommodate such a solution.

For this reason, another group of Ozon's films show how their protagonists seek refuge in an alternative world created through the imagination. *Swimming Pool* depicts the transformative effects of the creative process by showing how fantasy and reality become so mingled in the mind of Sarah Morton as she writes her new book that by the end neither she nor we can tell which is which. Significantly, it is immersion in this creative process that allows Sarah to escape from her father-hunger. At the beginning of the film, when she visits her publisher–another older man who is a father-figure–she complains to him: "You don't look after me any more." By the end of the film, she informs him that she does not need him anymore, having published her "different" book elsewhere.

Angel and *In the House* similarly depict protagonists who escape into a fantasy world they construct for themselves. Angel's romantic fantasies make her very rich, allowing her to escape the "hideousness" of her prior existence in Norley, where she lived with her mother above a grocery store–the father, significantly, again being absent. This film, however, unlike *Swimming Pool*, raises a question about how lasting such a solution can be. In addition to the source, Ozon has Angel, as she is dying, say to her lesbian devotee, Nora, "So you think I've lived the wrong life? Do you think it's all really a dream? None of it was real." To which Nora replies: "No sweet Angel, of course it was real–your life has been magnificent. You live in Paradise House and you're a great writer. You are impassioned, passionately loved." By this point, the film has developed a sufficient number of ironies for the spectator to see that such a viewpoint is illusory. Angel herself realizes this in her dying words: "The only person who ever really loved me, Nora, was you." Thus, in *Angel* Ozon paradoxically undermines his own strategy for dealing with the painfulness of life, even while extravagantly indulging it in the luxurious realization of the film.

In the House betrays no such ambivalence. Like Angel, Claude lives in abject lower-class conditions, but this time with a disabled father for whom he must care, the mother having left them when Claude was a child–another instance of reversal. Writing a story is a means by which Claude can attract the attention of an alternative father, in the form of his teacher, Germain, who takes an interest in him and becomes his mentor. Through the process of the evolving fiction, in which reality and fantasy again become confused, both Claude and Germain become obsessed with the story, to the point where Germain is ruined. At the end of the film, the two are shown sitting together on a park bench, looking at a block of apartments and wondering who lives in them. Concurring with Claude that "there's always a way in," Germain agrees to help him, which prompts Claude to utter the final words of the film: "Mr Germain had lost everything. His wife, his job. But I was there, at his side. Ready to tell him another story. *To be continued.*" It would appear, then, that despite the doubt expressed in *Angel*, this film reaffirms the creation of fiction as a means of replacing a missing but desired parent-son relationship with a fantasmatic one that is sustaining, irrespective of the disadvantages it may entail relative to life in the real world.

Standing back from these works, one can see that they present fantasies of self-discovery, self-disclosure, and self-repair. This process of fantasmatic construction encompasses the evacuation of unwanted violent and sadistic impulses as well as the incorporation of wish fulfillment fantasies. It also allows for the registration of doubt and skepticism in addition to hopes for the future. *Water Drops on Burning Rocks, 5x2,* and *Hideaway*, for example, all express perturbation at the thought that the protagonist is in search of something elusive that might never be found–reflected in the impermanence or disintegration of treasured relationships, or in a fear that finding a satisfactory relationship is impossible. On occasions, the protagonists engage in compensatory transgression or take refuge in eroticism as a means of self-medication, but here, too, even as with the escape provided by creativity itself, the effectiveness of the solution being entertained is put in doubt, as the ambiguities of the ending of Ozon's recent film, *Young & Beautiful*, confirms. In spite of intrusions of ambivalence, though, there is a feeling that the fantasies in these films are working toward a solution. At the very least, they manifest a determination not to allow the potential emotional perturbations that motivate them from gaining a tyrannical ascendancy.

To what extent is Ozon conscious of what he has done in the fictions he has created? Without further comment from the filmmaker himself, it is impossible to determine this. From time to time, Ozon refers to psychoanalysts he has consulted on various aspects of his fictive representations, as when dealing with Isabelle's "visceral need" to repeat her compulsive sexual encounters in *Young & Beautiful*,[35] which would suggest that he is aware of a psychological explanation for the syndromes he depicts. On other occasions, though, he emphasizes the unconscious dimension of his creative process: "It's a long journey, you know. I really believe in the work of the unconscious. You have an idea, you think about it. You dream about it . . . . for me, it's my way of working."[36] This would suggest, to the contrary, that much of the work that goes into the creation of his fictive fantasies takes place at an unconscious level, which is consistent with the patterns of recurring symbolic figuration that the analysis in this chapter has revealed. Whatever the case, Ozon's oeuvre demonstrates how the imaginative capacity of the human brain draws on its creative powers to invent fictions that enable both the creator and those who receive his or her fictive representations to deal with the emotional promptings that evolution has developed to ensure their psychic survival.

Conclusion

The neuropsychoanalytic synthesis proposed in this book suggests that the twin processes of fictive creation and reception are much more multidimensional than previous theories have allowed. More than the rational part of the mind is involved in the creation of literary and cinematic fictions, and texts do not write themselves. A multitude of factors enter into the process that eventuates in a fictive representation: the emotions activated by specific contexts that motivate the creation of a story; the models of perception and response that have become wired into the brain as a result of their biographical circumstances; the memories, both unconscious and conscious, that supply images constituting the symbolic figurations out of which narratives are constructed; the application of rational reflection during the shaping of the story and its interpretation; the polyphonic associations that inhere in the representation for both the author/auteur and the reader/spectator; and the intersubjective transaction that takes place between the author/auteur and the respondent during the process of reception. All of these things make a work of fiction a much more complex entity than can be explained simply in terms of the machineries of language, the computational facility of humans' rational capacities, the influence of socially encoded and constructed discursive practices, or the somatic reactions aroused in the reader/spectator by the embodied simulations found in fiction.

The functions that fictive representations serve, for both those who create them and those who consume them, involve a purpose that is far more immediate than merely attesting to the differential mechanisms or language or the primacy of cultural discourses. Human beings invent stories, I have suggested, as a means of addressing preoccupations fundamental to the experience of being human. Because these preoccupations arise from emotions hardwired into the human brain, being activated by certain situations encountered in the external environment, they turn out to be recurrent, and many of them relate to universal experiences: the excitement inherent in curiosity and exploration; the panic aroused by disturbed attachments and the prospect of separation or abandonment; the grief that results from loss; the rage kindled when something valued or desired is withheld or taken away; the fear induced by the perception of threatening danger; the passion that drives one to seek the object of one's desire; and the curiosity that impels one to test the viability of something different or new. Such experiences are ubiquitous in fiction, suggesting the existence of certain universals that arise from the mammalian brain with which evolution has equipped human beings—universals which make the postmodern rejection of any form of "essentialism" too extreme. There may be nothing essential in the cultural beliefs and practices that different societies adopt—and in exposing this fact, postmodernist relativism has done the world a service—but there certainly *is* something "essential" in the forces that drive human beings to seek to restore and enhance their emotional equilibrium through the creation and consumption of stories. In this respect, I believe, the evolutionary critics are right in proposing that literature (and by extension cinema) constitutes an adaptation—a tool designed by evolution to help ensure humans' psychic health and, as a consequence, their biological survival.

Then again, there is the sheer joy that authors experience from the act of creation. As Jean Genet wrote:

> Through writing I have attained what I was seeking. What will guide me, as something learned, is not what I have lived, but the tone in which I tell of it. Not the anecdotes, but the work of art. Not my life, but the interpretation of it. It is what language offers me to evoke it, to talk about it, render it. To achieve my legend.[1]

This kind of deep satisfaction is felt by many authors, and it is what compels them to keep on creating new works, year after year—not merely because it gives them insight into themselves, but because it enables them to impart some shape and meaning to their existence, and to gain some deep satisfaction from the act of doing so. Commensurately, through the power of literature to "transport" one, or the power of cinema to induce a form of "hypnosis," the reader/spectator is able to share in this authorial experience through the imaginative creativity invested in his or her response.

In fact, it is the human ability to construct fantasies composed of images arranged into symbolic figurations, through the expressive language of "montage," as Eisenstein conceived it, that enables apperception, accommodating affective intelligence, itself. While the impulse for this creative activity arises from the emotions, there is nothing simple or mechanistic about the creative process. Indeed, the coexistence of diverse, sometimes competing emotions in the mind of an author and the ability to blend them in countless idiosyncratic ways—combined with the endless differences between individuals in terms of the biographical experiences that supply the storehouse of memories from which an author draws his or her images—means that there are limitless possibilities in the creative process, which is infinitely variable from one artist to another. Some authors seem more profound than others, and some fictive works strike us as richer and more complex than others. This is because the inventive capacity of an accomplished author is greater, and his or her emotional experience more complex, as one sees with Shakespeare and Truffaut, whose fictive works strike us as paradoxical in their blend of competing emotions.

The theory propounded in this book has many implications for society and its institutions. If fiction has the functions I have been ascribing to it, then it is important for society to encourage and foster its creation, as well as to support the exposure of its members to fictive representations at appropriate stages of their education. The intersubjective dimension in fictive works means that they are capable of inducing empathy, and empathy in turn leads to an expansion of the imagination, and hence promotes tolerance and an ethic of care. The experience of literary and cinematic works, therefore, has a civilizing function that works to the good of a society at large.

For this reason, educational institutions have a particular responsibility to preserve this function. Furthermore, at the very least, those academic disciplines involved in the study of literature, cinema, and other forms of fictive representation should ensure that their curricula and methodological approaches allow sufficient scope for scholars and students to explore the nature and working of the creative processes involved in authorship and reception that I have been describing. Imaginative fictions are far more than entertainment: they are a strategy that human beings have devised, as the human brain enlarged and became more complex, to help ensure their very survival. To return to Sir Philip Sidney, from whose *Apology for Poetry* the title of this book is taken, "poetry" (that is, fictive representation) takes precedence among other branches of learning because it makes men and women "know that goodness whereunto they are moved," which is "the noblest scope to which ever any learning was directed."[2]

NOTES

INTRODUCTION

1. Matthew Arnold, "The Study of Poetry," in *The Complete Prose Works of Matthew Arnold*, vol. 9, ed. R. H. Super (Ann Arbor: University of Michigan Press, 1973), 161–162.
2. For an overview of the evolution of "Grand Theory," see D. N. Rodowick, "An Elegy for Theory," *October* 122 (Fall 2007): 91–109.
3. Christopher Butler, *Postmodernism: A Very Short Introduction* (Oxford, U.K.: Oxford University Press, 2002), 25.
4. See, for example, David Bordwell and Noël Carroll, *Post-Theory: Reconstructing Film Studies* (Madison: University of Wisconsin Press, 1996).
5. Sergei Eisenstein, *The Problems of Film Direction* (Honolulu, HI: University Press of the Pacific, 2004), 27.
6. André Bazin, *What Is Cinema?* vol. 1, trans. Hugh Gray (Berkeley: University of California Press, 2004), 62.
7. Sergei M. Eisenstein, *The Psychology of Composition*, ed. and trans. Alan Upchurch (London: Methuen, 1988), 3.
8. Ibid., 8, 12.
9. Eisenstein, *Problems of Film Direction*, 45.
10. See Dudley Andrew, "Foreword to the 2004 Edition," in André Bazin, *What Is Cinema?*, vol. 2, trans. Hugh Gray (Berkeley: University of California Press, 2004), xx–xxii.
11. See Julia Vassilieva, "Eisenstein/Vygotsky/Luria's Project: Cinematic Thinking and the Integrative Science of Mind and Brain," *Screening the Past* 38 (December 2013), http://www.screeningthepast.com/2013/12/eisenstein-vygotsky-luria's-project-cinematic-thinking-and-the-integrative-science-of-mind-and-brain/.
12. Vassilieva, "Eisenstein/Vygotsky/Luria's Project.
13. Antonio Damasio, *Self Comes to Mind: Constructing the Conscious Brain* (New York: Pantheon Books, 2010), 71.
14. Eric Kandel, "Biology and the Future of Psychoanalysis: A New Intellectual Framework for Psychiatry Revisited," *American Journal of Psychiatry* 156, no. 4 (1999): 505–524.

15. See, in particular, Mark Solms and Oliver Turnbull, *The Brain and the Inner World: An Introduction to the Neuroscience of Subjective Experience* (New York: Other Press, 2002).

16. See, for example, Joseph Carroll, *Literary Darwinism: Evolution, Human Nature, and Literature* (New York: Routledge, 2004).

17. See Isabel Jaén and Julien Jacques Simon, eds., *Cognitive Literary Studies: Current Themes and Directions* (Austin: University of Texas Press, 2012).

18. Damasio, *Self Comes to Mind*, 177.

19. Ibid., 3.

20. See, in particular, Jaak Panksepp, *Affective Neuroscience: The Foundations of Human and Animal Emotions* (New York: Oxford University Press, 1998); and Panksepp and Lucy Biven, *The Archaeology of Mind: Neuroevolutionary Origins of Human Emotions* (New York: W. W. Norton, 2012).

21. Philip Sidney, *An Apology for Poetry or The Defence of Poesy*, ed. Geoffrey Shepherd (Manchester, U.K.: Manchester University Press, 1973), 100.

22. John Milton, *The Reason of Church Government*, in *John Milton: Complete Poems and Major Prose*, ed. Merritt Y. Hughes (Indianapolis, IN: Odyssey Press, 1957), 669.

1. CHANGING CONFIGURATIONS IN THEORIES OF FICTIVE REPRESENTATION

1. Aristotle, "The Origins of Poetry," from *Poetics* (chap. 1), in *Classical Literary Criticism*, ed. D. A. Russell and Michael Winterbottom (Oxford: Oxford University Press, 1989), 54.

2. Ibid., 57.

3. Plutarch, "De Gloria Atheniensium," in *Moralia*, vol. 4, 346F, Loeb Classical Library ed. (Cambridge, MA: Harvard University Press, 1936), 501.

4. Horace, *Ars Poetica*, lines 333–334, *Satires, Epistles and Ars Poetica*, trans. H. Rushton Fairclough (Cambridge, MA: Loeb Classical Library, 1942), 478.

5. Ibid., lines 343–344, 478.

6. Ibid., line 361, 480. For further comment on the views of these classical theorists, see Leonard Barkan, *Mute Poetry, Speaking Pictures* (Princeton, NJ: Princeton University Press, 2013), 28–48.

7. Plato, *The Republic and Other Works* (bk. 10), trans. B. Jowett (New York: Dolphin Books, 1960), 297.

8. Ibid., 299.

9. Augustine, *On Christian Doctrine*, trans. J. F. Shaw (New York: Dover Publications, 2009), 3.

10. *L'Ovide moralisé*, lines 13225–13226. See Joel N. Feimer, "Medea in Ovid's *Metamorphoses* and the *Ovide Moralisé*: Translation," *Florilegium* 8 (1986): 40–55, http://journals.hil.unb.ca/index.php/flor/article/viewFile/18844/20658.

11. See R. Howard Bloch, *The Scandal of the Fabliaux* (Chicago: University of Chicago Press, 1986), 11.

12. For a detailed examination of the intersection of these forces, see Alistair Fox, *The English Renaissance: Identity and Representation in Elizabethan England* (Oxford, U.K.: Blackwell Publishers, 1997).

13. Thomas More, *The Yale Edition of the Complete Works of St. Thomas More, Volume 6: A Dialogue Concerning Heresies*, ed. Thomas M. C. Lawler, Germain Marc'hadour, and Richard C. Marius (New Haven: Yale University Press, 1981), 46.

14. Ibid., 56.
15. Ibid., 46–47.
16. Philip Sidney, *An Apology for Poetry or The Defence of Poesy*, ed. Geoffrey Shepherd with an introduction and notes by R. W. Maslen (Manchester: Manchester University Press, 1973), 108.
17. Ibid., 101.
18. Stephen Halliwell, *The Aesthetics of Mimesis: Ancient Texts and Modern Problems* (Princeton, NJ: Princeton University Press, 2002), 22.
19. Ibid.,100–101.
20. Ibid., 103.
21. Ibid., 106.
22. Ibid., 107.
23. Ibid.
24. Stephen Gosson, *The schoole of abuse conteining a plesaunt inuectiue against poets, pipers, plaiers, iesters, and such like caterpillers of a comonwelth; setting vp the hagge of defiance to their mischieuous exercise, [and] ouerthrowing their bulwarkes, by prophane writers, naturall reason, and common experience: a discourse as pleasaunt for gentlemen that fauour learning, as profitable for all that wyll follow virtue* (London: Thomas Woodcocke, 1579). Both Sidney and Gosson use "poetry" in the broader Elizabethan sense, as signifying any representation that results from fictive invention or is heightened by the artifice of rhetoric.
25. Alexander Pope, *The Poetical Works of Alexander Pope, Esq, to which is prefixed the Life of the Author* (London: J. Walker, 1808), 50.
26. William Wordsworth, "Preface to the *Lyrical Ballads*," in Russell Noyes, *English Romantic Poetry and Prose* (New York: Oxford University Press, 1956), 358.
27. Samuel Taylor Coleridge, *Biographia Literaria* (chap. 13), in *The Portable Coleridge*, ed. I. A. Richards (New York: Viking Press, 1950), 516.
28. Isaiah Berlin, *The Crooked Timber of Humanity: Chapters in the History of Ideas*, ed. Henry Hardy (Princeton: Princeton University Press, 2013), 96–97.
29. See Ian Watt, *The Rise of the Novel: Studies in Defoe, Richardson, and Fielding* (Berkeley: University of California Press, 1957).
30. This slogan was popularized by the poet Ezra Pound (see Michael North, "The Making of It New," *Guernica*, August 15, 2013, http://www.guernicamag.com/features/the-making-of-making-it-new/).
31. T. S. Eliot, "Tradition and the Individual Talent," *Perspecta* 19 (1982, repr.): 36–42, 39.
32. Ibid., 42.
33. Ibid., 37.
34. For arguments linking the Enlightenment to fascism, see Max Horkheimer, *Eclipse of Reason* (London: Continuum, 2004 [1957]), and Horkheimer, Theodor W. Adorno, and Gunzelin Schmid Noerr, *Dialectic of Enlightenment: Philosophical Fragments* (Stanford, CA: Stanford University Press, 2002).
35. Robert Stam, *Film Theory: An Introduction* (Malden, MA: Blackwell, 2000), 181.
36. Christian Metz, *The Imaginary Signifier: Psychoanalysis and the Cinema* (Bloomington: Indiana University Press, 1982), 151.
37. Ibid., 116.
38. Ibid.

39. Slavoj Žižek, *Enjoy Your Symptom! Jacques Lacan in Hollywood and Out* (New York: Routledge, 2001), 216.

40. Gilles Deleuze, "Bergson's Conception of Difference," in *Desert Islands: And Other Texts, 1953–1974* (Paris: Semiotexte, 2004), 32–33.

41. Frank B. Farrell, *Why Does Literature Matter?* (Ithaca, NY: Cornell University Press, 2004), 5.

42. Roland Barthes and Stephen Heath, *Image, Music, Text* (New York: Hill and Wang, 1977), 142–148.

43. Hall, *Representation*, 1–11.

44. Ibid., 6.

45. See Christopher Bollas, *The Infinite Question* (London: Routledge, 2009), loc. 197 (Kindle ed.).

46. Sigmund Freud, Interpretation of Dreams (pt. 1), in James Strachey, Sigmund Freud, and Anna Freud, *The Standard Edition of the Complete Psychological Works of Sigmund Freud,* trans. James Strachey et al., vol. 4 (London: Vintage, 2001).

47. Ibid., 282.

48. Ernest Jones, *Hamlet and Oedipus* (London: V. Gollancz, 1949).

49. Norman Norwood Holland, *5 Readers Reading* (New Haven, CT: Yale University Press, 1975), xi.

50. Harold Bloom, *The Western Canon: The Books and School of the Ages* (London: Papermac, 1995), 350, 358.

51. Holland, *Literature and the Brain*, 235, 239–240.

52. Peter Brooks, *Reading for the Plot: Design and Intention in Narrative* (Cambridge, MA: Harvard University Press, 1992), xiii, 112.

53. Ibid., 48.

54. Ibid., 100.

55. Ibid., 102.

56. Ibid., 103.

57. Ibid.

58. Jacques Lacan, "Le séminaire sur 'La Lettre volée,'" in *Écrits* (Paris: editions du Seuil, 1966), 11–61; trans. Jeffrey Mehlman as "Seminar on 'The Purloined Letter,'" in *French Freud: Structural Studies in Psychoanalysis,* Yale French Studies, 48 (New Haven, CT: Yale University, 1972).

59. Jacques Lacan, *The Psychoses: The Seminar of Jacques Lacan,* ed. Jacques-Alain Miller, Book III 1955–1956, trans. Russell Grigg (New York: Norton, 1993), 274.

60. Slavoj Žižek, *Enjoy Your Symptom! Jacques Lacan in Hollywood and Out,* rev. ed. (New York: Routledge, 2001), 52.

61. Ibid., 216.

62. Two recent books, both of which emphasize the role of the body in responses to fiction, suggest a growing backlash against the Lacanian/Žižekian version of psychoanalytic theory: Luke Hockley, *Somatic Cinema: The Relationship between Body and Screen—A Jungian Perspective* (New York: Routledge, 2014), and Agnieszka Piotrowska, ed., *Embodied Encounters: New Approaches to Psychoanalysis and Cinema* (New York: Routledge, 2014).

63. Hanna Segal, "A Psychoanalytic Approach to Aesthetics," in *The Work of Hanna Segal: A Kleinian Approach to Clinical Practice* (New York: J. Aronson, 1981), 185–206, esp. 188.

64. Ibid., 189.

65. Ibid.
66. Northrop Frye, *Anatomy of Criticism: Four Essays* (Princeton, NJ: Princeton University Press, 1957), 17.
67. Ibid., 16ff.
68. See Terry Eagleton, *After Theory* (New York: Basic Books, 2003), 2.
69. David Bordwell and Noël Carroll, *Post-Theory: Reconstructing Film Studies* (Madison: University of Wisconsin Press, 1996), xiii.
70. See D. N. Rodowick, "An Elegy for Theory," *October* 122 (Fall 2007): 91–109.
71. See Torben Kragh Grodal, *Embodied Visions: Evolution, Emotion, Culture, and Film* (Oxford, U.K.: Oxford University Press, 2009).
72. F. Elizabeth Hart, "Foreword," in Jaén and Simon, *Cognitive Literary Studies*, x–xi.
73. Patrick Colm Hogan, *The Mind and Its Stories: Narrative Universals and Human Emotion* (Cambridge, U.K.: Cambridge University Press, 2003), 9.
74. Ibid., 4.
75. Patrick Colm Hogan, "Introduction" in *How Authors' Minds Make Stories* (Cambridge, U.K.: Cambridge University Press, 2013).
76. Brian Boyd, *On the Origin of Stories: Evolution, Cognition, and Fiction* (Cambridge, MA: Belknap Press of Harvard University Press, 2009), 15.
77. Ibid., 86–89.
78. Ibid., 157–158.
79. Arthur P. Shimamura, ed., *Psychocinematics: Exploring Cognition at the Movies* (Oxford, U.K.: Oxford University Press, 2013).
80. Paul B. Armstrong, *How Literature Plays with the Brain: The Neuroscience of Reading and Art* (Baltimore: Johns Hopkins University Press, 2013), loc. 28 (Kindle ed.).
81. An even more uncompromisingly functionalist account of film as an embodied process is presented in Shimamura, *Psychocinematics*.
82. Torben Kragh Grodal, *Moving Pictures: A New Theory of Film Genres, Feelings, and Cognition* (Oxford: Clarendon Press, 1999), 278, 281.
83. Ibid. For a critique of Grodal's theory, see Nicolas Tredell, *Cinemas of the Mind: A Critical History of Film Theory* (Cambridge: Icon, 2002), 205–214.
84. Grodal, *Embodied Visions*, loc. 73 (Kindle ed.).
85. Grodal, *Moving Pictures*, 281.
86. Sidney, *Apology for Poetry*, 103.
87. Joseph E. LeDoux, *Synaptic Self: How Our Brains Become Who We Are* (New York: Viking, 2002), 202. For LeDoux's detailed discussion of the shortcomings of cognitivist approaches, see 23–24.
88. Patricia Ticineto Clough and Jean O'Malley Halley, eds., *The Affective Turn: Theorizing the Social* (Durham, NC: Duke University Press, 2007).
89. Eric Kandel, "Biology and the Future of Psychoanalysis: A New Intellectual Framework for Psychiatry Revisited," *American Journal of Psychiatry* 156, no. 4 (1999): 505–524.
90. Ibid.
91. Ibid.
92. Holland, *Literature and the Brain*, 22, 42–43.
93. Joseph Newirth, *Between Emotion and Cognition: The Generative Unconscious* (New York: Other Press, 2003), 150.
94. Goodwyn, *The Neurobiology of the Gods*, 6, 21.

95. Ibid., 4–6.
96. Holland, *Literature and the Brain,* 153–159.
97. Allan N. Schore, *Affect Regulation and the Repair of the Self* (New York: W. W. Norton, 2003), loc. 58 (Kindle ed.).
98. Ibid., loc. 93.
99. Ibid.
100. Ibid., loc. 5711.
101. J. M. Davies, "Dissociation, Repression and Reality: Testing in the Countertransference. The Controversy over Memory and False Memory in the Psychoanalytic Treatment of Adult Survivors of Sexual Abuse," *Psychoanalytic Dialogues* 6, no. 2 (1996): 189–218, esp.197.
102. Jaak Panksepp, "What Is an Emotional Feeling? Lessons about Affective Origins from Cross-Species Neuroscience," *Motivation and Emotion* 36, no. 1 (2012): 4–15. Panksepp's theory of the emotions is fully developed in Panksepp, *Affective Neuroscience,* and in Panksepp and Lucy Biven, *The Archaeology of Mind: Neuroevolutionary Origins of Human Emotions* (New York: W. W. Norton, 2012).
103. Schore, *Affect Regulation,* loc. 110 (Kindle ed).
104. Mark Solms and Oliver Turnbull, *The Brain and the Inner World: An Introduction to the Neuroscience of Subjective Experience* (New York: Other Press, 2002), 117.
105. Among Bollas's writings, the books that I have found most relevant to this project are *The Shadow of the Object: Psychoanalysis of the Unthought Known* (New York: Columbia University Press, 1987); *Being a Character: Psychoanalysis and Self Experience* (New York: Hill and Wang, 1992); *The Freudian Moment* (London: Karnac, 2008); and *The Evocative Object World* (New York: Routledge, 2009).
106. Joyce McDougall, "The Psychosoma and the Psychoanalytic Process," in *Plea for a Measure of Abnormality* (New York: Brunner/Mazel, 1992), 337–396.
107. LeDoux, *Synaptic Self,* 319.
108. Aristotle, *Poetics,* in *Classical Literary Criticism,* ed. D. A. Russell and Michael Winterbottom (Oxford: Oxford University Press, 1989), 57.
109. John Milton, *The Reason of Church Government* (bk. 2), in *John Milton: Complete Poems and Major Prose,* ed. Merritt Y. Hughes (Indianapolis; New York: The Odyssey Press, 1957), 669.
110. Panksepp, *Archaeology of Mind,* 10.

2. WHY DOES FICTIVE REPRESENTATION EXIST?

1. Eric R. Kandel, *The Age of Insight: The Quest to Understand the Unconscious in Art, Mind, and Brain: From Vienna 1900 to the Present* (New York: Random House, 2012), 450.
2. Joseph E. LeDoux, *Synaptic Self: How Our Brains Become Who We Are* (New York: Viking, 2002), 24.
3. Antonio R. Damasio, *Self Comes to Mind: Constructing the Conscious Brain* (New York: Pantheon Books, 2010), 198.
4. Ibid., 199.
5. Jaak Panksepp and Mark Solms, "What is Neuropsychoanalysis? Clinically Relevant Studies of the Minded Brain," *Trends in Cognitive Sciences* 16, no.1 (January 2012): 6–8.
6. See Jaak Panksepp, *Affective Neuroscience: The Foundations of Human and Animal Emotions* (New York: Oxford University Press, 1998), 42–43. My account of the brain and its affective systems is drawn from Panksepp's book.

7. Ibid., 43.

8. David Servan-Schreiber, *Healing without Freud or Prozac: Natural Approaches to Curing Stress, Anxiety and Depression without Drugs and without Psychoanalysis* (London: Rodale, 2004), 31–32.

9. Damasio, *Self Comes to Mind*, 25.

10. Antonio R. Damasio, *Looking for Spinoza: Joy, Sorrow, and the Feeling Brain* (Orlando, FL: Harcourt, 2003), 35.

11. Ibid., 8.

12. Damasio, *Self Comes to Mind*, 54.

13. Charles Darwin, *The Expression of the Emotions in Man and Animals*, ed. Francis Darwin (Cambridge, U.K.: Cambridge University Press, 2009), chap. 3, esp. 70–87.

14. Panksepp, *Affective Neuroscience*, 144–280; see also Jaak Panksepp and Lucy Biven, *The Archaeology of Mind: Neuroevolutionary Origins of Human Emotions* (New York: W. W. Norton, 2012), passim.

15. Jaak Panksepp, "Brain Emotional Systems and Qualities of Mental Life: From Animal Models of Affect to Implications for Psychotherapeutics," in *The Healing Power of Emotion: Affective Neuroscience, Development, and Clinical Practice*, ed. Diana Fosha, Daniel J. Siegel, and Marion Fried Solomon (New York: W. W. Norton, 2009), 1–26, esp. 9–10.

16. Mark Solms and Oliver Turnbull, *The Brain and the Inner World: An Introduction to the Neuroscience of Subjective Experience* (New York: Other Press, 2002), 118.

17. Ibid., 119.

18. Ibid., 123.

19. Ibid., 123–124.

20. Ibid., 126–130.

21. Ibid., 132–133.

22. D. W. Winnicott, *Playing and Reality* (London: Routledge, 2005 [1971]), 52, quoting Marion Milner in "Aspects of Symbolism in Comprehension of the Not-Self," *International Journal of Psychoanalysis* 33, no. 2 (1952): 181–194.

23. Jaak Panksepp, "Cross-Species Affective Neuroscience Decoding of the Primal Affective Experiences of Humans and Related Animals," *PLoS One* 6, no. 9 (2011): e21236.

24. Panksepp, *Affective Neuroscience*, 249.

25. Joseph LeDoux, *Synaptic Self: How Our Brains Become Who We Are* (New York: Viking, 2002), 323–324.

26. See Kandel, *The Age of Insight*, 377.

27. Damasio, *Self Comes to Mind*, 177.

28. Solms and Turnbull, *The Brain and the Inner World*, 83, citing J. A. Bargh and T. L. Chartrand, "The Unbearable Automaticity of Being: Assumptions upon which much contemporary psychological research rests are shown to be impossible. Moment-to-moment psychological life – evaluations, judgments, motivation, social interactions, emotions, and goal-oriented behavior – must occur through nonconscious means if they are to occur at all," *American Psychologist* 54, no. 7 (1999): 462–479.

29. See Eric R. Kandel, *In Search of Memory: The Emergence of a New Science of Mind* (New York: W. W. Norton, 2006), loc. 5372ff (Kindle ed.).

30. Christopher Bollas, *The Shadow of the Object: Psychoanalysis of the Unthought Known* (New York: Columbia University Press, 1987), 241.

31. LeDoux, *Synaptic Self*, 322.

32. Ibid.

33. Ibid., 323.
34. Servan-Schreiber, *Healing without Freud or Prozac*, 40–41.
35. Mauro Mancia, *Feeling the Words: Neuropsychoanalytic Understanding of Memory and the Unconscious*, trans. Judy Baggott (Hove, U.K.: Routledge, 2007), 19.
36. George Lakoff and Mark Johnson, *Metaphors We Live By* (Chicago: University of Chicago Press, 2003), 244.
37. Ibid., 255–256.
38. Ibid., 256.
39. Ibid., 244.
40. Sigmund Freud, "Considerations of Representability," *The Interpretation of Dreams*, in James Strachey, Sigmund Freud, and Anna Freud, *The Standard Edition of the Complete Psychological Works of Sigmund Freud*, trans. James Strachey et al., vol. 5 (London: Vintage, 2001), 339–349. On "figurability," see Jean Laplanche and J. B. Pontalis, *Vocabulaire De La Psychanalyse* (Paris: Presses Universitaires de France, 1967), 119; also see César Botella and Sara Botella, *The Work of Psychic Figurability: Mental States without Representation* (Hove, U.K.: Brunner-Routledge, 2005).
41. See Mauro Mancia, ed., *Psychoanalysis and Neuroscience* (Milan: Springer, 2006), 4–5.
42. Panksepp and Biven, *The Archaeology of Mind*, 214.
43. Mancia, *Feeling the Words*, 57.
44. Damasio, *Self Comes to Mind*, 132; Kandel, *In Search of Memory*, loc. 4277.
45. Daniel J. Siegel, *Pocket Guide to Interpersonal Neurobiology: An Integrative Handbook of the Mind* (New York: W. W. Norton, 2012), 239, 241.
46. Mancia, *Feeling the Words*, 57.
47. Kandel, *In Search of Memory*, loc. 4305.
48. Panksepp, *The Archaeology of Mind*, 214.
49. Ibid., 214–215.
50. Mancia, *Feeling the Words*, 58.
51. Ibid., 71–72.
52. Mancia, *Psychoanalysis and Neuroscience*, 5.
53. Ibid.
54. Mancia, *Feeling the Words*, 118.
55. Panksepp, *The Archaeology of Mind*, 215.
56. Mancia, *Psychoanalysis and Neuroscience*, 11–12.
57. Deleuze, *Desert Islands*, 33.
58. Edmund White, "Edmund White Speaks with Edmund White," *The Review of Contemporary Fiction* 16, no. 3 (1996): 13–20.
59. See Siegel, *Pocket Guide to Interpersonal Neurobiology*, 249.
60. Louis J. Cozolino, *The Neuroscience of Psychotherapy: Healing the Social Brain* (New York: W. W. Norton, 2010), 164.
61. Ibid.
62. See Daniel J. Siegel, "An Interpersonal Neurobiology of Psychotherapy: The Developing Mind and the Resolution of Trauma," in *Healing Trauma: Attachment, Mind, Body, and Brain*, ed. Marion Fried Solomon and Daniel J. Siegel (New York: W. W. Norton, 2003), 7–15.
63. Bruno Dumont, "Cannes Questionnaires #3: Bruno Dumont," May 17, 2011, https://mubi.com/notebook/posts/cannes-2011-cannes-questionnaires-3-bruno-dumont.

64. "Ingmar Bergman at AFI," October 31, 1975, supplement to *The Virgin Spring* (Criterion Collection), DVD.

65. Bollas, *The Infinite Question* (London: Routledge, 2009), loc. 92 (Kindle ed.).

66. Siegel, "Interpersonal Neurobiology," 15.

67. See Allan N. Schore, "Right-Brain Affect Regulation: An Essential Mechanism of Development, Trauma, Dissociation, and Psychotherapy," in Diana Fosha, Daniel J. Siegel, and Marion Fried Solomon (eds.), *The Healing Power of Emotion: Affective Neuroscience, Development, and Clinical Practice* (New York: W. W. Norton, 2009), 112–144.

68. See Kandel, *Age of Insight*, 366.

69. On the cognitive processes involved, see John F. Kihlstrom, Jennifer Dorfman, and Lillian Park, "Implicit and Explicit Memory and Learning," in *The Blackwell Companion to Consciousness*, ed. Max Velmans and Susan Schneider (Oxford, U.K.: Blackwell, 2007), 525–539.

70. Kandel, *Age of Insight*, 394.

71. Quoted in Kandel, *Age of Insight*, 447.

72. Philip Sidney, *An Apology for Poetry or The Defence of Poesy*, ed. Geoffrey Shepherd (Manchester, U.K.: Manchester University Press, 1973), 100–101.

3. THE WELLSPRINGS OF FICTIVE CREATIVITY

1. Jaak Panksepp and Lucy Biven. *The Archaeology of Mind: Neuroevolutionary Origins of Human Emotions* (New York: W. W. Norton, 2012), 95, 98.

2. D. W. Winnicott, *Playing and Reality*, reprint, London: Routledge, 2005 [1971], 73.

3. Ibid., 69.

4. See Daniel J. Siegel, *Pocket guide to Interpersonal Neurobiology: An Integrative Handbook of the Mind* (New York: W. W. Norton, 2012), passim. For an account of the earlier evolution of attachment theory, see Inge Bretherton, "The Origins of Attachment Theory: John Bowlby and Mary Ainsworth," *Developmental Psychology* 28, no. 5 (1992): 759–775.

5. See Marion Fried Solomon and Stan Tatkin, *Love and War in Intimate Relationships: Connection, Disconnection, and Mutual Regulation in Couple Therapy* (New York: W. W. Norton, 2011), xiv–xvii, 44.

6. Allan N. Schore, "Early Relational Trauma, Disorganized Attachment, and the Development of a Predisposition to Violence," in *Healing Trauma: Attachment, Mind, Body, and Brain*, ed. Marion Fried Solomon and Daniel J. Siegel (New York: W. W. Norton, 2003), 106–167, esp. 112.

7. Ibid., 116–117.

8. Ibid., 117–118.

9. Winnicott, *Playing and Reality*, 89; see also Winnicott, *The Maturational Processes and the Facilitating Environment; Studies in the Theory of Emotional Development* (New York: International Universities Press, 1965).

10. Ibid., 152.

11. Ibid., 108.

12. Ibid., 152–153.

13. See Joyce McDougall, *Theaters of the Mind: Illusion and Truth on the Psychoanalytic Stage* (New York: Brunner/Mazel, 1991), 7–8.

14. McDougall, "The Psychosoma and the Psychoanalytic Process," in Joyce McDougall, *Plea for a Measure of Abnormality* (New York: Brunner/Mazel, 1992), 339.

15. Ibid., 340.
16. Ibid., 361–370.
17. Ibid., 370.
18. Ibid., 363.
19. Ibid.
20. McDougall, "The Psychosoma and the Psychoanalytic Process," 338.
21. Ibid., 337–396.
22. Ibid., 438, 451.
23. David Servan-Schreiber, *Healing without Freud or Prozac: Natural Approaches to Curing Stress, Anxiety and Depression without Drugs and without Psychoanalysis* (London: Rodale, 2004), 88–89, 92.
24. See Jörn Donner, "Ingmar Bergman on Life and Work" (documentary, 1998), in *Wild Strawberries* (Criterion Collection), DVD.
25. Quoted in Jonah Weiner, "The Impossible Body: Storyboard P, the Basquiat of Street Dancing," *The New Yorker*, January 6, 2014, 22–28, esp. 23.
26. Ibid., 25–26.
27. "Interview with François Ozon on *In the House*," *Premiere Scene*, http://www.premierescene.net/ps-movie-interviews/in-the-house-interviews.html.
28. McDougall, "The Psychosoma and the Psychoanalytic Process," 372.
29. Quoted in Barbara Arrowsmith-Young, *The Woman Who Changed Her Brain and Other Inspiring Stories of Pioneering Brain Transformation* (New York: Free Press, 2012), loc.1222–1237 (Kindle ed.).
30. See Jaak Panksepp, "Brain Emotional Systems and Qualities of Mental Life," in Diana Fosha, Daniel J. Siegel, and Marion Fried Solomon (eds), *The Healing Power of Emotion: Affective Neuroscience, Development, and Clinical Practice* (New York: W. W. Norton, 2009), 1–26, esp. 3.
31. Ibid.
32. Ibid., 6.
33. Antonio R. Damasio, *Self Comes to Mind: Constructing the Conscious Brain* (New York: Pantheon Books, 2010), 295.
34. Ibid.
35. Ibid., 296.
36. Colin Robinson, "The Loneliness of the Long-Distance Reader," *New York Times*, January 4, 2014, http://www.nytimes.com/2014/01/05/opinion/sunday/the-loneliness-of-the-long-distance-reader.html?_r=0.
37. See Allociné, http://www.allocine.fr/films/decennie-2010/.
38. Rod A. Martin, *The Psychology of Humor: An Integrative Approach* (Amsterdam: Elsevier Academic Press, 2007), 5–15.
39. Ibid., 10.
40. Ibid.
41. Panksepp, "Brain Emotional Systems," 16.
42. Martin, *Psychology of Humor*, 16.
43. Allociné.
44. Randall D. Marshall, "Introduction," in *The Psychology of Terrorism Fears*, ed. Samuel J. Sinclair and Daniel Antonius (New York: Oxford University Press, 2012), 3.
45. Ibid., 11.
46. Quoted in ibid., 6; Siegel, *Pocket Guide to Interpersonal Neurobiology*, 162.

47. John G. Cawelti, *Adventure, Mystery, and Romance: Formula Stories as Art and Popular Culture* (Chicago: University of Chicago Press, 1976).

4. THE MATERIALS OF FICTIVE INVENTION

1. Antonio R. Damasio, *Self Comes to Mind: Constructing the Conscious Brain* (New York: Pantheon Books, 2010), 17.
2. Ibid., 17–18.
3. On volition, see Mark Solms and Jaak Panksepp, "Foreword," in Georg Northoff, *Neuropsychoanalysis in Practice: Brain, Self, and Objects* (Oxford: Oxford University Press, 2011), vii–viii.
4. Damasio, *Self Comes to Mind*, 71.
5. Ibid., 133.
6. Ibid., 174.
7. Christopher Bollas, *The Infinite Question* (London: Routledge, 2009), loc. 443 (Kindle ed.).
8. Ibid.
9. Damasio, *Self Comes to Mind*, 210.
10. Sergei M. Eisenstein, *Problems of Film Direction* (Honolulu: University Press of the Pacific, 2004), 27.
11. Ibid., 27.
12. Ibid., 23–24.
13. Sergei Eisenstein, *Film Form: Essays in Film Theory*, ed. and trans. Jay Leyda (New York: Harcourt, 1949), 248.
14. Eisenstein, *Problems of Film Direction*, 11.
15. Ibid., 12–14.
16. Ibid., 24–25.
17. Ibid., 34.
18. Ibid., 24.
19. Ibid., 45.
20. Damon Smith, "Bruno Dumont, *Hors Satan*," interview, *Filmmaker*, January 17, 2013, http://www.filmmakermagazine.com/62955-bruno-dumont-hors-satan/#.Uvp8DXkxH8s.
21. See Susanne Katherina Knauth Langer, *Philosophy in a New Key: A Study in the Symbolism of Reason, Rite and Art* (Cambridge, MA: Harvard University Press, 1942), 466.
22. Ibid.
23. William Shakespeare, *Romeo and Juliet*, act 1, scene 4, lines 106–115.
24. Sigmund Freud, *Studies on Hysteria*, in Sigmund Freud, James Strachey, and Anna Freud, *The Standard Edition of the Complete Psychological Works of Sigmund Freud* (London: Hogarth Press. 1953), 2:290.
25. "That little short is my style in a nutshell. I'm proud of that little short. I was just in Greece only to be reminded that my forebears had those two masks: one laughing and the other crying. They're not two separate things." See David Stratton, *"Paris, je t'aime* Interview," *At the Movies*, http://www.abc.net.au/atthemovies/txt/s1888271.htm.
26. See Daniel N. Stern, *Forms of Vitality: Exploring Dynamic Experience in Psychology, the Arts, Psychotherapy, and Development* (Oxford: Oxford University Press, 2010).
27. Ibid., 4, 23.

28. George Lakoff and Mark Johnson, *Metaphors We Live By* (Chicago: University of Chicago Press, 2003), 247–256.

29. George Lakoff and Mark Johnson, *Philosophy in the Flesh: The Embodied Mind and Its Challenge to Western Thought* (New York: Basic Books, 1999), 57.

30. Lakoff and Johnson, *Metaphors We Live By*, 257.

31. See ibid., 50–54.

32. Alexander Pope, *An Essay on Criticism* (pt. 2), in *The Poems of Alexander Pope*, ed. John Butt (London: Methuen, 1963), 155, lines 365–373.

33. Stern, *Forms of Vitality*, 23.

34. Ibid., 11.

35. William Shakespeare, *The Sonnets*, ed. William Burto (New York: Signet, 1964), 169.

36. I have argued elsewhere that such problems arose, in part, because of an unresolved clash of value systems that was intrinsic to the English reformation. See Alistair Fox, *The English Renaissance: Identity and Representation in Elizabethan England* (Oxford, U.K.: Blackwell Publishers, 1997).

37. Stern, *Forms of Vitality*, 93.

38. Gideon Bachmann, "'Every Sexual Relationship Is Condemned': An Interview with Bernardo Bertolucci apropos *Last Tango in Paris*," *Film Quarterly* 26, no. 3 (1973): 2–9.

39. Ric Gentry, "Introduction: Vittorio Storaro, Cinematographer as Painter with Light and Motion," *Post Script* 29, no. 2 (2010): 3.

40. Ibid.

41. George Herbert, *The English Poems of George Herbert*, ed. C. A. Patrides (London: Everyman, 1974), 188.

42. Jean Renoir, *My Life and My Films*, trans. Norman Denny (New York: Da Capo Press, 1974), 55.

43. Ibid., 67.

44. Ibid., 250.

45. Ibid., 11.

46. Christopher Bollas, *Being a Character: Psychoanalysis and Self Experience* (New York: Hill and Wang, 1992), 17.

47. Ibid.

48. Ibid., 21.

49. Christopher Bollas, *The Freudian Moment* (London: Karnac, 2008), loc. 319 (Kindle ed.).

50. Daniel J. Siegel. "An Interpersonal Neurobiology of Psychotherapy: The Developing Mind and the Resolution of Trauma," in *Healing Trauma: Attachment, Mind, Body, and Brain*, edited by Marion Fried Solomon and Daniel J. Siegel (New York: W. W. Norton, 2003), 1–56.

51. Bollas, *The Freudian Moment*, loc. 452 (Kindle ed.).

52. Ibid., loc. 475.

53. Ibid., loc. 510–529.

54. Paul B. Armstrong, *How Literature Plays with the Brain: The Neuroscience of Reading and Art* (Baltimore: Johns Hopkins University Press, 2013), loc. 43 (Kindle ed.).

55. Jaak Panksepp and Lucy Biven, *The Archaeology of Mind: Neuroevolutionary Origins of Human Emotions* (New York: W. W. Norton, 2012), 62.

56. Bollas, *The Freudian Moment*, loc. 465 (Kindle ed.).

57. Maurice Gee, *The Plumb Trilogy: Plumb, Meg, Sole Survivor* (Auckland, New Zealand: Penguin, 1995), 254.

58. Judith Holloway, "A Fat Boy, a Creek and a Personal Responsibility," *New Zealand Books* 3, no. 5 (1995): 22–24.

59. See Colleen Reilly, "An Interview with Maurice Gee," *Sport* 5 (Spring 1990): 80–86, esp. 85.

60. See Alan Duff, *Both Sides of the Moon* (Auckland, New Zealand: Vintage, 2000), 16. Duff recounts the autobiographical origins of this novel in *Out of the Mist and Steam: A Memoir* (Auckland, New Zealand: Tandem Press, 1999). For an extended discussion, see Alistair Fox, *The Ship of Dreams: Masculinity in Contemporary New Zealand Fiction* (Dunedin, New Zealand: Otago University Press, 2008).

61. Jörn Donner, "Ingmar Bergman on Life and Work" (documentary, 1998), in *Wild Strawberries* (Criterion Collection), DVD.

62. Ibid.

63. See Alistair Fox, *Jane Campion: Authorship and Personal Cinema* (Bloomington: Indiana University Press, 2012).

64. Ibid., 56–57.

65. Edith Campion, "To Black Cat," *Islands* 8, no. 3 (1980): 238.

66. Marie Colmant, "Jane et Janet, face à face," *Libération*, April 24, 1991.

67. Jane Campion, "Director's Commentary," *An Angel at My Table*, DVD (Criterion Collection).

68. George Lakoff, "How Unconscious Metaphorical Thought Shapes Dreams," in *Cognitive Science and the Unconscious*, ed. Dan J. Stein (Washington, D.C.: American Psychiatric Press, 1997), 108.

5. THE INFORMING ROLE OF FANTASY

1. Sigmund Freud, *Interpretation of Dreams* (pt. 1), in James Strachey, Sigmund Freud, and Anna Freud *The Standard Edition of the Complete Psychological Works of Sigmund Freud*, trans. James Strachey et al., vol. 5 (London: Vintage, 2001), 492.

2. Sigmund Freud, *A Metapsychological Supplement to the Theory of Dreams*, in James Strachey, Sigmund Freud, and Anna Freud, *The Standard Edition of the Complete Psychological Works of Sigmund Freud*, trans. James Strachey et al., vol. 15 (London: Vintage, 2001), 3034.

3. See, for example, Melanie Klein, *Envy and Gratitude and Other Works 1946–1963* (London: Vintage, 1988), 5–6 (Kindle ed.).

4. Ibid., 58.

5. Morris N. Eagle, *Attachment and Psychoanalysis: Theory, Research, and Clinical Implications* (New York: Guilford Press, 2013), 65.

6. Ibid., 64.

7. See Ethel Spector Person, *By Force of Fantasy: How We Make Our Lives* (New York: Basic Books, 1995), 5; see also Brett Kahr, *Sex and the Psyche: The Truth about Our Most Secret Fantasies* (London: Penguin, 2007), 311–336.

8. Ibid., 159.

9. César Botella and Sára Botella, *The Work of Psychic Figurability: Mental States without Representation* (Hove, U.K.: Brunner-Routledge, 2005), xviii.

10. Sigmund Freud, *Interpretation of Dreams* (pt.1), in James Strachey, Sigmund Freud, and Anna Freud, *The Standard Edition of the Complete Psychological Works of Sigmund Freud*, trans. James Strachey et al., vol. 4 (London: Vintage, 2001), 161.

11. Ibid., 157–159.
12. Jaak Panksepp and Lucy Biven, "Preface," in *The Archaeology of Mind: Neuroevolutionary Origins of Human Emotions* (New York: W. W. Norton, 2012), loc. 171 (Kindle ed.).
13. Ibid.
14. Ibid., 345.
15. Ibid., 314.
16. Ibid., 355.
17. Person, *By Force of Fantasy*, 36.
18. Ibid., 14.
19. Ibid., 14–15.
20. See Marion Fried Solomon, *Narcissism and Intimacy: Love and Marriage in an Age of Confusion* (New York: W. W. Norton, 1989), 87–88.
21. See Person, *By Force of Fantasy*, 23.
22. See Linda S. Kauffman, *Discourses of Desire: Gender, Genre, and Epistolary Fictions* (Ithaca, NY: Cornell University Press, 1986), 159–176.
23. See Alistair Fox, *Jane Campion: Authorship and Personal Cinema* (Bloomington: Indiana University Press, 2012), chap. 3.
24. Jane Campion, "Director's Commentary," *Sweetie* (Criterion Collection), DVD.
25. Ibid.
26. Bob Strauss, "Tart Family Ties in *Sweetie*," *San Francisco Chronicle*, February 25, 1990.
27. See Fabien S. Gerard, T. Jefferson Kline, and Bruce Sklarew, eds., *Bernardo Bertolucci Interviews* (Jackson: University Press of Mississippi, 2000), 103; and John Naish, "Bertolucci on the Couch," *The Times* (London), October 29, 2005, 7.
28. John Tulsa, "Interview with Film Maker Bernardo Bertolucci," BBC Radio 3, http://www.bbc.co.uk/radio3/johntusainterview/bertolucci_transcript.shtml.
29. Naish, "Bertolucci on the Couch"; Bernardo Bertolucci and Andrea Sabbadini, "An Additional Lens: Bernardo Bertolucci in Conversation with Andrea Sabbadini–May 1997," *British Psychoanalytic Society*, http://www.psychoanalysis.org.uk/bertolucci.htm.
30. John W. Whitehead, "Besieged by the Past: The Return of Bernardo Bertolucci," *Gadflyonline*, August 1999, http://www.gadflyonline.com/archive/August99/archive-bertolucci.html.
31. Ibid.
32. Donald Ranvaud and Enzo Ungari, *Bertolucci by Bertolucci* (London: Plexus, 1987), 222.
33. Whitehead, "Besieged by the Past."
34. Ranvaud and Ungari, *Bertolucci by Bertolucci* 222.
35. Philip Matthews, "Leaving Sequence," *The Listener* (Wellington, New Zealand), August 19, 1995, 45.
36. Bernardo Bertolucci and Andrea Sabbadini, "Psychoanalysis: The 11th Muse (A Conversation)," *Psychoanalytic Inquiry* 27, no.4 (2007): 381–394.
37. Jean-Francois Pluijgers, "Amos Kollek, un poisson hors de l'eau," *LaLibre.be*, June 18, 2002, http://www.lalibre.be/culture/cinema/amos-kollek-un-poisson-hors-de-l-eau-51b878dfe4b0de6db9a730df.
38. Ibid.
39. Fabienne Ferreira, "Entretien avec Amos Kollek sur son Film *Fiona*," *Cinémotions* [n.d.], http://www.cinemotions.com/interview/1311, reprinted from Epicentre Films press kit.

40. Ibid.
41. Ibid.
42. Raúl Ruiz, *Poetics of Cinema: 1 Miscellanies*, trans. Brian Holmes (Paris: Dis Voir, 1995), 111.
43. Ibid.
44. Ibid., 112.
45. Ibid., 114.

6. THE SHAPING OF FICTIVE SCENARIOS BY THE AUTHOR

1. For a comprehensive overview, see James Phelan and Peter J. Rabinowitz, eds., *A Companion to Narrative Theory* (Malden, MA: Blackwell, 2005).
2. See David Bordwell, *Narration in the Fiction Film* (Madison: University of Wisconsin Press, 1985).
3. See, in particular, Peter Brooks, *Reading for the Plot: Design and Intention in Narrative* (Cambridge, MA: Harvard University Press, 1992).
4. See Christian Metz, *The Imaginary Signifier: Psychoanalysis and the Cinema* (Bloomington: Indiana University Press, 1982).
5. Rick Altman, *A Theory of Narrative* (New York: Columbia University Press, 2008).
6. See Holland, *Literature and the Brain* (Gainesville, FL: PsyArt Foundation, 2009), 154, 183–185.
7. Ibid., 185.
8. Brooks, *Reading for the Plot*, 37.
9. Ibid., 103.
10. Christopher Bollas, "Creativity and Psychoanalysis," in *A Spirit That Impels: Play, Creativity, and Psychoanalysis*, edited by Gerard Fromm (London: Karnac, 2014), 3–20.
11. I have adapted this schema from George Lakoff and Mark Johnson, *Metaphors We Live By*, Chicago: University of Chicago Press, 2003), 77–78
12. Helen Frances, "Facts, Fairytales and the Politics of Storytelling," Gaylene Preston Productions, www.gaylenepreston.co.nz/Articles_FactsFairytales.html, reprinted from *Cineaste* (Autumn 2005)
13. Ibid. I was first alerted to the personal element in Preston's films by Hilary Radner in a paper, "No Country for Women? The Place of Gaylene Preston's *Perfect Strangers* (2003) in New Zealand Cinema," delivered at the Contemporary Women's Cinema Conference: Global Scenarios and Transnational Contexts, University of Roman Trè, Rome, May 2013.
14. Quotations are drawn from *The Faerie Queene: Book One*, ed. Carol V. Kaske (Indianapolis, IN: Hackett Publishing Company, 2006).
15. *The Faerie Queene*, bk I, Canto 4, l. 8; Book I, Canto 10, ll. 3ff.
16. Ibid., Book I, Canto 11, l. 3.
17. Jane Campion, "Director's Commentary," *In the Cut* (2003) (Sony Pictures, 2004), DVD.
18. Jane Campion, "Director's Commentary," *Sweetie* (2011) (Criterion Collection).
19. Ibid.
20. Marie Colmant, "Jane et Janet, face à face," interview with Jane Campion on *An Angel at My Table* (1990), *Libération*, April 24, 1991.

21. Michel Ciment, "Jane Campion: La mort dans le jardin," *Positif* 347 (January 1990), 8–19; reprinted as "Two Interviews with Jane Campion," in Virginia Wright Wexman, *Jane Campion: Interviews* (Jackson: University Press of Mississippi, 1999), 43.

22. Michel Ciment, "Les racines du moi," *Positif* 362 (April 1991), 4–14 ; reprinted as "The Red Wigs of Autobiography: Interview with Jane Campion," in Wexman, *Jane Campion*, 67.

23 "Interview exclusive de la réalisatrice Jane Campion et de la productrice Jan Chapman," *La Leçon de piano*, disk 2 (1993) (TF1 Video, 2003), DVD.

24. I have delineated these at length in Alistair Fox, *Jane Campion: Authorship and Personal Cinema* (Bloomington: Indiana University Press, 2011).

25. Sébastien Ors, Philippe Tancelin, Valérie Jouve, and Bruno Dumont, *Bruno Dumont* (Paris: Éditions Dis Voir, 2001), 11.

26. Ibid., 45.

27. Ibid., 102.

28. Ibid., 12.

29. "Bruno Dumont on Hadewijch" (interview) *Hadewijch* (New Wave Films, 2009), DVD.

30. Daniel Kasman, "Cannes Questionnaires #3: Bruno Dumont," *MUBI*, May 22, 2011, https://mubi.com/notebook/posts/cannes-2011-cannes-questionnaires-3-bruno-dumont.

31. Ibid.

32. Ibid.

33. Jaak Panksepp and Lucy Biven, *The Archaeology of Mind: Neuroevolutionary Origins of Human Emotions* (New York: W. W. Norton, 2012), 314.

34. See Anne Gillain, *François Truffaut: The Lost Secret*, trans. Alistair Fox (Bloomington: Indiana University Press, 2013 [1991 in French]).

35. Melissa P[anarello], *One Hundred Strokes of the Brush before Bed*, trans. Lawrence Venuti (London: Serpent's Tail, 2004).

36. Ibid., 1.

37. Ibid., 14.

38. Joyce McDougall, *Plea for a Measure of Abnormality* (New York: Brunner/Mazel, 1992), 303

39. Panarello, *One Hundred Strokes*, 1–3.

40. Ibid., 7.

41. Ibid., 11, 22.

42. Panarello has candidly admitted the autobiographical source of the sexual addiction depicted in the novel and its masochistic nature: "I often describe my experience as like that experienced by alcoholics and drug addicts, to the extent that they know what they are doing is not good for them and they don't particularly enjoy it, but it becomes an addiction: you are addicted to your pain and start feeling pleasure in your pain, and depending on it" (quoted in Benedicte Page, "Lost in the Woods," *The Bookseller*, April 19, 2004.

43. *One Hundred Strokes*, 112–113.

44. Ibid., 132.

45. Ibid., 154.

46. "Le processus a été très douloureux.... Mais le fait d'extérioriser mes propres douleurs, de parler du viol que j'ai subi, a été une forme de thérapie et m'a libérée d'une sorte

de drogue," quoted in Stéphane Penouel, "Parler de sexe n'est pas scandaleux" (interview), *Le Matin*, 25 mars, 2004.

7. THE EXPLOITATION OF GENERIC TEMPLATES AND INTERTEXTS AS VEHICLES FOR AFFECT REGULATION

1. See Rick Altman, *Film/Genre* (London: BFI Publishing, 1999); and Raphaëlle Moine, *Film Genre*, trans. Alistair Fox and Hilary Radner (Malden, MA: Blackwell, 2008), 55–61.
2. Raúl Ruiz, *Poetics of Cinema* (Paris: Dis Voir, 2005), 58.
3. Some scholars have argued for an earlier composition, in the 1640s or 1650s, but they are unconvincing in light of the close thematic and verbal parallels with both *Paradise Lost* and *Paradise Regained*. See Barbara Kiefer Lewalski, *The Life of John Milton: A Critical Biography*, rev. ed. (Oxford: Blackwell, 2003), 492.
4. See his Sonnet VII ("How Soon Hath Time"), c. 1632.
5. On Milton's polemical career, see Arthur E. Barker, *Milton and the Puritan Dilemma, 1641–1660* (Toronto: University of Toronto press, 1942).
6. See Gordon Campbell, *John Milton* (Oxford: Oxford University Press, 2007), 49.
7. Ibid., 71–72.
8. I cite the edition given in *John Milton: Complete Poems and Major Prose*, ed. Merritt Y. Hughes (Indianapolis: Odyssey Press, 1957), from which all subsequent quotations are taken, referenced by line numbers.
9. John Milton, *The Reason of Church Government Urged against Prelaty*, in *John Milton: Complete Poems and Major Prose*, ed. Merritt Y. Hughes (Indianapolis: Odyssey Press, 1957), 669.
10. Paul Valéry, *Mauvaises Pensees et autres* (Paris: Gallimard, 1942), 79.
11. Serge Tisseron, *Un Psy au cinema* (Paris: Belin, 2013), 182.
12. "Spiegel Interview with Tom Cruise and Steven Spielberg . . . " *Spiegel Online International*, http://www.spiegel.de/international/spiegel/spiegel-interview-with-tom-cruise-and-steven-spielberg-actor-tom-cruise-opens-up-about-his-beliefs-in-the-church-of-scientology-a-353577.html.
13. "War of the Worlds," *Reverse Shot*, http://www.reverseshot.com/article/war_worlds.
14. *Spielberg on Spielberg* (Lorac Productions, Turner Classic Movies, 2007).
15. Mike Benton, *The Comic Book in America: An Illustrated History* (Dallas: Taylor Publishing, 1989), 22.
16. "Interview with François Ozon," *François Ozon: le site officiel*, http://www.francois-ozon.com/en/interviews-the-new-girlfriend/494-entretien-avec-francois-ozon.
17. Ibid.
18. "François Ozon: I Don't Suffer," interview, *The Talks*, http://the-talks.com/interviews/francois-ozon/.
19. "Interview with François Ozon."
20. On the generic attributes of romantic comedy, see Hilary Radner, *Neo-Feminist Cinema: Girly Films, Chick Flicks, and Consumer Culture* (New York: Routledge, 2010), 26–41.
21. "François Ozon: I Don't Suffer."
22. "Interview with François Ozon."
23. Ibid.

8. THEORIES OF RECEPTION IN THE TWENTIETH AND TWENTY-FIRST CENTURIES

1. Louise M. Rosenblatt, *Literature as Exploration* (New York: D. Appleton-Century, 1938), 23.

2. Louise M. Rosenblatt, *the Reader, the Text, the Poem: The Transactional Theory of the Literary Work* (Carbondale: Southern Illinois University Press, 1994 [1978]).

3. Ibid. (1994), ix.

4. Both essays, co-written with Monroe C. Beardsley, are reprinted in William K. Wimsatt, *The Verbal Icon: Studies in the Meaning of Poetry* (Lexington: University of Kentucky Press, 1954), 3–20, 21–40.

5. See, for example, Janet Staiger, *Interpreting Films: Studies in the Historical Reception of American Cinema* (Princeton, NJ: Princeton University Press, 1992).

6. See the discussion of cognitivist theory in chapter 1.

7. Staiger, *Interpreting Films*, 9.

8. Brian Boyd, *On the Origin of Stories: Evolution, Cognition, and Fiction* (Cambridge, MA: Belknap Press of Harvard University Press, 2009), 157–158.

9. Wolfgang Iser, *Prospecting: From Reader Response to Literary Anthropology* (Baltimore: Johns Hopkins University Press, 1989), 4.

10. Ibid., 6. See also Wolfgang Iser, *The Implied Reader: Patterns of Communication in Prose Fiction from Bunyan to Beckett* (Baltimore: Johns Hopkins University Press, 1974); and Iser, *The Act of Reading: A Theory of Aesthetic Response* (Baltimore: Johns Hopkins University Press, 1978).

11. Stanley Eugene Fish, *Is There a Text in This Class: The Authority of Interpretive Communities* (Cambridge, MA: Harvard University Press, 1980).

12. Norman Norwood Holland, *The Dynamics of Literary Response* (New York: Oxford University Press, 1968), 75.

13. Norman Norwood Holland, *5 Readers Reading* (New Haven, CT: Yale University Press, 1975), 13.

14. Ibid., 16.

15. Christian Metz, *The Imaginary Signifier: Psychoanalysis and the Cinema* (Bloomington: Indiana University Press, 1982), 48–49.

16. Ibid., 45, 49.

17. Stuart Hall, "Encoding/Decoding," in *Media and Cultural Studies: Keyworks*, ed. Meenakshi Gigi Durham and Douglas Kellner (Malden, MA: Blackwell, 2006), 164, 169.

18. Stuart Hall, ed., *Representation: Cultural Representations and Signifying Practices—Culture, Media, and Identities* (London: Sage in association with the Open University, 1997).

19. Stuart Hall, "The Work of Representation," in *Representation: Cultural Representations and Signifying Practices—Culture, Media, and Identities*, ed. Stuart Hall (London: Sage in association with the Open University, 1997), 42, 44.

20. Janet Staiger, *Perverse Spectators: The Practices of Film Reception* (New York: New York University Press, 2000), 1.

21. Ibid., 1–2.

22. Mark Turner, "The Art of Compression," in *The Artful Mind: Cognitive Science and the Riddle of Human Creativity*, ed. Mark Turner (Oxford, U.K.: Oxford University Press, 2006), 101.

23. Keith Oatley, *Such Stuff as Dreams: The Psychology of Fiction* (Malden, MA: Wiley-Blackwell, 2011), 167.

24. Ibid., 169.
25. Ibid., 163.
26. Patrick Colm Hogan, *Cognitive Science, Literature, and the Arts: A Guide for Humanists* (New York: Routledge, 2003), 256.
27. Boyd, *On the Origin of Stories*, 157–158.
28. Lawrence M. Zbikowski, "The Cognitive Tango," in *The Artful Mind: Cognitive Science and the Riddle of Human Creativity*, ed. Mark Turner (Oxford, U.K.: Oxford University Press, 2006), 115.
29. Keith Oatley, *Best Laid Schemes: The Psychology of Emotions* (Cambridge, U.K.: Cambridge University Press, 1992), 98.
30. Hogan, *Cognitive Science*, 240.
31. Significant publications in this domain include Stefan Andriopoulos, *Besessene Körper: Hypnose, Körperschaften und die Erfindung des Kinos* (Munich: Fink, 2000); Ruggero Eugeni, *Semiotica dei media: Le forme dell'esperienza* (Rome: Carocci, 2010); Raymond Bellour, *Le Corps du cinéma: hypnoses, émotions, animalités* (Paris: POL, 2009); Rae Beth Gordon, *Why the French Love Jerry Lewis: From Cabaret to Early Cinema* (Stanford, CA: Stanford University Press, 2001).
32. Ruggero Eugeni, *Semiotica dei media: Le forme dell'esperienza* (Rome: Carocci, 2010). I quote from his online article, "A Semiotic Theory of Media Experience," https://www.academia.edu/399281/A_Semiotic_Theory_of_Media_Experience, which presents a summary in English of the theory presented in this book.
33. Ibid.
34. Ibid.
35. Adriano D'Aloia and Ruggero Eugeni, "Introduction," in *Cinéma & Cie*, special issue, *Neurofilmology: Film Studies and the Challenge of Neuroscience* 14, no. 22/23 (Spring/Fall 2014), https://www.academia.edu/11355271/Neurofilmology._Film_Studies_and_the_Challenge_of_Neuroscience.
36. See Eugeni, "A Semiotic Theory of Media Experience."
37. See Vivian Sobchack, *Carnal Thoughts: Embodiments and Moving Image Culture* (Berkeley: University of California Press, 2004).
38. Raymond Bellour, *Le Corps du cinéma: Hypnoses, émotions, animalités* (Paris: Pol, 2009). All quotations from Bellour are my own.
39. Hilary Radner and Cecelia Novero, Introduction to "From Hypnosis to Animals by Raymond Bellour," edited and translated by Alistair Fox, *Cinema Journal* 53, no. 3 (2014): 4."
40. Bellour, *Corps du cinéma*, 430.
41. Ibid., 422.
42. Ibid., 291.
43. Raymond Bellour, "Avec Daniel Stern, chap. 6, 151–177.
44. Ibid., 297.
45. Ibid., 311.
46. Mireille Berton, "Cinéma et hypnose," in Raymond Bellour, *Le Corps du cinéma: Hypnoses, émotions, animalités*; Stefan Andriopoulos, *Besessene Körper*; Ruggero Eugeni, *La relazione d'incanto: Studi su cinema e ipnosi*; Rae Beth Gordon, *Why the French Love Jerry Lewis: From Cabaret to Early Cinema*," *1895* 58 (2009), http://1895.revues.org/3971.
47. Ibid.
48. Michele Aaron, *Spectatorship: The Power of Looking On* (London: Wallflower, 2007), 1–2.

9. A NEUROPSYCHOANALYTIC THEORY OF RECEPTION

1. Allen Thiher, *The Power of Tautology: The Roots of Literary Theory* (Madison NJ: Fairleigh Dickinson University Press, 1997), 138.

2. Daniel N. Stern, *The Interpersonal World of the Infant: A View from Psychoanalysis and Developmental Psychology*, with a new introduction by the author (New York: Basic Books, 2000 [1985]), xvii.

3. Antonio R. Damasio, *Self Comes to Mind: Constructing the Conscious Brain* (New York: Pantheon Books, 2010).

4. Stern, *Interpersonal World of the Infant*, xxv.

5. From here on I use the term "respondent" to refer to the reader/spectator because it designates the agency of both the creator in generating meaning and the reader/spectator in generating meaning in response to the creator's meaning via the nature of his or her subjective response.

6. Christian Keysers, *The Empathic Brain: How the Discovery of Mirror Neurons Changes Our Understanding of Human Nature* (sold by Amazon Digital Services, 2011), 44 (Kindle ed.).

7. Ibid., 24, 45.

8. Ibid., 27, 66.

9. Ibid., 98.

10. Ibid., 108, 112.

11. Ibid., 123.

12. On the nature of affective attunement, see Lawrence J. Brown, *Intersubjective Processes and the Unconscious: An Integration of Freudian, Kleinian and Bionian Perspectives* (London: Routledge, 2011), 6.

13. Keysers, *The Empathic Brain*, 55.

14. Vittorio Gallese, "Intentional Attunement: Embodied Simulation and Its Role in Social Cognition," in *Psychoanalysis and Neuroscience,* ed. Mauro Mancia (Milan: Springer, 2006), 269–301.

15. Ibid., 270.

16. Ibid., 271.

17. Ibid., 273.

18. Ibid., 278.

19. Ibid.

20. Ibid.

21. Stern, *Interpersonal World of the Infant*, 128, citing C. Trevarthan and P. Hubley, "Secondary Intersubjectivity: Confidence, Confiders and Acts of Meaning in the First Year," in *Action, Gesture and Symbol*, ed. A. Lock (New York: Academic Press, 1978).

22. Ibid., 125.

23. Ibid., 126.

24. Ibid., 129.

25. For a description of the signaling behaviors that take place within the mother/child dyad, see Stern, *Interpersonal World of the Infant*, 129–131.

26. "Interaffectivity" is a term used by Stern, ibid., 133.

27. Sergei M. Eisenstein, *Problems of Film Direction* (Honolulu: University Press of the Pacific, 2004), 25.

28. Ibid.

29. Ibid., 26.
30. Ibid.
31. A term used by Brown, *Intersubjective Processes and the Unconscious*, 111.
32. Ibid., 8.
33. Stern, *Interpersonal World of the Infant*, 134.
34. Ibid., 125.
35. See Morris N. Eagle, *Attachment and Psychoanalysis: Theory, Research, and Clinical Implications* (New York: Guilford Press, 2013), 14 passim.
36. See, in particular, John Bowlby, *Attachment and Loss*, 3 vols. (New York: Basic Books, 1969); and John Bowlby, *A Secure Base: Clinical Applications of Attachment Theory* (London: Routledge, 1988).
37. For a cogent summary, see Eagle, *Attachment and Psychoanalysis*, 15.
38. Norman Norwood Holland, *5 Readers Reading* (New Haven, CT: Yale University Press, 1975), 23.
39. Norman Norwood Holland, *Literature and the Brain* (Gainesville, FL: PsyArt Foundation, 2009), 42.
40. Ibid., 42–43.
41. See Christopher Bollas, *The Shadow of the Object: Psychoanalysis of the Unthought Known* (New York: Columbia University Press, 1987), 243–244.
42. I am here adapting ideas drawn from Bollas, *Shadow of the Object*, 245–246, which discusses them in relation to psychotherapeutic practice.
43. "A Conversation with Clark Gregg and Chuck Palahniuk," commentary (2009) on *Choke*, (20th Century Fox, 2008), DVD.
44. Ibid.
45. Bollas, *The Shadow of the Object*, chap. 1.
46. Ibid., 14.
47. Ibid., 107–108, 124.
48. Ibid., 124.
49. Ibid., 65.
50. For this and what follows, I am indebted to Ethel Spector Person, *By Force of Fantasy: How We Make Our Lives* (New York: Basic Books, 1995), 5ff.
51. Ibid.
52. Ibid., 189.

10. INTERSUBJECTIVE ATTUNEMENT, FILIATION, AND THE RE-CREATIVE PROCESS

1. Throughout this chapter, I refer to Henri Pierre Roché's novel by its French title *Jules et Jim* and to François Truffaut's cinematic adaptation by its American release title *Jules and Jim*, so as to distinguish between the two.
2. Jean-Luc Godard, *Godard on Godard,* ed. Jean Narboni and Tom Milne (New York: Da Capo Press, 1972), 241–242.
3. See Lawrence J. Brown, *Intersubjective Processes and the Unconscious: An Integration of Freudian, Kleinian and Bionian Perspectives* (London and New York: Routledge, 2011) 111–112.
4. See Sook-Lei Liew and Lisa Aziz-Zadeh, "The Human Mirror Neuron System, Social Control, and Language," in *Handbook of Neurosociology*, ed. David D. Franks and Jonathan H. Turner (New York: Springer, 2013), 199.

5. Brown, *Intersubjective Processes and the Unconscious*, 6.
6. Ibid., 8.
7. See Anne Gillain, ed., *Le Cinéma selon François Truffaut* (Paris: Flammarion, 1988), 29.
8. For detailed accounts of Truffaut's biography, see Antoine de Baecque and Serge Toubiana, *Truffaut*, trans. Catherine Temerson (Berkeley: University of California Press, 2000).
9. Catherine Du Toit, *Henri-Pierre Roché: à la recherche de l'unité perdue, le devenir d'un écrivain* (Ph.D. thesis, University of Pretoria, 2006), http://upetd.up.ac.za/thesis/available/etd-04142009-163147/unrestricted/01chapter1.pdf.
10. This relationship cannot be verified; a senior French academic informed me that the rumor was commonplace in Paris while Truffaut was still alive.
11. de Baecque and Toubiana, *Truffaut*, 45.
12. Erik Morse, "Time and Again," *Frieze*, March 1, 2011, http://www.frieze.com/issue/print_article/time-again/; Ho Yi, "'Learn to Understand': Tai Ming-Liang," *Taipei Times*, October 8, 2009 http://www.taipeitimes.com/News/feat/archives/2009/10/08/2003455433.
13. "The Filmmakers' Portrait Series: Christophe Honoré," *Cool*, August 16, 2012, http://www.cool-ny.com/en/archives/1353.
14. "Xavier Dolan on George Stroumboulopoulos Tonight: Interview," http://www.cbc.ca/strombo/videos/xavier-dolan-1.
15. See Joyce McDougall, *The Many Faces of Eros: A Psychoanalytic Exploration of Human Sexuality* (New York: W. W. Norton, 1995), 181–191.
16. For details of this relationship, see Robert Stam, *François Truffaut and Friends: Modernism, Sexuality, and Film Adaptation* (New Brunswick, NJ: Rutgers University Press, 2006).
17. Henri-Pierre Roché, *Carnets 1 (1920–1921): Les Années "Jules et Jim,"* avant-propose de François Truffaut (Marseilles: A. Dimanche,1990); also see also Stam, *François Truffaut and Friends*, 84.
18. See Henri-Pierre Roché, *Jules et Jim*, trans. Patrick Evans, with an essay by François Truffaut (London: Marion Boyars, 2006), 243; also see Stam, *François Truffaut and Friends*, 86–87.
19. Ibid., 82.
20. See de Baecque and Toubiana, *Truffaut*, 41.
21. Ibid., 82.
22. See Catherine Du Toit, *Henri-Pierre Roché*, 203.
23. Anne Gillain, *François Truffaut: The Lost Secret*, trans. Alistair Fox (Bloomington: Indiana University Press, 2013), 89.
24. Ibid., 81.
25. I am using here a metaphor employed by Catherine Du Toit in *Henri-Pierre Roché*, 12.
26. Ibid., 12–23.
27. Henri-Pierre Roché, unpublished untitled manuscript, quoted in ibid., 12.
28. Quoted in ibid., 14.
29. Ibid., 13. For Truffaut's observation about his mother's embitterment, see Gillain, *Le Cinéma selon François Truffaut*, 15–16.
30. Henri-Pierre Roché, journal entry, January 2, 1922. Quoted in Du Toit, *Henri-Pierre Roché*, 18.

31. Ibid., 19.
32. Henri-Pierre Roché, journal entry, July 3, 1931, quoted in ibid., 19.
33. Ibid., 22.
34. Henri-Pierre Roché, *Two English Girls and the Continent* [Deux anglaises et le continent], trans. Walter Bruno (Cambridge, WI: Cambridge Book Review Press, 2004), 107.
35. Quoted in Stam, *François Truffaut and Friends*, 107.
36. Gillain, *Le Cinéma selon François Truffaut*, 15.
37. Quoted in de Baecque and Toubiana, *Truffaut*, 11.
38. Gillain, *Le Cinéma selon François Truffaut*, 30.
39. de Baecque, *François Truffaut*, 140–141.
40. Gillain, *François Truffaut: The Lost Secret*, 258.
41. François Truffaut, *Correspondance*, ed. Gilles Jacob (Paris: 5 Continents/Hatier, 1988), 467.
42. Roché, *Two English Girls*, 185.
43. Ibid., 196.
44. Vittorio Gallese, "Intentional Attunement: Embodied Simulation and Its Role in Social Cognition," in *Psychoanalysis and Neuroscience*, ed Mauro Mancia (Milan: Springer, 2006), 269–301, especially 270–271.
45. de Baecque and Toubiana, *Truffaut*, 170.
46. Ibid., 169.
47. Ibid., 176.
48. Stam, *François Truffaut and Friends*, 102.
49. "Je ne suis jamais conscient de l'aspect global du sujet quand je le sélectionne et quand je le traite. D'habitude je le comprends longtemps après avoir fait le film. J'avais une relation très difficile avec ma famille, en particulier avec ma mère, et j'ai compris il y a seulement quelques années que j'ai fait *Jules et Jim* pour lui plaire et obtenir son approbation. L'amour jouait un grand rôle dans sa vie, et comme *Les 400 Coups* était pour elle comme un coup de couteau dans le dos, j'ai fait *Jules et Jim* dans l'espoir de lui montrer que je la comprenais." Gillain, *Le Cinéma selon François Truffaut*, 144.
50. See Gillain, *François Truffaut: The Lost Secret*, 89.
51. Stam, *François Truffaut and Friends*, 103.
52. de Baecque and Toubiana, *Truffaut*.
53. Roché, *Jules et Jim*, 72.
54. Gillain, *François Truffaut: The Lost Secret*, xxxii, 15, 288.
55. Alistair Fox, "Emotion and the Authorial Fantasmatic: An Introduction to the English Edition of Anne Gillain's *François Truffaut: The Lost Secret*," in Gillain, *François Truffaut: The Lost Secret*, 15.
56. See Gillain, *François Truffaut: The Lost Secret*, 82–95.
57. Ibid., 89.
58. See Gillain, *François Truffaut: The Lost Secret*, 251–274.

11. THE CONVERSION OF AUTOBIOGRAPHICAL EMOTION INTO SYMBOLIC FIGURATION

1. Joseph Carroll, "Intentional Meaning in *Hamlet*: An Evolutionary Perspective," *Style* 44, nos. 1 and 2 (2010): 230–260.

2. Patrick Colm Hogan, "The Mourning Brain: Attachment, Anticipation, and Hamlet's Unmanly Grief," in *Cognitive Literary Studies: Current Themes and New Directions*, ed. Isabel Jaén and Julien Jacques Simon (Austin: University of Texas Press, 2012), 101.

3. Ibid.

4. François de Belleforest, *Le Cinqviesme Tome des histoires tragiqves, contenant vn discours mémorable de plusieurs histoires, le succez & euenement desquelles est pour la plus parr recueilly des choses aduenuës de nostre temps* (Paris: J. Hulpeau, 1572), 149–191. The English quotations are taken from *The Hystorie of Hamblet*, a translation published in 1608, after Shakespeare's play was written, and reprinted in the Kindle edition of *The Norse Hamlet*, ed. Soren Filipski (n.p.: Hythloday Press, 2013). For the quotation, see *The Hystorie of Hamblet*, loc. 1144).

5. *The Hystorie of Hamblet*, loc. 684.

6. Belleforest, *Histoires tragiques*, 5:5, 190r–190v.

7. *The Hystorie of Hamblet*, loc. 1422.

8. On the relationship of these versions, see Shakespeare, *The First Quarto of Hamlet*, ed. Kathleen O. Irace (New York: Cambridge University Press, 1998), 1–27.

9. Thomas Nashe referred to Seneca as affording "whole *Hamlets*." See *The Works of Thomas Nashe*, ed. R. B. McKerrow (London: A. H. Bullen, 1904), 315–316. Geoffrey Bullough, identifying features shared by Shakespeare's *Hamlet* and Thomas Kyd's *The Spanish Tragedy* (1592), has surmised that the earlier play might have been written by Kyd, but this is now impossible to prove. See Bullough, *Narrative and Dramatic Sources of Shakespeare*, vol. 7 (London: Routledge and Kegan Paul, 1973), 16–17.

10. See Bullough, *Narrative and Dramatic Sources of Shakespeare*, 16–17.

11. *Hamlet*, 3.2.217–218. All quotations are from *The Tragedy of Hamlet Prince of Denmark*, ed. Sylvan Barnet (New York: Signet, 1998). References are to act, scene, and line.

12. Caroline Spurgeon, *Shakespeare's Imagery and What It Tells Us* (Cambridge, U.K.: Cambridge University Press, 1935), 317–318.

13. *Hamlet*, 1.5.71–72; 3.4.148–150. All quotations from *Hamlet* are from *The Tragedy of Hamlet Prince of Denmark*, ed. Sylvan Barnet (New York: Signet, 1998).

14. Ibid., 1.1.7–8.
15. Ibid., 1.1.62–63.
16. Ibid., 1.2.129–130.
17. Ibid., 3.1.136–138.
18. Ibid., 1.2.133–136.
19. Ibid., 3.1.58–77.
20. Ibid., 3.1.154–157.
21. Spurgeon, *Shakespeare's Imagery*, 318–319.
22. *Hamlet*, 3.2.328–329.
23. Ibid., 1.4.44–87.
24. Ibid., 1.5.149–163.
25. Ibid., 3.4.106–138.
26. Ibid., 3.1.88–90, 144–152.
27. Ibid., 3.1.90–92, 103, 131.
28. Ibid., 3.4.93–96.
29. Ibid., 5.1.257–273, 5.2.78–79.

30. For a useful overview of earlier psychoanalytic interpretations of *Hamlet*, see Norman Holland, *Psychoanalysis and Shakespeare* (New York: McGraw-Hill, 1964), 163–206.

31. Jaak Panksepp, *Affective Neuroscience: The Foundations of Human and Animal Emotions* (New York: Oxford University Press, 1998), 212.
32. *Hamlet*, 1.5.188–189.
33. Ibid., 5.2.10–11.
34. Ibid., 5.2.220–225; 242–245.
35. E. K. Chambers, *William Shakespeare: A Study of Facts and Problems* (Oxford, U.K.: Clarendon, 1930), 18.
36. See Stephen Greenblatt, "The Death of Hamnet and the Making of Hamlet," *New York Review of Books,* October 21, 2001.
37. Ibid.
38. Katherine Duncan-Jones, *Ungentle Shakespeare: Scenes from his life* (London: Arden Shakespeare, 2001), 132–133.
39. Ella Freeman Sharpe, "The Impatience of Hamlet," *International Journal of Psycho-Analysis* 10 (1929): 270–279.
40. William Shakespeare, *Much Ado About Nothing,* 4.1.39, *The Complete Pelican Shakespeare: The Comedies and the Romances,* ed. Alfred Harbage (Harmondsworth: Penguin Books, 1969).
41. Shakespeare, *The Winter's Tale,* ibid., 1.2.145.
42. William Shakespeare, *Othello,* 4.2.57–58, *The Complete Pelican Shakespeare: The Tragedies,* ed. Alfred Harbage (Harmondsworth: Penguin Books, 1969).
43. Shakespeare, *Macbeth,* ibid., 1.7.31.
44. Shakespeare, *Antony and Cleopatra,* ibid., 4.7.11.
45. William Shakespeare, *Coriolanus,* ed. Reuben Bower (New York: The New American Library, 1966), 1.3.3–5.
46. Ibid., 1.3.37–41.
47. Ibid., 1.1.37–39.
48. Ibid., 1.4.26–27.
49. Ibid., 3.2.15–16.
50. Ibid., 5.3.182–189.

12. TRACKING A PERSONAL MYTH THROUGH AN OEUVRE

1. Linda Hutcheon, *Formalism and the Freudian Aesthetic: The Example of Charles Mauron* (Cambridge, U.K.: Cambridge University Press, 2006).
2. Charles Mauron, *Des métaphores obsédantes au mythe personnel: Introduction à la psychocritique* (Paris: J. Corti (Rennes Impr. réunies), 1963), 108. All passages quoted from this work are given in English translation, and the translations are my own.
3. Ibid., 109.
4. Ibid., 213.
5. Ibid., 109.
6. Ibid.
7. Ibid., 209.
8. Ibid., 217, 210.
9. Ibid., 210.
10. Ibid., 222.
11. Ibid., 212.
12. Ibid., 211.

13. Stéphane Goudet, "Le court métrage en France: François Ozon," *Positif* 432 (December 1997): 93–95.
14. "Entretien avec François Ozon," *Studio Magazine*, May 1998, http://www.francois-ozon.com/en/interviews-sitcom.
15. Interview with Charlotte Rampling, *Swimming Pool* (Magna Pacifica, 2004), DVD.
16. "Entretien avec François Ozon," *Studio Magazine*.
17. "*In the House* (Dans le maison)—Director François Ozon Interview," *Premiere Scene*, https://www.youtube.com/watch?v=UcoMrZc4KiI.
18. For a detailed analysis of Ozon's short films, see Alistair Fox, "Auteurism, Personal Cinema, and the Fémis Generation: The Case of François Ozon," in *A Companion to Contemporary French Cinema*, ed. Raphaëlle Moine, Hilary Radner, Alistair Fox, and Michel Marie (Malden, MA: Wiley-Blackwell, 2014).
19. "Interviews about *Swimming Pool*," *François Ozon: Le site officiel*, http://www.francois-ozon.com/en/interviews-swimming-pool.
20. "Interviews about *Time to Leave*," *François Ozon: le site officiel*, http://www.francois-ozon.com/en/interviews-time-to-leave, accessed April 9, 2014.
21. "François Ozon—*Time to Leave*," *Groucho Reviews*, May 19, 2006, http://www.grouchoreviews.com/interviews/165.
22. Thibault Schilt, "An Interview with François Ozon, in *François Ozon* (Urbana: University of Illinois Press, 2011), 167.
23. See "Lettre de François Ozon à Marina de Van," May 20, 1996, http://www.francois-ozon.com/en/interviews-see-the-sea/79-lettre-de-francois-ozon-a-marina-de-van.
24. "Interviews about *Time to Leave*."
25. "Theatergram" is a term coined by Louise George Clubb, based on her study of early-modern Italian plays, in *Italian Drama in Shakespeare's Time* (New Haven, CT: Yale University Press, 1989).
26. "Interviews about *Water Drops on Burning Rocks*, *François Ozon: le site officiel*, http://www.francois-ozon.com/en/interviews-time-to-leave, accessed April 9, 2014.
27. "Interviews about *Time to Leave*."
28. Arthur Rimbaud, "Nuit en enfer," in *Une Saison en enfer* (In Libro Veritas), http://www.inlibroveritas.net/lire/oeuvre28232.html.
29. "Interview with François Ozon," http://www.francois-ozon.com/en/interviews-ricky/155-francois-ozon.
30. "François Ozon—*Time to Leave*," *Groucho Reviews*.
31. "Interviews about *Swimming Pool*."
32. Ibid.
33. For the sources of Ozon's fascination with this character, see "François Ozon: Le cineaste que aime les femmes," *aufeminin.com*, http://www.aufeminin.com/mag/culture/d1258.html.
34. "The HeyUGuys Interview: French Director François Ozon Discusses His Latest Film Jeune & Jolie," *HeyUGuys*, November 28, 2013, http://www.heyuguys.co.uk/interview-francois-ozon-jeune-et-jolie.
35. See Hannah Park, "Adolescence & Adultery—François Ozon Speaks," *On the Box*, March 17, 2014, http://blog.onthebox.com/2014/03/17/francois-ozon.
36. "You Think I Should Die? François Ozon on *In the House*," *Filmmaker*, April 18, 2013, http://filmmakermagazine.com/68911-you-think-i-should-die-francois-ozon-on-in-the-house/#.UocvX14xH8s.

CONCLUSION

1. Jean Genet, *The Thief's Journal,* trans. Bernard Frechtman (New York: Grove Press, 1964), 205.

2. Sidney, Philip. *An Apology for Poetry or The Defence of Poesy,* ed. Geoffrey Shepherd (Manchester, U.K.: Manchester University Press: 1973), 103.

SELECT BIBLIOGRAPHY

Aaron, Michele. *Spectatorship: The Power of Looking On*. London: Wallflower, 2007.
Altman, Rick. *A Theory of Narrative*. New York: Columbia University Press, 2008.
———. *Film/Genre*. London: BFI Publishing, 1999.
Andrew, Dudley. "Foreword to the 2004 Edition." In *What Is Cinema?* Vol. 2. Edited by André Bazin. Translated by Hugh Gray. Berkeley: University of California Press, 2004, xx–xxii.
Andriopoulos, Stefan. *Besessene Körper. Hypnose, Körperschaften und die Erfindung des Kinos*. Munich: Fink, 2000.
Armstrong, Paul B. *How Literature Plays with the Brain: The Neuroscience of Reading and Art*. Baltimore: Johns Hopkins University Press, 2013.
Arnold, Matthew. *The Complete Prose Works of Matthew Arnold*. Vol. 9. Edited by R. H. Super. Ann Arbor: University of Michigan Press, 1973.
Arrowsmith-Young, Barbara. *The Woman Who Changed Her Brain and Other Inspiring Stories of Pioneering Brain Transformation*. New York: Free Press, 2012.
Augustine. *On Christian Doctrine*. Translated by J. F. Shaw. New York: Dover Publications, 2009.
Bargh, J. A., and T. L. Chartrand. "The Unbearable Automaticity of Being: Assumptions upon which much contemporary psychological research rests are shown to be impossible. Moment-to-moment psychological life--evaluations, judgments, motivation, social interactions, emotions, and goal-oriented behavior--must occur through nonconscious means if they are to occur at all," *American Psychologist* 54, no. 7 (1999): 462–479.
Barkan, Leonard. *Mute Poetry, Speaking Pictures*. Princeton, NJ: Princeton University Press, 2013.
Barker, Arthur E. *Milton and the Puritan Dilemma, 1641–1660*. Toronto: University of Toronto Press, 1942.
Barthes, Roland, and Stephen Heath. *Image, Music, Text*. New York: Hill and Wang, 1977.
Bazin, André, ed. *What Is Cinema?* Vol. 1. Translated by Hugh Gray. Berkeley: University of California Press, 2004.

Bellour, Raymond. "From Hypnosis to Animals by Raymond Bellour." Edited and translated by Alistair Fox, with an introduction by Hilary Radner and Cecelia Novero, *Cinema Journal* 53, no. 3 (2014): 4.
———. *Le Corps du cinéma: Hypnoses, émotions, animalités*. Paris: Éditions P.O.L., 2009.
Benton, Mike. *The Comic Book in America: An Illustrated History*. Dallas: Taylor Publishing, 1989.
Bergman, Ingmar, and Marianne Ruuth. *Images: My Life in Film*. New York: Arcade Publishing, 2011.
Berlin, Isaiah, and Henry Hardy. *The Crooked Timber of Humanity: Chapters in the History of Ideas*. Princeton: Princeton University Press, 2013.
Bertolucci, Bernardo, and Andrea Sabbadini. "Psychoanalysis: The 11th Muse (A Conversation)," *Psychoanalytic Inquiry* 27, no. 4 (2007): 381–394.
Bloch, R. Howard. *The Scandal of the Fabliaux*. Chicago: University of Chicago Press, 1986.
Bloom, Harold. *The Western Canon: The Books and School of the Ages*. London: Papermac, 1995.
Bollas, Christopher. *Being a Character: Psychoanalysis and Self Experience*. New York: Hill and Wang, 1992.
———. "Creativity and Psychoanalysis." In *A Spirit That Impels: Play, Creativity, and Psychoanalysis*. Edited by Gerard Fromm (London: Karnac, 2014), 3–20.
———. *The Evocative Object World*. New York: Routledge, 2009.
———. *The Freudian Moment*. London: Karnac, 2008.
———. *The Infinite Question*. London: Routledge, 2009.
———. *The Shadow of the Object: Psychoanalysis of the Unthought Known*. New York: Columbia University Press, 1987.
Bordwell, David. *Narration in the Fiction Film*. Madison: University of Wisconsin Press, 1985.
Bordwell, David, and Noël Carroll. *Post-Theory: Reconstructing Film Studies*. Madison: University of Wisconsin Press, 1996.
Botella, César, and Sara Botella. *The Work of Psychic Figurability: Mental States without Representation*. Hove, U.K.: Brunner-Routledge, 2005.
Bowlby, John. *A Secure Base: Clinical Applications of Attachment Theory*. London: Routledge, 1988.
———. *Attachment and Loss*. 3 vols. New York: Basic Books, 1969.
Boyd, Brian. *On the Origin of Stories: Evolution, Cognition, and Fiction*. Cambridge, MA: Belknap Press of Harvard University Press, 2009.
Bretherton, Inge. "The Origins of Attachment Theory: John Bowlby and Mary Ainsworth," *Developmental Psychology* 28, no. 5 (1992): 759–775.
Brooks, Peter. *Reading for the Plot: Design and Intention in Narrative*. Cambridge, MA: Harvard University Press, 1992.
Brown, Lawrence J. *Intersubjective Processes and the Unconscious: An Integration of Freudian, Kleinian and Bionian Perspectives*. London: Routledge, 2011.
Bullough, Geoffrey. *Narrative and Dramatic Sources of Shakespeare*. Vol. 7. London: Routledge and Kegan Paul, 1973.
Butler, Christopher. *Postmodernism: A Very Short Introduction*. Oxford, U.K.: Oxford University Press, 2002.
Campbell, Gordon. *John Milton*. Oxford, U.K.: Oxford University Press, 2007.

Carroll, Joseph. "Intentional Meaning in *Hamlet:* An Evolutionary Perspective," *Style* 44, nos. 1 and 2 (2010): 230–260.
Cawelti, John G. *Adventure, Mystery, and Romance: Formula Stories as Art and Popular Culture.* Chicago: University of Chicago Press, 1976.
Chambers, E. K. *William Shakespeare: A Study of Facts and Problems.* Oxford, U.K.: Clarendon, 1930.
Chatman, Seymour. "What Novels Can Do That Films Can't (and Vice Versa)," *Critical Enquiry* 7, no. 1 (1980): 121–140.
Ciment, Michel. *Jane Campion par Jane Campion.* Paris: Cahiers du cinéma, 2014.
Clough, Patricia Ticineto, and Jean O'Malley Halley, eds. *The Affective Turn: Theorizing the Social.* Durham, NC: Duke University Press, 2007.
Clubb, Louise George. *Italian Drama in Shakespeare's Time.* New Haven, CT: Yale University Press, 1989.
Coleridge, Samuel Taylor. *The Portable Coleridge.* Edited by I. A. Richards. New York: Viking Press, 1950.
Cozolino, Louis J. *The Neuroscience of Psychotherapy: Healing the Social Brain.* New York: W. W. Norton, 2010.
D'Aloia, Adriano, and Ruggero Eugeni. "Introduction," *Cinéma & Cie,* Special issue, *Neurofilmology: Film Studies and the Challenge of Neuroscience* 14, no. 22: https://www.academia.edu/11355271/Neurofilmology._Film_Studies_and_the_Challenge_of_Neuroscience.
Damasio, Antonio R. *Looking for Spinoza: Joy, Sorrow, and the Feeling Brain.* Orlando, FL: Harcourt, 2003.
——. *Self Comes to Mind: Constructing the Conscious Brain.* New York: Pantheon Books, 2010.
Darwin, Charles. *The Expression of the Emotions in Man and Animals.* Edited by Francis Darwin. Cambridge, U.K.: Cambridge University Press, 2009.
Davies, J. M. "Dissociation, Repression and Reality: Testing in the Counter-transference. The Controversy over Memory and False Memory in the Psychoanalytic Treatment of Adult Survivors of Sexual Abuse," *Psychoanalytic Dialogues* 6, no. 2 (1996): 189–218.
de Baecque, Antoine, ed. *Truffaut.* Translated by Catherine Temerson. Berkeley: University of California Press, 2000.
de Belleforest, François. *Le Cinqviesme Tome des histoires tragiqves, contenant vn discours mémorable de plusieurs histoires, le succez & euenement desquelles est pour la plus parr recueilly des choses aduenuës de nostre temps.* Paris: J. Hulpeau, 1572.
Deleuze, Gilles. *Desert Islands: And Other Texts, 1953–1974.* Paris: Semiotexte, 2004.
Duff, Alan. *Both Sides of the Moon.* Auckland, New Zealand: Vintage, 2000.
——. *Out of the Mist and Steam: A Memoir.* Auckland, New Zealand: Tandem Press, 1999.
Duncan-Jones, Katherine. *Ungentle Shakespeare: Scenes from His Life.* London: Arden Shakespeare, 2001.
Durham, Meenakshi Gigi, and Douglas Kellner, eds. *Media and Cultural Studies: Keyworks.* Malden, MA: Blackwell, 2006.
Du Toit, Catherine. *Henri-Pierre Roché: à la recherche de l'unité perdue, le devenir d'un écrivain.* PhD thesis, University of Pretoria, 2006, http://upetd.up.ac.za/thesis/available/etd-04142009-163147/unrestricted/01chapter1.pdf.
Eagle, Morris N. *Attachment and Psychoanalysis: Theory, Research, and Clinical Implications.* New York: Guilford Press, 2013.

———. *From Classical to Contemporary Psychoanalysis: A Critique and Integration.* New York: Routledge, 2011.
Eagleton, Terry. *After Theory.* New York: Basic Books, 2003.
Eisenstein, Sergei M. *Film Form: Essays in Film Theory.* Edited and translated by Jay Leyda. New York: Harcourt, 1949.
———. *Problems of Film Direction.* Honolulu: University Press of the Pacific, 2004.
———. *The Psychology of Composition.* Edited and translated by Alan Upchurch. London: Methuen, 1988.
Eliot, T. S. "Tradition and the Individual Talent," Reprint, *Perspecta* 19 (1982): 36–42.
Eugeni, Ruggero. "A Semiotic Theory of Media Experience," https://www.academia.edu/399281/A_Semiotic_Theory_of_Media_Experience.
———. *Semiotica dei media: Le forme dell'esperienza.* Rome: Carocci, 2010.
Farrell, Frank B. *Why Does Literature Matter?* Ithaca, NY: Cornell University Press, 2004.
Feimer, Joel N. "Medea in Ovid's *Metamorphoses* and the *Ovide Moralisé*: Translation," *Florilegium* 8 (1986): 40–55.
Filipski, Soren, ed. *The Norse Hamlet.* N.p.: Hythloday Press, 2013.
Fish, Stanley Eugene. *Is There a Text in This Class: The Authority of Interpretive Communities.* Cambridge, MA: Harvard University Press, 1980.
Fosha, Diana, Daniel J. Siegel, and Marion Fried Solomon, eds. *The Healing Power of Emotion: Affective Neuroscience, Development, and Clinical Practice.* New York: W. W. Norton, 2009.
Fox, Alistair. "Auteurism, Personal Cinema, and the Fémis Generation: The Case of François Ozon." In *A Companion to Contemporary French Cinema.* Edited by Alistair Fox, Michel Marie, Raphaëlle Moine, and Hilary Radner. Malden, MA: Wiley-Blackwell, 2014, 205–229.
———. *The English Renaissance: Identity and Representation in Elizabethan England.* Oxford, U.K.: Blackwell Publishers, 1997.
———. *Jane Campion: Authorship and Personal Cinema.* Bloomington: Indiana University Press, 2012.
———. *The Ship of Dreams: Masculinity in Contemporary New Zealand Fiction.* Dunedin, New Zealand: Otago University Press, 2008.
Freud, Sigmund, James Strachey, Anna Freud and others. *The Standard Edition of the Complete Psychological Works of Sigmund Freud.* 24 volumes. London: Hogarth Press. 1953.
———. *Studies on Hysteria.* Translated and edited by James Strachey in collaboration with Anna Freud, assisted by Alix Strachey and Alan Tyson. Reprint of vol. 2 of *The Standard Edition of the Complete Psychological Works of Sigmund Freud.* New York: Basic Books, 1957.
Frye, Northrop. *Anatomy of Criticism: Four Essays.* Princeton, NJ: Princeton University Press, 1957.
Gallese, Vittorio. "Intentional Attunement: Embodied Simulation and Its Role in Social Cognition." In *Psychoanalysis and Neuroscience.* Edited by Mauro Mancia. Milan: Springer, 2006, 269–301.
Gee, Maurice. *The Plumb Trilogy: Plumb, Meg, Sole Survivor.* Auckland, New Zealand: Penguin, 1995.
Genet, Jean. *The Thief's Journal.* Translated by Bernard Frechtman. New York: Grove Press, 1964.

Gerard, Fabien S., T. Jefferson Kline, and Bruce Sklarew, eds. *Bernardo Bertolucci Interviews*. Jackson: University Press of Mississippi, 2000.
Gillain, Anne. *Le Cinéma selon François Truffaut*. Paris: Flammarion, 1988.
——. *François Truffaut: The Lost Secret*. Translated by Alistair Fox. Bloomington: Indiana University Press, 2013.
Godard, Jean-Luc. *Godard on Godard*. Edited by Jean Narboni and Tom Milne. New York: Da Capo Press, 1972.
Goodwyn, Erik D. *The Neurobiology of the Gods: How Brain Physiology Shapes the Recurrent Imagery of Myth and Dreams*. Hove, U.K.: Routledge, 2012.
Gordon, Rae Beth. *Why the French Love Jerry Lewis: From Cabaret to Early Cinema*. Stanford, CA: Stanford University Press, 2001.
Goudet, Stéphane. "Le court métrage en France: François Ozon," *Positif* 432 (December 1997): 93–95.
Grodal, Torben Kragh. *Embodied Visions: Evolution, Emotion, Culture, and Film*. Oxford, U.K.: Oxford University Press, 2009.
——. *Moving Pictures: A New Theory of Film Genres, Feelings, and Cognition*. Oxford, U.K.: Clarendon Press, 1997.
Hall, Stuart, ed. *Representation: Cultural Representations and Signifying Practices. Culture, Media, and Identities*. London: Sage, in association with the Open University, 1997.
Halliwell, Stephen. *The Aesthetics of Mimesis: Ancient Texts and Modern Problems*. Princeton, NJ: Princeton University Press, 2002.
Herbert, George. *The English Poems of George Herbert*. Edited by C. A. Patrides. London: Everyman, 1974.
Hockley, Luke. *Somatic Cinema: The Relationship between Body and Screen–A Jungian Perspective*. Abingdon, Oxon; New York: Routledge, 2014.
Hogan, Patrick Colm. *Cognitive Science, Literature, and the Arts: A Guide for Humanists*. New York: Routledge, 2003).
——. *How Authors' Minds Make Stories*. Cambridge, U.K.: Cambridge University Press, 2013.
——. "The Mourning Brain: Attachment, Anticipation, and Hamlet's Unmanly Grief." In *Cognitive Literary Studies: Current Themes and New Directions*. Edited by Isabel Jaén and Julien Jacques Simon. Austin: University of Texas Press, 2012, 89–104.
Holland, Norman Norwood. *5 Readers Reading*. New Haven, CT: Yale University Press, 1975.
——. *The Dynamics of Literary Response*. New York: Oxford University Press, 1968.
——. *Literature and the Brain*. Gainesville, FL: PsyArt Foundation, 2009.
Horace. *Satires, Epistles and Ars Poetica*. Translated by H. Rushton Fairclough. Cambridge, MA: Loeb Classical Library, 1942.
Horkheimer, Max. *Eclipse of Reason*. London: Continuum, 1957.
Horkheimer, Max, Theodor W. Adorno, and Gunzelin Schmid Noerr, *Dialectic of Enlightenment: Philosophical Fragments*. Stanford, CA: Stanford University Press, 2002.
Hutcheon, Linda. *Formalism and the Freudian Aesthetic: The Example of Charles Mauron*. Cambridge, U.K.: Cambridge University Press, 2006.
Iser, Wolfgang. *The Act of Reading: A Theory of Aesthetic Response*. Baltimore: Johns Hopkins University Press, 1978.
——. *The Implied Reader: Patterns of Communication in Prose Fiction from Bunyan to Beckett*. Baltimore: Johns Hopkins University Press, 1974.

———. *Prospecting: From Reader Response to Literary Anthropology*. Baltimore: Johns Hopkins University Press, 1989.
Jaén, Isabel, and Julien Jacques Simon, eds. *Cognitive Literary Studies: Current Themes and New Directions*. Austin: University of Texas Press, 2012.
Jones, Ernest. *Hamlet and Oedipus*. London: V. Gollancz, 1949.
Kahr, Brett. *Sex and the Psyche: The Truth about Our Most Secret Fantasies*. London: Penguin, 2007.
Kandel, Eric. *The Age of Insight: The Quest to Understand the Unconscious in Art, Mind, and Brain: From Vienna 1900 to the Present*. New York: Random House, 2012.
———. "Biology and the Future of Psychoanalysis: A New Intellectual Framework for Psychiatry Revisited," *American Journal of Psychiatry* 156, no. 4 (1999): 505–524.
———. *In Search of Memory: The Emergence of a New Science of Mind*. New York: W. W. Norton, 2006.
Kauffman, Linda S. *Discourses of Desire: Gender, Genre, and Epistolary Fictions*. Ithaca, NY: Cornell University Press, 1986.
Kermode, Frank, and John Hollander, eds. *Modern British Literature*. New York: Oxford University Press, 1973.
Keysers, Christian. *The Empathic Brain: How the Discovery of Mirror Neurons Changes Our Understanding of Human Nature*. N.p.: Amazon Digital Services, 2011.
Kihlstrom, John F., Jennifer Dorfman, and Lillian Park. "Implicit and Explicit Memory and Learning." In *The Blackwell Companion to Consciousness*. Edited by Max Velmans and Susan Schneider. Oxford, U.K.: Blackwell, 2007, 525–539.
Klein, Melanie. *Envy and Gratitude and Other Works 1946–1963*. London: Vintage, 1988.
Lacan, Jacques. *Écrits*. Paris: editions du Seuil, 1966.
———. *The Psychoses: The Seminar of Jacques Lacan*. Edited by Jacques-Alain Miller. Book III 1955–1956. Translated by Russell Grigg. New York: Norton, 1993.
Lakoff, George, and Mark Johnson. *Metaphors We Live By*. Chicago: University of Chicago Press, 2003.
———. *Philosophy in the Flesh: The Embodied Mind and Its Challenge to Western Thought*. New York: Basic Books, 1999.
Langer, Susanne, and Katherina Knauth. *Philosophy in a New Key: A Study in the Symbolism of Reason, Rite and Art*. Cambridge, MA: Harvard University Press, 1942.
Laplanche, Jean, and J. B. Pontalis. *Vocabulaire de la psychanalyse*. Paris: Presses Universitaires de France, 1967.
LeDoux, Joseph E. *Synaptic Self: How Our Brains Become Who We Are*. New York: Viking, 2002.
Lewalski, Barbara Kiefer. *The Life of John Milton: A Critical Biography*. Rev. ed. Oxford, U.K.: Blackwell, 2003.
Liew, Sook-Lei, and Lisa Aziz-Zadeh. "The Human Mirror Neuron System, Social Control, and Language" In *Handbook of Neurosociology*. Edited by David D. Franks and Jonathan H. Turner. New York: Springer, 2013.
Mancia, Mauro. *Feeling the Words: Neuropsychoanalytic Understanding of Memory and the Unconscious*. Translated by Judy Baggott. Hove, U.K.: Routledge, 2007.
———, ed. *Psychoanalysis and Neuroscience*. Milan: Springer, 2006.
Martin, Rod A. *The Psychology of Humor: An Integrative Approach*. Amsterdam: Elsevier Academic Press, 2007.

Mauron, Charles. *Des métaphores obsédantes au mythe personnel: Introduction à la psychocritique*. Paris: J. Corti (Rennes Impr. réunies), 1963.
McDougall, Joyce. *The Many Faces of Eros: A Psychoanalytic Exploration of Human Sexuality*. New York: W. W. Norton, 1995.
———. *Plea for a Measure of Abnormality*. New York: Brunner/Mazel, 1992.
———. *Theaters of the Mind: Illusion and Truth on the Psychoanalytic Stage*. New York: Brunner/Mazel, 1991.
McHugh, Kathleen. *Jane Campion*. Champaign: University of Illinois Press, 2007.
Metz, Christian. *The Imaginary Signifier: Psychoanalysis and the Cinema*. Bloomington: Indiana University Press, 1982.
Milner, Marion. "Aspects of Symbolism in Comprehension of the Not-Self," *International Journal of Psychoanalysis* 33, no. 2 (1952): 181–194.
Milton, John. *John Milton: Complete Poems and Major Prose*. Edited by Merritt Y. Hughes. Indianapolis: Odyssey Press, 1957.
Moine, Raphaëlle. *Film Genre*. Translated by Alistair Fox and Hilary Radner. Malden, MA: Blackwell, 2008.
Moore, Susanna. *In the Cut*. Sydney: Picador, 2004.
More, Thomas. *The Yale Edition of the Complete Works of St. Thomas More*. Vol. 6, *A Dialogue Concerning Heresies*. Edited by Thomas M. C. Lawler, Germain Marc'hadour, and Richard C. Marius. New Haven, CT: Yale University Press, 1981.
Nashe, Thomas. *The Works of Thomas Nashe*. Edited by R. B. Mckerrow. London: A. H. Bullen, 1904.
Newirth, Joseph. *Between Emotion and Cognition: The Generative Unconscious*. New York: Other Press, 2003.
Nichols, Bill. *Movies and Methods: An Anthology*. Berkeley: University of California Press, 1976.
Northoff, Georg. *Neuropsychoanalysis in Practice: Brain, Self and Objects*. Oxford, U.K.: Oxford University Press, 2011.
Noyes, Russell. *English Romantic Poetry and Prose*. New York: Oxford University Press, 1956.
Oatley, Keith. *Best Laid Schemes: The Psychology of Emotions*. Cambridge, U.K.: Cambridge University Press, 1992.
———. *Such Stuff as Dreams: The Psychology of Fiction*. Malden, MA: Wiley-Blackwell, 2011.
Ors, Sébastien, Philippe Tancelin, Valérie Jouve, and Bruno Dumont. *Bruno Dumont*. Paris: Éditions Dis Voir, 2001.
P[anarello], Melissa. *One Hundred Strokes of the Brush before Bed*. Translated by Lawrence Venuti. London: Serpent's Tail, 2004.
Panksepp, Jaak. *Affective Neuroscience: The Foundations of Human and Animal Emotions*. New York: Oxford University Press, 1998.
———. "Brain Emotional Systems and Qualities of Mental Life: From Animal Models of Affect to Implications for Psychotherapeutics." In *The Healing Power of Emotion: Affective Neuroscience, Development, and Clinical Practice*. Edited by Diana Fosha, Daniel J. Siegel, and Marion Fried Solomon. New York: W. W. Norton, 2009, 1–26.
———. "Cross-Species Affective Neuroscience Decoding of the Primal Affective Experiences of Humans and Related Animals," *PLoS One* 6, no. 9 (2011): e21236.
———. "What Is an Emotional Feeling? Lessons about Affective Origins from Cross-Species Neuroscience," *Motivation and Emotion* 36, no. 1 (2012): 4–15.

Panksepp, Jaak, and Lucy Biven. *The Archaeology of Mind: Neuroevolutionary Origins of Human Emotions*. New York: W. W. Norton, 2012.

Panksepp, Jaak, and Mark Solms. "What Is Neuropsychoanalysis? Clinically Relevant Studies of the Minded Brain," *Trends in Cognitive Sciences* 16, no. 1 (2012): 6–8.

Person, Ethel Spector. *By Force of Fantasy: How We Make Our Lives*. New York: Basic Books, 1995.

Phelan, James, and Peter J. Rabinowitz, eds. *A Companion to Narrative Theory*. Malden, MA: Blackwell, 2005.

Piotrowska, Agnieszka, ed. *Embodied Encounters: New Approaches to Psychoanalysis and Cinema*. Hove, U.K.: Routledge, 2014.

Plato. *The Republic and Other Works*. Translated by B. Jowett. New York: Dolphin Books, 1960.

Plutarch, "De Gloria Atheniensium." In *Moralia*, Vol. 4. Loeb Classical Libraryedition, Cambridge, MA: Harvard University Press, 1936.

Pope, Alexander. *The Poems of Alexander Pope*. Edited by John Butt. London: Methuen, 1963.

Radner, Hilary, and Cecelia Novero. Introduction to "From Hypnosis to Animals by Raymond Bellour," edited and translated by Alistair Fox, *Cinema Journal* 53, no. 3 (2014): 4.

Renoir, Jean. *My Life and My Films*. Translated by Norman Denny. New York: Da Capo Press, 1974.

Roché, Henri-Pierre. *Carnets 1 (1920–1921): Les Années "Jules et Jim."* Avant-propose de François Truffaut. Marseilles: A. Dimanche; Austin: Harry Ransom Humanities Research Center of the University of Texas, 1990.

——. *Jules et Jim*. Translated by Patrick Evans, with an essay by François Truffaut. London: Marion Boyars, 2006.

——. *Two English Girls and the Continent* [Deux Anglaises et le Continent]. Translated by Walter Bruno. Cambridge, WI: Cambridge Book Review Press, 2004.

Rodowick, D. N. "An Elegy for Theory," *October* 122 (Fall 2007): 91–109.

Rosenblatt, Louise M. *Literature as Exploration*. New York: D. Appleton-Century, 1938.

Ruiz, Raúl. *Poetics of Cinema: 1 Miscellanies*. Translated by Brian Holmes. Paris: Dis Voir, 1995.

Russell, D. A., and Michael Winterbottom, eds. *Classical Literary Criticism*. Oxford, U.K.: Oxford University Press, 1989.

Schilt, Thibault. *François Ozon*. Champaign: University of Illinois Press, 2011.

Schore, Allan N. *Affect Regulation and the Repair of the Self*. New York: W. W. Norton, 2003.

——. "Early Relational Trauma, Disorganized Attachment, and the Development of a Predisposition to Violence." In *Healing Trauma: Attachment, Mind, Body, and Brain*. Edited by Marion Fried Solomon and Daniel J. Siegel. New York: W. W. Norton, 2003, 106–167.

——. "Right-Brain Affect Regulation: An Essential Mechanism of Development, Trauma, Dissociation, and Psychotherapy." In *The Healing Power of Emotion*. Edited by Diana Fosha, Daniel J. Siegel, and Marion Solomon. New York: W. W. Norton, 112–144.

Segal, Hanna. *The Work of Hanna Segal: A Kleinian Approach to Clinical Practice*. New York: J. Aronson, 1981.

Servan-Schreiber, David. *Healing without Freud or Prozac: Natural Approaches to Curing Stress, Anxiety and Depression without Drugs and without Psychoanalysis*. London: Rodale, 2004.

Shakespeare, William. *Coriolanus*. Edited by Reuben Bower. New York: The New American Library, 1966.
———. *The Complete Pelican Shakespeare: The Comedies and the Romances*. Ed. Alfred Harbage. Harmondsworth: Penguin Books, 1969.
———. *The Complete Pelican Shakespeare: The Tragedies*. Ed. Alfred Harbage. Harmondsworth: Penguin Books, 1969.
———. *The First Quarto of Hamlet*. Edited by Kathleen O. Irace. New York: Cambridge University Press, 1998.
———. *The Sonnets*. Edited by William Burto. New York: Signet, 1964.
———. *The Tragedy of Hamlet Prince of Denmark*. Edited by Sylvan Barnet. New York: Signet, 1998.
Sharpe, Ella Freeman. "The Impatience of Hamlet," *International Journal of Psycho-Analysis* 10 (1929): 203–213.
Shimamura, Arthur P. *Psychocinematics: Exploring Cognition at the Movies*. Oxford, U.K.: Oxford University Press, 2013.
Sidney, Philip. *An Apology for Poetry or The Defence of Poesy*. Edited by Geoffrey Shepherd. Manchester, U.K.: Manchester University Press, 1973.
Siegel, Daniel J. "An Interpersonal Neurobiology of Psychotherapy: The Developing Mind and the Resolution of Trauma." In *Healing Trauma: Attachment, Mind, Body, and Brain*. Edited by Marion Fried Solomon and Daniel J. Siegel. New York: W. W. Norton, 2003, 7–15.
———. *Pocket guide to Interpersonal Neurobiology: An Integrative Handbook of the Mind*. New York: W. W. Norton, 2012.
Sinclair, Samuel J., and Daniel Antonius. *The Psychology of Terrorism Fears*. New York: Oxford University Press, 2012.
Sobchack, Vivian. *Carnal Thoughts: Embodiments and Moving Image Culture*. Berkeley: University of California Press, 2004.
Solms, Mark, and Oliver Turnbull. *The Brain and the Inner World: An Introduction to the Neuroscience of Subjective Experience*. New York: Other Press, 2002.
Solomon, Marion Fried. *Narcissism and Intimacy: Love and Marriage in an Age of Confusion*. New York: W. W. Norton, 1989.
Solomon, Marion Fried, and Daniel J. Siegel, eds. *Healing Trauma: Attachment, Mind, Body, and Brain*. New York: W. W. Norton, 2003.
Solomon, Marion Fried, and Stan Tatkin. *Love and War in Intimate Relationships: Connection, Disconnection, and Mutual Regulation in Couple Therapy*. New York: W. W. Norton, 2011.
Spenser, Edmund. *The Faerie Queene: Book One*. Edited by Carol V. Kaske. Indianapolis: Hackett Publishing, 2006.
Spurgeon, Caroline. *Shakespeare's Imagery and What It Tells Us*. Cambridge, U.K.: Cambridge University Press, 1935.
Staiger, Janet. *Interpreting Films: Studies in the Historical Reception of American Cinema*. Princeton, NJ: Princeton University Press, 1992.
———. *Perverse Spectators: The Practices of Film Reception*. New York: New York University Press, 2000.
Stam, Robert. *Film Theory: An Introduction*. Malden, MA: Blackwell, 2000.
———. *François Truffaut and Friends: Modernism, Sexuality, and Film Adaptation*. New Brunswick, NJ: Rutgers University Press, 2006.

Stamenov, Maxim I., and Vittorio Gallese, eds. *Mirror Neurons and the Evolution of Brain and Language*. Amsterdam: John Benjamins Publishing, 2002.
Stead, C. K. *Kin of Place*. Auckland, New Zealand: Auckland University Press, 2002.
Stern, Daniel N. *Forms of Vitality: Exploring Dynamic Experience in Psychology, the Arts, Psychotherapy, and Development*. Oxford, U.K.: Oxford University Press, 2010.
——. *The Interpersonal World of the Infant: A View from Psychoanalysis and Developmental Psychology, with a New Introduction by the Author*. New York: Basic Books, 2000.
Stern, Donnel B. *Unformulated Experience: From Dissociation to Imagination in Psychoanalysis*. Hillsdale, NJ: Analytic Press, 2003.
Strachey, James, Sigmund Freud, and Anna Freud. *The Standard Edition of the Complete Psychological Works of Sigmund Freud*. Translated by James Strachey et al. London: Vintage, 2001. 24 vols. Thiher, Allen. *The Power of Tautology: The Roots of Literary Theory*. Madison, NJ: Fairleigh Dickinson University Press, 1997.
Tisseron, Serge. *Un Psy au cinema*. Paris: Belin, 2013.
Tredell, Nicolas. *Cinemas of the Mind: A Critical History of Film Theory*. Cambridge, U.K.: Icon, 2002.
Truffaut, François. *Correspondance*. Edited by Gilles Jacob. Paris: 5 Continents/Hatier, 1988.
Turner, Mark. "The Art of Compression." In *The Artful Mind: Cognitive Science and the Riddle of Human Creativity*. Edited by Mark Turner. Oxford, U.K.: Oxford University Press, 2006.
Valéry, Paul. *Mauvaises pensées et autres*. Paris: Gallimard, 1942.
Vassilieva, Julia. "Eisenstein/Vygotsky/Luria's Project: Cinematic Thinking and the Integrative Science of Mind and Brain," *Screening the Past* 38 (December 2013): http://www.screeningthepast.com/2013/12/eisenstein-vygotsky-luria's-project-cinematic-thinking-and-the-integrative-science-of-mind-and-brain/.
Verhoeven, Deb. *Jane Campion*. London: Routledge, 2009.
Watt, Ian. *The Rise of the Novel: Studies in Defoe, Richardson, and Fielding*. Berkeley: University of California Press, 1957.
Wexman, Virginia Wright. *Jane Campion: Interviews*. Jackson: University Press of Mississippi, 1999.
White, Edmund. "Edmund White Speaks with Edmund White," *The Review of Contemporary Fiction* 16, no. 3 (1996): 13–20.
Wimsatt, William K. *The Verbal Icon: Studies in the Meaning of Poetry*. Lexington: University of Kentucky Press, 1954.
Winnicott, D. W. *The Maturational Processes and the Facilitating Environment: Studies in the Theory of Emotional Development*. New York: International Universities Press, 1965.
——. *Playing and Reality*. London: Routledge, 2005 [1971].
Zbikowski, Lawrence M. "The Cognitive Tango." In *The Artful Mind: Cognitive Science and the Riddle of Human Creativity*. Edited by Mark Turner. Oxford, U.K.: Oxford University Press, 2006, 115–132.
Žižek, Slavoj. *Enjoy Your Symptom! Jacques Lacan in Hollywood and Out*. New York: Routledge, 2001.

FILMOGRAPHY

5x2 (François Ozon, 2004)
8 Women (François Ozon, 2002)
"14ᵉ Arrondissement" (Alexander Payne), segment in *Paris, je t'aime* (various directors, 2006)
The 400 Blows (François Truffaut, 1959)
2012 (Roland Emmerich, 2009)
An Angel at My Table (Jane Campion, 1990)
Angel (François Ozon, 2007)
Anna Karenina (Joe Wright, 2012)
Bad Teacher (Jake Kasdan, 2011)
Batman Begins (Christopher Nolan, 2005)
Blue Is the Warmest Color (Abdellatif Kechiche, 2013)
Blue Valentine (Derek Cianfrance, 2010)
Bridget (Amos Kollek, 2002)
Bright Star (Jane Campion, 2009)
Camille Claudel 1915 (Bruno Dumont, 2013)
Captain America: The First Avenger (Joe Johnston, 2011)
The Chronicles of Narnia: The Lion, the Witch and the Wardrobe (Andrew Adamson, 2005)
Contagion (Steven Soderbergh, 2011)
Criminal Lovers (François Ozon, 1999)
The Dark Knight (Christopher Nolan, 2008)
The Dark Knight Rises (Christopher Nolan, 2013)
Dans Paris (Christophe Honoré, 2006)
Days of Glory (Rachid Bouchareb, 2006)
Diana (Oliver Hirschbiegel, 2013)
The Dreamers (Bernardo Bertolucci, 2003)
Fanny and Alexander (Ingmar Bergman, 1982)
Fiona (Amos Kollek, 1998)
Friends with Benefits (Will Gluck, 2011)
The Green Room (François Truffaut, 1978)

Hadewijch (Bruno Dumont, 2009)
Heartbreaker (Pascal Chaumeil, 2010)
Hideaway (François Ozon, 2009)
Humanité (Bruno Dumont, 1999)
I Killed My Mother (Xavier Dolan, 2009)
I'm the Proudest Girl in the World! (Julian Roffman, 1944)
In the Cut (Jane Campion, 2003)
In the House (François Ozon, 2012)
Intouchables (Olivier Nakache, 2011)
Jules and Jim (François Truffaut, 1962)
The King's Speech (Tom Hooper, 2010)
Knocked Up (Judd Apatow, 2007)
The Life of Jesus (Bruno Dumont, 1997)
La Fille de l'eau (Jean Renoir, 1924)
La Première Nuit (Georges Franju, 1958)
The Last Metro (François Truffaut, 1980)
Last Tango in Paris (Bernardo Bertolucci, 1972)
Man of Steel (Zack Snyder, 2013)
The Man Who Loved Women (François Truffaut, 1977)
Megafault (David Michael Latt, 2009)
Mommy (Xavier Dolan, 2014)
My Worst Nightmare (Anne Fontaine, 2011)
Nana (Jean Renoir, 1926)
No Strings Attached (Ivan Reitman, 2011)
Olympus Has Fallen (Fuqua, 2013)
Pacific Rim (Guillermo del Toro, 2013)
Pardonnez-moi (Maïwenn, 2010)
Paris, je t'aime (various directors, 2006)
Perfect Strangers (Gaylene Preston, 2003)
Persona (Ingmar Bergman, 1966)
Photo de famille (François Ozon, 1988)
The Piano (Jane Campion, 1993)
The Place Beyond the Pines (Derek Cianfrance, 2013)
Polisse (Maïwenn, 2011)
The Portrait of a Lady (Jane Campion, 1996)
Potiche (François Ozon, 2010)
Resident Evil, series (Paul W. S. Anderson, 2002, 2004, 2007, 2010, 2013)
Ricky (François Ozon, 2009)
The River (Jean Renoir, 1951)
Shame (Steve McQueen, 2011)
See the Sea (François Ozon, 1997)
Sitcom (François Ozon, 1998)
The Soft Skin (François Truffaut, 1964)
The Spider's Stratagem (Bernardo Bertolucci, 1970)
Sue (Amos Kollek, 1997)
Sweetie (Jane Campion, 1989)
Swimming Pool (François Ozon, 2003)

Time to Leave (François Ozon, 2005)
Tomboy (Céline Sciamma, 2011)
Top of the Lake, television series (Jane Campion, 2013)
Under the Sand (François Ozon, 2000)
Une nouvelle amie [The New Girlfriend] (François Ozon, 2014)
Une robe d'été [A Summer Dress] (François Ozon, 1996)
Une rose entre nous (François Ozon, 1994)
War of the Worlds (Steven Spielberg, 2005)
War Stories Our Mothers Never Told Us (Gaylene Preston, 1995)
The Water Diary (Jane Campion, 2006)
Water Drops on Burning Rocks (François Ozon, 2000)
White House Down (Roland Emmerich, 2013)
The Wolf of Wall Street (Martin Scorsese, 2013)
World War Z (Marc Forster, 2013)
The Women on the 6th Floor (Philippe le Guay, 2011)
Young & Beautiful (François Ozon, 2012)

INDEX

"14e Arrondissement" (Payne), 78–81
2012 (Emmerich), 66
5x2 (Ozon), 219, 234
8 Women (Ozon), 223, 230

Aaron, Michele, 155
affective fallacy, 145
affective systems, 53
affective turn, the, 156
Allen, Woody, 59, 217
Altman, Rick, 111
A Midsummer Night's Dream (Shakespeare), 211
Amygdala, memory, and, 45
An Angel at My Table (Campion), 93, 119
An Apology for Poetry (Sidney), 15, 241
An Essay on Criticism (Pope), 83
Angel (Ozon), 230, 233, 235, 236
animality, 153
Antony and Cleopatra (Shakespeare), 212
Aristotle, 6, 9, 13, 14, 37, 60, 131, 192
Armstrong, Paul B., 28
Arnold, Matthew, 1–2, 18, 192
Ars Poetica (Horace), 10
arts, role of, 61
A Summer Dress (Ozon), 219
attachment, 55, 165; classifications, 166; disturbances, impact of, 56; styles, 56
Augustine, Saint, 11, 13

authorial intention, 162
"A Wreath" (Herbert), 87

Bad Teacher (Jake Kasdan), 65
Balzac, Honoré de, 177, 178
Barthes, Roland, 21, 111
Batman (Kane and Finger), 136, 137
Batman Begins (Nolan), 135
Batman franchise, 135
Bazin, André, 3–4, 176
Belleforest, François, 195–197
Bellour, Raymond, 153–154, 162
Bergman, Ingmar, 51, 59, 92, 105, 217
Bergson, Henri, 153
Berlin, Isaiah, 17
Bertolucci, Attilio, 104
Bertolucci, Bernardo, 59, 85, 86, 104–106
Berton, Mireille, 154
Beyond the Pleasure Principle (Brooks), 23
Bion, Wilfred, 25
blockbuster films, 129, 135–139
Bloom, Harold, 23
Blue Is the Warmest Color (Kechiche), 63
Blue Valentine (Cianfrance), 63
Boccaccio, Giovanni, 12
Bollas, Christopher: evocative objects, theory of, 51, 90; transformational object, theory of, 168; transubstantial object, theory of, 112; unconscious, view

Bollas, Christopher (*continued*)
  of, 36, 90–91; mentioned, 6, 7, 22, 25, 35, 44, 108, 118
Bordwell, David, 27, 111
Bory, Jean-Louis, 185
Botella, César, 98
Botella, Sára, 98
Both Sides of the Moon (Duff), 92
Bowlby, John, 165–166
Boyd, Brian, 28, 150
brain, the: brainstem and, 48; cognitive, 41; emotional, 41, 48; left hemisphere of, 51; limbic system in, 48; linear processing, and, 51; neocortex, and, 41, 44, 48; neomammalian, 41; neural clusters in, 45; neural network integration, and, 50; neurons in, 45; old mammalian, 41; reptilian, 41; right hemisphere of, 47, 51; triune, 41; visual systems, and, 45
Brando, Marlon, 105
Bridget (Kollek), 106–107, 141
Bright Star (Campion), 93, 119
Brontë, Charlotte, 102
Brooks, Peter, 24, 111
Brown, Lawrence J., 175
Bullough, Geoffrey, 198
Butler, Christopher, 2

Camille Claudel 1915 (Dumont), 121
Campion, Edith, 93
Campion, Jane, 93, 103, 105, 118–120
Captain America franchise, 135
Captain America: The First Avenger (Johnston), 135
Caravaggio (Michelangelo Merisi), 85
CARE subsystem, 43
Carnets (Roché), 177, 185, 191
Carroll, Joseph, 194
Cawelti, John G., 68
Cento colpi di spazzola prima di andare a dormire (Panarello). See *One Hundred Strokes of the Brush before Bed*
Chaucer, Geoffrey, 12
Choke (Gregg), 167
Choke (Palahniuk), 167
Christian-humanism, 12–13
cinema: generic categories and, 62; market share of genres in, 67

Clarendon Code, 133
Close, Bartholomew, 130
Cocteau, Jean, 176, 177, 179
cognitivism, 40
cognitivist criticism, 27–30
Coleridge, Samuel Taylor, 17
Constantine, Emperor, 11
Contagion (Soderbergh, 2011), 66
Coriolanus (Shakespeare), 212; mother-son relations in, 213, 214
Cozolino, Louis J., 49
creativity: function of, 56; process of, 71
Criminal Lovers (Ozon), 219, 221–222, 225, 227, 230, 232, 234

Damasio, Antonio: self-formation, view of, 159; mentioned, 4, 6, 40, 42, 61, 71
Dans Paris (Honoré), 178
Dante Alighieri, 126
Darwin, Charles, 28, 42
David, Liliane, 188
Davies, J. M., 35
da Vinci, Leonardo, 73
Days of Glory (Bouchareb), 54
Decameron (Bocaccio), 12
De casibus virorum illustrium (Boccaccio), 12
De Doctrina Christiana (Augustine), 11
Defensio pro populo Anglicano (Milton), 130
Defensio Secunda (Milton), 130
De gloria Atheniensium (Plutarch), 10
Deleuze, Gilles, 20, 152
Deneuve, Catherine, 124
Des métaphores obsédantes au mythe personnel (Mauron), 215
Diana (Hirschbiegel), 63
displacement, 101, 106
Dolan, Xavier, 179
Duff, Alan, 92
Dumont, Bruno, 75, 116, 120–122
Du Toit, Catherine, 182, 183

Eagle, Morris N., 96
Eikon Basilike (anon.), 130
Eikonoklastes (Milton), 130
Eisenstein, Sergei: creative process, view of, 73; montage principle, and, 72; reception, view of, 164; mentioned, 3, 4, 74
Eliot, T. S., 18, 19, 21

embodied simulation, 151, 161
emotional systems, 41–43, 53–55, 64–67
Enlightenment, the, 18, 19
Eugeni, Ruggero, 152
Euripides, 134
evocative objects, 51, 89–94
evolutionary bioculturalism, 27
executive systems, 43
experiential turn, the, 152, 156

fabliau tradition, the, 12
Fanny and Alexander (Bergman), 92
fantasy, 95–101; affective systems, and, 99, 100; defense mechanism as, 96; definition of, 95, 97; Freud's theory of, 95; functions of, 97, 101; mechanisms of, 98; popular fiction, and, 100; separation distress, and, 99
Farrell, Frank, 20–21
Fassbinder, Rainer Werner, 217
FEAR system, 43, 59, 64, 65, 67
Ficino, Marsilio, 39
fictive representation: functions of, 49–50, 55, 57, 61, 68, 238; metaphoric thought as, 112; symbolic mediation as, 58
figurability, 98, 99
Finger, Bill, 136
Fiona (Kollek), 106, 107, 141
formalism, 21
forms of vitality. *See* vitality affects
Franju, Georges, 124
Freud, Sigmund: fantasies, view of, 98; figurability, theory of, 46; *Hamlet*, view of, 22; mind, theory of, 22; representability, view of, 98; unconscious, view of, 35; mentioned, 15, 34, 55, 95
Friends with Benefits (Gluck), 65
Frye, Northrop, 11, 21, 26, 27

Gallese, Vittorio, 161–162
Gaskell, Elizabeth, 54
Gee, Maurice, 91
Genet, Jean, 176–179, 239
genre: action thriller, 65–66, 138; alien invasion, 136, 138; comedies, 64, 65; definition of, 128–129; dramas, 63; horror/terror films, 66; slasher movies, 67; social motivations, and, 136; superheroes

in, 67; templates for the containment of anxiety as, 136
Gesta Danorum (Saxo Grammaticus), 195
Gillain, Anne, 123, 190, 191
Godard, Jean-Luc, 175, 179
Goodwyn, Erik, 34
Gorboduc (Sackville and Norton), 198
Gosson, Stephen, 15
Great Depression, the, 18
Greenblatt, Stephen, 209
Gregg, Clark, 167
Grodal, Torben, 29
Gruault, Jean, 190

Hadewijch (Dumont), 121
Hall, Stuart, 21, 148–149
Halliwell, Stephen, 14
Hamlet (Shakespeare): associative metaphors in, 200–202; attachment relations in, 194; emotional dysregulation in, 206; family triangles in, 200; fathers in, 198; informing fantasy of, 206–209; *Jules and Jim*, parallels with, 193; psychological function of, 210; Senecan revenge tragedy as, 198; Shakespeare's biography, and, 209–211; Shakespeare's personal myth, and, 211–214; source, and, 197–198, 209; structural shaping of, 198–200; textual versions of, 197; mentioned, 22, 84, 193
Hart, F. Elizabeth, 27
Heartbreaker (Chaumeil), 65
Heger, Constantin, 102
Herbert, George, 87
Hessel, Franz, 180, 184
Hessel, Helen (née Grund), 180, 181, 188
Hessling, Catherine, 87, 88
Hideaway (Ozon), 219, 225
Histoires tragiques (Belleforest), 195, 197
Hitchcock, Alfred, 177, 178
Hogan, Patrick Colm, 27, 150, 151, 194
Holland, Norman, 22, 23, 34, 111, 147, 166
Holy Smoke (Campion), 119
Holzer, Jenny (multimedia artist), 66
homeostasis, 42, 43, 48, 61, 67
Homer, 19
Honoré, Christophe, 178
Horace (Quintus Horatius Flaccus), 10, 12

How Authors' Minds Make Stories (Hogan), 28
How Literature Plays with the Brain (Armstrong), 28
Humanité (Dumont), 121
Hutcheon, Linda, 215

I Killed My Mother (Dolan), 179
images: affect-inducing power of, 49–50; evocative power of, 51; function of, 50
I'm the Proudest Girl in the World! (Roffman), 170
intentional attunement, 162
intentional fallacy, 111, 144, 145
interaffectivity, 164
interfantasy, 165–166, 171
intersubjectivity: definition of, 163; intersubjective attunement, and, 174, 175; intersubjective transaction, process of, 163; intersubjective transfer, and, 164
intertexts, 129
In the Cut (Campion), 93, 118, 120
In the House (Ozon), 225, 227, 228, 230, 231, 235, 236
Intouchables (Nakache), 65
introjection, 166
introjective identification, 101, 167
introjective subjectification, 90
Iron Man (Favreau), 135, 137, 138
Iron Man 2 (Favreau), 135
Iron Man 3 (Black), 135
Iser, Wolfgang, 146

Jaén, Isabel, 5
J'ai tué ma mère (Dolan). See *I Killed My Mother*
Jane Eyre (Brontë), 102
Jones, Ernest, 22
Jules and Jim (Truffaut): adaptation as, 187–190; fantasmatic scenario in, 190–192; mother as influence on, 188; personal memories in, 189; Roché's novel, compared with, 189; *The Last Metro*, and, 191; *The Man Who Loved Women*, and, 191; *The Soft Skin*, and, 191; mentioned, 112, 174
Jules et Jim (Roché), 174, 180–182, 184, 189
Jung, Carl, 26, 27, 34

Kandel, Eric, 4–5, 32–33, 39, 40
Kane, Bob, 136
Keysers, Christian, 161
Klein, Melanie: phantasies, view of, 96; mentioned, 23, 25, 95
Knocked Up (Apatow), 65
Kollek, Amos, 106–107, 141
Kollek, Teddy, 106
Kris, Ernst, 52
Kyd, Thomas, 198

Lacan, Jacques, 11, 20, 24, 95; unconscious, theory of, 20
Lachenay, Robert, 178
La Divina Commedia (Dante), 126, 127
La Fille de l'eau (Jean Renoir), 86–87
Lakoff, George, 45, 82
Langer, Susanne, 75
La Première Nuit (Franju), 124
Last Tango in Paris (Bertolucci), 104–106
Léaud, Jean-Pierre, 105, 178
LeDoux, Joseph, 6, 32, 37, 40, 44, 47
Lee Kang-sheng, 178
Lejrekrøniken (Chronicle of the Kings of Lejre), 195
limbic system, 41, 48
literary Darwinism, 27, 28
literary genres, 67
Literature and the Brain (Holland), 33
Literature as Exploration (Rosenblatt), 145
Lives of the Noble Grecians and Romans (Plutarch), 212
L'Ovide moralisé (anon.), 11
Luria, Alexander, 4, 60
LUST system, 43, 59
Lyrical Ballads (Wordsworth), 16

Macbeth (Shakespeare), 212
Mancia, Mauro, 35, 45, 47
Manningham, John, 210
Man of Steel (Snyder, 2013), 135
Mauron, Charles, 211; personal myth, theory of, 215–217
McDougall, Joyce: creativity, view of, 56; mentioned, 5, 7, 35, 36, 57, 60
Megafault (Latt), 66
Melancholia (von Trier), 63

memory, 45; autobiographical, 47, 51; episodic, 46; explicit, 44, 45, 46; hippocampus, and, 45; implicit, 45, 46; memory systems, and, 47; trauma, and, 47; working, 47
Metamorphoses (Ovid), 12
metaphors, 82; conceptual, 46; Lakoff's theory of, 45–46
Metz, Christian, 20, 147, 153
Milton, John, 129–135; arrest and imprisonment of, 130; definition of tragedy of, 131; failure of Puritan revolution, and, 131; identification with Samson of, 131, 134; poetry, view of, 60; Secretary for Foreign Tongues as, 130; traumatic experience of, 131; mentioned, 6, 8, 11, 37, 139, 192
mimēsis, 14
mirror neurons: functions of, 160, 161; mentioned, 175
modernism, 18, 19
Mommy (Dolan), 179
Monferrand, Janine de. *See* Truffaut, Janine
montage principle, 72–74
More, Thomas: visual imagery, view of, 13; mentioned, 10, 14, 103
Moreau, Jeanne, 187, 189
Morgenstern, Madeleine, 187, 188
Much Ado About Nothing (Shakespeare), 211
My Worst Nightmare (Fontaine), 65

Nana (Renoir), 88
Nana (Zola), 88
narrative: cognitivist theories of, 111; nature of, 110; psychoanalytic theories of, 111; structuralist theories of, 110
neoclassicism, 16
neurofilmology, 152
neuropsychoanalysis, 5
Newirth, Joseph, 34
Nicholls, Arthur Bell, 102
North, Sir Thomas, 212
North and South (Gaskell), 54
No Strings Attached (Reitman, 2011), 65
"Nuit en enfer" (Rimbaud), 230

Oatley, Keith, 150
Oedipus Rex (Sophocles), 22

Olympus Has Fallen (Fuqua, 2013), 66, 136, 137
One Hundred Strokes of the Brush before Bed (Panarello), 125–127, 139
On the Origin of Stories (Boyd), 28
Origin of the Species (Darwin), 28
Orlando furioso (Ariosto), 127
Ovid (Publius Ovidius Naso), 12
Ozon, François: cinegrams in films of, 226–228; fantasmatic elements in films of, 229–232, 234, 236; incestuous relationships in films of, 231; motivations for filmmaking of, 217–218; pairings and doublings in films of, 224; mentioned, 60, 139–142, 217, 225

Pacific Rim (del Toro), 66
Panarello, Melissa, 125–127
PANIC/GRIEF system, 43, 64
Panksepp, Jaak: emotional systems, view of, 42–44, 64, 99; episodic memory, view of, 46–47; mind, view of, 35–36, 39, 91; mentioned, 5, 6, 37, 40, 53, 206
Paradise Lost (Milton), 15, 129, 131, 134
Paradise Regained (Milton), 15, 129, 131, 132, 134
Pardonnez-moi (Maïwenn), 63
Paris, je t'aime (various directors), 78, 81
Payne, Alexander, 78, 81
Perfect Strangers (Preston), 114–116, 127
Persona (Bergman), 92
philosophy of difference, 48; critical theory, and, 48
Photo de famille (Ozon), 218, 221
Plato, 10, 13, 14
PLAY system, 43, 54, 64
Plumb Trilogy (Gee), 91
Plutarch, 9, 212
Poe, Edgar Allan, 24
Poetics (Aristotle), 9
Polisse (Maïwenn), 63
Poltava (Pushkin), 73
polysemia, visual, 107
Pope, Alexander, 16, 82
postcolonialism, 19
postmodernism, 2, 19–20
poststructuralism, 19, 48

Post-Theory (Bordwell), 27
Potiche (Ozon), 223
Powell, Mary (wife of John Milton), 132
Preston, Gaylene, 114, 115
Preston, Tui, 115
priming effect, 52
projection, 166
projective identification, 101, 103, 166
projective subjectification, 90
projective transidentification, 165
psychoanalytic criticism, 22–27
Pushkin, Alexander Sergeyevich, 73

Radner, Hilary, 153
RAGE system, 43, 64
Rampling, Charlotte, 217
Real Steel (Levy), 161, 171
reception, 144–145; cognitivist theories of, 149–151, 155; discursive theories of, 148; hypnosis, and, 153; intersubjective transfer in, 156; neuropsychoanalytic theory of, 158; psychoanalytic theories of, 147–148; reader-response theory, and, 145, 146–147
Renaissance, the, 12
Renard, Denise, 181
Rendell, Ruth, 129, 140
Renoir, Jean, 88
Republic (Plato), 10
Resident Evil series (Anderson), 66
reversal, strategy of displacement as, 106
Richard III (Shakespeare), 210
Ricky (Ozon), 219, 231, 234
Rimbaud, Arthur, 176, 177, 179, 230
Roché, Clara, 182–183
Roché, Henri-Pierre, 177; Don Juanism of, 183; mother, relationship with, 182–183
Roché, Pierre, 183
romanticism, 16, 17, 18
Romeo and Juliet (Shakespeare), 76, 78; vitality affects in, 84
Rosenblatt, Louise, 145
Ruiz, Raúl, 108, 129

Sadler, Hamnet, 209
Samson Agonistes (Milton): tragedy as, 129–135; mentioned, 15, 139

Saussure, Ferdinand de, 19
Saxo Grammaticus, 195
Schneider, Maria, 105
School of Abuse (Gosson), 15
Schore, Allan, 6, 35, 36, 55
SEEKING system, 42, 53, 59
See the Sea (Ozon), 219, 224, 231
Segal, Hanna, 25, 26
self-experience, 51
self-formation, 159
sensorimotor domains, 45
sensorimotor patterns, 46
Servan-Schreiber, David, 6, 44
Shakespeare, Hamnet, 209
Shakespeare, Judith, 209
Shakespeare, William: personal myth of, 211; mentioned, 11, 76, 83. See also *Hamlet*
Shame (McQueen), 54, 63
Sharpe, Ella Freeman, 211
Shimamura, Arthur P., 28
Shuster, Joe, 136
Sidney, Philip: theory of poetry of, 13–15; mentioned, 5, 11, 30, 52, 72, 192
Siegel, Daniel J., 35, 66
Siegel, Jerry, 136, 139
Simon, Julien Jacques, 5
Simonides of Ceos, 9
Sitcom (Ozon), 219, 220, 225, 228, 229, 231, 232, 234
Sobchack, Vivian, 152
Solms, Mark, 35, 36, 40, 43
Sonnets (Shakespeare), 83, 214
Sophocles, 134
spatialization, 126
Spenser, Edmund, 116, 117, 127
Spielberg, Steven, 136, 138
splitting, 101, 103
Spurgeon, Caroline, 200, 202
Staiger, Janet, 149
Stam, Robert, 19
Stern, Daniel, 81, 83, 85, 89, 153, 163, 165
Stolen Kisses (Truffaut), 123
Storaro, Vittorio, 85
Storyboard P (dancer), 60
storytelling: functions of, 61; metaphor as, 113; origins of, 71; preoccupations of, 62–64; transitional object as, 58

Stowe, Harriet Beecher, 54
subjectification, 90
subjective objects, 90
Sue (Kollek), 106, 141
superhero movies: fantasmatic enactments of revenge as, 138; functions of, 138; superheroes in, 135–136; *Superman* as personification of America, 137
Superman (Siegel and Shuster), 136
Sweetie (Campion), 93, 103, 118
Swift, Jonathan, 16
Swimming Pool (Ozon), 218, 219, 220, 225, 230, 232, 235
symbolization: discursive symbols, and, 75; presentational symbols, and, 75; psychic function of, 56; symbolic figuration, 50–52; symbolic structuration, 50; mentioned, 50, 56, 74–78
symbolopoietic process, 47

Taylor, Elizabeth (novelist), 233
The 400 Blows (Truffaut), 123, 124, 179, 188
The Avengers (Whedon, 2012), 135, 138
The Canterbury Tales (Chaucer), 12; "The Miller's Tale," 12; "The Reeve's Tale," 12
The Chronicles of Narnia (Adamson), 171
The Conformist (Bertolucci), 104
The Dark Knight (Nolan), 135
The Dark Knight Rises (Nolan, 2013), 135
The Dreamers (Bertolucci), 104
The Faerie Queene (Spenser), 116–118, 139
The Green Room (Truffaut), 192
The Interpretation of Dreams (Freud), 22
The King's Speech (Hooper), 63
The Last Metro (Truffaut), 122–125
The Life of Jesus (Dumont), 121
The Man Who Loved Women (Truffaut), 185
The Matrix (Andy Wachowski), 25
The Mind and Its Stories (Hogan), 28
The New Girlfriend (Ozon), 139–142; informing fantasy of, 140; Ozon's motives in, 141
The Piano (Campion), 119, 120
The Portrait of a Lady (Campion), 93, 120
The Psychology of Composition (Eisenstein), 4
"The Purloined Letter" (Poe), 24

The Ready and Easy Way to Establish a Free Commonwealth (Milton), 130
The Reason of Church Government (Milton), 134
The River (Renoir), 88
The Soft Skin (Truffaut), 191
The Sonnets (Shakespeare), 84, 210
The Spanish Tragedy (Kyd), 198
The Spider's Stratagem (Bertolucci), 104
The Tenure of Kings and Magistrates (Milton), 130
The Thief's Journal (Genet), 176
The Water Diary (Campion), 93
The Winter's Tale (Shakespeare), 211
The Wolf of Wall Street (Martin Scorsese), 63
The Women on the 6th Floor (Le Guay), 65
Time to Leave (Ozon), 220, 222, 224, 225, 227, 228, 232, 234
Tisseron, Serge, 136
Tomboy (Sciamma), 63
Top of the Lake (Campion), 119
transformational objects, 168
trauma, 47
traumata, 56
Troilus and Cressida (Shakespeare), 212
Truffaut, François: affiliation networks, and, 176; childhood of, 185; family background of, 177; Jeanne Moreau, and, 187; mother, relations with, 185, 186; narcissistic deprivation of, 186; Roché, parallels with life of, 186; mentioned, 122–125, 178
Truffaut, Janine, 178, 182, 184–186
Truffaut, Roland, 123, 184, 188, 189
Tsai Ming-Liang, 178
Two English Girls and the Continent (Roché), 183

Uncle Tom's Cabin (Stowe), 54
unconscious, the: multi-modal conception of, 91; nature of, 90; received unconscious, 90; unrepressed unconscious, 47; mentioned, 44
Under the Sand (Ozon), 219, 234
Une nouvelle amie (Ozon). See *The New Girlfriend*

Une robe d'été (Ozon), 140. See also *A Summer Dress*
Une rose entre nous (Ozon), 227, 233
Utopia (More), 13, 103

Verlaine, Paul, 177
Victor (Ozon), 226
visualization, 75
vitality affects, 81–89; cinema in, 85, 88; functions of, 89; poetry in, 87

War of the Worlds (Spielberg), 66, 136, 137
War Stories Our Mothers Never Told Us (Preston), 115
Water Drops on Burning Rocks (Ozon), 227, 236
Wells, H. G., 136

White, Edmund, 49
Whitehead, John W., 105
White House Down (Emmerich), 66, 136, 137
Wimsatt, William K., 145
Winnicott, D. W.: play, theory of, 54; mentioned, 6, 25, 43, 56
Wordsworth, William, 16
World War I, 18
World War II, 19
World War Z (Forster), 66

Young & Beautiful (Ozon), 63, 220, 226, 227, 233, 237

Zimbardo, Philip, 66
Žižek, Slavoj, 20, 24, 25
Zola, Émile, 88

ALISTAIR FOX

is Professor Emeritus of English at the University of Otago, New Zealand. He is author of *Jane Campion: Authorship and Personal Cinema* (IUP, 2011), translator of Anne Gillain's *François Truffaut: The Lost Secret* (IUP, 2013), and editor, with Raphaëlle Moine, Hilary Radner, and Michel Marie, of *A Companion to Contemporary French Cinema*.

www.ingramcontent.com/pod-product-compliance
Lightning Source LLC
Chambersburg PA
CBHW021804220426
43662CB00006B/173